# SOCIAL WELFARE PROGRAMS

## Narratives from Hard Times

### RAYMOND ALBERT
*Bryn Mawr College*

### LOUISE SKOLNIK
*Adelphi University*

*Nassau County (NY)*
*Health and Human Services*

**THOMSON**

™

**BROOKS/COLE**

Australia • Brazil • Canada • Mexico • Singapore • Spain
United Kingdom • United States

# THOMSON

## BROOKS/COLE

Executive Editor: Lisa Gebo
Assistant Editor: Alma Dea Michelena
Editorial Assistant: Sheila Walsh
Technology Project Manager:
    Barry Connolly
Executive Marketing Manager:
    Caroline Concilla
Marketing Assistant: Rebecca Weisman
Senior Marketing Communications
    Manager: Tami Strang
Project Manager, Editorial Production:
    Rita Jaramillo
Creative Director: Rob Hugel
Art Director: Vernon Boes

Print Buyer: Doreen Suruki
Permissions Editor: Sarah Harkrader
Production Service: Buuji, Inc.
Copy Editor: Pam Suwinsky
Cover Designer: Nina Lisowski
Cover Image from top clockwise:
    Viviane Moos/Corbis, Bojan Brecelj/
    Corbis, Joel Stelteheim/Corbis,
    Billy Suratt/Getty Images,
    Sean Gallup/Getty Images
Cover Printer: Malloy Incorporated
Compositor: Buuji, Inc.
Printer: Webcom

Printed in Canada
1  2  3  4  5  6  7  09  08  07  06  05

For more information about our products,
contact us at:
Thomson Learning Academic Resource Center
1-800-423-0563

For permission to use material from this text
or product, submit a request online at
http://www.thomsonrights.com.

Any additional questions about permissions
can be submitted by e-mail to
thomsonrights@thomson.com.

Thomson Higher Education
10 Davis Drive
Belmont, CA 94002-3098
USA

Library of Congress Control Number: 2005926923
ISBN 0-534-35918-3

*To our clients, who had the courage and commitment
to teach us about coping with hard times*

# CONTENTS

CHAPTER 3

**Temporary Assistance to Needy Families**   40

CHAPTER 4

**Public Housing and Homelessness**   91

CHAPTER 5

**Unemployment Insurance**   139

CHAPTER 6

**Supplemental Security Income**   174

# PREFACE

This text has been written to help social workers understand the social programs affecting and informing professional practice with those individuals who have been economically dislocated. These are the near-poor and poor who are situated on the fringes of the economy and who find themselves dependent upon federal governmental assistance programs to meet one or more of their and their families' basic needs for food, clothing, shelter, and/or medical care.

The book presents not only the parameters of the major national programs supporting this group, but also the subjective experience of recipients and the impact of program participation on their lives. We give prominence to clients' voices as a way to gain insight into the meaning they assign to program participation and its consequences. Clients' stories provide the connection between the often-segregated professional knowledge realms of practice and policy.

We facilitate students' understanding of the interplay between the two arenas by introducing them to the specific programmatic elements that directly affect clients' participation and to the programs' legal contexts in terms of relevant legislation, judicial decisions, and regulations.

The unemployed, the underemployed, the poor—these are populations traditionally served by social workers. Their numbers and needs are climbing, due to a stubbornly weak economy that casts aside many, a shift in job opportunities for the working poor, and a concomitant decline in real wages. Funding cutbacks have exacerbated their plight, cutbacks spurred by a national political leadership that falsely glorifies autonomy and individual responsibility and eschews governmental support of social programs. Another issue for the economically dislocated has been the consequences of the 1996 welfare reform initiative, whose legacy persists in the paradigmatic notion that the marketplace is the preferred defense against poverty.

The economy since the late 1990s has brought into focus the importance of social work's attention to the needs and experiences of the economically dislocated. This population constitutes a significant portion of social program recipients, and we are likely to continue to see their numbers rise with each economic indicator that portends more economic insecurity. Indeed, as of spring 2005, the current American economic landscape remains a source of concern, with stock market fluctuations, general worry over the economy's ability to resurge, and escalating expenditures for defense related to the war in Iraq and its aftermath.

In this text, we examine the following social programs for the economically dislocated: Temporary Assistance to Needy Families (TANF), Section 8 Housing Choice Vouchers and Public Housing, unemployment insurance, Supplemental Security Income (SSI), food stamps, and Medicaid. Collectively, these constitute the most significant elements of a social safety net and, as such, the best defense against destitution. They are, in short, the programs to which the poor and near-poor turn to weather distressingly difficult economic times.

To illustrate the relationship between people's lives and these programs, we have selected several narratives that we believe reveal the interplay between life circumstances and governmental assistance. While our sample is not representative, the stories reflect common human themes and experiences that will, we believe, resonate with the reader who works with any of these programs' recipients.

## ORGANIZATION OF THE TEXT

The structure of the text is designed to illustrate the connection between each program's legal context, its salient operational elements, and the personal narratives of recipients. The text begins in Chapter 1 with an overview of the problem of the economically dislocated. Chapter 2 then moves to a brief overview of American legal processes. The reader becomes acquainted both with the processes by which legislatures, regulatory agencies, and courts conduct their business and with strategies for deciphering the "products" that emerge from these processes (statutes, regulations, judicial opinions). These materials are the cornerstone for fully understanding social programs, which have their genesis in a legal rule, usually a statute. The legislation lays out congressional goals that then must be given life (that is, be implemented) by an administrative agency, which announces its intentions through regulations that become operationalized as program initiatives. When conflict arises about statutory meaning or adverse impact of regulations, the court exists as the final arbiter of both legislative and regulatory language. To better illustrate this process, in Chapter 2 we use material related to welfare law. We hope this helps readers grasp the legal processes by giving them examples with which most are familiar. We anticipate that this chapter will enable the reader to make sense of the law, to grasp the reality of American distinct legal processes and their interaction, and to develop rudimentary competency in reading legal documents. The subsequent chapters presume these prerequisite skills.

Chapters 3 through 8 each examine one of the aforementioned social programs, and each chapter is structured to move the reader through several levels of comprehension, from legal context, to program context, to clients' stories, to a brief discussion of what we learn from their stories. The format for Chapters 3 to 8 is as follows:

- An examination of the legal context for the program (statutory authority, illustrative regulations, selected and representative judicial decisions)
- The program context (overview, application and eligibility, benefits, and due process)
- The clients' stories (their words, based on in-person interviews, about the interaction of their life choices and history and their participation in social programs)
- What clients' stories teach us (illuminating themes that emerge from the personal narratives)

Finally, Chapter 9 concludes by briefly reinforcing the collective themes that emerged from the narratives and by exploring the implications for social work practice.

What distinguishes this text? Its key features are (1) the focus on participants' perception of their lives in relation to their receipt of government largess, (2) the attention given to the legal context of these programs, (3) the effort to explicate the underlying "lessons" that our participants pass on to us through their narratives, and (4) the discussion about implications of social policy and social programs for professional practice. Our intention is to depict the social welfare system's impact on recipients, thereby bridging the gap between social policy and social work practice. Given social work students' reliance on experiential learning, our approach should be meaningful for those who seek to integrate real-world perspectives with classroom content.

In light of the impact of the legal context on social work practice, the effort to instruct about law and its influential role is especially significant. Careful reflection on the materials included in Chapter 2, along with some confidence in their grasp of the materials in the subsequent chapters, should allow students to understand the legal and policy issues informing professional practice. These materials may appear foreign, or perhaps even daunting, but the presentation lays out rudimentary concepts, and the reader is instructed on how to make sense of legal processes and of the products—judicial opinions, legislation, and regulations—that emerge from these processes.

In the preface of his text, *The Reluctant Welfare State* (2005), Bruce Jansson discusses the merits of coupling the teaching of social welfare history and policy courses. He argues that the connection between social justice perspectives and the requisite competencies for policy reform is a necessary foundation for professional education. Moreover, Jansson's text, *Becoming an Effective Policy Advocate* (2003), underscores this relationship by focusing on the requisite policy and law-related knowledge and techniques for policy practice and intervention. Our text complements history and policy courses by providing students with an appreciation of the legal context of the social programs that are the typical focus of this part of the foundation social work curriculum. The emphasis on the connection between social programs and their direct impact on people's lives makes the text useful in reinforcing the ecological perspective that is so central to the foundation practice curriculum.

The text is designed for use by both BSW and MSW students. We envision it as a supplemental text in BSW-level practice and policy courses and in MSW generalist and foundation policy and practice courses. It also can be incorporated into courses at any level of professional education dealing with the nexus between social work and law. Moreover, by laying out the program context and legal dimensions of the clients' stories, our text will achieve some of the foundation program objectives articulated in the Educational Policy and Accreditation Standards (EPAS) of the Council on Social Work Education. Specifically, we give attention to the interplay among the clients, the lessons we glean from their stories, and the programs that govern their experiences; by doing so we enable the reader to better accomplish EPAS objectives, such as:

- Practice without discrimination and with respect, knowledge, and skills related to clients' age, class, color, culture, disability, ethnicity, family structure, gender, marital status, national origin race, religion, sex, and sexual orientation
- Understand the forms and mechanisms of oppression and discrimination and apply strategies of advocacy and social change that advance social and economic justice

- Analyze, formulate, and influence social policies

Consequently, our text, as indicated previously, is a useful supplement in any of the courses typically associated with the foundation curriculum content.

## ACKNOWLEDGMENTS

This text could not have found its way into print without the support and assistance of numerous persons. Our sincere appreciation to remarkable administrative assistants—Vicki Gerstenfeld, Dorothy Hanley, Barbara Prins, Marlene Scheer, and Judith Vazquez. We are especially grateful to our students at Adelphi University and Bryn Mawr College who inspired us to develop this approach to illuminating the legal context of policy and practice and of illustrating the close interconnections among policy, people's lives, and social work practice. Special thanks to Nassau County Executive Thomas R. Suozzi, whose "No Wrong Door" vision shows us that hard times for clients can be ameliorated by a human public welfare delivery system.

Our editors, Lisa Gebo and Alma Dea Michelena, have been enthusiastic, understanding, and patient. In addition, thank you to the reviewers of the text who made invaluable and astute suggestions for enhancing its value to students: Joel Blau, SUNY–Stony Brook; Carl D. Holland, Illinois State University; David F. Humphers, Emeritus Professor, California State University, Sacramento; and Janine Mariscotti, LaSalle University.

We gratefully acknowledge those without whom we could not have written the text; namely, the extraordinary individuals who shared their stories with us.

Our families sustained and encouraged us, and for this we say thank you with love.

# ABOUT THE AUTHORS

Raymond Albert received his undergraduate degree from the University of Pennsylvania and his JD and MSW degrees from the University of Connecticut, where he was one of the first dual-degree graduates. In addition to serving as Co-Dean at Bryn Mawr College Graduate School of Social Work and Social Research, Professor Albert is the Director of the Law and Social Policy (LSP) program. He teaches several courses in the LSP program, in addition to teaching a course on social legislation and on community practice in the Master of Social Services program. He also is the author of *Law and Social Work Practice: A Legal Systems Approach* (2000).

From 1976 to 2002, Dr. Louise Skolnik was a professor in the master's and doctoral programs, Director of the Social Services Center, and Associate Dean at the Adelphi University School of Social Work. In 2002, she was granted an academic leave from Adelphi to accept an appointment as Deputy Commissioner of the Nassau County Department of Social Services and in 2004 was named the county's Director of Human Services. In this capacity, she is helping to implement Nassau County's unique "No Wrong Door" integration of its Health and Human Services Departments. Dr. Skolnik is the author of Public Assistance and Your Client (1982) and coauthor of *Understanding Social Welfare* (third and fourth editions, 1993 and 1997).

# INTRODUCTION

We live in hard times for society's economically vulnerable. Although strong economic conditions in the 1990s brought material security to many people, millions of others were unable to meet their basic needs for food, housing, shelter, medical care. With the economic recession of the early 2000s, the hard times intensified for society's vulnerable populations. As of early 2005, the difficult times continue. Some individuals and families have never participated in the American economic mainstream because of disability, inadequate education, discrimination, premature parenting responsibilities, refugee status, or some combination thereof. Others have worked but have never received sufficient income or few if any work-related benefits. Still others have participated in the world of work for many years but find their economic security shattered by unemployment, old age, catastrophic illness, or domestic violence. Collectively, these are the unemployed, the underemployed, the poor—populations traditionally served by social workers. Their numbers and needs have remained high in recent years as a result of such factors as corporate downsizing, shifts in job opportunities for the working poor, funding cutbacks in antipoverty programs, and the uncertain impact of new welfare reform legislation.

Society's safety net initiatives were designed to meet the basic needs of these economically insecure individuals and families. Aid to

Families with Dependent Children (AFDC), Medicaid, Food Stamps, Supplemental Security Income (SSI), Unemployment Insurance, and public housing programs emerged between the 1930s and the late 1960s, an era associated with varying degrees of active governmental intervention designed to ameliorate poverty.

Beginning in the 1970s and culminating in the 1990s, the federal government unceremoniously and unapologetically retreated from the social welfare arena. The retreat continues, as the Republican Party sweep of the presidency and Congress in fall 2005 signals a determination to further displace of non-market remedies to poverty and economic dislocation.

The 1980s, for example, introduced an anti-welfare state approach that appears quite consistent with similar rhetoric in 2005. Block, Cloward, Ehrenreich, and Piven's (1987) observations still resonate:

> Over the last decade, the welfare state has become the target of a concerted ideological attack. From the expanding network of conservative think tanks and foundations on up to the President [Reagan] himself, the same themes are reiterated: that social welfare measures are a drag on the economy, an incentive to immorality, and a cruel hoax on the needy themselves. In the process, even the phrase "the welfare state" has been discredited. . . . What has been momentarily forgotten, in the disarray created by the conservative attack, is that the welfare state is the only defense many people have against the vicissitudes of the market economy. Capitalism, from the beginning, has confronted people with the continual threat of economic dislocation: downturns in the business cycle periodically throw millions out of work; shifting patterns of investment plunge some regions (or industries) into depression while others boom; long-term structural changes in the economy—such as the shift away from agriculture and, more recently, from heavy manufacturing—leave millions stranded with obsolete skills and scanty resources. The only "logic" of the market is change and disruption; and for many of us, the only protection lies in the programs of the welfare state. (p. ix)

It takes no leap of imagination to connect this characterization of Reagan's worldview with that of George W. Bush, elected to his second term in November 2004.

In 1996, AFDC, the core assistance program for poor families introduced in the Social Security Act, was eliminated and was replaced with the time-limited Temporary Assistance to Needy Families (TANF). TANF's underlying premise is that government's social welfare role should be minimal and focused on swiftly moving the needy to a state of self-reliance through employment. Failure to succeed is seen as related to the individual's weakness, not to societal conditions or economic uncertainty. This perspective permeates the contemporary sociopolitical environment and, we propose, will make for harder times for people who are poor or near-poor. As of 2005, as this welfare-reform initiative nears its 10th anniversary, the Congress continues to extend funding and remains committed to former President Bill Clinton's promise to "end welfare as we know it."

It is within this context of a planned diminution of the welfare state that this book has been written. Its purpose is to help social workers practice with a population that can be characterized as the economically dislocated. The book presents not only the parameters of the major national programs supporting this group, but the subjective experience of the recipients of these programs and the impact on their lives. We give prominence to clients' voices as a way to gain insight into the meaning they assign to program participation and its consequences. Clients' stories provide the connection between the often segregated professional knowledge realms of practice and policy. It is from these stories that both policy implications for practice and an understanding of the program emerge.

This text concentrates on practice concerned with helping clients cope with problems in living related to a nonexistent or inadequate attachment to the labor market. The clients' stories underscore the unique features of social work practice at the juncture of the economy and its impact on client systems. Here, the principal concern is to help clients devise strategies to reconnect to the labor market and/or to cope with the consequences of their joblessness or underemployment. Typically, the knowledge and associated skill base for this type of practice is based on an understanding of the contours of assorted social programs and their legal context. Our hope is that by sharing the recipient's perspectives on program participation, we will help the reader appreciate the requisite policy, programmatic, and legal knowledge for professional practice with the economically dislocated.

In this text, we present clients' stories, their experiences as participants in social programs, and the life histories that provide the backdrop for their economic dislocation and subsequent social program participation. The reader is informed of the structure and functions of these programs, including relevant legislation and related judicial decisions. Practice issues are addressed in relation to a review of clients' situations. We use a framework for analysis that we believe informs both the description of the program and the discussion of practice issues.

In the following section of the chapter, we provide a profile of families at risk and the current sociopolitical attitude toward them. We also discuss briefly the social constructionist perspective that informs our use of clients' narratives.

## A PROFILE OF FAMILIES AT RISK

The individuals whose stories comprise this book share several characteristics, chief among them their economic status: they are poor or near-poor and they participate in an assortment of "safety net" social programs. Notable is the diversity of their impoverishment, which suggests that poverty or near-poverty can take many forms. Some of our participants maintain an attachment to the labor market while receiving social program benefits; others are unemployed and rely entirely on public assistance. The duration of their dependency varies, as well. Unfortunately, in the anti-welfare state climate that has persisted since the 1990s, their receipt of public aid is used to define them in a limited way, to imply that they are the flawed sum of their social program benefits. Reality, and our research, suggests this notion is as simplistic as it is repugnant.

The persons we interviewed possess an insightful grasp of their economic situation, one that accommodates both a self-perception as productive members of society and receipt of public assistance. They don't see themselves as living a contradictory existence. That they meet federal poverty guidelines or that they meet the criteria for the so-called working poor says little about who they really are and how they construct their social reality as they try to remain afloat. They maintain their attachment to mainstream social values and their dedication to self-reliance. They have a life and a conception of themselves within their social environment apart from their economic status, and they anticipate—and are trying to achieve—a better life for themselves and their children. Their impoverishment and social program participation exists alongside their commitment to the work ethic. Ultimately, their conception of themselves as legitimate citizens, worthy of all that such a designation entails, reveals them as survivors who are determined to cope with and overcome their current economic hard times.

O'Hare (1996) among others, noted nearly a decade ago the contradiction of individuals who work but are poor. At that time, when the poverty threshold for a family of four was $15,967, nearly 6 million children lived in families with poverty-level incomes despite the fact that at least one parent worked at least 50 weeks that year. "The biggest reason for their growth," O'Hare argued, "is declining job opportunities for adults who have not been to college. Thirty-eight percent of working-poor families have not graduated from high school, and another 35 percent have only a high school degree. Between 1973 and 1993, entry-level wages fell 30 percent for men with a high school degree, and 18 percent for women" (p. 1). A corollary to this bleak profile is the reality reported by the U.S. Census Bureau (2003), which reports that 3 out of 4 Americans experience a 5 percent fluctuation in their economic well-being—in either direction—from one year to the next. Although factors such as changes in family circumstances can affect economic status, changes in financial well-being are also correlated with shifts in income.

This picture has not changed dramatically in the intervening years. As of August 2004, according to the National Jobs for All Coalition, the economic indicators for those at risk were disturbing:

- Net job loss since the March 2001 recession . . . . . . . . . . . . . 1.2 million
- Official unemployment, as of July 2004 . . . . . . . . . . . . . . . . 8.2 million
- Additional jobs created *if* employment had grown
  by the average growth of the last three recessions . . . . . . . . . 6.2 million
- Real wages, for year ending June 2004 . . . . . . . . . . . 0.7 percent decline
- Median household income for 2003
  versus 2000 . . . . . . . . . . . . . . . . . . . . . . . . . . $43,318 versus $44,853
- Number of people in poverty for 2003
  versus 2000 . . . . . . . . . . . . . . . . . . . . . 35.9 million versus 31.6 million

- Those without health insurance for 2003
  versus 2000 . . . . . . . . . . . . . . . . . . . . . . . 45 million versus 40 million
  (Unemployment data are from the U.S. Bureau of Labor Statistics; other
  data from U.S. Census and Economic Policy Institute.)

Changes in economic well-being can also be measured in terms of participation in social programs. Data from the 2002 round of the National Survey of America's Families, according to an Urban Institute study by Nelson (2004), show that food hardship affected 51 percent of low-income parents in 2002. Housing hardship among single low-income parents increased from 32 percent in 1997 to 35 percent in 2002. The report concludes that:

> Food and housing hardship are important indicators of well-being. Patterns in these indicators drawn from the three rounds of the NSAF indicate that food hardship among low-income parents is likely to increase during weaker economic times. Housing hardship rates appear less sensitive than food hardship rates to economic fluctuations overall, but housing hardship increased for single parents during the recent downturn. Low-income single parents are especially vulnerable to food and housing hardship because their wages must cover all of their families' costs—a difficult feat with one paycheck.

Michael Leachman in a November 2004 press release from the Oregon Center for Public Policy (2004) reported that Oregon has lost 161,000 jobs since the economic downturn began in the late 1990s. Whatever gains that accrued to the state during the 1990s boom were entirely eradicated by the early 2000s, as the state witnessed a decline in its median income and an incline in the number of poor. The Census Bureau reported that real median household income remain unchanged between 2002 and 2003, at $43,318. The official poverty rate rose from 12.1 percent to 12.5 percent during the same period, alongside a similar rise in the percentage of those without health coverage from 15.2 percent to 15.6 percent (U.S. Census Bureau, 2003). Similar trends emerged from a National League of Cities (2003) study, which also showed that structural changes in the economy since the 1990s have limited the opportunities of low-wage workers, with larger percentages of these workers earning poverty-level or near-poverty-level wages and experiencing diminished prospects for advancement.

# THE ECONOMIC AND POLITICAL ENVIRONMENT
# OF THE NARRATIVES

## Income Inequality

Changes in economic conditions comprise an important context for the individuals whose life histories are contained in this book. The persons we interviewed have dealt with the vagaries of the American economy, and, as their stories attest, they have coped with the attendant consequences. The impact of these changing circumstances on the lives of our participants, along with the meaning they assign to their ability to cope and respond to an unpredictable economy, reveal much about the real-life human consequences of participation in social programs.

Economic prospects for all Americans have taken on a peculiar cast since the mid-1970s. To be sure, income inequality in America is perennial, but the two decades following World War II saw *both* rising incomes, spurred by a vigorous postwar economy, and inequality. As Levy (1987) suggests, the healthy 1947–73 economy enabled the whole income distribution to rise despite the constancy of income inequality, because good economic times allowed everyone to improve their situations.

Since then, the subtle transition to two main economic classes, the well-off and the not-so-well-off, can be witnessed in their respective income profiles. As the National League of Cities (2003) study attests:

> The real wages of workers with a high school education declined dramatically in the 1980s and did not start to pick up until the late 1990s; today, they remain lower than they were in the mid-1970s. The country has seen an ongoing loss of well-paid, lower-skilled manufacturing jobs—over 2 million manufacturing jobs have been lost since 2000. . . . Traditional avenues of advancement—like career ladders and seniority—are no longer assured for low-wage workers or for many other employees. This trend is exacerbated by the ongoing decline in unionization which has reduced the bargaining power of low-wage workers and decreased their access to health and retirement benefits. In addition, the amount of temporary and contract work—offering no benefits or job stability—doubled in the 1990s. Finally, the combination of high levels of immigration and welfare leavers entering the low-wage workforce may contribute to increasing the supply of labor and decreasing wages at the lower-end of the wage scale. (p. 7)

It is interesting that nearly two decades ago the National Conference of Catholic Bishops (1986), in its pastoral letter on the economy, cited both unequal income distribution and the impoverishment of national policy as the imperative for a new moral position. Their position was as unambiguous as it was prescient. Although it may very well be, in the view of Michael B. Katz (1989), that the bishops' document is "the finest modern American application of the principles of distributive justice to the problem of poverty" (p. 183), the political developments of the 1990s and early 2000s certainly suggest that the bishops' concerns are no longer "on the screen" of the American public, which, through its elected officials, seems to have taken a more laissez-faire approach to the matter.

A divide between Americans who anticipate continued rising income and those with opposite expectations is a current reality. Those in the former category have seen their incomes steadily increase (albeit at an incline less steep than what they experienced in the postwar period prior to 1973), and they anticipate similar advancement. Those in the latter category, including many who might characterize themselves as middle class, have experienced a wage slowdown and evaporating opportunities that portend not only stagnation but serious risk of falling behind. They experience a palpable fear of backsliding, with well-grounded concerns about receding further to the economic fringe. Scholars from Newman (1993) to Ehrenreich (2001) and Wolff (2002) tell the story of this very real economic insecurity and its consequences.

As recently as April 2002, the Economic Policy Institute (EPI) reported that the overall economic growth of the 1980s and 1990s and their associated low-unemployment levels were not enough to override the historically wide gap between high- and low-income families. Moreover, while this trend has been well documented at the national level, the EPI investigation, "Pulling Apart: A State-by-State Analysis of Income Trends" (2002) found that "it was not only the poor who failed to share fully in national prosperity. Over the past two decades, the gap between high-income families and families in the middle fifth of income distribution also grew in 44 states." Resulting hardships affect not only those who shared their stories with us but people from all walks of life. The "depth and tenacity" of the problem is revealed in the economy's persistent failure to mitigate the ever-widening income gap. As the report's author indicates, "Exceptionally low unemployment rates brought gains to low wage workers and fairly broad-based wage growth, especially in the last few years of the 1990s. Still, high-income families gained the most in the 1990s, and inequality grew over the decades" (Economic Policy Institute, 2002).

## Joblessness

Other related economic trends have converged to adversely affect the life chances of many low-income individuals, thus making them vulnerable to participation in the sort of social programs that are profiled in this text. Wilson (1996), for example, cites, among other variables, the increase caused by heightened levels of joblessness in the so-called new poverty neighborhoods, which he defines as "poor, segregated neighborhood[s] in which a substantial majority of individual adults are either unemployed or have dropped out of the labor force altogether" (p. 19). The threat to economic security is not located solely in Chicago, the site of Wilson's research; citing worrisome trends in the disappearance of jobs, Wilson (1996) argues that the nation's other largest central cities are at risk as well:

> For the first time in the twentieth century most adults in many inner ghetto neighborhoods are not working in a typical week. The disappearance of work has adversely affected not only individuals, families, and neighborhoods, but the social life of the city at large as well. Inner-city joblessness is a severe problem that is often overlooked or obscured when the focus is placed mainly on poverty and its consequences. Despite increases in the concentration of poverty since 1970, levels of joblessness in some neighborhoods are unprecedented.
>
> The consequences of high neighborhood joblessness are more devastating than those of high neighborhood poverty. A neighborhood in which people are poor but employed is different from a neighborhood in which people are poor and jobless. Many of today's problems in the inner-city ghetto neighborhoods—crime, family dissolution, welfare, low levels of social organization, and so on—are fundamentally a consequence of the disappearance of work. (p. xiii)

Certain structural trends in the economy, such as the globalization of the American economy, the deindustrialization of urban areas, the increase in the number of jobs requiring high-tech skills, and the skills mismatch between those seeking jobs and the skill requirements of available jobs contribute to the challenges faced by the individuals who shared their stories with us for this text. One of the consequences of these trends, cited by Schwartz and Volgy in 1992 and based on interviews they conducted in the early 1990s, was the emergence of a growing class of working poor, stuck in the lowest levels of the job market. These persons work year round and full time, but nonetheless find themselves in poverty and unable to afford basic necessities, such as food, medical coverage, housing, and clothing. Like Wilson (1987, 1996), Schwartz and Volgy suggested several causes of so-called working poverty, including discrimination against minorities and women, lack of skill because of poor educational opportunities, and the paucity of well-paying jobs related to the loss of America's competitive edge in the global market (p. 22).

Finally, according to a Census Bureau report on Dynamics of Economic Well-Being: Poverty, 1996–1999 (2003), poverty dynamics are quite variable, as the following highlights from the report indicate:

- On average, nearly 40.9 (±0.7) million people were poor in a given month in 1996, representing an average monthly poverty rate of 15.5 (±0.3) percent. By 1999, the number of people who were poor fell to 34.8 (±0.8) million, indicating an average monthly poverty rate of 12.8 (±0.3) percent in that year.

- About 34.2 (±0.4) percent of people were poor for at least 2 months during the panel, but only 2.0 (±0.1) percent were poor every month of the 4-year period between 1996 and 1999.

- Reflecting declines in poverty from 1996 and 1999, more people exited poverty (14.8 (±0.5) million) over that time than entered poverty (7.6 (±0.4) million)—as measured by examining people's poverty status in those 2 years using annual income and poverty thresholds.

- Of those who were poor in 1996 (using an annual poverty measure), 65.1 (±1.2) percent remained poor in 1997, 55.5 (±1.3) percent were poor in 1998, and 50.5 (±1.3) percent were poor in 1999. Of those who were not poor in 1996, only 2.9 (±0.2) percent became poor in 1997, 3.3 (±0.2) percent were poor in 1998, and 3.5 (±0.2) percent were poor in 1999.

- Poverty transitions occur more frequently when using a monthly rather than an annual poverty measure, indicating greater short-term fluctuations in income. Based on a monthly poverty measure (and excluding spells underway in the first interview month of the panel), 51.1 (±0.7) percent of poverty spells were over within 4 months, and about four-fifths were over after a year.

- Non-Hispanic Whites had lower poverty rates (measured using a variety of time frames), shorter median spell lengths, lower poverty entry rates, and higher poverty exit rates than Blacks and Hispanics. Patterns for Blacks and Hispanics were generally similar; Blacks showed a higher prevalence of poverty along a couple of measures (median spell length and poverty entry rate), lower according to one (episodic poverty), and were not different from Hispanics among yet others (average monthly poverty, chronic poverty, and poverty exit rate).

- Children tended to have higher poverty rates than adults 18 to 64 and people 65 and over. There were two exceptions: people 65 and over had higher chronic poverty rates (poor for the entire panel) and lower exit rates than the other two age groups, likely indicating less variability in their income over the panel.
- People in married-couple families tended to have lower poverty rates than people in other family types. Conversely, people in families with a female householder were more likely to be poor than others along all measures.
- People in suburbs had lower poverty rates than people in central cities or in nonmetropolitan territory across nearly all measures.

Collectively, these trends have implications for a sector of American workers at risk of downward economic mobility. Their potential or actual slide into social program participation exists alongside their expectation of a more permanent attachment to the labor market. Their inability to secure this attachment contributes to their perceptions about their receipt of public assistance.

## Changing Political Values

Societal perspectives with respect to those who, for one reason or another, must seek refuge in social program participation shifted in the 1990s, and this change has consequences for the lives we depict in this book. The political framework for this dramatic change was captured effectively by, among others, Kaus (1992) and Katz (1989), both of whom depicted the shift in the intellectual foundations that have historically supported the welfare state and its associated programs. Their observations remain powerful. Kaus made the case for what he termed "social equality," a state of existence based on "class-mixing" institutions that would bring together persons of different classes, thereby reinforcing their shared bonds rather than highlighting their differences. Kaus's proposed remedy, however, turned on a significant behavioral change among the poor and others outside the resource mainstream, including assumption of greater personal responsibility. Katz, on the other hand, addressed the notion that has framed public discourse about social welfare: the assignment of the poor into categories of "deserving" versus "undeserving." His chronicle of the evolution of the philosophical underpinnings of the "war on poverty" to the "war on welfare" suggests that by the 1990s there existed a readiness for a paradigm shift in our thinking about social welfare, one that set the stage for the bipartisan assault on programs in aid of the working poor and those on welfare.

One need look no further than the Personal Responsibility Work Opportunity Reconciliation Act (PRWORA) of 1996 for the most dramatic evidence of the transition in the political context for those who participate in social programs. This 1996 legislative initiative had its roots not only in traditional Republican rhetoric about personal responsibility and eradicating the "culture of poverty" but also in the campaign promise of then-Democratic presidential candidate Bill Clinton, who vowed to "end welfare as we know it." The focus of this promise was welfare, that is, cash assistance for poor persons, but the dismantling of the social welfare apparatus and the concomitant imposition of greater personal responsibility was also incorporated into the resultant legislation. Again, it is within this context that the lives chronicled in this text have unfolded.

What propels this fixation with the character flaws of the poor and near-poor? Ellwood's (1988) classic, *Poor Support,* laid out the values framework that resonates still and was evident in the rhetoric of the most recent presidential campaign and its fixation on "values."

- *Autonomy of the individual:* Americans believe that they have a significant degree of control over their destinies and, at a minimum, that people can provide for themselves if they are willing to make the necessary sacrifices. The rags-to-riches American dream permeates our culture. Rugged individualists win respect even if their behavior borders on the eccentric or even the criminal.
- *Virtue of work:* The work ethic is fundamental to our conceptions of ourselves and our expectations of others. People ought to work hard not only to provide for their families, but because laziness and idleness are seen as indications of weak moral character. The idle rich command as much disdain as jealousy; the idle poor are scorned.
- *Primacy of family:* The nuclear family is still the primary social and economic unit, and, certainly, its foremost responsibility is to raise children. Families are expected to socialize children, to guard their safety, to provide for their education, to impose discipline and direction, and to ensure their material well-being while they are young. The husband and wife are also expected to support each other.
- *Desire for and sense of community:* The autonomy of the individual and primacy of the family tend to push people in individualistic and often isolating directions. But the desire for community remains strong in everything from religion to neighborhood. Compassion and sympathy for others can be seen as flowing from a sense of connection with and empathy for others. (p. 16)

The challenge for those we interviewed is the reconciliation of these value tenets with their current economic status. To be sure, they certainly share these values, despite the fact that a superficial glance at their present conditions might indicate otherwise. Therein lies the rationale for asking them to share with us the meaning they assign not only to their lives but, equally important, their lives in relation to their participation in social programs. The interviews reveal the aspirations, frustrations, and challenges confronting the participants and therefore insights for social workers who come in contact with them.

# METHODOLOGY

In conducting our interviews, we covered considerable ground, including such issues as our participants' lives before their receipt of welfare and related assistance, their current reactions to such participation, their perspectives of the impact on their sense of self-reliance and independence, their assumptions about the values that inform the welfare reform debate, and their projections about their future. Using their current participation in social programs as a lens, we seek insight into our participants' life stories as these stories impinge on their current situations. As Martin (1995) points out:

> The inner narrative at any given time can be accessed to provide insight into the individual's inner life. It is not necessary that the story begin with the earliest years or even that chronological order and other historic points be scrupulously maintained. The "truth" lurks in the patterns and connections between life events as revealed in the telling of the story. Thus oral history, which formalizes the story-telling process with the interviewer-social worker intervening as midwife, can provide a bridge between the problems social workers and their clients seek to confront and the clients' own solutions. (p. 9)

Each interview took several hours, and each participant received financial compensation for his or her time and expenses. Each participant was asked to complete a consent agreement, which describes the purpose and scope of the interview as well as the fact that the contents of the exchange would be incorporated in this text. The confidentiality of the interviewee was assured by the changing of names, locations, and any other identifying information. We devised a protocol for the interviews, largely for organizational purposes and to ensure some degree of consistency between our efforts (we divided the interviews between us). All interviews were tape-recorded and subsequently transcribed, and these transcriptions, along with our field notes, comprised the basis for our analysis.

## The Participants

Our selection of participants warrants explanation. We first identified the key social program areas most relevant to the poor or near-poor: Temporary Assistance to Needy Families, Medicaid, Food Stamps, Supplemental Security Income, Unemployment Insurance, and housing. While this set does not represent the entire universe of social programs, it includes those most important to the life circumstances of the economically dislocated. Having selected the programs, we next turned our attention to the selection of participants. Our aim was to use a relatively small number of participants, but nonetheless capture an array of viewpoints and depict the diversity among program participants. Recognizing that representativeness per se is less central as a research value where oral history is concerned, our principal purpose was to lay out the phenomenological perspective of each participant and to do so in sufficient detail as to capture the truth of his or her narrative, that is, his or her story.

While one might argue that a larger sample universe would yield greater, arguably more representative insight, our view is that we have chosen our participants with sufficient care so as to provide an illustrative set of narratives.

## Conceptualizing "Social Construction" and the Analysis of the Histories

The analytical challenge we confronted stemmed from our desire not only to let the participants speak for themselves but also to provide some conceptual overlay to their life histories. To be sure, we lean in the direction of the former, as against the latter, but we believe there is something to be gained by explicating the lessons gleaned from our efforts. Perhaps the most instructive aspect of these narratives is the meaning the respondents assign to their lives in the light of their participation in social programs. Their construction of their circumstances, then, is the focus of our attention.

The social construction of reality (Berger & Luckmann, 1966) informs our approach to understanding our respondent' experiences. In this perspective, the multiple factors—social, cultural, historical, psychological, value—influencing each human being's perception and understanding of the world are recognized (Gergen, 1985). The interaction of our respondents with their social environment, including resource programs, is guided by social factors that shape their self-perception and social reality.

The conceptual framework discussed previously resonates with social work's person-in-environment orientation. The social work profession has a long-standing preoccupation with these mutually shaping influences, and our hope is to make evident this interaction in the lives of our participants. We anticipate that our respondents' stories will help us understand whether and how participants' perceptions of social welfare programs and their relationship with them are consonant with the legislative intent and shifting societal attitudes toward those in need.

## THE IMPLICATIONS FOR PROFESSIONAL PRACTICE

Our intention throughout the text is to enable social work professionals to use the insights gleaned from the program descriptions and these client narratives in their professional practice, particularly that part that focuses on helping clients to cope with problems in living caused by economic dislocation, by a lack of an attachment to the labor force. This conception of practice, which emphasizes the social work role as one that opens the door to resources that clients require, is not bound by modality, field of practice, social problem, or professional category identity (clinician, community organizer, psychotherapist, and so on). Rather, it is grounded in the very straightforward assumption that clients in any practice setting can become economically dislocated, and consequently social workers must be able to help them understand, access, and utilize appropriate social programs. Contemporary models of social work practice reinforce this perspective. The ecological (Germain & Gitterman, 1980); empowerment (Solomon, 1976); ecosystems (Meyer, 1983); interactional (Shulman, 2005); strengths (Saleebey, 2005); and structural (Goldberg-Wood & Middleman, 1989) models, among others, all perceive the provision of resources and the improvement of resource systems as an essential component of the domain of professional social work.

In light of the current political-economic climate, where the very concept of a right to governmental protection and basic needs provision has been challenged, it is imperative that clients receive professional support as they seek access to and utilize existing resources.

# 2 CHAPTER | UNDERSTANDING LEGAL PROCESSES

This chapter lays out the key features of the legal system, focusing particularly on legislative, regulatory, and judicial processes. The objective is to acquaint the reader with the rudiments of legal processes and their associated outcomes and to provide an overarching legal context for the programs that are explored in later chapters. The logic of this approach is straightforward: *Legislation* is the governing framework for social programs. Congress, or a state legislature, enacts a *statute* to address a particular social problem, such as care for the disabled under the Supplemental Security Income (SSI) program. This legislation, in turn, frames the programs to be provided and the associated funding allocation. However, although legislation describes what must be done, it is not self-enforcing. Implementation and enforcement of legislation is the province of administrative or regulatory (these terms are used interchangeably) agencies.

*Administrative agencies* are brought into existence through legislation and exist to put legislation into effect; that is, the legislature enacts a statute and turns to the appropriate regulatory body to implement statutory objectives. For example, Congress enacts the Personal Responsibility and Work Opportunity Reconciliation Act (PRWORA) and then turns to the Department of Health and Human Services (DHHS) to implement legislative provisions, such as the Temporary Assistance to Needy Families (TANF) Program, which is one of the first titles under the new law. How is implementation achieved? Through regulations, which are rules that are issued by *regulatory agencies* that have the binding force of law.

Courts are the third of three institutions that comprise the American legal system. Using an *adversarial judicial process* grounded in decision-making based on *precedent* or *stare decisis,* courts exist to settle disputes, which are often based on disagreements about the application of statutes and/or regulations. That is, anyone who feels adversely affected by a legislative or regulatory rule can seek redress in a court of law. For example, California's statutory provision that allowed for two-tier welfare benefit levels based on the recipients' length of residency within the state was challenged as unconstitutional because it promoted unequal treatment and interfered with the fundamental right to travel. In the 1999 case of *Saenz v. Roe,* the U.S. Supreme Court invalidated the California legislation and, in the process, also held as unconstitutional a related provision of the PRWORA.

Having laid out the essential elements of the American legal system, we turn now to a brief description of the processes associated with each. In the course of this description, we also discuss how to read and analyze legislation, regulations, and judicial opinions.

## THE LEGISLATIVE PROCESS: LEGISLATIVE AUTHORITY, STRUCTURE, AND FUNCTION

State and federal legislatures have similar structures.[1] Both have two chambers (Nebraska, with only one chamber, is the exception among the states), which provide for different tenures for its members, that is, varying terms of office (for example, the U.S. Senate members are elected for six-year terms; House members, for two years). There are currently 100 members of the U.S. Senate and 435 members of the U.S. House of Representatives. The size of each state's chambers varies. Each legislature exercises its lawmaking authority as stated in its constitution. For example, Article I of the U.S. Constitution defines the scope of congressional lawmaking authority: "All legislative Powers herein granted shall be vested in a congress of the United States, which shall consist of a Senate and House of Representatives. . . . [It] shall make all Laws which shall be necessary and proper for carrying into Execution [their enumerated] Powers, and all other Powers vested by this Constitution in the government of the United States, or in any Department or Officer thereof" (U.S. Constitution, Article I).

The legislative process depicts, essentially, the process by which a bill (proposed legislation) becomes a law. The typical events range from the bill's introduction in a committee within a legislative chamber (that is, House of

---

1. The materials on legal processes and legal research resources are excerpted from Raymond Albert, *Law and Social Work Practice: A Legal Systems Approach* (New York: Springer Publishing Co., 2000). Reprinted with permission.

# HOW A BILL BECOMES A LAW
# IN THE UNITED STATES CONGRESS

**2.1**

### A. Legislation is Introduced

Any member can introduce a piece of legislation.

> House—Legislation is handed to the clerk of the House or placed in the hopper.
>
> Senate—Members must gain recognition of the presiding officer to announce the introduction of a bill during the morning hour. If any senator objects, the introduction of the bill is postponed until the next day.
>
> > The bill is assigned a number. (e.g. HR1 or S1).
> >
> > The bill is labeled with the sponsor's name.
> >
> > The bill is sent to the Government Printing Office and copies are made.
> >
> > Senate bills can be jointly sponsored.
> >
> > Members can cosponsor the piece of Legislation.

### B. Committee Action

The bill is referred to the appropriate committee by the Speaker of the House or the presiding officer in the Senate. Most often the actual referral decision is made by the House or Senate parliamentarian. Bills may be referred to more than one committee and it may be split so that parts are sent to different committees. The Speaker of the House may set time limits on committees. Bills are placed on the calendar of the committee to which they have been assigned. Failure to act on a bill is equivalent to killing it. Bills in the House can only be released from committee without a proper committee vote by a discharge petition signed by a majority of the House membership (218 members).

COMMITTEE STEPS:

1. Comments about the bill's merit are requested by government agencies.
2. Bill can be assigned to subcommittee by Chairman.
3. Hearings may be held.
4. Subcommittees report their findings to the full committee.
5. Finally there is a vote by the full committee—the bill is "ordered to be reported."
6. A committee will hold a "mark-up" session during which it will make revisions and additions. If substantial amendments are made, the committee can order the introduction of a "clean bill" which will include the proposed amend-

---

Representatives or Senate) to its consideration by other committees, to hearings held by various committees, to remarks about the bill uttered by individual legislators on the floor of the House or Senate, to the final vote on the bill by one or both chambers, to final signing into law. (A detailed discussion of this process for the U.S. Congress can be found at http://www.talktogov.com/howabill.htm., and the process is illustrated in Box 2.1.)

ments. This new bill will have a new number and will be sent to the floor while the old bill is discarded. The chamber must approve, change or reject all committee amendments before conducting a final passage vote.

7. After the bill is reported, the committee staff prepares a written report explaining why they favor the bill and why they wish to see their amendments, if any, adopted. Committee members who oppose a bill sometimes write a dissenting opinion in the report. The report is sent back to the whole chamber and is placed on the calendar.

8. In the House, most bills go to the Rules committee before reaching the floor. The committee adopts rules that will govern the procedures under which the bill will be considered by the House. A "closed rule" sets strict time limits on debate and forbids the introduction of amendments. These rules can have a major impact on whether the bill passes. The rules committee can be bypassed in three ways: (1) members can move rules to be suspended (requires 2/3 vote) (2) a discharge petition can be filed (3) the House can use a Calendar Wednesday procedure.

**C. Floor Action**

1. Legislation is placed on the Calendar
   House: Bills are placed on one of four House Calendars. They are usually placed on the calendars in the order of which they are reported yet they don't usually come to the floor in this order—some bills never reach the floor at all. The Speaker of the House and the Majority Leader decide what will reach the floor and when. (Legislation can also be brought to the floor by a discharge petition.)
   Senate: Legislation is placed on the Legislative Calendar. There is also an Executive calendar to deal with treaties and nominations. Scheduling of legislation is the job of the Majority Leader. Bills can be brought to the floor when ever a majority of the Senate chooses.

2. Debate
   House: Debate is limited by the rules formulated in the Rules Committee. The Committee of the Whole debates and amends the bill but cannot technically pass it. Debate is guided by the Sponsoring Committee and time is divided equally between proponents and opponents. The Committee decides how much time to allot to each person. Amendments must be germane to the subject of a bill—no riders are allowed. The bill is reported back to the House (to itself) and is voted on. A quorum call is a vote to make sure that there are enough members present (218) to have a final vote. If there is not a quorum, the House will

*continued*

The process for states is comparable to that used by the U.S. Congress. Box 2.2, detailing the legislative process for the Kentucky General Assembly, will suffice to illustrate the workings of state legislatures. The excerpt comes from the Louisville *Courier-Journal*, and it provides a realistic lay-language description of the process, including some sentiments about how ideas make their way into the legislature.

adjourn or will send the Sergeant at Arms out to round up missing members. Senate: Debate is unlimited unless cloture is invoked. Members can speak as long as they want and amendments need not be germane—riders are often offered. Entire bills can therefore be offered as amendments to other bills. Unless cloture is invoked, Senators can use a filibuster to defeat a measure by "talking it to death."

3. Vote—the bill is voted on. If passed, it is then sent to the other chamber unless that chamber already has a similar measure under consideration. If either chamber does not pass the bill then it dies. If the House and Senate pass the same bill then it is sent to the President. If the House and Senate pass different bills they are sent to Conference Committee. Most major legislation goes to a Conference Committee.

**D. Conference Committee**
1. Members from each house form a conference committee and meet to work out the differences. The committee is usually made up of senior members who are appointed by the presiding officers of the committee that originally dealt with the bill. The representatives from each house work to maintain their version of the bill.
2. If the Conference Committee reaches a compromise, it prepares a written conference report which is submitted to each chamber.
3. The conference report must be approved by both the House and the Senate.

**E. The President**
The bill is sent to the President for review.
1. A bill becomes law if signed by the President or if not signed within 10 days and Congress is in session.
2. If Congress adjourns before the 10 days and the President has not signed the bill then it does not become law ("Pocket Veto.")
3. If the President vetoes the bill it is sent back to Congress with a note listing his/her reasons. The chamber which originated the legislation can attempt to override the veto by a vote of two-thirds of those present. If the veto of the bill is overridden in both chambers then it becomes law.

**F. The Bill Becomes A Law**
Once a bill is signed by the President or his veto is overridden by both houses it becomes a law and is assigned an official number.

The authority to act, however, does not speak to the issue of competency: Can a legislative institution effectively execute what it has the exclusive power to do? As citizens, we turn to legislatures to address numerous social problems, but in so doing we threaten to strain their competency. On the one hand, legislatures are perceived as the rule-making mechanism closest to the people and, consequently, express the vagaries of public opinion (Hurst, 1982). On

| 2.2 | HOW A BILL BECOMES LAW: KENTUCKY GENERAL ASSEMBLY |

## HOW A BILL BECOMES LAW: KENTUCKY GENERAL ASSEMBLY

### 1. A Bill Starts as an Idea

It can be an idea from an individual, a group or a lawmaker. Few bills involve sweeping changes—many propose small changes to existing law. To survive, bills must have some support among lawmakers and their leadership.

### 2. A Bill Is Introduced

Only a member of the General Assembly can introduce a bill. Anyone can submit an idea to a legislator. However, each legislator has thousands of constituents, and hundreds of special-interest groups hire lobbyists to compete for legislators' attention.

### 3. First Steps

After a bill is introduced, it is assigned to a standing committee for review. Many bills simply go to the most logical spot—for example, a bill on law enforcement would go to the Judiciary Committee. But lawmakers also can bury a bill by sending it to a committee whose chairman may refuse to call it up for consideration.

### 4. Committee Action

Committee chairmen have great power to advance or kill a bill. A chairman can quietly kill a bill by not calling it up—or by waiting till too late in the session to effectively consider it. Once a bill is called up for hearing, supporters or opponents can testify in front of the committee. If the committee approves the bill, it goes to either the House or the Senate.

### 5. To the Floor

A bill gets its first and second reading on the floor of the House or Senate, depending on where it was introduced. That essentially serves as notice it's coming up for a vote by the full chamber. After second reading, it goes to the Rules Committee, which can schedule it for a final vote. Debate—and often, a host of amendments—follow.

### 6. Voting

A vote to pass a bill is always by roll call. Floor debate beforehand seldom sways the final vote on a bill since most lawmakers have made up their minds by then. For a bill to pass, it must have a majority of those voting and at least two-fifths of all members—40 in the 100-seat House and 16 in the 38-member Senate. For bills that have an immediate effective date, a majority of the body—at least 51 House members or 20 senators—is required. In odd-numbered years, bills to raise taxes or spend money must get a three-fifths vote—60 in the House and 23 in the Senate.

### 7. After It's Passed

If a bill is passed, it's sent to the other chamber for approval, where it goes through much the same process. On a complex or important piece of legislation, new

*continued*

amendments may be attached. Both the House and Senate must agree on the same version of a bill before it becomes law. If they can't agree, the bill goes to a conference committee with members from each chamber. That committee usually comes up with a compromise version of the bill. That version must still be approved a final time by the House and Senate. If both approve the bill, it goes to the governor.

**8. Action by the Governor**
The governor has 10 days, excluding Sundays, to act. He can sign a bill into law, allow it to become law without his signature or veto it. If vetoed, the bill returns to the General Assembly, which can enact it into law through a majority vote of each chamber—51 in the House, 20 in the Senate.

Source: *Louisville Courier-Journal.* Available at http://www.courier-journal.com/legislature/2003preview/Feb02/stories/ke013103s358838.htm

the other hand, legislatures are also settings for compromise (Dworkin, 1979; Nunez, 2004). The rules that emerge typically reflect the negotiations among diverse and competing interests. In this way, one of the most attractive legislative features, "representation of public interests," can produce two seemingly incompatible tendencies: receptivity to evolutionary social norms and a narrowing of that receptivity caused by the need to reach a consensus on competing normative views.

Legislatures must rely heavily on administrative agencies for policy implementation, so the connection between legislative intention and implementation cannot be overstated. This remains the case especially for judicial interpretation of legislation, where a court seeks to apply a rule of law derived from a statute. In these circumstances, the court is compelled to discern and articulate the legislature's will. "Statutes are binding statements of law," argue Hanks, et al (1994 ). "One can imagine a different system, but in the one we have, legislatures can overturn decisions by courts but courts cannot rewrite or ignore legislature. This is the principle of 'legislative supremacy.' Subject to constitutional limitations, statutes trump other sources of law" (pp. 227–228).

## HOW TO READ A STATUTE OR BILL

Legislation (or proposed legislation, that is, a bill) contains certain structural features, the key components of which are as follows:

*   *Identifying designation:* House or Senate Bill number or Public Law number. Both state and federal bills or statutes have similar designations.
*   *Title:* The legislation's subject—"A Bill to . . ."; "An Act to . . ."
*   *Enacting clause:* A statement that the legislature adopts as law the language that follows this clause—"Be it enacted by . . . that . . ." Essen-

tially, that which follows this clause is the law the legislature wishes to enact.

- *Purpose or findings:* The facts and issues that comprise the reason for the legislation; it's a statement of the "evil" or problem the legislation seeks to address. Because it follows the "enacting clause," the purpose is part of the legislation and is frequently codified as such.
- *Definitions:* Terms that have special meanings within the statute.
- *Purview:* The body of the law; it contains the substantive provisions, the available remedies under, and provisions for administrative implementation or enforcement.

Box 2.3, an excerpt of the public law that was enacted as the 1996 welfare reform legislation, lays out the elements of a statute and what those elements reveal about the nature and intent of lawmakers.

How does one make sense of these elements? Naturally, the actual text of the legislation is the logical place to begin the analysis. But the text is not always clear, and in these circumstances it becomes necessary for a court to interpret the intention of the legislature. The task can be daunting, as the legislature does not always explicate its goals and objectives, and a court must compensate for its ignorance by looking for clues, often found in the statutory language or in the hearings that occurred as the bill was moving through the legislative process. While no perfect formula exists for statutory analysis, Statsky (1984) offers the following considerations for uncovering the meaning of legislation.

- *Statutory text is unclear.* The ambiguity is sometimes by design; but more often than not it is due to poor draftsmanship or the limitations of language. The search for meaning will require interpretation.
- *Legislative intent (that is, what the legislature intended to achieve) will always be beyond our grasp.* Under the best circumstances intent will be elusive because one can never definitively discern the intention of the legislature as it deliberates a bill. The documents that comprise the legislative trial can put "intent" within our reach, but on the more complicated issues, it can easily elude our grasp.
- *Statutes should be read one word at a time.* Proceed through them line by line, attending to each punctuation mark and qualification; the grammatical marks and the language are not idle choices but often drivers for what the legislature hopes will take effect.

## THE ADMINISTRATIVE PROCESS: KEY FEATURES
## OF ADMINISTRATIVE AUTHORITY

We turn now to the administrative or regulatory process, which results in regulations that put into effect the will of the legislature. Statutes are not self-enforcing; the legislature specifies in the legislation it enacts the broad goals it wants to achieve and delegates authority to the administrative agency to carry out its intentions. Social work professionals intersect with these agencies through the

EXAMPLE OF A PUBLIC LAW:
ELEMENTS OF A STATUTE (P.L. 104-193)

### SECTION 1. SHORT TITLE.
This Act may be cited as the **"Personal Responsibility and Work Opportunity Reconciliation Act of 1996"**.

### SEC. 2. TABLE OF CONTENTS.
The table of contents for this Act is as follows:

TITLE I—BLOCK GRANTS FOR TEMPORARY ASSISTANCE FOR NEEDY FAMILIES

TITLE I—BLOCK GRANTS FOR TEMPORARY ASSISTANCE FOR NEEDY FAMILIES

### Sec. 101. FINDINGS.
The Congress makes the following findings:

(1) Marriage is the foundation of a successful society.
(2) Marriage is an essential institution of a successful society which promotes the interests of children.
(3) Promotion of responsible fatherhood and motherhood is integral to successful child rearing and the well-being of children.
(4) In 1992, only 54 percent of single-parent families with children had a child support order established and, of that 54 percent, only about one-half received the full amount due. Of the cases enforced through the public child support enforcement system, only 18 percent of the caseload has a collection.
(5) The number of individuals receiving aid to families with dependent children (in this section referred to as "AFDC") has more than tripled since 1965. More

---

regulations that guide their daily practice, especially in fields such as child welfare, juvenile justice, and mental health. Occasionally, a party adversely affected by a regulation will challenge it in court, at which point a judge interprets the regulation to determine that it is consistent with legislative objectives. This judicial interpretation underscores the essential linkage between regulations and statutes; the former must be framed to implement the latter.

Administrative agencies exist at local, state, and federal levels, and their primary charge is to implement legislative goals. They were created as a repository of the expertise required to achieve the legislature's aims and, in the process, advance the interest of the public. The institutional arrangement that produces this outcome follows from the legislature's single mandate to make the law—a constitutionally inspired provision that recognizes that the legislature must ultimately turn to the administrative agency to implement its objectives. This situation results in agencies being responsible for enacting more law

than two-thirds of these recipients are children. Eighty-nine percent of children receiving AFDC benefits now live in homes in which no father is present.

(A) (i)   The average monthly number of children receiving AFDC benefits—
        (I)    was 3,300,000 in 1965;
        (II)   was 6,200,000 in 1970;
        (III)  was 7,400,000 in 1980; and
        (IV)   was 9,300,000 in 1992.
     (ii)  While the number of children receiving AFDC benefits increased nearly threefold between 1965 and 1992, the total number of children in the United States aged 0 to 18 has declined by 5.5 percent.

(B) The Department of Health and Human Services has estimated that 12,000,000 children will receive AFDC benefits within 10 years.

(C) The increase in the number of children receiving public assistance is closely related to the increase in births to unmarried women. Between 1970 and 1991, the percentage of live births to unmarried women increased nearly threefold, from 10.7 percent to 29.5 percent.

(6)  The increase of out-of-wedlock pregnancies and births is well documented as follows:

(A) It is estimated that the rate of nonmarital teen pregnancy rose 23 percent from 54 pregnancies per 1,000 unmarried teenagers in 1976 to 66.7 pregnancies in 1991. The overall rate of nonmarital pregnancy rose 14 percent from 90.8 pregnancies per 1,000 unmarried women in 1980 to 103 in both 1991 and 1992. In contrast, the overall pregnancy rate for married couples decreased 7.3 percent between 1980 and 1991, from 126.9 pregnancies per 1,000 married women in 1980 to 117.6 pregnancies in 1991. [The detailed presentation of evidence regarding the crisis of out-of-wedlock births is omitted here.]

Therefore, in light of this demonstration of the crisis in our Nation, it is the sense of the Congress that prevention of out-of-wedlock pregnancy and reduction in out-of-wedlock birth are very important Government interests and the policy contained in part A of title IV of the Social Security Act (as amended by section 103(a) of this Act) is intended to address the crisis.

than the legislature; however, this is not to suggest that agencies operate without constraints. The reverse is true: they operate within the context of the enabling legislation that governs their activities.

Administrative agencies promulgate (issue) regulations that have the force of law to inform the public about new standards of conduct to which they must conform. Agency officials must be similarly cognizant of these changes, given their responsibility to implement the regulations. Both agency officials and those affected by agency decisions must recognize the interaction between legislative goals and their accomplishment through agency regulations.

An agency must carry out its statutory mandate within the bounds of the authority delegated to it by the legislature. The regulations thus promulgated have the force of law. And when an agency exceeds its statutory authority, its conduct is *ultra vires* (that is, beyond the scope of its authority) and therefore void. This arrangement demonstrates, on the one hand, the tension created by our need to reconcile the administrative process with the separation of powers doctrine and, on the other hand, our determination to have some governmental institution handle complex social problems. Moreover, the delegation of authority is not unlimited. Agency conduct must be gauged against the enabling legislation's original intent and related policy goals. An agency, consequently, can only make and enforce such rules as are necessary to put into effect legislative policy. Congress and state legislatures retain jurisdiction over delegated authority through mechanisms such as legislative oversight, budget appropriations, confirmation power over executive branch officials, and the ability to rescind the delegation.

## STAGES IN THE ADMINISTRATIVE PROCESS

### The Administrative Procedures Act

The Administrative Procedures Act (5 U.S.C. § 551 *et seq.*) grew out of New Deal experiments with the use of administrative agencies to handle social problems. It was enacted in 1946 and was welcomed as a major instrument in maintaining fairness. It provides an important framework for guaranteeing due process in administrative procedures. The act spells out the conditions under which the public can participate in, among other things, the administrative rule-making process.

### The Rule-Making Process

Rule making involves developing regulations for future implementation. The agency issues three types of rules:

1. *Procedural rules,* which identify an agency's organization, describe its method of operation, and spell out the requirements of its practice for rule making and adjudicative hearings. . . . These housekeeping rules are usually authorized by the agency's enabling act and are binding on the agency.
2. *Interpretative rules,* which are issued by an agency to guide both its staff and regulated parties as to how the agency will interpret its statutory mandate. They . . . are issued only after interested persons are given notice and an opportunity to be heard.
3. *Substantive rules,* which are, in effect, administrative statutes. [These are the regulations typically encountered by social workers and other professionals in practice.] In issuing a substantive rule, the administrator exercises lawmaking power delegated to him or her by the legislature. Notice and hearings must usually precede issuance of the rule. (Robinson & Gellhorn, 1972)

The rule-making process unfolds in two stages. The *first stage* deals with the proposed rules, which must be published prior to implementation in order to allow sufficient time for public comment. This event fulfills the requirement for notice to the public before the rule is made final, and is accomplished by publishing the proposed rule. (Federal regulations are published in the *Federal Register*; state regulations are found in comparable documents published by state agencies.) The comments from interested parties generally address their perceptions about how the rules will affect them. The comment period is limited to a specified time (for example, 30 days). Comments can be offered in writing, or in some cases at a public hearing. The *second stage* deals with the compilation and analysis of public responses following the comment period. The agency then announces its final rules or regulations, which proceed through a similar notice and comment period. The process culminates in the publication of the final regulations and the date on which they will take effect.

Box 2.4 presents an excerpt from the *Federal Register,* the source for initial publication of a federal regulation, to illustrate the scope of a typical rule. The full text of the regulation is not included, but the text that is supplied signals the stance of the Department of Health and Human Services regarding the requirements for verifying the alien registration status as a precondition to receipt of federal program benefits. The regulation was issued against the background of the 1996 welfare reform legislation and is written to be consistent with the goals that Congress sought to achieve.

## HOW TO READ AND ANALYZE REGULATIONS

Regulations are published in the *Federal Register* (for federal regulations) and in a counterpart document at the state level. Such publication gives the public an opportunity to read and comment on rules that affect their behavior, and agencies integrate any feedback from the public into their final announcement of regulations. However, the purpose and intent of a regulation cannot always be discerned by simply reading it. Regulations are designed to enact legislation, and there must be consistency between the two. Where inconsistency exists—for example, when an agency issues a regulation that might arguably go beyond what the legislature intended—it becomes necessary to reconcile the two rules, and this process of reconciliation often entails interpreting what both the regulatory agency and the legislation intended. Statsky (1975) offers some compelling advice for solving this sort of problem:

> Because a regulation exists, you cannot assume that it is valid. Simply because the agency is giving an official interpretation of its regulations (in connection with the facts of your case), you cannot assume that that interpretation is correct, even though the same agency that passed the regulation is the agency that is now interpreting it. (p. 140)

Statsky's analytical framework is comprised of four questions, all of which are designed to provoke critical consideration of the regulation in the light of the relevant statutory authority:

SCOPE OF A TYPICAL RULE

FEDERAL REGISTER
Vol. 63, No. 149
Proposed Rules
DEPARTMENT OF JUSTICE (DOJ)
Immigration and Naturalization Service
8 CFR Part 104
[INS No. 1902-98; AG Order No. 2170-98]
RIN 1115-AE99
Verification of Eligibility for Public Benefits
Part III
63 FR 41662

**DATE:** Tuesday, August 4, 1998

**ACTION:** Proposed rule.

**SUMMARY:** This rule amends the Immigration and Naturalization Service ("Service") regulations by establishing a new part requiring certain entities that provide Federal public benefits (with certain exceptions) to verify, by examining alien applicants' evidence of alien registration and by using a Service automated verification system that the applicants are eligible for the benefits under welfare reform legislation. The rule also sets forth procedures by which a State or local government can verify whether an alien applying for a State or local public benefit is a qualified alien, a nonimmigrant, or an alien paroled into the United States for less than 1 year, for purposes of determining whether the alien is eligible for the benefit. In addition, the rule establishes procedures for verifying the U.S. nationality of individuals applying for benefits in a fair and nondiscriminatory manner.

---

1. Is there some statute in existence that gives the agency authority to pass regulations on the *general subject matter* of the regulation before you?
2. Is there a statute that is the authority for the *particular* regulation before you?
3. Is the *agency's interpretation* of its own regulation consistent with the statute upon which it is based?
4. Is *your interpretation* of the regulation consistent with the statute?

Exhibit 2.5 provides an opportunity to evaluate the connection between the intent of the legislature and the implementation of that intention through issuing a regulation. It is an excerpt from the language of the 1996 welfare reform legislation, restricting welfare and public benefits for aliens. Compare the statutory language of Box 2.5, taking special note of congressional findings regarding welfare and immigration, with the text of the regulation presented in Box 2.4, which was issued to implement this provision of the law.

DATES: Written comments must be submitted on or before October 5, 1998.

SUPPLEMENTARY INFORMATION:
*Statutory Authority*
Section 432 of the Personal Responsibility and Work Opportunity Reconciliation Act of 1996 ("PRWORA"), Pub. L. 104-193, as amended by section 504 of the Illegal Immigration Reform and Immigrant Responsibility Act of 1996 ("IIRIRA"), Pub. L. 104-208, and by section 5572 of the Balanced Budget Act of 1997, Pub. L. 105-33, 8 U.S.C. 1642, requires the Attorney General to promulgate regulations requiring verification that a person applying for a Federal public benefit (subject to certain exceptions) is a qualified alien and is eligible to receive the benefit. The same statutory provision requires the Attorney General to promulgate regulations that set forth the procedures by which a State or local government can verify whether an alien applying for a State or local public benefit is a qualified alien, a nonimmigrant under the Immigration and Nationality Act, 8 U.S.C. 11001 et seq. (the "Act"), or an alien paroled into the United States for less than 1 year, for purposes of determining whether the alien is eligible for the benefit. In addition, 8 U.S.C. 1642(a)(2) requires the Attorney General to establish procedures for a person applying for a Federal public benefit to provide proof of citizenship in a fair and nondiscriminatory manner.

*Background*
[The section on background is omitted here.]

*Analysis of the Rule*
The rule is designed to provide effective, flexible, efficient, fair, nondiscriminatory, and user-friendly methods by which government agencies and their contractors, agents, or designees (other than nonprofit charitable organizations) that provide public benefits ("benefit granting agencies") may carry out their responsibilities to ensure that those benefits are provided only to those persons eligible to receive them under Federal law. . . .

Consider whether the regulation is consistent with the legislation, whether it appears to give effect to congressional intentions, as implicit in the statutory language.

# THE JUDICIAL PROCESS: CASE LAW, PRECEDENT, AND COURT HIERARCHY

Courts hear an array of disputes, and resolve them by referring to rules gleaned from prior cases. The disputing parties end up in court because they cannot (or will not) resort to violent force, because they cannot reach a mutually acceptable compromise, because they feel entitled to their "day in court," or some combination of all of these. Motivation notwithstanding, they seek a court-imposed solution. In so doing, the parties may agree more or less with

**2.5**  |  EXCERPT FROM P.L. 104-193

SECTION 1. SHORT TITLE.
This Act may be cited as the **"Personal Responsibility and Work Opportunity Reconciliation Act of 1996"**.

TITLE IV—RESTRICTING WELFARE AND PUBLIC BENEFITS FOR ALIENS

*Sec. 400. STATEMENTS OF NATIONAL POLICY CONCERNING WELFARE AND IMMIGRATION.*
The Congress makes the following statements concerning national policy with respect to welfare and immigration:
(1) Self-sufficiency has been a basic principle of United States immigration law since this country's earliest immigration statutes.
(2) It continues to be the immigration policy of the United States that—
     (A) aliens within the Nation's borders not depend on public resources to meet their needs, but rather rely on their own capabilities and the resources of their families, their sponsors, and private organizations, and
     (B) the availability of public benefits not constitute an incentive for immigration to the United States.
(3) Despite the principle of self-sufficiency, aliens have been applying for and receiving public benefits from Federal, State, and local governments at increasing rates.
(4) Current eligibility rules for public assistance and unenforceable financial support agreements have proved wholly incapable of assuring that individual aliens not burden the public benefits system.
(5) It is a compelling government interest to enact new rules for eligibility and sponsorship agreements in order to assure that aliens be self-reliant in accordance with national immigration policy.
(6) It is a compelling government interest to remove the incentive for illegal immigration provided by the availability of public benefits.
(7) With respect to the State authority to make determinations concerning the eligibility of qualified aliens for public benefits in this title, a State that chooses to follow the Federal classification in determining the eligibility of such aliens for public assistance shall be considered to have chosen the least restrictive means available for achieving the compelling governmental interest of assuring that aliens be self-reliant in accordance with national immigration policy.
Subtitle A—Eligibility for Federal Benefits

*Sec. 401. ALIENS WHO ARE NOT QUALIFIED; ALIENS INELIGIBLE FOR FEDERAL PUBLIC BENEFITS.*
(a) In General.—Notwithstanding any other provision of law and except as provided in subsection (b), an alien who is not a qualified alien (as defined in section 431) is not eligible for any Federal public benefit.

the judicial remedy, but their ultimate satisfaction with the outcome will depend on whether they feel they are treated fairly. And in our legal system, fairness is conveyed when similar disputes receive similar treatment.

This method of dispute resolution produces *case law*—where rules applied in a dispute today are gleaned from earlier disputes between A and B, and, consequently, these rules may in turn become relevant to future conflicts between C and D. Case law development is encapsulated in the concept of decision-making based on precedent, also referred to as *stare decisis,* which focuses on consistency of result. The doctrine of *stare decisis,* derived from a Latin phrase meaning "to stand by precedents and not to disturb settled points," simultaneously reinforces the binding effect of judicial decisions and emphasizes the way legal rules become authoritative in a particular jurisdiction (that is, a geographic area that contains a hierarchy of courts, such as a state or within the federal system). The resulting uniformity is due to the requirement that courts within a jurisdiction be bound by the decisions rendered by their particular jurisdiction, especially when those decisions emerge from a higher court.

Court systems exist at the federal and at the state level. Although each varies slightly, their hierarchy is similar. Lower-level decisions can be reviewed by higher levels, and the process ends with some "court of last resort." And each lower-level court is bound by the precedents established in a higher level. For example, a federal trial court (that is, District Court) is bound by the rulings of the federal Circuit Court of Appeals for its circuit (a geographical region). A state's highest appellate court, usually referred to as a Supreme Court, announces decisions that must be followed by all lower state courts.

## State Court Structure

- *"Inferior" or "petty" courts:* The lowest court is designated to handle very minor disputes, usually involving small amounts of money. These "petty" courts generally take the form of a justice of the peace, a district justice, or a municipal court. Their jurisdiction (the matters they may hear) is cast in terms of the dollar amount in dispute; that is, the claims can only be heard by these courts if they don't exceed a certain dollar amount. (Small claims disputes are a prime example.) Though referred to as "inferior," they are the forum where most "everyday disputes" are heard. They thus provide necessary access for those who otherwise might be locked out of the civil process.
- *Trial courts of general jurisdiction:* The next level is the court of general jurisdiction, the one empowered to hear all cases without regard to money limitations. Again, the names vary; some are referred to as Superior Courts, others, Courts of Common Pleas.
- *Appellate courts:* These courts review lower court decisions. They are intermediary tribunals and are most often known as Courts of Appeal. Their decisions are reviewed by the state's highest court.

- *Supreme courts:* The state Supreme Court is the state's "court of last resort." It reviews all lower level decisions and announces the final word on the state's law.

## Federal Court Structure

The federal hierarchy is like the states' in that there are trial and appellate levels. Unlike the states heirarchy, however, each level is referred to by the same name in each of the country's geographical regions.

- *District Court:* These are the federal trial courts. They are courts of general jurisdiction, although there are some cases that they alone can hear (for example, so-called federal questions and disputes where the amount in controversy exceeds $10,000). There are 95 judicial districts in the United States.
- *Courts of Appeal:* Known as Circuit Courts of Appeal, these intermediate appellate tribunals hear appeals from the District Courts. The country is divided into 11 circuits.
- *U.S. Supreme Court:* The ultimate "court of last resort," the Supreme Court announces the "law of the land." It hears appeals from lower-level federal courts and from state supreme courts. It may also hear, at its discretion, cases that petition for a *writ of certiorari* (a request for the record of a lower court with the expectation of granting a review of a lower court's decision).

## HOW TO READ AND ANALYZE A CASE

### The Structure of a Judicial Opinion

A judicial opinion must be analyzed to discover the court's rule selection and its accompanying rationale. Every opinion specifies the parties, the facts, the issues before the court, the lower court decisions, the court's decision or holding, and the court's reasoning for its decision.

*Briefing* is a technique designed to break down an opinion into its component parts. The technique relies on a series of questions that may be used to capture the opinion's essential elements.

- Who are the parties in the dispute? What does each want?
- On what legal theory does each base its claims?
- How was the dispute handled in lower courts? Who appealed and why?
- What are the facts, as the court describes them?
- What is the legal issue the court is being asked to decide?
- What is the court's decision? (Also known as the *holding,* which is sometimes designated by a phrase such as "the court holds that . . .") Essentially, to "hold" is to "declare the conclusion of law reached by the court as to the legal effects of the facts decided" (Black, 1968).

- What reasons does the court offer to support its decision? What are its sources of authority (precedents)?
- How does the dissenting (or concurring) opinion, if there is one, depart from the majority?
- To what extent does the decision follow from the cited precedents? How does the court discuss precedents? Does it persuasively discuss its treatment of precedents?
- What guidance will the opinion offer future courts? How will this decision be treated as a precedent in the future?

Each of these questions can be answered after reading any opinion; collectively they will yield a comprehension of the opinion's meaning, scope, and impact. The latter questions are particularly helpful in assessing the opinion in relation to divergent rule interpretations and for reconciling an opinion with cases that precede or follow it.

To demonstrate how to read a judicial decision and to illustrate the benefits of "briefing" a case, consider the following judicial opinion, *City of Chicago v. Shalala,* which examines the constitutionality of the section of the 1996 welfare reform act, the Personal Responsibility and Work Opportunity Reconciliation Act, that added a citizenship requirement for receipt of welfare. In other words, this provision makes it illegal to grant welfare benefits to immigrants. Consider the manner in which the court handles the legislation in question and, more important, *how* it interprets the statute to reach its conclusion. The decision in Box 2.6 was handed down by the Illinois District Court in 1998. It was appealed to the U.S. Supreme Court, where the petition for *writ of certiorari* (a request to hear the appeal) was denied on May 27, 2000.

## RESOURCES FOR FINDING THE LAW

Legal research can be placed in three general categories: (1) primary sources (original legal documents for federal and state statutes, regulations, and judicial decisions); (2) "finding tools" (indexes, digests, looseleaf services, citators, and similar devices that help you locate and update statutes, regulations, and judicial decisions); and (3) secondary sources (sources that help you better understand the primary sources and assist your search for and use of them). Some sources can be placed into two categories, for example, looseleaf services and citators are both finding tools and secondary sources.

### Primary Sources: Statutes and Regulations

**Federal Bills**    The official source for the text of these bills while they proceed through Congress is the *Congressional Record,* which records Congress's daily activities. The text will typically cover the bill's essentials, such as bill number, sponsor, and title. The full version of the bill is often published as part of the official committee hearings.

| 2.6 | ILLUSTRATIVE JUDICIAL OPINION |

## CITY OF CHICAGO v. SHALALA, (Ill. D.C.: 1998)
## UNITED STATES DISTRICT COURT OF ILLINOIS

*Summary:* This decision deals with the newly enacted welfare reform law of 1996, specifically the issue of whether the act can lawfully prohibit giving welfare benefits to immigrants, thus making citizenship a requirement for welfare receipt. The court in this case rejected the constitutional challenge, thus allowing the statutory provisions that added citizenship requirement for receiving welfare.

*The implications of the law:* The decision below suggests that the court cannot arbitrarily determine on its own whether to uphold the constitutionality of a statute. Rather, the court must use its understanding of the legislature's intentions and use that insight to draw conclusions about the legally appropriate course of action. In the decision below, it was important for the court to indicate that Congress has the power to regulate matters pertaining to so-called "alien" or noncitizens. Further, they note that they have in the past upheld the notion the Congress need not provide the same welfare benefits to aliens that it affords its citizens. Moreover, the court specifically said that Congress' action was constitutional in the light of the goals it set for the welfare reform act and that there was a "rational basis" for concluding that aliens should be denied benefits if Congress' goal was to foster self-reliance and thereby relieve the burden (i.e., the costs) of the welfare system. Denying benefits to aliens thus becomes a cost-saving move directly associated with the Congressional goal of improving the welfare system's efficacy and also promoting self-sufficiency among welfare recipients—and there was nothing in the United States Constitution that prohibited Congress from achieving such legislative goals.

OPINION BY: Blanche M. Manning This case challenges the constitutionality of § 402 of the Personal Responsibility and Work Opportunity Reconciliation Act of 1996, P.L. 104-193. . . .For the following reasons . . . the court rejects the plaintiffs-intervenors' constitutional challenge to the Welfare Reform Act. . . .

### Background
*A. The Welfare Reform Act*
The Welfare Reform Act is a comprehensive legislative package designed to revamp federally funded welfare programs. Its provisions pertaining to legal resident aliens were drafted in light of the increasing number of immigrants on the welfare rolls and the associated sharp increases in costs, and were meant to eliminate the incentive of public benefits as a motive for immigration to the United States.

Section 402 of the Welfare Reform Act added a citizenship requirement, subject to certain limited exceptions, to the eligibility criteria of: (1) the Supplemental Security Income program ("SSI"); (2) the Food Stamp program; (3) the Temporary Assistance for Needy Families program ("TANF"); (4) the Medicaid program; and (5) the Social Services Block Grant program ("SSBG").

The Seventh Circuit recently upheld the constitutionality of the Welfare Reform Act, rejecting claims that the limitations on food stamp eligibility imposed by the Welfare Reform Act violated the rights of legal resident aliens to due process. In *Shvartsman* [a prior judicial decision], a class of impoverished legal permanent resident aliens who had applied for citizenship before their eligibility for benefits terminated under the Welfare Reform Act claimed that the Act violated their due process rights. Specifically, they argued that the statutory transition period, coupled with the INS's [Immigration and Naturalization Service] delay in processing their citizenship applications, prevented them from having a fair opportunity to prove their continuing eligibility to receive food stamp benefits.

The Seventh Circuit rejected this argument, holding that the plaintiffs had failed to establish a property interest. The court reasoned that the right to access adjudicatory [that is, a court] procedures exists because it serves to protect the plaintiffs' underlying legal claims, not because litigants have property interests in the procedures themselves. The court also explained that the procedures necessary to recertify aliens' eligibility to receive benefits could not themselves create property rights, or the scope of the due process clause would be "virtually boundless." Thus, the court concluded that the plaintiffs had failed to establish a property interest and, therefore, the transition procedures implementing the new citizenship requirement did not violate their due process rights. * * *

### B. The Parties' Claims

[T]he court will describe the parties' claims and sort out the various bars to the plaintiffs [the party who sues] and plaintiffs-intervenors' claims before reaching the merits of the few claims that are ultimately left. The court notes, however, that its merits analysis would have applied equally to all of the constitutional challenges to the Welfare Reform Act.

### 1. The Plaintiffs

In its three-count complaint, the City challenges the constitutionality of the Welfare Reform Act, arguing that it violates the Fifth Amendment due process and equal protection rights of permanent legal resident aliens by prohibiting those persons from receiving food stamps and Supplemental Security Income ("SSI"). The City also argues that the Welfare Reform Act purports to authorize the State of Illinois to discriminate against permanent legal resident aliens and thus violates the due process and equal protection rights of permanent legal resident aliens and violates the principle of separation of powers.

The City seeks a declaration that the Welfare Reform Act violates their rights to due process and equal protection, as well as the principle of separation of powers. They ask the court to enjoin the defendants from enforcing the Welfare Reform Act or otherwise denying benefits to previously eligible legal permanent resident aliens. . . . * * *

### 2. The Defendants

The defendants [the party being sued by the plaintiff] seek to dismiss both the City and the intervenors' complaints. . . . [T]hey note that . . . Congress has the power to condition aliens' eligibility for welfare benefits on the character and duration of their residence and to draw distinctions between aliens and citizens.* * *

*continued*

| 2.6 | ILLUSTRATIVE JUDICIAL OPINION (CONTINUED) |

**Discussion**
*A. Standard on 12(b)(6) Motion to Dismiss* \* \* \*

*2. TANF, Medicaid, and SSBG Claims*
The rational basis standard applies because Congress has plenary powers over immigration matters, as "over no conceivable subject is the legislative power of Congress more complete than it is over the admission of aliens." [R]estrictions on eligibility for welfare programs are within the ambit of immigration matters. Indeed, the Supreme Court has specifically noted that Congress need not "provide all aliens with the welfare benefits provided to its citizens. Moreover, federal legislation regarding alien age-based immigration laws is not comparable to state legislation, which may be subject to different standards of review. In short, the court agrees with the detailed and well-reasoned opinions in [earlier cases] regarding the proper standard of review.

Because rational basis scrutiny is the appropriate standard of review, the court turns to whether the Welfare Reform Act is indeed rational. Legislation must be upheld if there is "any reasonably conceivable state of facts that could provide a rational basis for the classification." The Seventh Circuit instructs that, when determining whether a statute survives rational basis review, courts do not have a "license . . . to judge the wisdom, fairness, or logic of legislative choices."

Congress enacted the Welfare Reform Act to encourage self-reliance and ease the burdens on the welfare system, stating that:

> The Congress makes the following statements concerning national policy with respect to welfare and immigration:
>
> (1) Self-sufficiency has been a basic principle of United States immigration law since this country's earliest immigration statutes.
> (2) It continues to be the immigration policy of the United States that—
>     (A) aliens within the Nation's borders not depend on public resources to meet their needs, but rather rely on their own capabilities and the resources of their families, their sponsors, and private organizations, and
>     (B) the availability of public benefits not constitute an incentive for immigration to the United States.
> (3) Despite the principle of self-sufficiency, aliens have been applying for and receiving public benefits from Federal, State, and local governments at increasing rates.
> (4) Current eligibility rules for public assistance and unenforceable financial support agreements have proved wholly incapable of assuring that individual aliens not burden the public benefits system.

A related and unofficial source for finding the text of these bills and their legislative history is the *United States Code Congressional and Administrative News (U.S.S.C.A.N.)*. Published by West Publishing Company, the U.S.S.C.A.N. refers you to the congressional committees that considered the bill and reprints of final committee reports.

(5) It is a compelling government interest to enact new rules for eligibility and sponsorship agreements in order to assure that aliens be self-reliant in accordance with national immigration policy.

(6) It is a compelling government interest to remove the incentive for illegal immigration provided by the availability of public benefits.

(7) With respect to the State authority to make determinations concerning the eligibility of qualified aliens for public benefits in this chapter, a State that chooses to follow the Federal classification in determining the eligibility of such aliens for public assistance shall be considered to have chosen the least restrictive means available for achieving the compelling governmental interest of assuring that aliens be self-reliant in accordance with national immigration policy.

Restricting non-citizens' ability to receive welfare benefits bears a rational relationship to achieving these goals as there appears to be a logical connection between the means (restricting aliens' access to welfare programs) and Congress' end (fostering self-reliance and easing the burden on the welfare system). Moreover, the fact that the Welfare Reform Act impacts certain permanent resident aliens by denying them benefits unless and until they become citizens does not affect the court's conclusion that the Welfare Reform Act survives rational basis review. It is well established that Congress may address the part of a problem that it deems the most acute.

In addition, Congressional line drawing necessarily implies that people with differing circumstances will be placed on either side of the line. This court is not empowered to second-guess Congress' decision as to where to place that line. Despite the fact that the plaintiffs contend that the Welfare Reform Act will harm legal resident aliens, this court cannot act as a super-Congress and rewrite legislation that is rationally related to Congress' stated purpose.

Finally, in the interests of completeness, the court briefly notes that it disagrees with the plaintiffs-intervenors' argument that the Welfare Reform Act should be invalidated because its alienage restrictions were based on animus towards non-citizens. It is legitimate to distinguish between citizens and aliens, as demonstrated by the fact that Title 8 of the United States Code is founded on the legitimacy of this distinction.

Moreover, as discussed above, the goals of the Welfare Reform Act appear to be rationally linked to the purpose identified by Congress. Thus, the plaintiffs-intervenors cannot establish that the Welfare Reform Act is "inexplicable by anything but animus toward the class that it affects." Thus, the provisions of the Welfare Reform Act affecting non-citizens' ability to obtain welfare benefits must stand.

### Conclusion

For the above reasons, the . . . court rejects the plaintiffs-intervenors' constitutional challenge to the Welfare Reform Act. . . .

The two previous paragraphs refer to "official" versus "unofficial" sources. The difference between these two terms is based on the publisher of the legal document. An *official* source refers to a document published by the government. The *unofficial* version is published by a commercial publisher, and is generally the preferred source because it is more frequently updated and it can refer the researcher to valuable collateral sources. The distinction is primarily relevant for purposes of citation. Often both official and unofficial sources are cited together.

**Federal Statutes**   Once enacted, a statute is published as a "slip law"—a printed copy of a bill passed by the legislature that is distributed immediately once signed by the executive—which can be found in two official sources. The *U.S. Statutes at Large* arranges the laws chronologically, in the order they became law. The *United States Code (U.S.C.)* is arranged under 50 titles, and is organized by subject.

Two related and unofficial sources are the *United States Code Annotated (U.S.C.A.)* and the *United States Code Service*. The *U.S.C.A.* is organized mostly by the West Key Number System, which is described following, and includes annotations—references to related judicial decisions that have interpreted a particular section of the *U.S.C.* One can gain access to these decisions through (1) the popular names index, (2) individual subject index for a particular title, or (3) general subject index.

Both sources can be updated. For the *U.S.C.A.*, there are the "pocket parts," "supplementary pamphlets," and "special pamphlets." Further updates of the *U.S.C.A.* and its pamphlets are provided by the *U.S.S.C.A.N.* and its supplementary pamphlets. The *United States Code Service* works like the *U.S.C.A.*, but refers to Lawyer's Cooperative materials rather than West.

**Federal Regulations**   The official source is the *Federal Register*, which provides a uniform system for announcing federal regulations and legal notices. It also contains helpful supplementary information, such as the name of the federal public law under which each regulation was issued.

After their issuance, federal regulations are arranged topically and published in the *Code of Federal Regulations (C.F.R.)*. The *C.F.R.* is a compilation of the regulations issued in conjunction with federal statutes. It is divided into titles that encompass broad topical areas. Changes in the *C.F.R.* can be found in a monthly pamphlet called the *Cumulative List of C.F.R. Sections Affected*, which describes the *C.F.R.* sections modified by the new final or proposed regulations. A final check is provided by the *Cumulative List of Parts Affected*, which can be found in the most recent issue of the *Federal Register*.

**State Statutes**   The publications for state statutes are comparable to those on the federal level. There are both official and unofficial versions. The state's *Code* usually compiles state law under different topics. The unofficial publications are mostly modeled after the *U.S.C.A.* and include references to judicial decisions and legislative history. They also contain references to relevant secondary sources such as legal periodicals and encyclopedias. There are usually indexes that provide access to the various state law titles, and "key words" can be used to find the right volume, which in turn refers to a general subject index that can be used to find to various sections of the law. They can be updated with pocket parts and supplements.

**State Regulations**    Many states have a system of reporting and codifying regulations that is comparable to the federal structure. Typically, there will be a publication, such as the *Pennsylvania Bulletin,* for publicizing proposed and final rules. The final regulations are likely to be compiled in a code, such as the *Pennsylvania Code,* which organizes the accumulated regulations by subject.

## Judicial Decisions

**Federal Decisions**    The official source for U.S. Supreme Court decisions is the *United States Reports.* There are no official versions for other federal courts, and any decisions that are published can be found in the West *National Reporter System.*

There are two unofficial sources for Supreme Court decisions: the Lawyer's Cooperative *United States Supreme Court Reports* and West's *Supreme Court Reporter.* Both are annotated and used frequently. In addition to these sources, the most recent decisions are published weekly by two looseleaf services: the *Commerce Clearing House Supreme Court Bulletin* and the *United States Law Week.*

**State Decisions**    The official sources report state opinions for the trial, appellate, and supreme court. The unofficial source, which is reported as part of West's *National Reporter System,* publishes only the appellate and state supreme court decisions.

The *National Reporter System,* therefore, is a particularly useful source for state decisions. It is relatively easy to use and allows access to all state appellate decisions. The *West Key Number Digest System*—subject index to case law—is the most widely used method for locating state and federal decisions. The digests are essentially subject indexes to case law. The West system divides the entire body of case law into seven main divisions, 30 subheadings, and more than 400 digest topics (and each topic is divided into numerous key numbers). Once you have located the key number that covers the point of law in which you are interested, it will give you access to all the cases that discuss that particular point.

Under the West system, there are three search methods that can be used with all West digests.

1. *Descriptive Word Index:* If you know the facts of a problem but not the name of the related case, you can find an appropriate key number through the descriptive word index. Use the subject you are searching for as the heading and then look under that to find the proper key number. A subsequent search under that number will describe other cases, if any, on point.
2. *Table of Cases:* If you know the case that deals with the issue you are researching, the table will indicate the topic and key numbers under which the various points of law in the case have been classified. Through the key number, you will also find other relevant cases.

3. *Words and Phrases:* This table lists all words and phrases that have been judicially defined. It may provide another entry into the topic area in which you are interested.

The search through the *National Reporter System* is supplemented by "advance sheets" (copies of decisions that will be subsequently printed in bound volumes) that accompany each reporter and enable the researcher to remain current. To match a decision reported in the *National Reporter System* with one of the official versions—in those instances when it is necessary to go back and forth between the two—one uses the West's *National Blue Book*.

## Finding Tools

There are numerous digests, looseleaf services, popular name tables, citators, and so on, that are used to locate specific statutes, regulations, or decisions. Some have been mentioned previously (for example, the "advance sheets," and the "supplementary pamphlets"), and are perhaps best thought of as providing access to primary sources. For example, the *American Digest* a comprehensive finding tool that digests cases from all federal and state courts and indexes them according to points of law. The *American Digest* is divided into units (the *Century Digest,* the *Decennial Digest,* and the *General Digest*), which cover designated time periods. The *Century Digest* covers cases between 1658 and 1897. The *Decennials* cover 10-year periods from 1897 to 1976 (for example, the 8th *Decennial Digest* covers cases between 1966 and 1976). More recent cases are found in the *General Digest,* which appears first as a monthly supplement to the *Decennials*.

## Secondary Sources

Many of the secondary sources are particularly helpful for non-lawyers. Among the most useful are citators, encyclopedias, periodicals, treatises, and looseleaf services.

- *Shepard's Citator:* This citator can identify the treatment of a statute, a case, a regulation, or other legal authority (for example, law review article). The task is accomplished by referring to all the places it (the statute, case, or regulation, and so on) has been mentioned (cited). This process has become known as "Shepardizing," and its importance cannot be overstated: law changes, and this citator provides a strategy to identify the most authoritative law.
- *Legal Encyclopedias:* These are arranged alphabetically by topic and work much like a general encyclopedia. They are particularly good to get a fast overview on a particular legal topic. The two must prominent are West's *Corpus Juris Secundum* (tied to the West Key system) and Lawyer's Cooperative *American Jurisprudence*. Both have general indexes for gaining access to the topics, and the pocket part offers updated information.

- *Legal Periodicals:* These indexes refer to law review articles, typically but not exclusively published by law schools, which analyze an array of legal issues. The articles are located through the *Index to Legal Periodicals,* the *Current Law Index,* or the *Legal Resources Index.*
- *Treatises:* Treatises are comprehensive treatments of a substantive topic, such as contracts or evidence.
- *Looseleaf Services:* A looseleaf service deals with one area of law (for example, family law), with one court or with a general legal topic. These services include important, and recent developments in statutory, regulatory, or case law. The *Clearing House Review* and the *Family Law Reporter* are two examples of such services.

## A UNIFORM SYSTEM OF CITATION

A *citation* is a protocol to find a legal document. Because the law evolves, it is important that there be some uniform method for finding legal rules. Generally, a citation describes the parties, the reporter or source where the information is located, the volume and edition of the reporter or source, the page number where the information is located, and the date. The citations are provided in both "official" and "unofficial" forms. For a more complete description of the rules for citation, see A *Uniform System of Citation.*

# 3 CHAPTER | TEMPORARY ASSISTANCE TO NEEDY FAMILIES

## THE LEGAL CONTEXT

### Authorizing Legislation

**The Personal Responsibility and Work Opportunity Reconciliation Act of 1996**  The Temporary Assistance to Needy Families (TANF) program (so-called welfare) is Title I of the Personal Responsibility and Work Opportunity Reconciliation Act of 1996 (PRWORA), Public Law 104-193, 42 U.S.C. § 601; it is one of the most significant pieces of social legislation since the enactment of the Social Security Act of 1935. Enacted into law by a Republican-controlled Congress and signed by (Democratic) President Bill Clinton, the act was the culmination of candidate Clinton's 1992 campaign pledge to "end welfare as we know it" and the embodiment of congressional and societal reaction against the perceive wastefulness and failure of the federal Aid to Families with Dependent Children (AFDC) program. Upon signing the bill into law on August 22, 1996, the president lauded the new law's goals and, befitting the act's focus on personal responsibility, the underlying message of reciprocal obligations between the government and welfare recipients.

> Today we are ending welfare as we know it, but I hope this day will be remembered not for what it ended, but for what it began: A new day that offers hope, honors responsibility, rewards work, and changes the terms

of the debate so that no one in America ever feels again the need to criticize people who are poor or on welfare, but instead feels the responsibility to reach out to men and women and children who are isolated, who need opportunity, and who are willing to assume responsibility, and give them the opportunity and the terms of responsibility. (President Bill Clinton at the Welfare Reform Bill signing, August 22, 1996)

As the former president's remarks attest, the legislation embodies a new attitude toward the arrangement between the poor who need governmental assistance and the government that supplies it. As described in the next section of the chapter, the PRWORA contains strong work requirements combined with supports for families moving from welfare to work, including increased funding for child care and continued eligibility for medical coverage. It also provides a performance bonus to reward states for achieving PRWORA's goals, state maintenance of effort requirements, and comprehensive child support enforcement provisions.

## The Balanced Budget Act of 1997

A related piece of legislation that has had an impact on TANF is the Balanced Budget Act (BBA) of 1997, Public Law 105-33, which contains provisions designed to move people from welfare to work and modified provisions in the welfare reform law. Specifically:

### WELFARE-TO-WORK JOBS CHALLENGE FUND.

The BBA included $3 billion to create a Welfare-to-Work Jobs Challenge fund to help states and local communities move long-term welfare recipients and certain non-custodial parents of children on welfare into lasting, unsubsidized jobs. These funds can be used for job creation, job placement and job retention efforts, including wage subsidies to private employers, and other critical post-employment support services. The Department of Labor provides oversight, but most of the dollars are placed through the Private Industry Councils into the hands of the localities who are on the front lines of the welfare reform effort. The Department of Labor awards 25 percent of the funds competitively to support innovative welfare-to-work projects.

### SERVICES TO LOW-INCOME PARENTS.

Amendments in 1999 to the Balanced Budget Act of 1997 expanded the definition of eligible non-custodial parents to include those who were unemployed or underemployed and having difficulty meeting child support obligations or had children who were receiving or eligible to receive food stamps, supplemental security income (SSI), or Medicaid. The amendments also required that parents receiving services also enter into and comply with a personal responsibility contract that includes cooperation with child support efforts. Both state formula and competitive grants are used to provide welfare-to-work services to non-custodial parents.

### WELFARE-TO-WORK TAX CREDIT.

This provision gives employers an added incentive to hire long-term welfare recipients by providing a credit equal to 35 percent of the first $10,000 in wages in the first year of employment, and 50 percent of the first $10,000 in the second year, paid to new hires who have received welfare for an extended period. The credit is for two years per worker to encourage not only hiring but job retention as well.

AMENDING PROVISIONS IN THE WELFARE LAW.

The BBA and the Noncitizen Technical Amendment Act of 1998 invested $11.5 billion to restore disability and health benefits to 380,000 legal immigrants who were in this country before welfare reform became law (August 22, 1996). The BBA also extended the SSI and Medicaid eligibility period for refugees and people seeking asylum from five years after entry to seven years, to give these residents more time to naturalize. The budget bill also modified some food stamp provisions by creating work slots and preserving food stamp benefits for those single, able-bodied recipients without dependents who are willing to work but, through no fault of their own, have not found employment. (U.S. Department of Health and Human Services, 2001)

## Regulatory Authority

As noted in Chapter 2, Congress does not implement the legislation it enacts; that responsibility belongs to the executive branch, or more specifically, to administrative agencies. These agencies, such as the Department of Health and Human Services (HHS), are legislative creations delegated by Congress to enforce or otherwise put into effect the legislative goals enshrined in statutes. As indicated earlier, these entities implement their statutory authority through issuance of regulations that have the force of law. They are not without limitations, however, insofar as their regulations may not be arbitrary, and must be grounded in and derived from specific congressional legislation; the issuance of regulations independent of appropriate legislation is invalid.

Regulations for TANF abound—an unsurprising outcome given the historic nature of the welfare reform law. Regulations are initially published by administrative agencies in the *Federal Register* (for federal agencies) or in a counterpart state publication. Eventually, all these find their way into the *Code of Federal Regulations* (C.F.R.), which is the official compilation of all regulations enacted by federal agencies, organized by Titles that refer to substantive topics. (Similar state counterpart documents, containing all state regulations, also exist.) Specifically, at Title 45 of the C.F.R., Part 260 (and its subsections), one finds the regulatory provisions that generally apply to the TANF program. As shown in Box 3.1, these regulations were published initially as final rules in the *Federal Register* on April 12, 1999, and derive their statutory authority from 42 U.S.C. § 601, which is the codification of the PRWORA, including the Title that pertains to the TANF program. (Regulations issued in connection with the BBA may be found at 42 C.F.R. 402.)

## Case Law

The enactment of the PRWORA replaced the federal Aid to Families with Dependent Children program with TANF, and simultaneously eliminated federal statutory and regulatory protections for welfare recipients that had been in place for nearly 30 years. "As states began to exercise their new authority

| 3 . 1 | EXAMPLE OF TANF REGULATION PUBLISHED IN *CODE OF FEDERAL REGULATIONS* |

TITLE 45—PUBLIC WELFARE
SUBTITLE B—REGULATIONS RELATING TO PUBLIC WELFARE
CHAPTER II—OFFICE OF FAMILY ASSISTANCE
(ASSISTANCE PROGRAMS), ADMINISTRATION FOR CHILDREN
AND FAMILIES, DEPARTMENT OF HEALTH AND HUMAN SERVICES
PART 260—GENERAL TEMPORARY ASSISTANCE
FOR NEEDY FAMILIES (TANF) PROVISIONS
SUBPART A—WHAT RULES GENERALLY APPLY
TO THE TANF PROGRAM?
45 CFR 260.20

§ 260.20 What is the purpose of the TANF program?
The TANF program has the following four purposes:
(a) Provide assistance to needy families so that children may be cared for in their own homes or in the homes of relatives;
(b) End the dependence of needy parents on government benefits by promoting job preparation, work, and marriage;
(c) Prevent and reduce the incidence of out-of-wedlock pregnancies and establish annual numerical goals for preventing and reducing the incidence of these pregnancies; and
(d) Encourage the formation and maintenance of two-parent families.

HISTORY: [64 FR 17720, 17878, Apr. 12, 1999]

AUTHORITY: AUTHORITY NOTE APPLICABLE TO ENTIRE PART: 42 U.S.C. 601, 601 note, 603, 604, 606, 607, 608, 609, 610, 611, 619, and 1308.

NOTES: [EFFECTIVE DATE NOTE: 64 FR 17720, 17878, Apr. 12, 1999, added Part 260, effective Oct. 1, 1999.]

to define the scope of their welfare programs for poor families," according to Mannix et al. (1999), "lawyers for these families began to confront the challenge of identifying other sources of law, such as state statutes, other federal statutes, and state and federal constitutional provisions, that can be used in litigation to protect families harmed by unfair state policies and practices."

Perhaps the most significant challenges to state policies enacted pursuant to TANF are those based on discrimination against state residents and on work program requirements. "With respect to welfare work issues," argue Mannix et al. (1999):

The U.S. Department of Labor (DOL) indication that federal employment laws generally apply to welfare recipients is a helpful advocacy too. Other pending or recent litigation has challenged specific state policies, including child exclusion policies, child support cooperation requirements, and the elimination of the child-support pass-through. . . . The full range of legal issues that will arise from state TANF implementation cannot yet be identified.

Several topics promise to be key, and will have a significant impact on TANF, depending on their treatment in the courts. For example, there are four judicial decisions that constitute the so-called pillars of welfare reform. These landmark cases were handed down between 1968 and 1970 and collectively spelled out welfare recipient rights, ranging from the right to be free from residency requirements in order to receive welfare, the right to some kind of hearing when one appeals the denial of welfare benefits, the right to be free from the imposition of morality tests as a prerequisite to receive welfare, and the rights of states to determine the maximum grant it will award welfare recipients. While the collective power of these decisions undeniably secures a range of rights to welfare recipients, these protections cannot be taken for granted. Indeed, the enactment of PRWORA will provide opportunities to challenge these cases and thereby threaten their status as good law. The mere passage of the welfare reform law is not itself a threat per se; rather, there are provisions within the law that bespeak Congress's intention to test the viability of those "pillars of welfare reform," and it will be up to the Supreme Court to determine whether these "pillars" endure.

Two of these four decisions, *Shapiro v. Thompson* (1969) and *Goldberg v. Kelly* (1970), are discussed following, in relation to two recent judicial decisions: *Saenz v. Roe* (1999) and *Washington Legal Clinic for the Homeless v. Barry* (1997), respectively. The *Shapiro* decision involved the imposition of residency requirements as a condition of receiving welfare benefits. The court ruled that these requirements interfered with the right to travel, and thus found the state legislation unconstitutional. In *Saenz v. Roe,* the court again addressed the issue of the constitutionality of residency requirements. Under PRWORA, Congress had fashioned a residency requirement that did not directly violate welfare recipients rights depicted in the earlier *Shapiro* case, but instead crafted a provision that invited the court to decide if *Shapiro* would remain good law. The *Goldberg* decision addressed the requirement that welfare recipients are entitled to some kind of hearing as part of an appeal of denial of benefits. In the *Washington Legal Clinic for the Homeless v. Barry* decision, the court confronted the issue of whether families seeking emergency shelter possessed a property interest for due process purposes. Due process, under the Fourteenth Amendment, is concerned with fairness between the individual and the government and the conditions under which the state may deprive an individual of life, liberty, or property. In the *Goldberg* decision, the court ruled that welfare benefits constituted a property interest worthy of due process protection and thus required states to provide "some kind of hearing" in connection with termination of benefits. The *Washington Legal Clinic for the Homeless v. Barry* decision, while not dealing with welfare benefits per se, does bring into focus the due process issues associated with the receipt of a social program benefit—emergency shelter—and the implications for the durability of *Goldberg* are the critical unknowns.

The two other "pillars"—*King v. Smith* (1968) and *Dandridge v. Williams* (1970)—are not presented here, but can be summarized as follows. The *King* decision deals with Alabama's "substitute father" regulation, which was ruled invalid because it defines "parent" in a manner that is inconsistent with Section 406(a) of the Social Security Act, and, in denying AFDC assistance to appellees on the basis of the invalid regulation, Alabama breached its federally imposed obligation to furnish aid to families with dependent children with reasonable promptness to all eligible individuals. This case also stands for the proposition that so-called morality tests for receipt of welfare are also illegal. The *Dandridge* opinion found Maryland's maximum grant regulation placing an absolute limit on the amount of a grant under AFDC, regardless of family size, was not in conflict with federal statute governing grants to states for aid to needy dependent children. "We do not decide today," the court argued,

> that the Maryland regulation is wise, that it best fulfills the relevant social and economic objectives that Maryland might ideally espouse, or that a more just and humane system could not be devised. . . . But the intractable economic, social, and even philosophical problems presented by public welfare assistance programs are not the business of this Court.

Here, the court endorsed the notion that states are in the best position to determine how they want to spend their limited resources on public assistance; by implication, they underscored the notion that there is no right to welfare, per se.

### The Illegality of Residency Requirements: *Shapiro v. Thompson*

The 1969 *Shapiro* case deals with the legality of residency requirements for receipt of welfare; the U.S. Supreme Court concluded that such requirements interfered with fundamental rights and were consequently unconstitutional. That decision was thrown into question by PRWORA's statutory provisions allowing states to implement two-tiered benefit levels, depending on residency. Unlike the *Shapiro* decision, where the residency restrictions resulted in so-called newcomers receiving zero benefits for the first 12 months of their residency in a new state, the PRWORA language gives states the discretion to establish a two-tiered, residency-based system but provides for the "newcomers" to receive benefits equal to those of the state whence they came for the initial 12 months in the new state. The U.S. Supreme Court heard oral arguments on the constitutionality of these provisions in January 1999, in the case of *Saenz v. Roe* (1999), and handed down their decision 6 months later, in June. As the judicial opinion presented in Box 3.2 attests, the court upheld *Shapiro* and thereby struck down the objectionable PRWORA language.

### The Right to a Hearing Prior to Termination of Benefits: *Goldberg v. Kelly* and *Washington Legal Clinic for the Homeless v. Barry*

The *Goldberg* case has long stood for the proposition that welfare recipients are entitled to "some kind of hearing" prior to termination of benefits. The court announced that the state's eligibility requirements created an entitlement

| 3.2 | DECISION OF THE U.S. SUPREME COURT ON RESIDENCY REQUIREMENTS FOR WELFARE RECIPIENTS: *SAENZ V. ROE* |

### SAENZ v. ROE, 526 U.S. 489 (1999)

*Summary: California, which has welfare benefit levels that are lower than the levels in 5 states but higher than the levels in 44 states and the District of Columbia, enacted in 1992 a statute that limited the amount of welfare benefits for a family that had resided in California for less than 12 months to the amount that would have been received by the family from the state of the family's prior residence. Subsequently, Congress enacted a Personal Responsibility and Work Opportunity Reconciliation Act of 1996 (PRWORA) provision that expressly authorized such durational residency requirements. A class action challenging the federal constitutionality of California's durational residency requirement and the PRWORA's authorization of the requirement was filed in the United States District Court for the Eastern District of California. After the District Court preliminarily enjoined the implementation of the California statute, the United States Court of Appeals for the Ninth Circuit, agreeing with the District Court that the class members might suffer irreparable harm if the California statute became operative, affirmed the issuance of the injunction without reaching the merits of the case.*

*On certiorari, the United States Supreme Court affirmed. It was held that (1) the state statute violated the interstate travel right, protected under the citizenship clause contained in 1 of the Federal Constitution's Fourteenth Amendment, of a newly arrived citizen of a state to the same privileges and immunities enjoyed by other citizens of the state, because (a) the citizenship clause does not allow for degrees of citizenship based on length of residence and does not tolerate a hierarchy of 45 subclasses of similarly situated citizens based on the location of their prior residence, and (b) the state's legitimate interest in saving money provided no justification for its decision to discriminate among equally eligible citizens; and (2) congressional approval, in 604(c), of such durational residency requirements as the requirement in question did not resuscitate the constitutionality of the state statute, as Congress has no affirmative power to authorize the states to violate the Fourteenth Amendment and is implicitly prohibited from passing legislation that purports to validate any such violation.*

**OPINION BY:** STEVENS

In 1992, California enacted a statute limiting the maximum welfare benefits available to newly arrived residents. The scheme limits the amount payable to a family that has resided in the State for less than 12 months to the amount payable by the State of the family's prior residence. The questions presented by this case are whether the 1992 statute was constitutional when it was enacted and, if not, whether an amendment to the Social Security Act enacted by Congress in 1996 affects that determination.

* * * In 1992, in order to make a relatively modest reduction in its vast welfare budget, the California Legislature enacted § 11450.03 of the state Welfare and Institutions Code. That section sought to change the California AFDC program by

limiting new residents, for the first year they live in California, to the benefits they would have received in the State of their prior residence. Because in 1992 a state program either had to conform to federal specifications or receive a waiver from the Secretary of Health and Human Services in order to qualify for federal reimbursement, § 11450.03 required approval by the Secretary to take effect. In October 1992, the Secretary issued a waiver purporting to grant such approval.

On December 21, 1992, three California residents who were eligible for AFDC benefits filed an action in the Eastern District of California challenging the constitutionality of the durational residency requirement in § 11450.03. Each plaintiff alleged that she had recently moved to California to live with relatives in order to escape abusive family circumstances. One returned to California after living in Louisiana for seven years, the second had been living in Oklahoma for six weeks and the third came from Colorado. Each alleged that her monthly AFDC grant for the ensuing 12 months would be substantially lower under § 11450.03 than if the statute were not in effect. Thus, the former residents of Louisiana and Oklahoma would receive $190 and $341 respectively for a family of three even though the full California grant was $641; the former resident of Colorado, who had just one child, was limited to $280 a month as opposed to the full California grant of $504 for a family of two.

The District Court issued a temporary restraining order and, after a hearing, preliminarily enjoined implementation of the statute. District Judge Levi found that the statute "produces substantial disparities in benefit levels and makes no accommodation for the different costs of living that exist in different states." Relying primarily on our decisions in *Shapiro v. Thompson,* he concluded that the statute placed "a penalty on the decision of new residents to migrate to the State and be treated on an equal basis with existing residents." In his view, if the purpose of the measure was to deter migration by poor people into the State, it would be unconstitutional for that reason. And even if the purpose was only to conserve limited funds, the State had failed to explain why the entire burden of the saving should be imposed on new residents. The Court of Appeals summarily affirmed for the reasons stated by the District Judge. We granted the State's petition for certiorari.

We now affirm.

The word "travel" is not found in the text of the Constitution. Yet the "constitutional right to travel from one State to another" is firmly embedded in our jurisprudence. Indeed, as Justice Stewart reminded us in *Shapiro v. Thompson,* the right is so important that it is "assertable against private interference as well as governmental action . . . a virtually unconditional personal right, guaranteed by the Constitution to us all." (concurring opinion).

In Shapiro, we reviewed the constitutionality of three statutory provisions that denied welfare assistance to residents of Connecticut, the District of Columbia, and Pennsylvania, who had resided within those respective jurisdictions less than one year immediately preceding their applications for assistance. Without pausing to identify the specific source of the right, we began by noting that the Court had long "recognized that the nature of our Federal Union and our constitutional concepts of personal liberty unite to require that all citizens be free to travel throughout the length and breadth of our land uninhibited by statutes, rules, or regulations which unreasonably burden or restrict this movement." We squarely held that it was "constitutionally impermissible" for a State to enact durational residency require-

*continued*

<table>
<tr><td>3.2</td><td>DECISION OF THE U.S. SUPREME COURT ON RESIDENCY REQUIREMENTS FOR WELFARE RECIPIENTS: *SAENZ V. ROE* (CONTINUED)</td></tr>
</table>

ments for the purpose of inhibiting the migration by needy persons into the State. We further held that a classification that had the effect of imposing a penalty on the exercise of the right to travel violated the Equal Protection Clause "unless shown to be necessary to promote a compelling governmental interest," and that no such showing had been made.

In this case California argues that § 11450.03 was not enacted for the impermissible purpose of inhibiting migration by needy persons and that, unlike the legislation reviewed in Shapiro, it does not penalize the right to travel because new arrivals are not ineligible for benefits during their first year of residence. California submits that, instead of being subjected to the strictest scrutiny, the statute should be upheld if it is supported by a rational basis and that the State's legitimate interest in saving over $10 million a year satisfies that test. Although the United States did not elect to participate in the proceedings in the District Court or the Court of Appeals, it has participated as amicus curiae in this Court. It has advanced the novel argument that the enactment of PRWORA allows the States to adopt a "specialized choice-of-law-type provision" that "should be subject to an intermediate level of constitutional review," merely requiring that durational residency requirements be "substantially related to an important governmental objective." The debate about the appropriate standard of review, together with the potential relevance of the federal statute, persuades us that it will be useful to focus on the source of the constitutional right on which respondents rely.

The "right to travel" discussed in our cases embraces at least three different components. It protects the right of a citizen of one State to enter and to leave another State, the right to be treated as a welcome visitor rather than an unfriendly alien when temporarily present in the second State, and, for those travelers who elect to become permanent residents, the right to be treated like other citizens of that State.

It was the right to go from one place to another, including the right to cross state borders while en route, that was vindicated in *Edwards v. California,* which invalidated a state law that impeded the free interstate passage of the indigent. We reaf-

---

and that this entitlement constituted a property interest of the sort protected by the Fourteenth Amendment. The PRWORA threatens to increase the pressure on states to resort to arbitrary behavior that could result in summary denial of benefits, particularly regarding work requirements and sanctions. Of special concern is PRWORA's assertion that it creates no entitlement to benefits, and this sets up a situation where a recipient may be viewed as not automatically entitled to the sort of procedural protections laid out in *Goldberg*. "The Supreme Court has made clear," argue Mannix et al. (1999), "that due process rights depend upon the nature of the interest created by the statute and may not be overcome by simply stating that recipients have 'no entitlement.'"

This conclusion will be critical in the TANF context, and may afford the only protection against arbitrary denial of benefits. Needless to say, the vital-

firmed that right in *United States v. Guest,* which afforded protection to the "'right to travel freely to and from the State of Georgia and to use highway facilities and other instrumentalities of interstate commerce within the State of Georgia.'" Given that § 11450.03 imposed no obstacle to respondents' entry into California, we think the State is correct when it argues that the statute does not directly impair the exercise of the right to free interstate movement. For the purposes of this case, therefore, we need not identify the source of that particular right in the text of the Constitution. The right of "free ingress and regress to and from" neighboring States, which was expressly mentioned in the text of the Articles of Confederation, may simply have been "conceived from the beginning to be a necessary concomitant of the stronger Union the Constitution created."

The second component of the right to travel is, however, expressly protected by the text of the Constitution. The first sentence of Article IV, § 2, provides:
**"The Citizens of each State shall be entitled to all Privileges and Immunities of Citizens in the several States."**

Thus, by virtue of a person's state citizenship, a citizen of one State who travels in other States, intending to return home at the end of his journey, is entitled to enjoy the "Privileges and Immunities of Citizens in the several States" that he visits. This provision removes "from the citizens of each State the disabilities of alienage in the other States." ("Without some provision . . . removing from citizens of each State the disabilities of alienage in the other States, and giving them equality of privilege with citizens of those States, the Republic would have constituted little more than a league of States; it would not have constituted the Union which now exists"). It provides important protections for nonresidents who enter a State whether to obtain employment, to procure medical services, or even to engage in commercial shrimp fishing. Those protections are not "absolute," but the Clause "does bar discrimination against citizens of other States where there is no substantial reason for the discrimination beyond the mere fact that they are citizens of other States." There may be a substantial reason for requiring the nonresident to pay more than the resident for a hunting license or to enroll in the state university, but our cases have not identified any acceptable reason for qualifying the protection afforded by the Clause for "the 'citizen of State A who ventures into State B' to settle there and establish a home."

[Chief Justice Rehnquist and Justice Thomas joined in a dissenting opinion, which is not included here.]

---

ity and durability of *Goldberg* also hangs in the balance. The reasoning behind this thinking is apparent in the decision presented in Box 3.3, *Washington Legal Clinic for the Homeless v. Barry* (1997), wherein the court stated that families seeking emergency shelter did *not* have a property interest for due process purposes. The D.C. statute provides that there is "no entitlement" to shelter, and the court said that this language does not itself preclude a finding of a property interest. Nonetheless, the court concluded that there is no constitutionally protected property interest because the city does not provide shelter for all eligible families and gives "unfettered discretion" to administrators to determine which eligible families get shelter, and no law prevents officials from distributing shelter in a way that leaves some eligible families unserved. It is not a great leap from this finding to the analogous situation of TANF benefits, and this may further put *Goldberg* in jeopardy.

| | OPINION OF APPELLATE COURT |
|---|---|
| 3.3 | ON THE RIGHT TO SHELTER: |
| | *WASHINGTON LEGAL CLINIC V. BARRY* |

## Washington Legal Clinic for the Homeless v. Barry, 107 F.3d 32 (1997)
## United States Court of Appeals for the District of Columbia Circuit

*Summary: The central question in this case is whether District of Columbia law creates a constitutionally protected entitlement to emergency family shelter. Although D.C. law established objective eligibility criteria for homeless families seeking shelter, for a combination of reasons the Court of Appeals held that homeless families lack an expectation of shelter sufficient to create a property right: the city does not provide enough shelter to meet the needs of all eligible families, it leaves allocation of limited shelter space among eligible families to the unfettered discretion of city administrators, and nothing in District law prohibits administrators from allocating space in such a way that not all eligible families receive shelter. Consequently, the Court reversed the lower court's due process ruling.*

**Opinion:** Circuit Judge Tatel.

\* \* \* Before addressing the district court's due process ruling, we emphasize what is at stake in this case and what is not. The quantity of emergency shelter available to homeless families is not at issue. The District does not attempt to supply shelter to all eligible families, nor does the Clinic seek the creation of additional shelter space. Because the city's emergency family shelters operate at capacity, a fact counsel for the District confirmed at oral argument, this case is not about available beds going empty while homeless families pursue Kafkaesque application procedures. Nor is this case about discrimination in the shelter allocation process; the district court found that the city's current procedures satisfy the Fifth Amendment's equal protection guarantee, a decision the Clinic does not appeal. The sole question before us is whether D.C. laws and regulations governing the city's emergency family shelter program create a constitutionally protected property interest in shelter, which in turn would require that the District's allocation and appeal procedures satisfy due process standards.

We begin with familiar principles. The Fifth Amendment's Due Process Clause prohibits the District of Columbia from depriving persons of "property, without due process of law." U.S. Const. amend. V. Individuals are entitled to due process, however, only if they have a constitutionally protected property interest. To have a property interest in a government benefit, "a person clearly must have more than an abstract need or desire for [the benefit]. He must have more than a unilateral expectation of it. He must, instead, have a legitimate claim of entitlement to it." Entitlements derive from "an independent source such as state law," i.e., statutes or regulations "that secure certain benefits and that support claims of entitlement to those benefits."

To determine whether a particular statute creates a constitutionally protected property interest, we ask whether the statute or implementing regulations place "substantive limitations on official discretion." Statutes or regulations limit official discretion if they contain "explicitly mandatory language, i.e., specific directives to the decisionmaker that if the regulations' substantive predicates are present, a particular outcome must follow." In *Goldberg v. Kelly*, for example, the Supreme Court held that because persons meeting state AFDC eligibility standards automatically qualified for benefits, eligible individuals had a protected property interest in the receipt of the benefits. Where, however, the legislature leaves final determination of which eligible individuals receive benefits to the "unfettered discretion" of administrators, no constitutionally protected property interest exists.

Applying these principles, we ask whether homeless families meeting the statutory qualifications for shelter are entitled to receive it. If so, as in *Goldberg*, eligible families would have a constitutionally protected property interest in shelter. But if not entitled to shelter because administrators have discretion to choose among otherwise eligible families, they would have no constitutionally protected interest.

As the Clinic observes, the eligibility standards set forth in the Overnight Shelter Act and its regulations are "fact based, objective criteria . . . [which] do not involve intangible assessments or discretionary factors." If all families meeting these criteria received shelter, we would agree with the district court and our dissenting colleague that applicants have a constitutionally protected entitlement to shelter. But that is not this case. * * *

Relying on traditional property law and citing contingent remainders, vested remainders subject to defeasance, and executory interests for illustration, the dissent argues that a property right can exist even though eligible families might not receive shelter. . . . In the realm of real property law, it is certainly true that improbability of vesting will not defeat a contingent future interest in property. . . . The question in this case, however, is not whether eligible families have a legally enforceable future interest in emergency shelter, but whether they have a constitutionally enforceable property right to emergency shelter. The common law of real property, where uncertainty of future vesting merely reduces the value of property, does not answer that question. Instead, we must look to principles of due process, where the uncertainty of shelter due to the exercise of administrative discretion prevents the creation of a constitutionally protected entitlement. The Supreme Court recognized a constitutionally protected property right in *Goldberg* because administrators had no discretion in the allocation of AFDC benefits—all statutorily eligible individuals automatically received benefits. By comparison, we held in *Tarpeh-Doe* that the regulations at issue there "fail[ed] to restrict sufficiently the decisionmaker's discretion to generate a protected [liberty or property] interest implicating the due process clause."

Pointing to procedures available to eligible families denied shelter, the dissent argues that the Shelter Office has insufficient discretion to defeat a constitutionally protected property right. . . . Acting on behalf of its clients, the Clinic regularly uses those procedures, often successfully, to challenge administrative determinations of ineligibility. . . . Such procedures, however, do not restrict the discretion the City Council has left to administrators to select the method of allocating scarce shelter space among eligible families, and it is the presence of that discretion which precludes a finding of an entitlement to emergency shelter. That eligible families reaching the top of the wait-list now receive shelter is of no constitutional significance because the Shelter Office can change its procedures tomorrow.

We agree with the dissent that in certain circumstances property rights may arise from administrative "rules or understandings." Equally clear, however, administra-

*continued*

tive actions may not create property rights where that result would "contravene the intent of the legislature." Here, the City Council's intent is plain: "Nothing in this chapter shall be construed to create an entitlement in any homeless person or family to emergency shelter. . . ." D.C. Code § 3-206.9(a); see also id. § 3-609 (same). While we doubt that blanket "no-entitlement" disclaimers can by themselves strip entitlements from individuals in the face of statutes or regulations unequivocally conferring them, the district's "no-entitlement" disclaimer reinforces our conclusion that District of Columbia law, by leaving allocation of limited shelter among eligible families to administrative discretion, creates no constitutionally protected entitlement to emergency shelter.

Moreover, outside the employment context, we have found no decision of the Supreme Court or of this Circuit holding that administrative rules or understandings existing wholly apart from legislation or regulations may create a property interest. We are not surprised by the lack of such decisions. In the absence of special circumstances neither alleged nor present in this case, such as where reliance on administrative action creates contractual responsibilities, obligations enforceable against the public fisc, i.e., entitlements, may arise only from the people acting through their legislators, not from administrative fiat.

We reverse the district court's ruling that District law creates a property interest in emergency family shelter and remand for further proceedings in accordance with this opinion. We affirm the district court's conclusion that the policy limiting unsolicited advocates' access to the Shelter Office waiting room to certain times of the week violates the First Amendment. So ordered.

The judicial decisions presented in Boxes 3.2 and 3.3 illustrate just two issues likely to surface in the courts and thus to affect the legal authority governing TANF. To be sure, other issues will be determinative of TANF's implementation, and Mannix et al. (1999) offer a comprehensive projection of potential post–TANF litigation topics that warrant attention: work programs, including preassignment issues and associated terms and conditions; Department of Labor guidelines; sanctions for noncompliance; child exclusion policies; child support enforcement; time-limited benefits; drug screening; and federalism issues.

### Issues Affecting the Future Legal Authority of TANF

Perhaps the single most significant matter facing TANF is its reauthorization. The enabling legislation was given a 5-year life, with reauthorization required in September 2002. However, as of summer 2005, no legislation has been passed regarding TANF's future. The 1996 statute expired on October 1, 2003. Since that time the program has continued to operate based on a series of continuing resolutions by Congress. The House did pass HR4, "The Personal Responsibility, Work, and Family Protection Act of 2003," on February 13, 2003, but the Senate version ("Personal Responsibility and Individual Development for Everyone (PRIDE)," has, as of summer 2005, not been passed. Therefore, TANF is still being operated under congressional extensions (National Association of Social Workers, 2004). The question remains whether new TANF legislation will substantially alter the original law. For example, the National Center on Poverty Law (2001) suggested that new legislation include:

- Refocus from caseload reduction to poverty reduction. TANF must aggressively reduce both the amount and depth of poverty, especially child poverty. TANF funding must be maintained at the current level (both the federal block grand and the states' maintenance-of-effort spending requirement) and increased every year for inflation.
- Eliminate the 5-year lifetime limit on receipt of assistance. If the lifetime limit is not eliminated, "stop the clock" for any individual or family that is in compliance with program requirements (for instance, while engaged in a work activity including training, education, or caregiving or addressing work/life barriers such as domestic or sexual violence, mental illness, substance abuse, or disability).
- Restore full access to benefits to legal immigrants.
- Promote education, training, work supports, and access to jobs that are permanent and sustainable and pay high wages and provide benefits.
- Assure access to services to address barriers such as mental illness, physical disability, substance abuse, and domestic and sexual violence.
- Support caregivers so that their children may be cared for in their own homes.
- Protect children born into poverty by prohibiting states from denying or limiting assistance to a child born into a family already receiving public assistance. This anti-child policy is commonly known as the "family cap" or the "child exclusion law."
- End the requirement that states send a portion of child support collected to the federal government and require states to pass through and disregard all child support payments made to current or past public assistance recipients and end the assignment of child support requirement.
- Limit sanctions to reducing assistance on a pro rata basis, in no case less than with the same number of children but no adults would receive.
- Support overcoming barriers and ensure that those with barriers are not denied, sanctioned, or terminated benefits for noncompliance due to a barrier.
- Make the Family Violence Option mandatory.
- Repeal the provision that currently prohibits individuals convicted of a drug-related felony from receiving TANF or food stamps.
- Remove unduly invasive restrictions on teen parents.
- Eliminate the out-of-wedlock studies, reports, and bonuses.
- Eliminate abstinence-only education funds, and replace them with funds for comprehensive, medically accurate sex education.

- Do not use TANF funds for the promotion of marriage. This is a highly personal matter that should be left to the individual, regardless of economic status. Promoting self-sufficiency through access to education, training, and high-wage employment for women and men, regardless of their marital, parental, or custodial status, is the better public policy.
- Repeal charitable choice and ban proselytization and employment discrimination by nongovernmental organizations that receive funds by contract, grants, or other forms of disbursement.
- Do not earmark funds for marriage, abstinence-only education, and charitable choice policies and programs; rather, allow states flexibility in terms of funding and implementation.
- Add funds to support transitional jobs programs.
- Guarantee safe, affordable, appropriate, quality child care for individuals in a TANF work activity.

Others have suggested that job training and education be incorporated into job search-employment activities (Martinson & Strawn, 2003), that child care funding be expanded, and that states not be required to enforce "full family" sanctions (children as well as parents are forced off assistance when parents have not met a regulation).

## THE PROGRAM CONTEXT

### Overview

Before the passage of the Personal Responsibility and Work Reconciliation Act of 1996, the federal assistance program for people in this situation was known as Aid to Families with Dependent Children. The 1996 legislation repealed AFDC, ending "welfare" as we had known it since 1935 and replacing it with a new program, Temporary Assistance for Needy Families. Also eliminated were the Emergency Assistance for Needy Families (EA) and the Job Opportunities and Basic Skills Training (JOBS) programs. In their place, states were given one sum of money (a block grant) to allocate as they determined.

The distinctions between AFDC and TANF are important to understand because of what they reveal about society's current perspectives on poverty. The words of the 1996 legislation's title—"personal responsibility"—and its income support program's name—"temporary assistance"—suggest an emphasis on individual behavioral change as the means to rapidly eliminate poverty. Implicit is the notion that largely prevailed until the Great Depression of the 1930s: that poor people through their own inadequacies cause their own financial dependency. Structural economic and social elements (low-wage jobs, racism, lack of health and child care, educational systems' deficits, and so on) are mostly ignored in TANF's design, with, for example, its lifetime limits to assistance, lack of federal guarantee to child care, and strict work requirements even for women with very young children. This focus on individual change through a no-nonsense, work-first approach for parents (mostly women) with young children is occurring at a time when the poverty rate for children has increased—17.6 percent in 2003, up from 16.2% percent in 2002 (U.S. Census Bureau, 2004). It has even been suggested that the well-being of children who are poor has become less of a priority than the modification of their parents' behavior (Marshall, 1997, p. 335).

The defining features of the TANF program are discussed in the next sections of the chapter. These are contrasted with the 61-year-old AFDC program that was supplanted by TANF, because the distinctions illuminate the essential characteristics of the current program.

**Block Grant Versus Entitlement Grant-in-Aid Funding**    AFDC funding was open-ended and involved cost sharing (that is, formula grant) between the federal and state governments (about 55 percent from the federal government and 45 percent from the states). TANF, in contrast, is funded through an annual block grant from the federal government. The fixed amount of federal dollars—$16.5 billion yearly from 1997 to 2002—is divided among the states. States are given an annual grant equal to the dollars they expended for AFDC, Emergency Assistance, and JOBS combined. The amount received is based on one of the following figures: the average of fiscal years (FY) 1992–94, the amount expended in fiscal year 1994, or the amount expended in fiscal year 1995. This block grant cannot be expanded; once a state depletes its annual allotment, it can serve additional persons only if it uses state funding.

This is related to the fact that, under TANF, applicants are not seen as entitled to aid, that is, there is no federal mandate that all who qualify receive benefits. PRWORA makes this explicit in Section 401(b), in which it is stated that the law "shall not be interpreted to entitle any individual or family assistance under any state program funded under this part" (P.L. 104-193, 110, Stat. 2105).

However, states have the option to provide assistance to all eligible applicants. Four states—Alaska, Hawaii, Rhode Island, and Vermont—have opted to reinstate the concept of entitlement to aid; New York's constitution includes an obligation to meet the basic needs of its citizenry. Twenty-eight states' TANF statutes do not refer to an entitlement to aid, and 17 states' statutes mimic the PRWORA and are explicit about the absence of such an entitlement.

In removing a federal statutory entitlement for aid to dependent children, TANF has opened the way for other actions against children who are poor. Unlike AFDC regulations, children whose parents are sanctioned (punished) by a loss of benefits because they have not complied with a TANF requirement can also lose benefits. Thirty-four states, for example, permit all family members to lose assistance if a parent violates work rules.

Block grant funding rewards states who reduce their TANF rolls, that is, states that serve fewer people can use unexpended monies for other purposes as permitted under the law. They can do this as long as they have spent at least 75 percent of the amount they spent in 1994 for the cash assistance and support programs TANF replaced (AFDC, EA, JOBS), child care, and other related activities. If a state fails to meet TANF work participation goals, it must spend 80 percent of its 1994 expenditure. This is known as maintenance-of-effort, or MOE. Implicit in the MOE requirement is permission for a 20–25 percent reduction (from 1994 spending) in state expenditures for persons who are needy.

A system whose funding basis gives incentives for client exclusion may have serious negative consequences for applicants and recipients. The TANF rolls have declined; between August 1996 and June 2000, there were 8,334,000 fewer recipients, a 59 percent decrease (Administration for Children and Families, 2000). While some of this reduction is clearly attributable to movement of recipients from welfare to work, some of the drop is also thought to be related to inappropriate denials to applicants and liberal use of sanctions against recipients. As of summer 2005, the full impact of the economic recession of the early 2000s on TANF has yet to be determined. Caseloads, however, have declined since 2002 despite rising poverty rates (Fremstad, 2003; Pear, 2002).

**State Discretion**    TANF gives states far more discretion in their use of federal funding than they had under AFDC. Indeed, Section 401(a) of the TANF legislation states that the law was designed to increase states' flexibility (Edelman, 1997). No longer are states mandated to meet a complex set of national regulations. Other than complying with time limit regulations, work participation rates, minimum maintenance-of-effort regulations, and a few other rules, states are free to design their own programs.

The plans states must submit to the Department of Health and Human Services do not ask for much information, and HHS, once it determines the plan is complete, has limited authority regarding the plan's contents (Center for Law and Social Policy, 1998). For example, each state sets its own rules on exemptions from work and time limitations and on the distribution of its block grant monies (including transfer to the child care and/or social services block grants). As we shall see, there is much variability among states not only on benefit levels but also on issues critical to clients' daily lives, including eligibility, work exemptions, and continuation of medical and child care assistance after acquiring a job.

**Time Limits**    The most dramatic change in public assistance policy is captured by the word *temporary* in the current program's title. No longer, as was true under AFDC, can families that are eligible under the law receive public assistance as often and for however long they qualify. Now the parent or guardian of a dependent child can only receive assistance for a *total* of *up to* 60 months during her adult lifetime. States can exercise the option to reduce the time limit below the 5-year federal maximum (as of 2000, 21 states have done so, with the briefest time period—21 months—having been adopted by Connecticut).

Twelve states use a fixed-period time limit in which a client's benefits are eliminated or reduced for a set time period and then resumed after that time period is over. Some of these states will grant assistance only for a total of 24 months in a 60-month time period; others stipulate that after 24 months on assistance, families cannot receive assistance for the next 36 months.

Under TANF, once an adult recipient reaches the state's time limit, she is *never* again eligible for TANF. By federal statute, time limits apply to all adult recipients, minors who are heads of a household, or minors married to an adult household head. All family members are penalized; children living in the household of an adult who has moved beyond the time limit are not eligible for assistance, unless a state chooses to continue their benefits. As of July 2000, only six states have opted to do so—Arizona, California, Indiana, Maine, Maryland, and Rhode Island.

This means that in every other state, children who are poor can only receive TANF benefits for up to 5 of their childhood years. One exception is children who live with adults who are not TANF recipients (for example, custodial grandparents). In addition, TANF (and all states) permit children to continue to receive assistance after an adult family member reaches the time limit *if* the children reside with another adult who is either not a recipient or is eligible for assistance. The adult who has already exhausted her TANF eligibility must *not* reside in the household. Mothers, therefore, may be forced to choose between living with their children or abandoning them so their children's basic needs are met. This provision clearly contradicts the professed "family values" objectives of the PRWORA.

In addition to exemptions related to children, TANF allows for other forms of time limit exemptions (periods during which the clock stops) and extensions (continuation of the federal TANF-funded assistance beyond the 60-month time limit).

Exemptions are allowed under three circumstances:

1. Months when only the household's children are receiving TANF
2. Months when a family resides in an Indian Reservation or Alaskan Native village in which there is 50 percent unemployment
3. Months when a minor parent (or pregnant minor) receives assistance (unless she is the head-of-household or married to the head-of-household)

Thirty-three states have adopted additional exemptions, the most frequent related to family situations involving disability or domestic violence.

Extensions of the time limit under federal TANF regulations may be granted to up to 20 percent of a state's caseload. Only five states have opted to have no extensions. The most frequently cited circumstances used by all the other states for time-limit extensions are domestic violence, continued un- or underemployment despite documented efforts to obtain employment, disability of a parent or caretaker, and/or caring for a disabled household member.

The time limit clock started ticking in October 1996. Families in the states with a 5-year limit who have been on TANF from its inception (many of them former AFDC recipients) reached their time limit by or after October 2001. Families in states with less than a 5-year limit reached the limit prior to October 2001. While extensions and exemptions have kept many on the rolls, in some states—most notably Connecticut—thousands of people have lost benefits.

The as yet unanswered question is what has happened to those who have left or been forced off the rolls. States have not introduced follow-up tracking mechanisms. What we do know is that those reaching the limits tend to be those most unable to obtain ongoing employment because of physical or mental health, child care, literacy, substance abuse, and other psychosocial barriers (Hernandez, 2000). The positive relationship between clients' psychosocial pressures and their inability to find employment has been documented in recent studies (Powers, 2003; Zedlowski, 2003). Data collected on comparable samples of AFDC recipients suggests that the 5-year lifetime limit—even in the most healthy economic times—is out of sync with the realities of clients' needs. While many AFDC recipients remained on assistance for less than 5 continuous years, most (69 percent) returned within 4 years of leaving the rolls (U. S. House of Representatives Committee on Ways and Means, 2000). Forty percent of children who received TANF did so for more than 5 years (Smith & Yeung, 1998, p. 2). Families who leave TANF because of time limits or sanctions have been found to be in more severe economic distress than other leavetakers (Fremstad, 2004).

**Work First**    While AFDC included work requirements, under TANF rapid job placement became the program's guiding goal. Work first—work before training; any work at any wage—was the program's designers' magic bullet to eradicate dependency.

Federally imposed standards are more evident here than in other sections of the law. In order to receive full federal funding, states must meet minimum work participation rates with 50 percent of their single-parent caseloads and 90 percent of their two-parent caseloads working as of fiscal year 2002. Prior to the economic downturn in 2001, states were approaching these goals. In FY 1999, for example, all states met the overall national participation rate (Administration for Children and Families, 2000). Despite weak economic conditions, both the Senate and House proposals for TANF reauthorization increase participation rate requirements from 55 percent in 2004 to 70 percent by 2008. Though new legislation was not passed by spring 2005, it seems very likely that higher work participation requirements will be included when it is.

Federal rules also require a work-trigger deadline of 24 months; by that point all recipients must be engaged in some job-related activity or lose benefits. States can lower the work-trigger date, and indeed 20 have chosen to do so. Ten require immediate involvement in a job or work-related effort, including workfare—nonpaid employment to work off the amount received in TANF benefits. Federal rules also require that recipients engage in some form of community service after receiving TANF for 2 months.

The required minimum work hours also are federally mandated. As of fiscal year 2000, single-parent households were to be engaged in 30 hours of work activity per week; two-parent families in 35–55 hours per week (the higher figure applied to families who also receive federally funded child care and those in which there is no adult with disabilities or adult caring for a child with severe disabilities). However, the House reauthorization bill (HR4) passed in 2003 requires 160 hours of work activity per month (that is, about 40 hours per week) for all families. The Senate bill, not yet passed as of summer 2004, includes a range of work hour requirements from 24 hours per week for a single parent with a child under 6, to 34 hours for all other single parents to 55 hours for a two-parent family with child care. The Bush administration recommends raising work requirements to 40 hours per week. Actual work activities are defined by the state, using federal guidelines. They can include unsubsidized employment (all wages paid by the employers); subsidized employment (states pay part of salary); the aforementioned workfare or work experience (client works off grant received); on-the-job training; job search and job readiness (but only for a maximum of 6 weeks); community service programs; job skills training directly linked to a position; provision of child care for a TANF recipient who is participating in a community service program.

Educational activities are not credited the way they were under AFDC, where enrollment in certain postsecondary education programs was allowed as a work-related activity. Permitted educational activities now are restricted to only 30 percent of a state's recipients, and these activities are narrowly defined: vocational educational training for a maximum of 12 months, secondary school attendance (for single or married teens), or education directly related to a job. It appears unlikely that the forthcoming reauthorization bill will include education as a countable work activity. The House version eliminates all education and training as a primary work-related activity. The Senate version permits vocational education or training for only 6 months out of a 24-month period.

Under TANF, few are exempt from the requirement to work (Abramovitz, 1997). Care of an infant or young child no longer is necessarily seen as a valid excuse. Under AFDC, a parent with a child under age 6 did not have to work; under TANF, there are *no* nationally set child care exemptions. As of 2001, all but five states required work participation of parents with children age 1 year or older. Eleven states mandated work for parents with children over *3 months* of age.

TANF's "work first" policy ignores several factors. TANF mandates work, but does not make child care a guaranteed benefit. The cost and availability of substitute care is not considered (Schumacher & Greenberg, 1999, pp. i–ii). The elimination of a national exemption standard for parenting a young child deprecates the value of the parenting role. In some instances, TANF recipients provide day care for the young children of other TANF recipients; serious questions have been raised about the rationale for and quality control involved in this practice. We have yet to experience the consequences of this "work outside the home" ethos that imbues TANF, but a 2001 study indicates that adolescent children of women who have moved from welfare to work have more behavioral and academic problems than a control group whose parents remain on assistance (Levin, 2001).

Moreover, the "work first" policy assumes that any employment experience will be an antidote to dependency. It ignores the demands of the highly technical contemporary job market and the commensurate necessity for education and training. TANF did not provide the states with the incentives and resources for the necessary skills training. As a consequence, many people are forced to move from welfare to minimum wage jobs with few if any benefits, limited job security, and none of the time flexibility and other supports mothers of young children require. TANF recipients with limited job skills as well as other barriers to employment (for example, substance abuse problems, illiteracy, learning disabilities) may find themselves unable to obtain or sustain employment, especially as economic conditions weaken (Edelman, 1997, pp. 52–53; Hasenfeld, 2000, p. 188; Martinson & Strawn, 2003). Data indicate that recent welfare leavers are not as likely to be employed as those who left before 2000. The percentage of former recipient families who receive no form of assistance and no income from work has risen between 1999 to 2002 (Loprest, 2003). Research has also found that the move from welfare to work does not necessarily mean a move out of poverty. Studies from Michigan, Pennsylvania, California, and Wisconsin found high poverty rates persisting for TANF leavers (Fremstad, 2004). With lifetime limits on the receipt of federally funded TANF and the uncertainty of whether and how states will choose to assist those who no longer are eligible for TANF, the question of how society will deal with those left in need remains unanswered.

**Family Policy Provisions**    AFDC's objective was to prevent the destitution of children whose parent was unable to provide for their basic needs generally because of the absence of the other parent. In its 60-year history, the program did not attempt to influence recipients' personal behaviors with regard to marriage and pregnancy. TANF, strongly influenced by the view that the irresponsible behaviors of unwed mothers caused their family's poverty (Hasenfeld, 2000, p. 187), included provisions to promote a two-parent wedded family formation. The family cap option, which permits states to refuse support to children born to TANF recipients, appears incompatible with family values. States are permitted to implement family caps without federal approval, and 23 have done so. The provision that children who leave the home of a TANF recipient who has reached her time limit can continue to receive benefits is also antithetical to family formation supports. In so doing, TANF became the first federal program whose intent was to impact on family structure, an arena traditionally viewed in the United States as beyond the reach of government (and still seen as such for citizens other than the poor). Among the TANF provisions designed to impact on family formation included:

- The top five states with the highest reduction in births outside of marriage (and an accompanying reduction in their abortion rates) are offered a fiscal incentive.

- States are prohibited from granting assistance to minor, unmarried parents unless they live with relatives or in another adult-supervised setting and participate in school or work activities.
- TANF dollars can be spent on family planning, but not on abortion services. TANF also provided dollars for abstinence education programs.
- Paternity and child support enforcement rules have been strengthened—failure to comply with state cooperation rules brings a 25 percent benefit reduction (and at state option ineligibility of the entire family).
- The more stringent eligibility standards that had been applied to two-parent families under AFDC were eliminated. However, work participation expectations are higher for these families, and may pose a challenge to states trying to meet their federally mandated work participation levels.

It is premature to assess the impact of these provisions. Studies reported in 2001 indicate an increase in two-parent families (both married and unmarried) among low-income African Americans between 1995 and 2000. Some of this shift was undoubtedly related to welfare reform, in particular its harsh rules—which forced women to look for or remain with partners for economic survival. Some of it may also be linked with the economic boom of the late '90s with its attendant increase in socioeconomic stability (Harden, 2001). Marriage promotion will undoubtedly be incorporated into whatever TANF reauthorization bill is ultimately passed. Unlike the original bill, which did not include funds specifically designed for these purposes, both the House and Senate reauthorization bills provide about $1 billion for "healthy marriage" program research activities (Center on Budget Policy and Priorities, 2003).

## Application and Eligibility

Under TANF, there are fewer nationally established criteria for eligibility than there were under AFDC. Most notably, deprivation of a child (due to such reasons as death, absence, or incapacitation of a parent) is no longer a criteria. Two-parent families are now as eligible as single-parent families, a change from AFDC eligibility standards.

In addition to being in financial need (as determined by each state), eligible families must—as under AFDC—include a minor child (defined as being under age 18 or under 19 if a full-time student in a secondary school or in a comparable vocational/technical training program). A family with a medically verified pregnant individual also qualifies. Unlike AFDC, where the woman needed to be 6 months pregnant to receive assistance, there is no such gestational age requirement under TANF. The following persons are *disqualified* as TANF eligible recipients (U. S. House of Representatives, Committee on Ways and Means, 2004):

- An applicant family that includes an adult who has, during her adult years already received 5 years (or less according to a state's lifetime limit) of TANF cash assistance is not eligible—unless the adult meets the hardship criteria established by the state for time limit extension (for example, for a disability or domestic violence). In determining whether the time limit has been exceeded, states are not to count months in which children were the only recipients, months in which the TANF services received were non-cash or a one-time-only emergency payment, or months in which the adult resided in a Native American or Alaska Native region with 50 percent of its adults unemployed. Included are months a minor received TANF benefits if the minor was head of household or married to the head of a household. Also included in the time limit calculation are months in which an adult received no cash benefits because the state was recouping money, months in which TANF was received in another state, and months in which an adult was sanctioned for noncompliance with work or other requirements by nonreceipt of assistance for herself but other members of her household continued to receive TANF cash assistance.

- Unmarried mothers who are under the age of 18 and their children who do not live in the home of a parent, legal guardian, or adult relative or, where there is no appropriate relative, in another adult-supervised, state-sanctioned living arrangement.

- An unmarried mother under age 18 who has a child at least 12 weeks old, is not a high school graduate, and is not attending high school or an alternative state-approved program.

- Legal immigrants who entered the United States after August 22, 1996; for these immigrants, states may choose to make them TANF eligible after they have been in the United States for 5 years. The 5-year exempt period does not pertain to refugees, veterans, asylees, or Cuban or Haitian entrants. Nineteen states have opted to include postenactment legal immigrants.

- Legal immigrants who arrived before August 22, 1996, and whose states have chosen not to exercise the option to include them as TANF eligible. This does not apply to refugees, asylees, veterans, or Cuban or Haitian entrants. Currently, all jurisdictions have chosen to include the immigrants here prior to August 1996.

- Persons who after August 22, 1996, are convicted of a drug-related felony and whose state does not choose to include them as eligible.

- Persons who lied about their residence when applying for TANF, Medicaid, the food stamp program, and/or Supplemental Security Income (SSI) from two or more states. Such persons are ineligible for TANF cash assistance for a period of 10 years.

- A person who does not cooperate in establishing her child's paternity, in cooperating with child support orders, or in assigning child or spousal support rights to the state will be denied assistance for herself and her family or have the benefit granted reduced by 25 percent unless the state exempts her because of good cause such as domestic violence.

- Children born to a current welfare recipient unless the state chooses to include them.

In contrast with AFDC federal regulations, TANF rules do not require that applicants be granted the right to file an application and to have their applications processed in a timely manner. Here again, states' discretion prevails; as of 2001, all states have chosen to permit every interested applicant to complete an application, and each state provides for the timely processing of applications (usually within 30–45 days). States, however, can and do require that applicants meet certain conditions before an application is filed or a determination made. For example, more than 30 states mandate that those awaiting a decision on their application engage in a work-related activity. Some states have also adopted diversion programs, in which those who attempt to apply for TANF are encouraged to seek help elsewhere (Casey, 1998, p. 11). With few exceptions, states use joint application forms enabling individuals to apply for Medicaid and food stamps as well as TANF.

While AFDC regulations required that a single state agency administer the program, TANF provides states with the "charitable choice/privatization" option. States can now contract with charitable, private, or religious organizations to run the states' TANF programs. This Clinton-era provision was a harbinger of the Bush administration's faith-based social service proposal.

## Benefits

The central benefit granted to TANF recipients is a cash allowance. The amount given is determined by each state and varies greatly from state to state (for example, in FY 2000, benefits ranged from a low of $170 monthly for a family of three in Mississippi to a high of $923 in Alaska for the same size family unit). TANF recipients usually receive their cash grant in the form of a monthly check, which covers what the state determines to be the costs of food, shelter, clothing, and other necessities of living. Sometimes, rent and/or utilities are paid directly to the landlord or utility company (through vouchers or restricted payments). The amount received is linked with the size of the family. Amounts may increase if a recipient has a baby, but as noted before, states can choose not to cover this child. Benefit amounts may decrease if an adult recipient is sanctioned because of lack of compliance with a TANF regulation (for example, to participate in work activities). The amount received is also affected by earned income, child support payments, and/or a child's Social Security benefits.

According to TANF rules, benefits that count toward the 5-year lifetime limit are cash, voucher, and other forms of reimbursements that provide for life's basic needs—food, shelter, clothing. Counseling, employment services, and short-term crisis benefits are not defined as countable assistance.

The adequacy of the amounts granted recipients was questionable under AFDC and under TANF is an even more problematic issue. Between July 1994 and January 2000, the value of benefits in real dollars decreased in most states. Adjusted for inflation, the federal government estimates an almost 11 percent loss of benefits (U.S. House of Representatives Committee on Ways and

Means, 2000, p. 382). Some states have cut benefits, others have not increased grants to keep up with inflation. Benefits may fall even further if economic conditions worsen. The block grant is capped; states may opt to serve more persons by lowering benefits. They also may keep benefits low to dissuade people from viewing TANF as a viable source of income, and to encourage families to leave the program (remember states are now fiscally rewarded for reducing their caseloads) (V. Albert, 2000).

In addition to the cash allowance, nearly all TANF recipients meet the Medicaid eligibility standards and, unless they reside with persons not receiving TANF, they are automatically eligible for food stamps. Eligibility for food stamps and Medicaid generally continues after a recipient leaves the cash assistance program. However, for reasons as yet not fully understood, there has been a marked decline in eligible families receiving these critical benefits once they leave the TANF rolls (Sweeney et al., 2000, p. 4; U.S. House of Representatives Committee on Ways and Means, 2000, p. 360). This has occurred even though state plans provide for transitional Medicaid for periods of 12 months.

**Sanctions**    As part of the tough posture taken toward recipients, TANF requires states to punish recipients who do not comply with work activity and/or child support enforcement requirements. States are penalized fiscally if they do not sanction these clients. States are also permitted to impose sanctions on recipients who fail to comply with any responsibility they have agreed to fulfill (for example, ensuring their children attend school). Sanctions take the form of a reduction or elimination of benefits for the adult recipient *or* the entire family. If clients demonstrate good cause—as defined by the state and federal government—they avoid a sanction. With regard to work sanctions, the federal definition of good cause is limited to situations in which single parents cannot find adequate child care for a child under age 6.

With regard to work-related sanctions, 36 states impose a partial sanction for an initial infraction; in 21 of these states, further instances of noncompliance results in termination of the entire family. The partial sanction may be a percentage of the total grant, the adult portion, or a flat figure.

Full-family sanction—the ending of all cash assistance—is permitted by 36 states, half of which allow such a sanction to take effect immediately even for a first instance of noncompliance. The sanction period varies by state, with the most frequent being a set period of 1–6 months. Seven states permit permanent discontinuance. Sanctions are lifted only if compliance is demonstrated through actions determined by each state—most frequently, clients must engage in the activity they failed to comply with for a set period of time.

## Due Process

With the removal of the federal entitlement to cash assistance for dependent children and their caretakers, and TANF's strict sanction policies, ensuring recipients due process safeguards against arbitrary decisions and actions becomes significant. Under AFDC, applicants and recipients were guaranteed the right to timely notice of state actions against them, to aid continuing until a hearing decision, and to an administrative hearing with procedural safeguards. Under TANF, while there is no such federal mandate, all states have continued a fair hearing process similar to the one they had in place under AFDC. However, fair hearing rights may be subject to states' limitations, and their future is still uncertain (see earlier decision, *Goldberg v. Kelly,* 1970).

## THE CLIENTS' STORIES

### Vivian

I'm a single mom with six children from the age of 18, 10, 9, 8, 2, and 1. I have a full-time job as a Maternal Child Health Advocate. I help fight infant mortality, as an outreach worker. I live in a three-bedroom apartment with just my children.

I was born in Germany. My father was in the service. I have a sister and two brothers, and we came over here to my mother's family when I was 9. I never met her family before that so it was all new to us. We were used to living good even though we had abuse in the family from my father. We still never missed a meal; we still, you know, had a roof over our head.

I have scars on me today from when my father used to beat me bloody. I remember when I was a child, I was looking out the window and I was tapping on the window and all of a sudden something just came across my back and just stung so bad, and I realized that my father had hit me in the back with a belt. And he just kept hitting me and hitting me, and I remember my mother arguing with him and cleaning me off and everything, and then eventually, it was a lot of time passed, but eventually we left him because she was getting broken ribs and black eyes, and I was getting bloody. I don't remember my sisters or anybody else getting hurt in that manner. . . .

I remember my mother dropping us off with her family. There was nothing we were used to but I remember my mom not being my mom like she used to be. Her family didn't treat us very well because they didn't know us. They didn't treat us well. They used to starve us, literally starve us and not wash our clothes. It was nothing we was used to. When I was younger living with my father, we had a maid, you know, and we had poodles overseas, I mean, I had two poodles named Fifi, one black one, one white one. When I came over here it was like hell. Like, you know, my mom dropped us in hell.

It was in the '70s. And we lived everywhere. Where I live today with my kids is the longest place I have ever stayed, and I have stayed there four years. You know, I was always alone. My sister was the favorite, and I was a big girl, chubby, so everybody teased me a lot, nobody really loved me but I was there, you know. But, as

I got older, when I really needed like a mother figure, a woman, you know my mom started working in bars and stuff like that. I don't remember being put under nobody's wing, nobody teaching me anything, how to save money, or you know anything. . . .

I dropped out in the seventh grade. I had trouble because I can't even spell today. It's hard for me to learn, but I can learn, I'm teachable, it's just that it's hard for me to learn.

I wouldn't tell people that I can't do it but they knew it if I was in their class. But nobody stepped up to the plate to say this child needs help. Nobody ever reached out until like recently when I did it for myself.

I dropped out, my mom was really heavy into her drinking, into her friends. She was getting welfare; she couldn't buy us clothes; she could hardly feed us. She'd get the food stamps in the beginning of the month, then at the end of the month everything would be gone so there was no money in the house, nobody to help us. My father never wrote us. My grandmother used to say my mother was the black sheep of the family. My mother used to tell us I'm the black sheep; they're not going to help me; they're not going to do nothing for my kids. And then she used to huddle us around and say that we're the five Musketeers and we got to stick together, but it didn't happen like that 'cause she wound up leaving me, 'cause I had dropped out of school and I started hanging out, and you know, I got loose. And I got pregnant when I was 17.

And I had my baby at 18 years old. And then when I had my baby, she packed her stuff and she rented her room and left us in there. My first baby and she left me, and I got on drugs then, crack cocaine, and so did my brothers and sister.

It was just us. 'Cause Mommy had left. We didn't have nobody now so we was just doing our thing. We were getting high, when we wanted something to eat we would have to go out there and ask folks to give us money. Then, eventually when I had my son, I was with his father, but then I got tired so I wanted a job, so I went out there and I tried. I was scared because I had no education, you know, I was scared. I was drinking when I first got the job. But I was scared because I didn't know that much, but I went and got a job anyway. My son was about 9 months old and then he got sick and went in the hospital. Somebody had fed him with dirty hands or something and his blood got infected, and they had to keep him in the hospital and then that's how I lost the job. Because I stayed at the hospital with my son.

His father was very abusive to me, and, so I had to run, even though I was on drugs, I still ran. And me and my son wound up in the shelter system, and I was still on drugs.

I was receiving the welfare, but I also wanted to go back to school and do everything. But I just didn't know how to do everything all by myself because I had this child, I knew I wanted to go to school. I knew everything I had to do but to put everything in perspective was so hard for me to do, you know? So I was on welfare for all them years.

I wound up having two children from this man I met in the shelter. He was very abusive. I wound up leaving him, too, because he didn't want to help me with the babies. I didn't want to live like I was living. We were staying in this little room. He wasn't helping; he would come in the house with drugs instead of Pampers and milk and stuff like that. We would get the welfare checks, but we were on drugs. We were sick. So when I left him I checked myself into a rehab. I just wanted to get away from him; and, I got away and I stayed in the rehab for three months. I have an aunt, my mother's brother's wife. I asked her can she please take the kids 'cause I knew she had six kids of her own and I knew she was responsible. I didn't ask my mom because I knew my mom wasn't going to do it. So my aunt took them and welfare paid her the food stamps and the benefits to take my kids temporarily while I was in the rehab. And I acquired Section 8 before I went in the rehab, and I have been on it ever since. So Section 8 has helped me a lot to get myself stable because, if it didn't, I'd still be living here and there and living with this fool and that fool. I have survival skills, I know how to survive as far as to utilize the agencies in my community, to go here and there for food and stuff like that. But it's a time where you want to grow out of that and, you want the agencies to help build you up. So when I got tired of that I started coming out of my house telling the agencies, "Look, I been on drugs for 12 years, I'm 11 years clean, I have such and such amount of kids, I have no education, I want to go back to school and I want to take care of my children."

I know I gotta work, I know I gotta take care, I know I gotta go to school, that's the first and foremost, I have to get an education because I need an education in order to do a job, but nobody will send me to school. And I took the test, the GED test, and I guessed the whole test, and I missed it by 24 points. And I went back and I said, "I need more help, please could you send me to get more help?" But they kept saying, "It's no help, there's no help for you, there's no help for you."

Social Services is good to help you like when you're in a bind. But that system is there to, how you say, keep you in one place and one place only. They say they want to help you but when you throw your opinions, or can you help me do it this way or that way, they go, "No. You either do it our way or there is no way, or you're going to find it outside somewhere else." So that's the attitude I had to find, I had to do their way, but I also had to go out there and find other baskets to put my eggs in, so to speak. You know what I'm saying? And, I'm not saying it didn't help a lot of people, I'm not saying it didn't help me 'cause it did help me when I had nobody, it fed me, it fed my children, but as far as that system, it's not set up right, I don't think. A lot of people that's on it today don't want to be on it, they don't want to be on it. If they had other options, they would try for other options than to deal with Social Service. But life is, everyone has dreams, everyone has goals, if they could find the right resources to help them with their goals, they would deter from Social Service because Social Service, they don't want you to have nothing. You can't have nothing, you can't be nobody on Social Service, but who they want you to be. If they say, "Only thing we going to pay for is nurse's aide," I don't like nurse's aide, I don't feel for nurse's aide, I don't, you know, that's not what I'm feeling, I don't have the interest in nurse's aide. "Well that's the only thing we'll pay for, and that's it. If you don't want to be a nurse's aide, you going to find help somewhere else." And that shouldn't be so. They do that because they know you need the help. They know you need the help.

They're making you go to work, okay, for the benefits. I mean they don't give you time to get on your feet. As soon as they know you got a job, they just snatch the rug from out of you, and you have to learn how to adjust. Once they find out you get a job, you have to learn the hard way how to start over and do without these services because you have a job now, so now you gotta learn how to do without Social Service.

I never had anything, believe me when I tell you, I never had anything. I always shop at Thrift Stores and always had to go to churches to get clothes. And, so when I got a job it was a good thing. Now I can keep laundry detergent in the house. Now I don't have to go to bus terminals and get tissue and beg for this and beg for that. So, I had a job, so I had to leave, 'cause I got pregnant again. I was going into pre-eclampsia and I couldn't work. So they fired me, I went through the union and everything to keep my job, but they was like, "We only take hard labor." If you can't do the hard labor, then they wanted me to resign. I didn't want to resign, I wanted to keep my job. But they fired me anyway, right? So I went on and had my baby. So I wasn't working. And I would pay the bills in the beginning of the month and we would get the little food stamps, and then at the end of the month I'd be broke.

We had Medicaid. Medicaid is excellent. We are still getting Medicaid. I had to buy Pampers and stuff like that, so at the end of the month I'd be, at the end of the week or the two weeks, I'd be broke. So I kept going to this program. And there's this director, and I would express my needs to her and she would always try to find me a job and try to do this and try to do that. Just like everybody else used to do, but hers was more like cradling. She would say, "Vivian, if you need anything, you get in contact with me."

Now I never had that in all the days that I've been through. I never had what she gave me. So I would go in there and I'd tell her I don't have no soap powder, no tissue and she would say, "Write out what you use, brand name, everything." And I go, she is different, because anybody else would say, we don't help with tissue, we don't help with soap. And I didn't want to be on welfare, I wanted me a job, I wanted to go back to school and I wanted to know how to raise my children, okay?

And Dr. Clark got me this job. I had been with the program for about 2 years. I've done so many things. She took me to Texas to the Children's Defense Fund. And last summer she said, "Listen Vivian, I think I got a job for you," that's how she talked, and she said, "Are you ready to come to work?" And then she told me to come on in to fill out this paperwork, and I've been there ever since. What I help women with today, is what I went through in the past. I don't treat them like they used to treat me. I have empathy for these women, I mean they come in they're hungry, or if they tell me they're hungry I will take a dollar out of my pocket and I will feed them because I know how I used to get treated. I have walked out of my house so determined so many days to get help for myself and to come home feeling worse than I felt. I have contemplated suicide, going out trying to get help for myself and going back home to the empty house. Until I met Dr. Clark. Today I'm a different person. I utilize everything. I'm not on welfare today, but I still have my Section 8 program in place. I still have my mental health service. I get Child Health Plus for my children. I still use my Family Services program for my children for their camp needs and everything. I'm not saying all agencies are bad, it's just sometimes the people that they put in there. They don't have sensitivity to people, so to speak, 'cause they never know where people are coming from and where they're trying to get to. It's not only Social Services; it's other agencies.

Right now I get up at 6 o'clock in the morning and I get the kids dressed, I get 'em fed and I get them out to day care by 8:30. I'm at work by 9 o'clock. I work from 9 to 5, and I come home. The kids come home from day care and the other two are at the Boys & Girls Club. I sometimes pick 'em up, but then I come home, I cook, I clean, I make them take showers and I help them with their homework and I make sure we get ready for tomorrow. And this is 5 days a week. If I have to take care of any business, I have to do that on my lunch break 'cause after I get off from work there's no more time. But the job is telling me that I have to get my GED but I need the work, so I'm trying to squeeze in school. I'm not going to say I'm gonna be back where I was, 'cause I'm never going back, 'cause I been out here, you know, for a while, I know I'm going to be struggling on how I'm going to take care of my kids, but I'm focusing more on my GED so I can go to college so I can get a better job to take care of my kids. That's my goal. And my day is very hectic. I try to clean on the weekends as much as I can, even during the day, but I don't get to bed 'til about 10:30 and then when I get to bed I be so tired, then the day come again, and then I'm starting over again. And nobody takes the kids, I have them, well, they go to school and everything, but when I come home it's like starting all over again. I'm trying to go to school if I can get help with my kids at night. And the day at my job is full because I'm helping other families and children.

I'm a Maternal Child Health Advocate. I'm trying to help other people find resources to help them in their lives. And I hate sending them to Social Services because I know Social Services sometimes doesn't help them.

I'm not going to say Social Services is wrong. It's just that they have a system to judge everybody the same way. And you can't fault them for that because they want to keep their guards up, you know, 'cause even the way they are now, the strict policy they have now, people still do fraud, you know. But I'm just saying, people have came from different lives, different lifestyles, everybody's not the same, a lot of people do want a lot of good things in life. They just need support, like me.

I have dreams for myself, I want my GED, I want to go to college, I want a good job, I dream of being a radiologist technician. And I want my children to go to college, I want us a home where I can grow roots and never move again. And I just want to live a comfortable life. I'm tired of being scared that I'm not going to make it, that I'm not going to be able to take care of my kids. I want to learn, once I learn my education, it's something nobody's going to ever take away from me. Just like the street education, nobody be able to take that away from me. So I know if I get that academically, it's something nobody could take away from me and my kids.

## Bette

I live with my husband and my son, and I also live with my mother and my brother. I have been married for 26 years. My husband, he works as a clerk. And my son, he's a police officer. My brother, he works for the transit, and my mother, well she's retired, and she's sick and I take care of her at this time.

As far as me working, right now I work for a community development program that is part of a Baptist church as the intake worker for the Weatherization Assistance Program. This program basically deals with assisting homeowners or tenants in receiving free services for their home, which entails heating system replacement of grading insulation and door replacement. It is a pleasure doing this program. And also I'm the registrar at a university off-site campus, which is located at the church. We offer an associate in religious studies, and business administration bachelor studies, master of divinity. And I'm a member of the church. And basically, you know, I just believe in the Lord and try to do the right thing and take care of my mother, who I have been taking care of approximately 15 years. I find that also rewarding because I also know that if it was me that she would take care of me, and I just feel it's the right thing, not only as a human being, but as a daughter to take care of parents.

My mother, she suffers from depression. She has arthritis. She has a home attendant, but also I try to be a great support system for my mother. I just don't trust the home attendant. I make sure that I fix her meals, make sure that she goes to the doctors, make sure that I do her shopping, make sure there's food in the house. I try to take care of every need, even down to her pound cakes and her candy bars. I make sure that she has that. I try to do whatever I can to make it comfortable for my mother. Even though she's sick, she's still my mother, and I love her and that's why I do what I'm supposed to do, and I want to do.

I can do all of this. I guess it's a Taurus thing, they say that we're systematic. I set myself with a system. I get up in the morning, I know what time I have to get up, for instance to cook dinner before I leave to come to work. I also try to schedule my day. I am not going to overtax myself. I'm not going to give myself high blood pressure. I know what time I have to leave to get to work. I stick to that schedule. When I get to work, I map my day out. What I can't do, there's another day. And this is the way I operate.

I work 4 days a week. I work from 1 o'clock in the afternoon to approximately 9 o'clock at night, and then when I go home I spend some time with my husband, give myself some time. Because I believe in giving myself some time. This is the time I sit and think by myself and nobody bothers me, and this is a help to me. This is my time, my shut down time, my soul's time, and also my time to pray. That's a big part of my life, too. God is a big part of my life. And I say this because as I look over my life I know that right now, if it wasn't for Him, I wouldn't even be talking to you. I would be six feet under. So, He's a big part of my life, and He's the one who gives me my strength and helps me to do what I'm supposed to do in my life. Without Him, I know I couldn't do it.

I was born in an urban area. I was raised with my parents. I had a great upbringing.

It was me, my brother, and my parents in the home. My father was a ship fitter. My mother was a homemaker. After I graduated from junior high school then my mother decided to go work in a school, serving lunches to school kids. My brother, when he graduated from high school he went into the Navy. My brother is younger than me, but sometimes he acts like he's older than me.

My mother and father's whole intent was for me to get a good education, and at the time, they felt Catholic schools provided the better education than the public school. Ironically, when I had to take the entrance exam for a Catholic high school, I literally sat at this test and tried to mark wrong answers. I was totally surprised when they called me and told me that I had passed and got into one of the best Catholic schools. I said, "How did this happen? I'm not supposed to be in this school," because I really wanted to go to public school with my friends and everything. But it worked out, because I made new friends. The reason why I say that is because I was predominantly raised in a black neighborhood. In elementary school I went to school with mostly all blacks, even though it was a Catholic school. When I got into high school it was like a whole new world for me. I was going to school now with all these Caucasians. At the time I was coming up it was time when there was a lot of violence going on, the civil rights movement was going on, and hangings were going on. When I walking into this high school, and I saw all these white people I literally was afraid to go to this school, because the perception I had. I thought I was going to be lynched, and I was afraid. I literally tried to fail all my courses in the freshman year, hoping I could get out of this school, because that's how scared I was. But then, as time went on, the ones that I tended to be afraid of became my best friends. I went to their homes. Their parents treated me well. They're still my friends and we keep in contact.

I was raised as a Catholic. First I was christened as African Orthodox, and then I became a Catholic because that was one of the requirements to go to Catholic school, and that's how I became a Catholic.

All my life I had wanted to be a phys ed teacher, so my favorite course was gym. My ambition was to go to either Howard University or Temple, because I knew they had a great physical education course, but at the time my parents couldn't afford to send me to college. I didn't have the scholastic skills to get a scholarship. I applied to get in colleges, but, you know, because of the finances I could not afford to go myself. I never made it to become a physical education teacher. That was my sole ambition. In fact, today, I still have that desire to be a physical education teacher.

My favorite sport was handball. I was pretty good at it. I got a couple of trophies there. When I was in high school I was on the bowling team. I got some trophies in that. I loved track. I loved basketball. You name the sport, I loved it. At my age, I still get out there and I bowl. Sometimes during the summer time I get out there and I play handball, play a little baseball. I still enjoy sports. I was a tomboy, and maybe I still have a little of that in me. I think there's nothing wrong with that. I think you need to have a little tomboy in you in order to cope with some of the problems in the world today. That's the way I feel.

After I graduated from high school I went to work for an insurance company, as a clerk, basically filing, and then I worked my way up to doing paid-up insurance claims. During that time I enrolled in a business school, in which I took a business course, and a little bit of computer programming. Then, after that I didn't enjoy the insurance company any more because I didn't care for the supervisor. Then after that I went to work for a bank. Then I met someone in my life who in a sense now I'm sorry I ever met that person because what that person did was introduce me to something that I never should have gotten involved in. That took a hold of my life. I stopped working. I'm talking about substance abuse. Before I got involved in substance abuse, I had a virus, and the virus had attacked my liver, and I had got viral hepatitis. At that time, I was so sick that literally I was given the last rites, and they really had expected me not to live. During recovery, like I said, I wasn't working at the time and I got involved. I did it for stupid reasons. Because, I had something stupid in my mind, for some reason I thought that my mother loved my brother more than me and it bothered me. For some stupid reason I felt as though, well if I get involved with this substance abuse, then maybe I will get some type of attention or I'll hurt them or whatever, but not realizing that I was hurting myself. So I got involved in that. I did not want to go back to work. I started doing other things to support my abuse. I don't mean robbing or anything like that. At the time I was using heroin. First I started snorting it. Then I started skin popping, and then I was introduced to mainlining.

At first, when you meet somebody they acquire it for you. They give it to you, and then after a while you learn where to go purchase it yourself. So, that's what I did.

I stopped working, because I had no desire to work, because your main focus is that high, and you're not thinking about working.

It's not your life any more. I didn't feel as though I had my life anymore. There wasn't a day when I could just get up, go to work, feel free, have fun. I couldn't do that. My day was, first of all, I went to bed that night thinking about getting up in the morning, getting that high, getting out in the street, selling the drugs for the high, and I felt like I was a prisoner within myself, and I didn't know how to get out. I had to have my fix. If you've never taken drugs before, you have to understand that if you don't have the drug you go through a period of withdrawal, you start feeling weak, you start sweating. The reason why you're going through withdrawal is because the drugs are trying to leave your system, and you need to have that fix to keep you going. You get some heroin where the comfort would only last for maybe two hours. Then you would have to go and you would have to have another fix. And you know some people have bigger habits, but basically I had to shoot up about two bags at one time. That's the reason why I had to go out there and get this money.

Getting back to the way I was brought up, one thing I knew I wasn't going to do was I wasn't going to rob, and I wasn't going to sell my body and become a prostitute for drugs. That just was not me. I would rather, you know, just sell it than to do those two instances I just mentioned. I stayed on drugs for maybe a year and a half, and then during that process I met my husband-to-be. In fact my best friend is the one who introduced me to her uncle, who became my husband. So now, my best friend is my niece also. I met him at his birthday party. That was the first time I met him. After we met, we had a relationship, and I became pregnant. When I became pregnant, I said, "Well you know I can't be on drugs and be pregnant at the same time. I can't do this." Also, my husband was a great support system for me because when he met me I was thinking about going on the methadone program, and he encouraged me to go on the methadone program. He also encouraged me and literally came with me to find jobs. I got a job working at the New York City Board of Education, which was provisional at the time, not permanent, but it was a job. Plus I had gotten to the point where I was just tired of taking drugs, of shooting up, because I had no life then. It's hard, you know, when you can't even go to family functions, you can't even go out to enjoy yourself because you're worrying about this. I was like embarrassed. If I was going to go out to a function I was afraid of people looking at me because they could automatically tell if you're high or not, and my eyes just gave everything away. I didn't want that. I didn't want to maybe have to leave a function or whatever, go into a bathroom, afraid I might get caught trying to get my fix. I started looking at other people. I started saying, "I want to be like this again. I want to be able to get up and go to work. I want to be able to enjoy my life. I'm tired of being a hostage for drugs." Everything just started coming into place, and I was like I'm tired of doing this. I've got to get my life back. Plus I was having a child. That was the biggest thing, to do right by my baby. So I got on the methadone program.

It happened I met a doctor who eventually became my son's pediatrician, and he was working with the methadone program. My whole fear was when my baby was born that he could be drug addicted or he could be addicted to the methadone or whatever, and that I didn't want. When I had my son I was at the time down to 5mg of the methadone. I looked at my baby and I saw my baby having tremors. That just tore my heart apart to see my baby like that. They had told me, "If you stop taking methadone just like this you're going to have problems forever." I prayed, I said, "God, I'm just going to stop this methadone, and I want you to help me, because if my baby could go through withdrawal, I can, too." I stopped. I give God the glory. I had no withdrawal symptoms. I had no problems coming off, and I was able to take care of my child. Again, I say God played an important part. The social worker at the hospital came to visit me and said that they probably wouldn't let me bring my baby home, because I was a drug-addicted mother. God stepped in. The doctor who was taking care of me during the methadone program spoke to the social worker, and I was able to bring my baby home. He was going through withdrawal, so they had to keep him in the hospital for about 3 weeks. They were also telling me that I needed to stay home and rest. No way. I got up every single morning, made sure I was there to feed my child every day. I don't know. I think they maybe took notice of that, that I was trying to be a sincere mother and how much I loved my child. I was able to bring him home. I started doing fine.

I was living in the family home. It was me, my husband, and of course my baby and my brother, and my mother. She was in the hospital at that time because that was when she had first suffered her bout of depression. When my son was about 3 months old we moved out of the house and we moved to Staten Island. During that time also, on top of my mother being sick, my father passed, and being married, a new baby, being out in a new part of the world that I was not accustomed to living in, I just became bored. Problems came down. As a comfort, I started drinking. I didn't realize how bad it was until I started having blackouts while I was drinking and not realizing sometimes that I was attacking my husband physically, and did not even remember I was doing this. At one point I got angry at my son. He was merely crying. I went in the room and I remember I just picked him up and threw him in the crib. I saw that and I was like, "Wait a minute here. What am I doing?" The drinking had taken such a toll on me. I would get up in the morning, I would have to drink about an 8-ounce glass of rum and Coke before I even got started for the day. I drank all day. It got to a point where I had to wake up every 3 hours it seemed during the night to get a drink. I couldn't even sleep during the night. This went on for maybe about a year and a half. I was on the verge of losing my job, losing my husband, losing my child. I didn't even feel like being a mother because this alcohol was taking such a toll on me. Then one day I just went to work and I sat at my desk. I said, "I'm tired of this." We had an alcohol abuse man who worked on our job. I went to see him that day, and I told him I want to stop drinking. That afternoon they put me in the hospital. They called my husband. He was like, "I don't know how I'm going to pay for this." But, again, God stepped in. My job paid for the entire bill. They paid for the hospital stay, and then I had to go to a rehab, where I was for 5 weeks. My job picked up the tab for that. To this day I could say that I have 26 years of sobriety. Still, I take a day at a time. After rehab, then I worked at a large advertising agency. I was there for almost 20 years. One day I came back from lunch and they told me my job was gone. For some reason I thought about drinking, but at the time also I had God in my life. So, what I did, instead of reaching for the bottle, I reached for the telephone to call my pastor. We sat down and we talked, and I got through that. After I lost the job, I went on unemployment. My unemployment ran out. Then I said, "What am I going to do?" I couldn't find a job because at the time inflation was rampant. Unemployment was high. This was in 1990. I had to make that dreadful move of going down to apply for public assistance.

My husband was working, but we were having problems. Just because you're with somebody doesn't mean that they're doing what they're supposed to be doing financially. One of the main reasons I had to make that move is because of the fact that I was not being supported financially, me or his son. So, this is something that I had to do.

The way the system is, if you have a husband or whatever, they do not want to assist you. So I had to do what I had to do. I had to go down to the public assistance and tell them that I was a single parent, which I did. I told them that my husband just left, we were separated, and I did not know where he was. Going to apply for public assistance for me was one of the most degrading things I had to do in my life, because first of all I felt as if I was treated, like I was a lazy individual who never worked in my life. The way they talk to you, they treat you like cattle. They literally have no respect for you. They talk down to you, and they have you fill out these enormous applications, all these pages. They ask you all these questions. They make you feel as though you're sitting on a witness stand for murder. I kept telling them I really don't want public assistance; I want a job. Of course, they could not find me a job. What I did is during that time I went to an adult learning center because I wanted to advance my skills. I took a computer course. Once I graduated from computer school they had promised they were going to find us a job. They did not. So, I was still on this public assistance. You know you hear people talk about how people on public assistance they're doing great and everything. Let me tell you how much a public assistance recipient receives to clear up any notion. First of all, for a family of two, you receive $125 a month for food stamps. That's to feed two people. I also received I think it was $250 for rent. In this day and time what apartments are you going to find for $250? Again, I said it was a good thing I had a roof over my head. I had to do this to survive. So, I stayed on the public assistance.

I was afraid for them to find out that I had lied. The reason why I had to do that was because as I stated previously, my husband did not support us. I needed to do something to help make ends meet.

I'll be honest with you. In a sense I felt as though I worked many years. I paid my taxes, I did my dues, I paid into the so-called system. I felt I was also deserving of something back. So, I did what I had to do for my family, basically not so much for me but for my son.

If I hadn't received public assistance we wouldn't have been able to eat like we were supposed to eat. I wouldn't have been able to take care of my son like I was supposed to take care of him. I wasn't too much of a factor. It was him. In public assistance they only give you but so much, but it's not enough. They put you through all these changes like they're going to give you the world, and they really don't, so it's a shame in a sense you had to get to a point where you could not tell them the truth. If you told them the truth, the least little income, they would start deducting from you. I could not afford that. Basically, I had to live a lie. I'm not proud that I had to live that lie, but it's what I had to do to survive. I think that's what life is about, surviving. It seemed like every time you went there, their motive was always trying to catch you up to find a reason to close your case. I dreaded that. Then it got to the point where they started a program where you had to work for your money. At the time when I went down to the appointment for the welfare work, the reason why I was excused is because I was also taking care of my mother. I had to bring letters from her doctors. They gave me forms that had to be filled out. They even wanted to come to the house to interview my mother. All this just to be excused from the welfare work program. Another thing I hated about this program is the workers used to come to your house. I hated the fact that they had to come looking through my house to see if I had somebody other than what I was stating living in the house, or what I had in the house. I just felt so degraded, them having to come checking me out like that. Then I was offered a job, and I said well it wasn't that much, but I was tired of going through this system. I was tired of having to go down for the recertification. I was tired of having the workers come to the home, asking the same things they asked you when you went down to be recertified.

What I had to do (about my husband) is I had to take everything like his clothes and hide them. Even the clock radio had to be hidden. Anything he had in the house that belonged to him I had to hide. I had to show no evidence that I had a male or another person in the house. I had to make it appear that it was just me and my son living in the home. My son was aware of this. Well I tried not to tell him so much, but basically when they came he was in school, which was good. I used to have to tell him that sometimes there are certain things not to say, which I tried to keep him a distance from what I was doing, because in all honesty I was not proud of what I was doing. I didn't care for the lying. I really didn't like the idea that I was on public assistance, because it was something at the time that I needed. The reason I'm saying this is because before I got on public assistance I remember I used to always look down on people who were on public assistance. I would even talk about them. Talk about, oh, they could do better than this. They just don't want to work, just want to be taking people's tax money, this, that and the other. Now, when I had to get on public assistance, I realize that I was so wrong; that there were a lot of people on there who could not help being on there, and who needed the support from the government. So my whole attitude changed towards people on public assistance, because now I was one.

After I was on public assistance I was offered a job. I said well, it wasn't that much money, but it was a door opening up where I could finally kiss public assistance good-bye. I told them good-bye in 1999.

Now that I'm not on public assistance it's like a heavy burden that's off me. I used to actually dread to get the mail because I was afraid I was going to see something. They always sent you some notice of intent to change, to come down for this appointment. There was always something. Now I don't mind getting the mail. It's just different things that were done to me. Now I feel independent again.

In 1999 I moved to this job. Ironically, when I was on public assistance and the way we were treated, I said, "God I want to be in a position one day when I can take and help people who are on public assistance, help them get a job, help work with them to make them feel as though they are somebody." When I went down there I felt like I was nobody, and that's the way they treated you. I felt as though every person deserves to be treated with respect and dignity and humanity. That's why when I got the opportunity to work with the Weatherization Program, helping people get their homes weatherized, or whatever, I make it a point that when they come in here the first thing I do is to try to make them comfortable, make them feel as though they are not coming into a Department of Social Service agency. They come in here sometimes nervous and frantic, with a lot of papers and stuff. My thing is to calm them down, let them know that I'm here to help you. That's where I'm at now. I basically want to help people now, to give them a sense of comfort and that every agency you go to, social agency or whatever, you're not always going to be treated like a leper. That's as basic as I could put it.

Right now my son is in the police academy. He's graduating in May. I'm proud and nervous. He's made the whole family very proud, especially his parents. Through it all, me and my husband are beginning to have a little better relationship. We're talking more. He's trying to do better financially, and I appreciate that. My mother, well, I still take care of Mom. I'm working right now like I said in the school and the weatherization. Also, now I help with the senior program, which I enjoy also. The golden age program at church is a very important part of my life. God is a very important part of my life. I'm a Baptist right now. I joined the Baptist faith in 1971, so I'm comfortable being a Baptist. I'm just enjoying life now, doing what I'm doing now. I just feel that those shackles of the substance abuse, I'm glad they're behind me. I just look back some time where I come from. I'm not trying to sound like I'm a religious fanatic, because I'm not, but I just appreciate what God has done for me. When I look back over my life and the many times that He has literally saved me to be here for a purpose, I don't know yet, but whatever it is, maybe it's doing what I'm doing.

The biggest thing I want is to be a grandmother. I'm waiting for that. So that I could have a couple of grandchildren and spoil them, send them back home to my son. I'm looking for that, basically just trying to live a good life and try to help people. I think that's my dream, just be happy, content, peaceful.

## Gayle

I'm definitely on the road of recovery. I live in an apartment, a two-bedroom apartment, my girls have their own room, I have my own room. It's very nice. I'm currently employed. I have no help from Social Service. It was hard for me in the beginning when I had to go on it. I now love being independent. I have my own car, I was so afraid of being by myself, but now I love it, I love it, and had I known I could feel this good about myself, you know, being single, being a single parent, I think I would have left a long time ago. I wouldn't have waited as long as I did.

In my church, I counsel women that are in domestic violent situations because they feel they have to stay in the same household. Coming from a religious point of view, they have to stay and they're supposed to try to work through it, but that's not so. God didn't call us to be abused. And, so I help out with that. My thing is, you leave. You leave the situation, especially if the batterer is not going to leave. You leave. Especially if there's children involved, because the children will pick up the habit. A female child could grow up to adopt that attitude that this is how her husband is supposed to treat her because this is how she's seen it. It's a learned behavior; males grow up to batter their wives.

It happened with my ex-husband. He grew up in that environment, he saw his mother get beat up, he even fought his father a few times because he said he walked into the house and saw his mother knocked out cold, you know, blood coming from her mouth, black eyes. And his mother finally divorced his father about 15 years of going through that, and she became a very bad alcoholic. So it's a cycle, it's a cycle that just repeats itself. But unlike his parents, and him, I'm breaking that chain of violence with my daughters. So now they're going to see that a woman doesn't sit there and take that. She does something about it.

I have a daughter who is going to be 6, and I have a 2-year-old, another little girl, and the 5-year-old experienced the violence. It started my last trimester of pregnancy; he did things like pushing me, but at that point I never really saw it as violence. And a few months after she was born, I remember he went into a rage, he didn't hit me yet, but he got angry about something. And I had her on the bed, thank God, and he kicked her bassinet and it cracked. An episode came where he had beaten me up really bad, and my daughter was lying in the bed with me, and she woke up and she saw him hitting on me. I had rolled on top of her and fell over on the other side, and at one point I kept yelling to him, you know, the baby. But he couldn't even hear me. He was just focused on hurting me. So she grew up seeing violence. There was a time where he left her in the house by herself to come to my job to fight me. And, I remember a coworker telling me, "Don't go home with him, we'll call the police." And I told my coworker, "I have to go back to the house because I know he left my daughter there." And she was 2 at the time. So when I came back to the house, there were holes in the walls, the phone had been smashed, and she was in the house by herself, crying. He had put her in a playpen so she couldn't get out, and there she was crying. Screaming, and she had to have been crying for hours. And that's when I said I have to find a way to leave him. At that point I knew it was really bad.

So now, she gets supervised visitations with her father and now she says to him, "Daddy, you know you should be nice to Mommy because Mommy's really good to us, and she takes care of us and, I'm so glad you're not mean to her anymore." And he asked her one day, "How come you don't want to come back to Daddy's house?" And she said, "I want you and Mommy to live together, but I'm afraid you're going to hit her again. And then Mommy's going to have to leave." So she knows, you don't stay in that environment. You leave. You can get up and move. When I went into a domestic violence shelter, I didn't think that she understood everything, and one night I was trying to get her to go to sleep, and she heard me crying. I thought she was asleep. But she heard me sobbing, and she got up and she came to my bed and she said, "Mommy, I know why you're crying." I said, "No, you don't. You know, Mommy's tired, just go back to sleep." And she said, "No, because you had to leave Daddy's house." And I said, "Well, yeah, we did have to leave." And she said, "We had to leave because Daddy keeps hitting you." And my heart broke because I didn't think she really understood as much as I thought. Now she's in school, she's a bright little girl, she's having lots of fun. She's in first grade. Her room is all pink, I painted her walls pink, she has a rose-colored carpet. She's being that little girl that she should be able to be, instead of trying to protect me.

The children have supervised visits with him once a week. It's in a big playroom and they get a corner of the room and there are two social workers that sit there and watch him. He's not allowed to ask if she misses him, he's not allowed to ask her where do I live, what's your phone number; he's not allowed to ask her if I'm dating. He's not allowed to ask her, "Do you want to come live with me?" He can't ask her any of those questions. He can only say to her, "How are you?" talk about school. He can't ask her where is her school, 'cause we're still in a confidential setting. And he can talk to her about whatever they're playing with at the time . . . so it's very strict. I'm not stopping him from seeing them; I want my daughters to know who their father is. I don't speak negative about him; I let them draw their own conclusions of who he is. I do let her know, though, that we can't live together because of his violent outbursts. She tells me, "Mommy, I think he's getting better because you know he's calmer now. (She knows the word calmer.) He seems calmer now, and you know, he's talking very nice, so I think he's getting better." And I told her that he did have a sickness, and if he's getting better that's good. When she goes to church, she prays for him.

Once I told him I wanted a divorce it was like everything started happening all over again. Once you get married you don't divorce, we're bonded for life, that type of talk. Bonding, you know, we're bonded for life. He must have felt, you know, Give me my space for a while, and he can go back to this family thing, without getting any help, without getting any counseling. He figured time would heal my wounds and I'd come back. Because he thought I was struggling, you know, he was the breadwinner in the family, and now that there are two children, I have to really be struggling. And, you know, he knew how I felt about welfare, and you know, just my whole persona of the whole idea or being on it. But I did it; I still did it. Two kids and all, I did it.

As a child, I grew up with both parents in the house, my mother was a nurse, my father was in the military and then he became a police officer, and so I had two dominant working parents. I have an older sister, a younger brother, and a younger sister. I loved my childhood. I had fun. I knew family values. I used to watch my mother cater to my father, and it's funny growing up, I always said I wanted to be just like my mother. She was very soft, very gentle. My father was the one who was very outspoken, he was much more domineering, much, much more domineering. He was a lot older than my mother. He was 20 years older than my mother. He's what you would call the man of the house. Mommy would try to negotiate for us. She would try to be the peacemaker. But whatever Daddy said goes. He never hit my mother, he never showed any violence toward my mother, but we used to get beatings from him. Growing up, as a teenager I didn't really like him. I moved out when I was 18. After I moved out we became friends. But I felt that I had lost time with him. It was like he didn't know how to ever say he was sorry, or he would say things to really hurt our feelings and I guess just expect us to just take it.

My father passed away about 7 years ago. He had a major stroke. My mother's still alive. Me and my mother are still the best of friends. She lives in another state. I'm here all on my own. My siblings are in another state. I was also raised in another state, and where I was raised also was, like everybody knew everybody. You could sleep on your porch. If there was a fire that happened in someone's house, everyone got together and helped build the house, or helped find shelter and clothes.

Now, see, the funny thing about it, me growing up, I never even heard about welfare. I never even knew what a food stamp was. Until I was about 18, 19, I never even saw one, you know, so to me, my perception of being on welfare was you had to be extremely poor. That was my whole perception of someone being on welfare. I guess because I saw how everyone helped out everyone. I had two working parents. I thought everyone was like that.

So when I had to go on welfare, once I left my husband, and I left my job, and I went into the domestic violence shelter and they told me that I had to, you know, go to DSS, I didn't even know what DSS was. I said, "So what is DSS, what kind of building is it in?" I thought it was a medical facility. I was embarrassed to tell them, I was too embarrassed to tell them I had no clue what DSS is. When they told me it was the Department of Social Service, I said, "Okay, why am I going there?" And when they said, "You have to get on welfare," I was horrified. I was mummified. I was speechless. I said to myself, "Oh, my God, I hit rock bottom." That's how I felt. I was so humiliated when I walked in there. I was 5 1/2 months pregnant when I left; my daughter was 3. I remember walking into this building with an advocate and having to stand on line and I purposely wanted to cover my belly. I was glad I was small because I was so embarrassed. My perception of people being on welfare, I thought that they were just, you know, young girls getting pregnant, not wanting to work, taking advantage of the system, literally living off the system. Just having welfare babies as, you know, they would call it.

And I didn't want to be classified as one, so I purposely wore a big sweatshirt to cover my belly and I remember the advocate telling me, "Wow, you don't even look like you're pregnant." I was so happy. I was so happy because I didn't want anyone to think, "Oh, this girl, she's lazy, she doesn't work, all she does is lay on her back and get pregnant and have these babies," and, you know, she's just taking advantage. I thought they were going to think of me the way I thought of people. And so in a way I guess you could say I had like a prejudice against them, and didn't even know it, and didn't even realize it. And I remember when I got to the window and I sat down and the advocate was speaking for me and then she said, "Well, I have to speak to her, she can talk, can't she?" And I felt, you know, okay. And when she said to me, "So you're 5½ months pregnant, right?" I said, "Yes", and she goes, "You have another child already?" I said, "Yes." She goes, "How old?" I said, "Three." She said, "Did you ever work in your life?" And I was so angry, because I moved out of my own house when I was 18, I had an apartment by the shore, I had my own car. I always had a job. It was only at this point in my life that I didn't work.

And so I told her, I said, "I been working ever since I was 18 years old, and had it not been for this situation, I would still be working." So, you know, I was very defiant, I was. I wanted to cry, that's how angry, that's how mad I was. You know, I wanted to say, "I'm not one of these girls that just don't care, that just don't give a damn, and I just want to have all these babies and that's it." I was humiliated. And then when she said, "You have to go and get your food stamps," I was like Oh, my God. You know, that's how I felt. I have to use food stamps? And once I got out of the shelter and I had to use my food stamps, I found a store that was open 24 hours; I wouldn't even go during the day because that's how embarrassed I was. I would strap my daughter to my chest, I would take her and we would leave about 11 o'clock, I would take a cab to the super-market, go food shopping, call a cab, and we'd go back to the house. So no one ever knew. When someone would say to me, when I was in line at the register, do I need change for food stamps, I would be so embarrassed. And I would say to them, "Did you have to do that? Did you have to say that?" I felt belittled. And it was like something that I had to get over because I kept saying, "You know, you're your worst enemy. You are your worst enemy. You're not on this thing because you chose to be on this thing; you were in a sit-uation and now you're trying to get yourself together, and Social Services are here to guide you, they're here to help you, they're here to assist you, and that's it."

You know you're not going to stay on this thing forever. Take it as assistance, because that's what it is. It's assisting the public who needs it. And I have to really drill this thing in my head and I pur-posely went out one day, during the day, to go food shopping, to like break this bondage of embarrassment. And I did it. And it was funny because after talking with some of the women in the church and telling them about how I felt, someone would say to me, "You felt like that too? I feel like that, too. I feel like that now." You know what I would say? "You know what, don't feel like it, because it's here to assist you." And now, now I thank God that I had it, because if I didn't, I wouldn't have been able to eat, I mean my children would have starved. It took almost a year for me to actually accept having to be on welfare, me having to use my food stamps, me actually going out and going shopping. It took about 10 months of me accepting where I was and not just accepting, but being able to adapt to where I was and be happy with myself, and be happy in my environment, and be happy, even in my situation.

He [her ex-husband] was a law enforcer. He was a cop. And my mother felt, he's a police officer, it was close to the military, so they felt this was ideal for me. He could take care of me, living in the city. He was someone who could protect me, take care of me, cater to me, all the above, you know, now the little girl's protected.

I told her I wanted to finish college. I wanted to get into the Air Force, and my mother kept saying, "No, he's a good man, you're going to let this good man go, and you know, take some time off, and have a baby, you don't want to wait until you're 30 years old to have a baby because then you're too old to do stuff." But that's how it is with the Asian population. Family is first, and then everything is secondary. And the first time he hit me, he slapped me, it wasn't until after we got married. We dated for 3 years; he never lifted a finger, never showed a streak of violence. I knew he was violent, but it went with the job, you know, he was a law enforcer so he had to be macho, he had to be domineering, he had to take control.

I remember the first time he slapped me, I was so embarrassed to tell anybody. I was shocked, I couldn't believe he did it because this man was so in love with me, you know, this was the man that I knew that was so in love with me, that would kill for me, you know, how could he slap me? But then maybe it was something I did, you know, maybe it was something that I really deserved because he's so good to me. But then, the way he started to talk to me was more or less like belittling me. "Well, you don't do anything anyway, you stay in this house, this house should be cleaned all the time, 'cause you don't, it's not like you have a job, it's not like you do anything." And then I started saying to myself, "You know what, before I knew you, I had a job. I always worked. If I could go back to work tomorrow I would do it."

I was an EMS [emergency medical service technician]. And, so that's what I did, I went back, after getting that type of talk, I went back to work. And he was so shocked that I went back to work, you know, and then for him being on the police force and me being in EMS, sometimes I would meet up with some of his coworkers. He became very jealous. If my coworker called me on a day off, you know, to ask me, "Are you going in on Monday?" or to make sure, he'd be like, "Why's he calling you?" And I would say, "'Cause he picks me up, you know; it's not like I pick him up, you always have the car." And the car that we were driving, mind you, my husband had bought for my birthday. But now I didn't even have control of the car that he bought for my birthday. And I saw all this happening, but it was like, I don't know what I was waiting for. I saw him becoming more controlling of my life. It happened gradually.

He had been hitting me, but I hid it. I learned to wear a mask. I learned to smile through it. He ended up coming one evening to my job. I was walking out, I was leaving and he came there and he grabbed me around my neck. And he was shaking me, and two cop cars had went by, but they knew him, so once he said, "Oh, this is my wife," they were like, "Oh, okay," and they kept going. He said, "I have a gun in the car, and if you don't get into the car right now, you're going to make me hurt you." He kept yelling at me when I got home about changing my schedule, and he's going to come up there every day until I change my schedule, so I just quit, I just quit altogether. I was so embarrassed. And I called my mother, and I told her, I need to get away from him. I said, "I want to come back home," and, you know, my mother, she's like, "That's your husband, you don't leave your husband, he's just trying to look out for your benefit." I fell into a bad depression. My hair started falling out 'cause I was very stressed out, and he figured having another baby would bring me back to life. And I didn't know how to get out. Then I was scared to death to get out, 'cause he told me, he said, "If you ever leave me, I'll kill you." And I kept saying, "Is this what love really is?" You know, how could true love threaten you to stay? I spoke with a pastor and he was like, "You try to work through this. Just keep praying and, you know, but that's your husband, that's your bed, you lie in it." You know, so I got pregnant and I kept waiting for something to happen.

I kept saying no, I'm not in a domestic violence relationship. Women like that get beat on all the time. But because it was sporadic, 2 or 3 months would go by, then something would happen. Then, like 4 months would go by, something would happen. And my perception of being in a domestic violence relationship was every week something would happen. And, but it was just my whole terrible awakening of, yes, it doesn't matter if it's months, it doesn't matter if it's even 6 months, once he lays his hands on you, once he belittles you by his words, and once he makes you feel like you're lower than dirt, he spit in my face, he stepped on me, he kicked me, you know, once, once those things happen, that is domestic, from the first time he slapped me, you know, but I wasn't knowledgeable about it, I was ignorant to the fact about domestic violence.

Five months I was in the shelter. You're only supposed to be there for 3, but I had my baby in the shelter. And she was the first baby born in the shelter, and even some of the staff in the shelter felt maybe I might call him once I went into the hospital because just that whole thing of a baby's here. One of the rudest awakenings was laying in that hospital while having my contractions and when they said to me, "We need a signature of you and your husband so we can give you an epidural," and I said, "Well, my husband's nowhere around," and they said, "Okay, well, give us his number and we'll call him." And I said, "You can't; I'm in a domestic violence shelter." And they called one of the house managers. She was taking classes with me, and she went and she met me there, and as I was pushing out, she cut the cord, and I said to myself, "Look at this stranger caring for me." And my biggest thing was having a baby on my own. I thought that was going to be the hardest thing in life for me to ever do. And once I did that, it was like, I think I'm going to make it.

After the 5 months they helped me to get housing. I came out, I moved into a new town, a new county, I knew absolutely nobody. I literally had to start from scratch. DSS helped me with money to buy furniture, and this is where I started to really appreciate the Department of Social Service, because if it had not been for them, I would have been in another rut, you know, of finances, because I didn't work. I was a new mother in a new town, didn't know anybody, I didn't know anything. I was leery of my neighbors. I was so sheltered, you know, for those 5 months I never went outside a house, so to try to get my daughter to interact outside of the house setting, I would walk her to McDonalds, I would walk her into the supermarket, 'cause we didn't do this for 5 months, well, actually 6 months. I never walked into a supermarket. Everything became so foreign. It seemed like a short period of time, but in that short period of time it was like, the milk is all the way over there. And I would spend hours in the supermarket just walking up and down the aisles. It was almost like I was an alien and I came to the planet Earth, and I was familiar with some things, but I had to refamiliarize myself with everything, with shopping, with buying clothes.

With the transitional housing, the victims' agency paid a portion, and Social Service paid the other portion. Once I started working I took over and paid the portion Social Services paid. The agency paid the majority of it until I could work myself up high enough to pay my own rent. So they assisted me for about a year and a half after me leaving the shelter, and they provided everything from counseling to housing.

I went back to work once the baby was about 10 months and I felt comfortable enough putting her in a day care, once I found a day care center that I was happy with. Social Service paid for day care. That's the only thing they pay for now is a portion of day care. I pay the other portion.

I went right back into what I left. I went back into EMS, but now I work for a hospital out here. And the environment is so much better. It's so much better. I was going to go into something different but then I said I was happy where I was, I liked what I was doing, and I want to go further now, I want to go into school for nursing, I want to go for my RN, I want to pick up where I left off and I'm not too old to do it, and I feel so good about myself, and actually I feel better about myself now than I did back then.

## WHAT OUR CLIENTS TEACH US

The stories of Vivian, Bette, and Gayle teach us about the challenges and triumphs in recipients' lives. Each woman's story is unique, but there are common threads that connect these women not only to each other but to the documented experiences of others in need in this society. The fact that each is a woman of color is not surprising; TANF recipients are primarily women, and minorities are overrepresented in the recipient population, particularly in urban or urban proximate regions (American Friends Service Committee, 2001). The proportion of adult recipients who are Hispanic or non-Hispanic black rose from 1994 to 2001 (53.6 % to 62.6%). In 2001, eight states had more than 80% non-white recipients (Georgia, Hawaii, Illinois, Louisiana, Maryland, New Jersey, New York, and Wisconsin). However, in 25 states, whites were the majority of families enrolled in TANF maintenance-of-effort (MOE) job-related activities (U.S. House of Representatives, Committee on Ways and Means, 2004). Historical and contemporary factors related to race and racism in American society, we propose, are discernable in these data.

1. *Significant obstacles to obtaining and retaining employment are not uncommon among public assistance recipients.* Indeed these barriers are often the reason assistance is required (Haveman, 1996; Olson & Pavetti, 1997). Each of our narrators reports a problem-in-living that has affected her economic independence. Gayle was employed as an emergency medical technician before emotional and physical spousal abuse forced her first to leave work and later to flee to a shelter for abused women. The relationship between domestic violence and economic vulnerability has been well documented (Brandwein, 1998), with studies revealing that more than half of welfare recipients had experienced episodes of abuse at the hands of a male significant other (Lyon, 1998).

Bette overcame substance abuse. She vividly describes how drugs and alcohol contributed to an erratic job history and total dependence on a spouse who (for reasons not made clear) refused to support her and their son. Both substance abuse and absence of financial support from a child's father are related to a woman's dependence on public assistance for survival. From 16 percent to 33 percent of TANF recipients are estimated to be affected by substance abuse problems (Kramer, 1998). The prevalence and serious economic consequences of resistance to paying child support are acknowledged in TANF's detailed provisions regarding this issue. TANF eligibility is in part predicated on establishing paternity so that the TANF provider can recover child support payments.

Vivian is a survivor of both drug addiction and child abuse. In addition, she has been diagnosed with learning disabilities. All three factors seem to have contributed to her dependence on public assistance. For Vivian, her inability to obtain her GED and her difficulties as a student were and remain a primary theme of life struggle. She is not alone. Research suggests that learning disabilities (minimal brain dysfunction) impact one-third of recipients (National Institute for Literacy, 1998, p. 202). And, like Vivian, 55 percent of women who receive welfare have not graduated from high school (Brown & Ganzglass, 1998).

The "work first" ethos of welfare reform has thrust an additional barrier to lifelong independence for these recipients. Under AFDC, those with low basic skills were encouraged to attend adult basic education and to obtain their GEDs. With a few exceptions, TANF regulations emphasize employment before or instead of skill training or degree-oriented education. For those with learning disabilities, such an ethos means placement in low-skill, low-paying, no benefit, insecure jobs and a high likelihood of redependency (Olson & Pavetti, 1997).

2. *Children provide sustenance, hope, and motivation for self-improvement.* Each of these women is a mother, and each has faced the daily pressures of childrearing, employment, and demands related to their economic dislocation. As with generations of recipients preceding them, it is their children who inspire these women to persist despite the stress and to take whatever steps are necessary to care for their children (Butler & Nevin, 1997).

Gayle leaves her abusive husband because of the potential harm to her children: "You leave . . . especially if there's a child involved," she says. Bette's move to sobriety and her decision to depend on public assistance are motivated by concerns about her son. She tells us she "did what I had to do . . . basically not so much for me but for my son." And Vivian, mother of six, struggles every day to provide for them. Her description of her day—one that begins at dawn when she dresses, feeds, and brings them to day care and school and ends late in the evening with showers and homework—reflects her heroic efforts on their behalf.

She says with determination, "I know I'm going to be struggling on how I'm going to take care of my kids, but I'm focusing more on my GED so I can go to college, so I can get a better job to take care of my kids. That's my goal."

3. *These stories challenge the stereotypic image of the lazy welfare recipient.* These women's hopes for themselves also bring into question the perspective implicit in TANF provisions—that welfare recipients must be pushed out of dependency through time limits, sanctions, and other punitive regulations. Each narrator positively views the world of work and sees a place for herself in it; Gayle is determined to build her medical career. "I want to go further now. . . . I want to go for my RN." Bette's life is defined by her position

in a faith-based community service center; her work there is the fulfillment of her ambitions. And Vivian's dreams center on completing her high school education and obtaining meaningful work. "I want my GED," she asserts with passion, "I want to go to college, I want a good job. . . . I dream of being a radiologist technician. Once I learn my education, it's something nobody's going to ever take away from me."

4. *External supports are crucial to these individuals' success.* Each recipient reports on the absence or toxic quality of familial supports. Each cites the availability of assistance from external resources as a—if not the—critical variable in her life's narrative. For Gayle, the availability of domestic violence services may have literally saved her life—a call to a hotline provided her with a safe residence, a range of psychosocial services (including a birth coach), and rent supplementation after she left the shelter. Gayle now volunteers as a spokesperson for the agency. Vivian speaks passionately about the director of a community agency whose help she sought for food and other supplies for her family: "I would express my needs to her and she would always try to find me a job and try to do this and try to do that. . . . Hers was more like cradling." The narrator's use of the word *cradling* is revealing. For this survivor of child abuse, the nurturance from this single social service provider became a powerful corrective experience, one that empowered her to move her life forward: "I have contemplated suicide . . . until I met Dr. Clark—today I'm a different person." For Bette, it was a spiritual connection ("God in my life") and employment in a faith-based organization that "saved" her and gave her life meaning. "When I look back over my life and the many times that He has literally saved me to be here for a purpose, I don't know yet, but whatever it is, maybe it's what I'm doing."

These organizations—a domestic violence agency, a community service center, a church—provided an empowering combination of emotional and concrete supports. Protection, shelter, food, job opportunities, rent, even soap powder and tissue given within a context of respect and caring, made a difference. Research confirms that institutions in the environment can be a key variable in the success of recipients' welfare-to-work journeys (DeBord, Canu, & Kerpelman, 2000; Weaver & Hasenfeld, 1997; Wijnberg & Weinger, 1998).

5. *Attitudes vary about the need to receive public assistance.* Our narrators' experiences with public assistance reflect different aspects of life on welfare. For Gayle, the major theme related to her own sense of shame and humiliation at being a recipient. Gayle brought to this situation her own middle-class preconceptions regarding "welfare": "When they said, 'You have to get on welfare,' I was horrified. I was mummified. I was speechless. I said to myself, 'Oh, my God, I hit rock bottom.' . . . My perception of people being on welfare . . . you know, young girls getting pregnant, not wanting to work, taking advantage of the system." Gayle's interaction with the Department of Social Services and her use of her benefits were influenced by this view. When the intake worker says, "Did you ever work in your life?" Gayle was "angry,"

"mad," "defiant." When she used food stamps, she would go at 11 o'clock in the evening "so no one ever knew." In retrospect, Gayle values the assistance, recognizing that "Social Services are here to guide you, they're here to help you." Unlike our two other clients, Gayle does not report on a negative experience with DSS workers. This may be related to the fact that, as a domestic violence survivor, she was not only accompanied by an advocate from the shelter, but also may have been viewed as "deserving" of assistance.

Vivian, a longtime recipient, is ambivalent about "that system." "It fed me," she recognizes, "it fed my children." But, she says, it "keeps you in one place and one place only." Vivian, with her longings for self-improvement, her self-esteem compromised by abuse and learning difficulties, focuses on the loss-of-control dimension of life on welfare. So she observes, "They say they want to help you but when you throw your opinions, or can you help me do it this way or that way, they go, 'No. You either do it our way or there is no way.'" Vivian also astutely notes one implication of the dependency and powerlessness built into the assistance system: "Once you follow the rules, and get a job, you receive no support, you are left entirely on your own. They don't give you time to get on your feet. . . . They just snatch the rug from out of you. . . . You have to learn the hard way how to start over and do without these services."

Bette turned to public assistance when her husband no longer financially supported her or her son. She chose, for reasons she did not share, not to leave him, but rather to present herself as a single parent to the public assistance department. Bette was a survivor of substance abuse and illness; she was, as she put it, unable to find another means of support, "had to do what I had to do. . . . I'm not proud that I had to live that lie, but it's what I had to do to survive." Her experiences on welfare are filtered through this deception. She notes, "It seemed like every time you went there their motive was always trying to catch you up to find a reason to close your case. I dreaded that." Home visits were particularly "hated" and challenging. "I just felt so degraded. . . . What I had to do is I had to take everything like his clothes and hide them." Bette, like Gayle, had prior negative perceptions about welfare recipients. Her own experience changed her preconceptions: "I realize that I was so wrong, that there were a lot of people on there who could not help being on there, and who needed the support from the government."

# PUBLIC HOUSING AND HOMELESSNESS

## CHAPTER 4

## THE LEGAL CONTEXT

### Authorizing Legislation: Public Housing

Public housing provision for low-income individuals emerges from federal law, the U.S. Housing Act and its various amendments, including most recently the Quality Housing and Work Responsibility Act of 1998, codified at 42 U.S.C. § 1437. Text of the law appears in Box 4.1.

### Authorizing Legislation: Homelessness

The Stewart B. McKinney Homeless Assistance Act (P.L. 100-77, 1987) is the first major federal legislation to deal with homelessness. In 2000, the act was renamed the McKinney-Vento Homeless Assistance Act. The McKinney Act, according to Foscarinis (1996), "marked the federal government's recognition that homelessness is a national problem requiring a federal response." Codified at 42 U.S.C. § 11301, *et seq.,* the legislation announces several key congressional findings and purpose and is presented in Box 4.2.

The scope and intention of the legislation is unambiguous: America faced an "unprecedented" housing crisis, effecting families and individuals, that precipitated an increase in homelessness. Finding no single cause of the problem, Congress nonetheless committed funding to states, localities, and nonprofit organizations to meet the "basic

|  | QUALITY HOUSING AND WORK |
|---|---|
| **4.1** | RESPONSIBILITY ACT |

§ 1437. Declaration of policy and public housing agency organization

(a) Declaration of policy. It is the policy of the United States—
    (1) to promote the general welfare of the Nation by employing the funds and credit of the Nation, as provided in this Act—
        (A) to assist States and political subdivisions of States to remedy the unsafe housing conditions and the acute shortage of decent and safe dwellings for low-income families;
        (B) to assist States and political subdivisions of States to address the shortage of housing affordable to low-income families; and
        (C) consistent with the objectives of this title, to vest in public housing agencies that perform well, the maximum amount of responsibility and flexibility in program administration, with appropriate accountability to public housing residents, localities, and the general public;
    (2) that the Federal Government cannot through its direct action alone provide for the housing of every American citizen, or even a majority of its citizens, but it is the responsibility of the Government to promote and protect the independent and collective actions of private citizens to develop housing and strengthen their own neighborhoods;
    (3) that the Federal Government should act where there is a serious need that private citizens or groups cannot or are not addressing responsibly; and
    (4) that our Nation should promote the goal of providing decent and affordable housing for all citizens through the efforts and encouragement of Federal, State, and local governments, and by the independent and collective actions of private citizens, organizations, and the private sector.

(b) Public housing agency organization.
    (1) Required membership. Except as provided in paragraph (2), the membership of the board of directors or similar governing body of each public housing agency shall contain not less than 1 member—

---

human needs and to engender respect for the human dignity of the homeless." The legislation details its intended target groups in 42 U.S.C. § 11302, as presented in Box 4.3.

The McKinney Act contains several titles, addressing not only the aforementioned general provisions (Title I) but the establishment of the Interagency Council on the Homeless (Title II), the Federal Emergency Management Agency (FEMA), Emergency Food and Shelter Program (Title III), housing assistance for emergency and transitional housing (Title IV), the identification and use of surplus federal property (Title V), health care for homeless persons (Title VI), education, training, and community services programs (Title VII), food assistance (Title VIII), and provisions for veterans (Title IX). Moreover, the act has been amended several times since its inception, notably in 1988, 1992, and 1994.

(A) who is directly assisted by the public housing agency; and

(B) who may, if provided for in the public housing agency plan, be elected by the residents directly assisted by the public housing agency.

(2) Exception. Paragraph (1) shall not apply to any public housing agency—

(A) that is located in a State that requires the members of the board of directors or similar governing body of a public housing agency to be salaried and to serve on a full-time basis; or

(B) with less than 300 public housing units, if—

(i) the agency has provided reasonable notice to the resident advisory board of the opportunity of not less than 1 resident described in paragraph (1) to serve on the board of directors or similar governing body of the public housing agency pursuant to such paragraph; and

(ii) within a reasonable time after receipt by the resident advisory board established by the agency pursuant to section 5A(e) [42 U.S.C.S. § 1437c-1(e)] of notice under clause (i), the public housing agency has not been notified of the intention of any resident to participate on the board of directors.

(3) Nondiscrimination. No person shall be prohibited from serving on the board of directors or similar governing body of a public housing agency because of the residence of that person in a public housing project or status as assisted under section 8 [42 U.S.C.S. § 1437f].

**HISTORY:**
(Sept. 1, 1937, ch 896, [Title I], § 2, as added Aug. 22, 1974, P.L. 93-383, Title II, § 201(a), 88 Stat. 653; Aug. 13, 1981, P.L. 97-35, Title III, Subtitle A, Part 2, § 322(c), 95 Stat. 402; June 29, 1988, P.L. 100-358, § 5, 102 Stat. 681; Nov. 28, 1990, P.L. 101-625, Title V, Subtitle C, § 572(2), 104 Stat. 4236; Oct. 21, 1998, P.L. 105-276, Title V, Subtitle A, § 505, 112 Stat. 2522.)

## Regulatory Authority: Public Housing

An example of relevant regulations pertaining to public housing appears in Box 4.4. The illustration is excerpted from the *Federal Register*, which is the initial source for publication of federal agency regulations. The final rule can be found in the *Code of Federal Regulations*, at 24 C.F.R. Parts 5, 960, 966, and 984.

## Regulatory Authority: Homelessness

The controlling regulations for the McKinney-Vento Homeless Assistance Act, as with other federal regulations, are contained in the *Code of Federal Regulations*. The relevant titles are scattered throughout the C.F.R., given the breadth of affected program elements. The regulation, presented in Box 4.5, illustrates one of a multitude of topics pertaining to homelessness.

| 4.2 | FINDINGS AND OURPOSE OF MCKINNEY-VENTO HOMELESS ASSISTANCE ACT |

(a)  Findings. The Congress finds that—

    (1)  the Nation faces an immediate and unprecedented crisis due to the lack of shelter for a growing number of individuals and families, including elderly persons, handicapped persons, families with children, Native Americans, and veterans;

    (2)  the problem of homelessness has become more severe and, in the absence of more effective efforts, is expected to become dramatically worse, endangering the lives and safety of the homeless;

    (3)  the causes of homelessness are many and complex, and homeless individuals have diverse needs;

    (4)  there is no single, simple solution to the problem of homelessness because of the different subpopulations of the homeless, the different causes of and reasons for homelessness, and the different needs of homeless individuals;

    (5)  due to the record increase in homelessness, States, units of local government, and private voluntary organizations have been unable to meet the basic human needs of all the homeless and, in the absence of greater Federal assistance, will be unable to protect the lives and safety of all the homeless in need of assistance; and

    (6)  the Federal Government has a clear responsibility and an existing capacity to fulfill a more effective and responsible role to meet the basic human needs and to engender respect for the human dignity of the homeless.

(b)  Purpose. It is the purpose of this Act—

    (1)  to establish an Interagency Council on the Homeless;

    (2)  to use public resources and programs in a more coordinated manner to meet the critically urgent needs of the homeless of the Nation; and

    (3)  to provide funds for programs to assist the homeless, with special emphasis on elderly persons, handicapped persons, families with children, Native Americans, and veterans.

## Case Law

The case law relevant to public housing is extensive, and no effort is made here to provide an exhaustive review. One judicial decision illustrates the types of issues that the court currently confronts regarding public housing residents: *Department of Housing and Urban Development v. Rucker* (2002), which considers the issue of lease termination where a public housing tenant is involved in drug-related activity.

The case law in which the McKinney Act was construed addresses an array of issues. The case presented in Box 4.7 is a selective examination of important aspects of the McKinney Act (as it was referenced at the time of this judicial decision) and, specifically, homelessness.

4·3    MCKINNEY-VENTO HOMELESS
ASSISTANCE ACT DEFINITION
OF HOMELESSNESS

§ 11302. General definition of homeless individual

(a) In general. For purposes of this Act, the term "homeless" or "homeless individual or homeless person" includes—

    (1) an individual who lacks a fixed, regular, and adequate nighttime residence; and

    (2) an individual who has a primary nighttime residence that is—

        (A) a supervised publicly or privately operated shelter designed to provide temporary living accommodations (including welfare hotels, congregate shelters, and transitional housing for the mentally ill);

        (B) an institution that provides a temporary residence for individuals intended to be institutionalized; or

        (C) a public or private place not designed for, or ordinarily used as, a regular sleeping accommodation for human beings.

(b) Income eligibility.

    (1) In general. A homeless individual shall be eligible for assistance under any program provided by this Act, only if the individual complies with the income eligibility requirements otherwise applicable to such program.

    (2) Exception. Notwithstanding paragraph (1), a homeless individual shall be eligible for assistance under Title I of the Workforce Investment Act of 1998.

(c) Exclusion. For purposes of this Act, the term "homeless" or "homeless individual" does not include any individual imprisoned or otherwise detained pursuant to an Act of the Congress or a State law.

## THE PROGRAM CONTEXT

### Overview

Our need for and right to a private, secure living space is commonly acknowledged. Yet for all too many Americans housing is inadequate, unsafe, or unavailable. An accurate count of the homeless is elusive, not only because it is a difficult population to locate, but also because of a lack of consensus on what defines a person as homeless—are families temporarily residing with relatives in tight quarters homeless? What about individuals who take turns sleeping in one room (First, Rife, & Toomey, 1995)?

At the turn of the 21st century it was estimated that a third of the nation's population lived in unaffordable, inadequate, or nonexistent housing (National Law Income Housing Coalition, 2005), and that approximately 800,000 people on any given night were homeless (Burt, 2001). Families with children are becoming a notably increasing proportion of those who, as

| | EXAMPLE OF A PUBLIC |
|---|---|
| **4·4** | HOUSING REGULATION |

Changes to Admission and Occupancy Requirements
in the Public Housing and Section 8 Housing Assistance Programs
Part III
64 FR 23460

DATE: Friday, April 30, 1999
ACTION: Proposed rule.
SUMMARY: This proposed rule addresses several changes related to admission and occupancy requirements of public housing and Section 8 assisted housing that were made by the Quality Housing and Work Responsibility Act of 1998 (referred to as the "1998 Act"). With respect to admission and occupancy, this rule includes important changes concerning choice of rent, community service and self-sufficiency in public housing. This rule also includes important changes concerning admission preferences and determination of income and rent in public housing and Section 8 housing assistance programs. Some of the provisions included in this rule are already in effect, as more fully discussed in HUD's Notice of Initial Guidance on the 1998 Act, published on February 18, 1999 ("Initial Guidance Notice"), and HUD's interim rule on the PHA Plan, also published on February 18, 1999 (PHA Plan interim rule). The provisions that are already in effect are identified in this rulemaking.

---

defined by the McKinney-Vento Homeless Assistance Act, "lack a fixed, regular, and adequate night-time residence" (42 U.S.C. § 11302(a)). The latest in a series of annual studies of urban homelessness found that, at 40 percent, families with children were the fastest growing sector of those without housing (U.S. Conference of Mayors, 2004). Homeless rates have been found to be as high or higher among families with children residing outside cities (Vissing, 1996). Resources to meet the needs of families and individuals who are homeless are insufficient. Eighty-one percent of 27 cities studied reported turning away homeless persons because of lack of sufficient emergency housing (U.S. Conference of Mayors, 2004). The increasing rates of those without housing (Johnson, 1995) and the related paucity of housing for Americans with no or low earnings are a result of multiple factors, including a shortage of affordable rental units, economic slowdowns, unrealistic public assistance rental allowances, discrimination, and unscrupulous landlords.

Moreover, the United States has never established a comprehensive approach to meeting housing needs, and existing programs are not entitlement based—that is, they are not mandated to provide shelter for all who meet eligibility criteria. Funding is limited to budget allocations, and waiting lists are common.

The federal government's involvement in housing was originally part of the response to the Great Depression. Prior to the 1930s, there were only scat-

| 4·5 | EXAMPLE OF A REGULATION<br>ON HOMELESSNESS |
|---|---|

### TITLE 24—HOUSING AND URBAN DEVELOPMENT
### SUBTITLE B—REGULATIONS RELATING TO HOUSING
### AND URBAN DEVELOPMENT
### CHAPTER V—OFFICE OF ASSISTANT SECRETARY
### FOR COMMUNITY PLANNING AND
### DEVELOPMENT, DEPARTMENT OF HOUSING
### AND URBAN DEVELOPMENT
### SUBCHAPTER C—COMMUNITY FACILITIES
### PART 582—SHELTER PLUS CARE
### SUBPART A—GENERAL
### 24 CFR 582.1

§ 582.1 Purpose and scope.

(a) General. The Shelter Plus Care program (S+C) is authorized by title IV, subtitle F, of the Stewart B. McKinney Homeless Assistance Act (the McKinney Act) (42 U.S.C. § 11403-11407b). S+C is designed to link rental assistance to supportive services for hard-to-serve homeless persons with disabilities (primarily those who are seriously mentally ill; have chronic problems with alcohol, drugs, or both; or have acquired immunodeficiency syndrome (AIDS and related diseases) and their families. The program provides grants to be used for rental assistance for permanent housing for homeless persons with disabilities. Rental assistance grants must be matched in the aggregate by supportive services that are equal in value to the amount of rental assistance and appropriate to the needs of the population to be served. Recipients are chosen on a competitive basis nationwide.

(b) Components. Rental assistance is provided through four components described in § 582.100. Applicants may apply for assistance under any one of the four components, or a combination.

**HISTORY:**
[58 FR 13892, Mar. 15, 1993; 61 FR 51168, 51169, Sept. 30, 1996]
**AUTHORITY:**
AUTHORITY NOTE APPLICABLE TO ENTIRE PART:
42 U.S.C. 3535(d) and 11403-11407b.
**NOTES:**
[EFFECTIVE DATE NOTE: 61 FR 51168, 51169, Sept. 30, 1996, which revised the first sentence in paragraph (a) and paragraph (b), became effective Oct. 30, 1996.]

---

tered efforts to improve housing conditions, with social reformers focusing primarily on legislation to improve tenements. During World War I, the federal government built and managed housing for those employed in war-related activities, and in 1934 the Public Works Administration (PWA) provided jobs and housing through sponsorship of the building of some large housing com-

## 4.6   JUDICIAL DECISION REGARDING PUBLIC HOUSING TENANTS

### DEPARTMENT OF HOUSING AND URBAN DEVELOPMENT v. RUCKER
### 122 S. Ct. 1230

*Summary:* In this case, the Oakland Housing Authority (OHA) instituted eviction proceedings in state court against four public housing tenants for violation of a lease provision obligating the tenants to assure that the tenant, any member of the household, a guest, or another person under the tenant's control, would not engage in any drug-related criminal activity on or near the premises. The lease provision tracked the language of a federal statute (42 USCS 1437d(l)(6)) requiring each public housing agency to utilize leases which provided that any criminal activity that threatens the health, safety, or right to peaceful enjoyment of the premises by other tenants or any drug-related criminal activity on or off such premises, engaged in by a public housing tenant, any member of the tenant's household, or any guest or other person under the tenant's control, shall be cause for termination of tenancy. As interpreted by the United States Department of Housing and Urban Development (HUD), the lease provision afforded local public housing authorities the discretion to evict for drug-related activity where the tenant did not know, could not foresee, or could not control behavior by other occupants of the unit.*

*The United States Supreme Court agreed to hear the case and concluded that the legislation in question could require lease terms that gave local public housing authorities the discretion to evict a tenant when a member of the household or a guest engaged in drug-related criminal activity, regardless of whether the tenant knew, or should have known, of the drug-related activity, because (1) the statute was unambiguous, (2) it was reasonable for Congress, having found that illegal drugs led to violence against tenants as well as deterioration of the physical environment, to permit no-fault evictions in order to provide public housing that was decent, safe, and free from illegal drugs, and (3) there were no serious constitutional doubts about Congress' affording local public housing authorities the discretion to conduct no-fault evictions for drug-related crime.*

CHIEF JUSTICE REHNQUIST delivered the opinion of the Court. With drug dealers "increasingly imposing a reign of terror on public and other federally assisted low-income housing tenants," Congress passed the Anti-Drug Abuse Act of 1988. The Act, as later amended, provides that each "public housing agency shall utilize leases which . . . provide that any criminal activity that threatens the health, safety, or right to peaceful enjoyment of the premises by other tenants or any drug-related criminal activity on or off such premises, engaged in by a public housing tenant, any member of the tenant's household, or any guest or other person under the tenant's control, shall be cause for termination of tenancy." Petitioners say that this statute requires lease terms that allow a local public housing authority to evict a tenant when a member of the tenant's household or a guest engages in drug-related criminal activity, regardless of whether the tenant knew, or had reason to know, of that activity. Respondents say it does not. We agree with petitioners.

Respondents are four public housing tenants of the Oakland Housing Authority (OHA). Paragraph 9(m) of respondents' leases, tracking the language of § 1437d(l)(6), obligates the tenants to "assure that the tenant, any member of the household, a guest, or another person under the tenant's control, shall not engage in . . . any drug-related criminal activity on or near the premises." Respondents also signed an agreement stating that the tenant "understands that if I or any member of my household or guests should violate this lease provision, my tenancy may be terminated and I may be evicted."

In late 1997 and early 1998, OHA instituted eviction proceedings in state court against respondents, alleging violations of this lease provision. The complaint alleged: (1) that the respective grandsons of respondents William Lee and Barbara Hill, both of whom were listed as residents on the leases, were caught in the apartment complex parking lot smoking marijuana; (2) that the daughter of respondent Pearlie Rucker, who resides with her and is listed on the lease as a resident, was found with cocaine and a crack cocaine pipe three blocks from Rucker's apartment; and (3) that on three instances within a 2-month period, respondent Herman Walker's caregiver and two others were found with cocaine in Walker's apartment. OHA had issued Walker notices of a lease violation on the first two occasions, before initiating the eviction action after the third violation.

United States Department of Housing and Urban Development (HUD) regulations administering § 1437d(l)(6) require lease terms authorizing evictions in these circumstances. The HUD regulations closely track the statutory language, and provide that "in deciding to evict for criminal activity, the [public housing authority] shall have discretion to consider all of the circumstances of the case. . . ." The agency made clear that local public housing authorities' discretion to evict for drug-related activity includes those situations in which "[the] tenant did not know, could not foresee, or could not control behavior by other occupants of the unit."

After OHA initiated the eviction proceedings in state court, respondents commenced actions against HUD, OHA, and OHA's director in United States District Court. They challenged HUD's interpretation of the statute under the Administrative Procedure Act, arguing that 42 U.S.C. § 1437d(l)(6) does not require lease terms authorizing the eviction of so-called "innocent" tenants, and, in the alternative, that if it does, then the statute is unconstitutional. The District Court issued a preliminary injunction, enjoining OHA from "terminating the leases of tenants pursuant to paragraph 9(m) of the 'Tenant Lease' for drug-related criminal activity that does not occur within the tenant's apartment unit when the tenant did not know of and had no reason to know of, the drug-related criminal activity."

A panel of the Court of Appeals reversed, holding that § 1437d(l)(6) unambiguously permits the eviction of tenants who violate the lease provision, regardless of whether the tenant was personally aware of the drug activity, and that the statute is constitutional. An en banc panel of the Court of Appeals reversed and affirmed the District Court's grant of the preliminary injunction. That court held that HUD's interpretation permitting the eviction of so-called "innocent" tenants "is inconsistent with Congressional intent and must be rejected. . . ."

We granted certiorari . . . and now reverse, holding that 42 U.S.C. § 1437d(l)(6) unambiguously requires lease terms that vest local public housing authorities with the discretion to evict tenants for the drug-related activity of household members and guests whether or not the tenant knew, or should have known, about the activity.

*continued*

| 4.6 | JUDICIAL DECISION REGARDING PUBLIC HOUSING TENANTS (CONTINUED) |

That this is so seems evident from the plain language of the statute. It provides that "each public housing authority shall utilize leases which . . . provide that any drug-related criminal activity on or off such premises, engaged in by a public housing tenant, any member of the tenant's household, or any guest or other person under the tenant's control, shall be cause for termination of tenancy." The en banc Court of Appeals thought the statute did not address "the level of personal knowledge or fault that is required for eviction.". . . Yet Congress' decision not to impose any qualification in the statute, combined with its use of the term "any" to modify "drug-related criminal activity," precludes any knowledge requirement. As we have explained, "the word 'any' has an expansive meaning, that is, 'one or some indiscriminately of whatever kind.'" Thus, any drug-related activity engaged in by the specified persons is grounds for termination, not just drug-related activity that the tenant knew, or should have known, about. * * *

Comparing § 1437d(l)(6) to a related statutory provision reinforces the unambiguous text. The civil forfeiture statute that makes all leasehold interests subject to forfeiture when used to commit drug-related criminal activities expressly exempts tenants who had no knowledge of the activity: "No property shall be forfeited under this paragraph . . . by reason of any act or omission established by that owner to have been committed or omitted without the knowledge or consent of the owner." Because this forfeiture provision was amended in the same Anti-Drug Abuse Act of 1988 that created 42 U.S.C. § 1437d(l)(6), the en banc Court of Appeals thought Congress "meant them to be read consistently" so that the knowledge requirement should be read into the eviction provision. But the two sections deal with distinctly different matters. The "innocent owner" defense for drug forfeiture cases was already in existence prior to 1988 as part of 21 U.S.C. § 881(a)(7). All that Congress did in the 1988 Act was to add leasehold interests to the property interests that might be forfeited under the drug statute. And if such a forfeiture action were to be brought against a leasehold interest, it would be subject to the pre-existing "innocent owner" defense. But 42 U.S.C. § 1437(d)(1)(6), with which we deal here, is a quite different measure. It is entirely reasonable to think that the Government, when seeking to transfer private property to itself in a forfeiture proceeding, should be

plexes. In 1937, the federal government's role in providing affordable housing was authorized through the passage of the U.S. Housing Act. This act covered the construction, management, and ownership of low-rent, low-cost housing for families, seniors, and people with disabilities. The act is still operative, although with modifications. The latest modification occurred in 1998 with the passage of the Quality Housing and Work Responsibility Act, which made, as we later discuss, significant changes in subsidized housing regulations.

Federal housing programs received further recognition and support when the U.S. Department of Housing and Urban Development (HUD) was created in 1965 as a cabinet-level agency. HUD administers most federal housing aid. Its programs include homeless assistance authorized under the Stewart B. McKinney Homeless Assistance Act of 1987 (later renamed the McKinney-

subject to an "innocent owner defense," while it should not be when acting as a landlord in a public housing project. The forfeiture provision shows that Congress knew exactly how to provide an "innocent owner" defense. It did not provide one in § 1437d(l)(6). * * *

Nor was the en banc Court of Appeals correct in concluding that this plain reading of the statute leads to absurd results. The statute does not require the eviction of any tenant who violated the lease provision. Instead, it entrusts that decision to the local public housing authorities, who are in the best position to take account of, among other things, the degree to which the housing project suffers from "rampant drug-related or violent crime," "the seriousness of the offending action," and "the extent to which the leaseholder has . . . taken all reasonable steps to prevent or mitigate the offending action," ibid. It is not "absurd" that a local housing authority may sometimes evict a tenant who had no knowledge of the drug-related activity. Such "no-fault" eviction is a common "incident of tenant responsibility under normal landlord-tenant law and practice." Strict liability maximizes deterrence and eases enforcement difficulties. . . .

And, of course, there is an obvious reason why Congress would have permitted local public housing authorities to conduct no-fault evictions: Regardless of knowledge, a tenant who "cannot control drug crime, or other criminal activities by a household member which threaten health or safety of other residents, is a threat to other residents and the project." With drugs leading to "murders, muggings, and other forms of violence against tenants," and to the "deterioration of the physical environment that requires substantial governmental expenditures," it was reasonable for Congress to permit no-fault evictions in order to "provide public and other federally assisted low-income housing that is decent, safe, and free from illegal drugs." * * *

We hold that "Congress has directly spoken to the precise question at issue." Section 1437d(l)(6) requires lease terms that give local public housing authorities the discretion to terminate the lease of a tenant when a member of the household or a guest engages in drug-related activity, regardless of whether the tenant knew, or should have known, of the drug-related activity.

Accordingly, the judgment of the Court of Appeals is reversed, and the cases are remanded for further proceedings consistent with this opinion. It is so ordered.

JUSTICE BREYER took no part in the consideration or decision of these cases.

---

Vento Homeless Assistance Act); home ownership support and loans, including those authorized by the 1990 Cranston-Gonzalez National Affordable Housing Act; and construction and rehabilitation initiatives.

In this chapter we focus on those HUD programs designed to make rental housing affordable for the economically dislocated. We have selected this emphasis because these programs are most relevant to persons who qualify for the other programs described in this book. We also have chosen to emphasize subsidized rental housing because it has been found to be the major variable in the elimination of homelessness (Bernstein, 2002).

Direct rental assistance is obtained through one of two methods. The first is acquisition of an apartment in a public housing complex specifically built for low-income families, seniors, and/or the disabled. As of the year 2000,

<table>
<tr><td>4·7</td><td>JUDICIAL DECISION INTERPRETING<br>THE MCKINNEY ACT</td></tr>
</table>

## LAMPKIN v. DISTRICT OF COLUMBIA, 27 F.3D 605 (1994)

*Summary: In this case, parents of homeless children residing in the District of Columbia sought to enforce provisions of the Stewart B. McKinney Homeless Assistance Act, which they argued conferred enforceable educational rights on homeless children. That is, they argued that their children were entitled to education under the Act. This District Court decision indicates that the court agreed with the parents and concluded that the McKinney Act does indeed ensure that children cannot be denied mainstream education simply because they are homeless and that states must assure that homeless children have access to a free, appropriate public education.*

### I. INTRODUCTION

The McKinney Act, was passed in 1987 in response to "the critically urgent needs of the homeless," including the proper education of their children. The Act is a mix of large visions and gritty detail, combining specific sections dealing with the provision of education to homeless children and youths with a broad congressional policy that "each State educational agency . . . assure that each child of a homeless individual and each homeless youth have access to a free, appropriate public education . . . [and that] homelessness alone . . . not be sufficient reason to separate students from the mainstream school environment."

To achieve this goal, the Secretary of Education is empowered to grant funds to States participating in the programs authorized by the McKinney Act. Grants may be used, among other purposes, to "establish or designate an Office of Coordinator of Education of Homeless Children and Youth" and to "prepare and carry out the State plan . . . [including] e.g., establishment of procedures for the resolution of disputes regarding the educational placement of homeless children and youths, assurance of their ability to participate in food programs, and undertaking to protect them from being isolated or stigmatized." [A related provision provides]:

(3)(A)  The local educational agency of each homeless child and each homeless youth shall either—
    (i)    continue the child's or youth's education in the school of origin—
        (I)    for the remainder of the academic year; or
        (II)    in any case in which a family becomes homeless between academic years, for the following academic year; or
    (ii)    enroll the child or youth in any school that nonhomeless students who live in the attendance area in which the child or youth is actually living are eligible to attend; whichever is in the child's best interest or the youth's best interest. (B) In determining the best interests of the child or youth for purposes of making a school assignment under subparagraph (A), consideration shall be given to a request made by a parent regarding school selection. . . .
(5)    Each homeless child shall be provided services comparable to services offered to other students in the school selected according to the provisions

of paragraph (3), including transportation services . . .; and school meals programs. . . .

(7)    Each local educational agency serving homeless children or youth that receives assistance under this subchapter shall coordinate with local social services agencies, and other agencies or programs providing services to such children or youth and their families.

Appellants here are homeless children living in the District of Columbia, which is deemed a State for purposes of the McKinney Act. They filed this action in the district court pursuant to 42 U.S.C. § 1983 (1988), which provides a cause of action against persons who infringe upon federal constitutional or statutory rights while acting "under color" of state law. . . . They seek an order requiring, among other things, that the District consider parents' requests and make "best interests" determinations when placing homeless children in schools; that it assure homeless children the transportation necessary to attend those schools; and that it ensure them access to various educational and school meal programs, and other services.

The district court found that the McKinney Act did not create an enforceable right of action under section 1983 and dismissed the complaint. Thus the sole question before us on appeal is whether the homeless children can enforce the relevant provisions of the McKinney Act pursuant to section 1983, a question we answer in the affirmative.

## II. DISCUSSION

Since 1980, the Supreme Court has recognized that section 1983 may be invoked to challenge violations of federal statutes. This rule has its exceptions: A statute will not be deemed enforceable under section 1983 if Congress did not intend to create any enforceable rights in it (which may be evidenced by the provision of a comprehensive remedial scheme in the statute itself) and where the statute "did not create enforceable rights, privileges, or immunities within the meaning of § 1983." These exceptions are more easily stated than applied, as will be apparent from the Supreme Court's recent decisions in *Wilder v. Virginia Hosp. Ass'n*, and *Suter v. Artist M.*.

### A. *Wilder v. Virginia Hospital Association*

In Wilder, the plaintiffs challenged the method by which the State of Virginia reimbursed health care providers under the Medicaid Act, 42 U.S.C. § 1396 et seq. (1988). In particular, the Court faced the question

whether the Boren Amendment to the Act, which requires reimbursement according to rates that a "State finds, and makes assurances satisfactory to the Secretary, are reasonable and adequate to meet the costs which must be incurred by efficiently and economically operated facilities," is enforceable in an action pursuant to § 1983.

Drawing on its decision in *Golden State Transit Corp. v. Los Angeles*, the Court established a test to determine whether a statutory provision creates a federal right enforceable under section 1983. First, the provision must have been intended to benefit the putative plaintiff. If it was so intended, the provision creates an enforceable right unless it [1] reflects merely a congressional preference for a certain kind of conduct rather than a binding obligation on the governmental unit . . . or [2] unless the

*continued*

| 4·7 | JUDICIAL DECISION INTERPRETING THE MCKINNEY ACT (CONTINUED) |

interest the plaintiff asserts is too vague and amorphous such that it is beyond the competence of the judiciary to enforce.

Once it has been determined that an enforceable right exists, the statute must be examined to determine whether "Congress has foreclosed such enforcement of the statute in the enactment itself." In applying this test to the Boren Amendment, the Court stated that there was little doubt that health care providers were its intended beneficiaries. The Court then reasoned that as the amendment was "cast in mandatory rather than precatory terms," it "imposes a binding obligation on States participating in the Medicaid program to adopt reasonable and adequate rates and . . . is enforceable under § 1983 by health care providers."

### B. Suter v. Artist M.

Two years later, the Court again addressed the availability of the section 1983 remedy. In *Suter v. Artist M.,* the Court was called upon to determine whether a provision of the Adoption Assistance and Child Welfare Act of 1980, 42 U.S.C. §§ 620-28, 670-79a (1988), could be enforced under section 1983. Under the Child Welfare Act, States seeking federal reimbursement of "a percentage of foster care and adoption assistance payments" "must submit a plan to the Secretary of Health and Human Services for approval." To be approved, a plan must meet sixteen requirements, the following among them:

> In each case, reasonable efforts will be made (A) prior to the placement of a child in foster care, to prevent or eliminate the need for removal of the child from his home, and (B) to make it possible for the child to return to his home. . . . In Suter, the plaintiffs sought to use section 1983 as the procedural vehicle to obtain substantive enforcement of this "reasonable efforts" provision. In examining the nature of the obligations created by the Child Welfare Act, the Court observed that the legitimacy of Congress' power to legislate under the spending power . . . rests on whether the State voluntarily and knowingly accepts the terms of the "contract." . . . If Congress intends to impose a condition on the grant of federal moneys, it must do so unambiguously.

Thus the critical inquiry in Suter was whether, "in light of the entire legislative enactment," the Child Welfare Act "unambiguously conferred upon [its] beneficiaries . . . a right to enforce the requirement that the State make 'reasonable efforts' to prevent a child from being removed from his home, and once removed to reunify the child with his family." * * *

### C. Private Enforcement of the McKinney Act

In applying this jurisprudence to the McKinney Act, the first question to ask is whether the statute was intended to benefit persons such as appellants' children. This point is not in dispute here: The parties all agree that the McKinney Act was enacted to benefit homeless children. That said, we must hold that the Act "creates an enforceable right unless it reflects merely a congressional preference for a certain kind of conduct rather than a binding obligation on the governmental unit." Mindful of the need "to analyze the statutory provisions in detail, in light of the entire legislative enactment, to determine whether the language in question creates enforceable rights, privileges, or immunities within the meaning of § 1983,". . . we must determine whether the Act creates rights that are substantively enforceable under section 1983.

Section 11432(f) of the McKinney Act provides:

> No State may receive a grant under this section unless the state educational agency submits an application to the Secretary at such time, in such manner, and containing or accompanied by such information as the Secretary may reasonably require.

The regulations issued by the Secretary stipulate that a State may not begin to obligate funds received pursuant to a federal grant until the later of the two following dates: "the date that the State plan is mailed or hand delivered to the Secretary in substantially approvable form" and "the date that the funds are first available for obligation by the Secretary."

The regulations further stipulate that a State shall comply with the State plan and applicable statutes, regulations, and approved applications, and shall use Federal funds in accordance with those statutes, regulations, plans, and applications. Here, of course, the "applicable statute" is the McKinney Act, and the obligations it imposes on participating States are clear. The Act requires that grants provided by the Secretary be used, . . . "to prepare and carry out the State plan," and that "each plan . . . assure . . . that local educational agencies within the State will comply with the requirements . . . [and] in turn provide highly specific instructions for meeting a variety of needs of homeless children and youths. This structure markedly contrasts with that of the Child Welfare Act. . . .

Although both Acts describe in detail the contents of the plan a participating State must adopt, only the McKinney Act provides specific directions for the plan's execution. It is this distinction that is ignored by our dissenting colleague, who concludes that "the genuine statutory duty of a recipient state under the McKinney Act is to prepare and carry out a plan, designed to achieve nine designated goals." While we agree that the McKinney Act requires the State to submit such a plan, it also differs significantly from the Adoption Act in that . . . the McKinney Act not only informs the State in great detail on how its plan is to be implemented, they impose obligations that are independent of the plan. These are set forth in specific, mandatory terms; and it is these that appellants seek to enforce.

Thus, paragraph (3) requires that

> the local educational agency of each homeless child and each homeless youth shall [assign the child or youth to a school which] is in the child's best interest or the youth's best interest. . . . In determining the best interests of the child or youth . . . consideration shall be given to a request made by a parent regarding school selection.

Succeeding paragraphs stipulate that "each homeless child shall be provided services comparable to services offered to other students in the school . . . ," and that records ordinarily kept by the school "shall be maintained" so as to be available when the child enters a new school district. Furthermore, they provide that

> each local educational agency serving homeless children or youth that receives assistance under this subchapter shall coordinate with local social services agencies, and other agencies or programs providing services to such children or youth and their families[,] and "shall designate a homelessness liaison."

*continued*

## 4.7 | JUDICIAL DECISION INTERPRETING THE MCKINNEY ACT (CONTINUED)

We read this language as "mandatory rather than hortatory." . . . In addition to the mandatory obligations listed in those seven paragraphs, the McKinney Act also provides that

> the Coordinator of Education of Homeless Children and Youth established in each State shall . . . once every 2 years, gather data on the number and location of homeless children and youth in the State . . . develop and carry out the State plan . . . [and] facilitate coordination between the State education agency, the State social services agency, and other agencies providing services to homeless children and youth and their families.

The language of these provisions is sufficiently clear to put the States on notice of the obligations they assume when they choose to accept grants made under the Act.

Moreover, as we noted earlier, the Secretary has promulgated regulations stipulating that for state-administered programs like the McKinney Act, "[a] State . . . shall comply with the State plan and applicable statutes, regulations, and approved applications, and shall use Federal funds in accordance with those statutes, regulations, plan, and applications." Here, the regulations merely reinforce our conclusion that States undertake well-defined obligations when they elect to accept funds under the McKinney Act.

Finally, the McKinney Act contains no statutory mechanisms for the administrative enforcement of the beneficiaries' rights, suggesting that Congress did not intend to create a private cause of action that is enforceable under section 1983. Thus there is nothing in the structure of the McKinney Act to suggest that its beneficiaries may not invoke section 1983 to enforce their rights under the Act.

One hurdle remains before we can declare that the rights conferred on homeless children by the Act are enforceable in federal court. Even if a statute confers rights

---

there were about 14,000 such developments, and these provided housing for about 2.8 million persons. HUD-funded public housing is operated by local governmental agencies usually referred to as local public housing authorities. Fifty percent of the households served in the 1.3 million occupied public housing apartments are families with children; 33 percent are elderly, childless occupants; and the remaining are persons with disabilities or those without children. A majority of these households are headed by women and by people of color (National Low Income Housing Coalition, 2001).

The other HUD-funded approach to rental assistance is the subsidizing of rental costs in the private housing rental market. In the past these subsidies (known as Housing Assistance Payments—HAP) have taken two forms: certificates and vouchers. With certificates, tenants sought a HUD-approved apartment whose rent could not exceed HUD's Fair Market Rent. The tenant paid 30 percent of household income toward the rent, and HUD paid any remaining amount. Certificates have been phased out and have been superseded by the voucher approach. Under what is now being called the Housing Choice Voucher program (also referred to as Section 8), the rent for the prion a beneficiary, their judicial enforcement requires that they not be overly "vague and amorphous." The District argues that the statutory requirement that a school be selected in accordance with the "best interests" of a homeless child is at least as vague as the "reasonable efforts" clause that the Court found too amorphous in [an earlier case].

This argument asserts, in essence, that the judiciary is incapable of determining the "best interests" of children, just as the plaintiffs in Wilder argued that the judiciary was incapable of determining what constitutes "reasonable and adequate" hospital rates. In response, the Court observed:

> That the [Boren] Amendment gives the States substantial discretion in choosing among reasonable methods of calculating rates may affect the standard under which a court reviews whether the rates comply with the amendment, but it does not render the amendment unenforceable by a court. While there may be a range of reasonable rates, there certainly are some rates outside that range that no State could ever find to be reasonable and adequate under the Act. Although some knowledge of the hospital industry might be required to evaluate a State's findings with respect to the reasonableness of its rates, such an inquiry is well within the competence of the Judiciary.

The obligations imposed by the McKinney Act involve, for the most part, the exercise of judgment by a local educational agency. A court, however, may discern whether the criteria or procedures adopted by the agency are reasonably designed to aid it in making the school placement decision. Moreover, we have little doubt that the court would also have the competence to determine whether the District had complied with its obligation to assign a particular homeless child to a school that was in his best interests. * * *

We conclude, from the foregoing, that section 11432(e)(3) of the McKinney Act confers enforceable rights on its beneficiaries and that appellants may invoke section 1983 to enforce those rights.

---

vately owned apartment can go above the Fair Market Rent. The subsidy can be based on rents that go to 110 percent of HUD's Fair Market Rent. However, in addition to 30 percent of household income, any rent amount in excess of HUD's rent scale must be paid by the tenant. The housing authority can determine whether the tenant's portion of the rent is reasonable in view of the tenant's income (generally no more than 40 percent of income), and can deny the client the use of the voucher for an apartment with an unreasonable rent.

This voucher program was enacted under the Quality Housing and Work Responsibility Act of 1998. In recent years, federal policy has clearly preferred household-based subsidies for use in the private market over public housing. From 1977 through 2000, the proportion of assisted low-income renters receiving these household subsidies rose from 8 percent to 32 percent (U. S. House of Representatives Committee on Ways and Means, 2001, p. 948). In 2000, nearly 50 percent of HUD's housing dollars went to private subsidy programs (U.S. Census Bureau, 2001). The Housing Choice Voucher program is also administered by HUD through local housing agencies or authorities.

Public housing starts are now relatively few, and most target housing for seniors. Housing for the disabled has become less available, because after 1992, senior housing complexes were no longer required to set aside a specified number of units for the disabled. Current housing policy attempts to discourage the concentration of very low- or no-income persons in any one housing complex or community. Under the 1998 Quality Housing Act, public housing authorities are required to include a policy regarding income mixing in their 5-year plans.

As of the early part of the 21st century, adequate, affordable housing remains a pressing issue for society's economically dislocated populations. The specter of homelessness remains a haunting presence in the daily lives of people with low and unstable incomes, and there is little hope that the situation will improve. As of 2005, the Section 8 Housing Choice Voucher program is being threatened by inadequate federal funding and pending budget and legislative proposals. If these are enacted, it has been estimated that as many as 370,000 fewer households could receive vouchers by 2010 (Center on Budget & Policy Priorities, 2005).

## Application and Eligibility

Applicants for rental assistance receive application forms from the local housing authority responsible for public housing and/or Section 8 rental subsidies. HUD requires a written application process and the signature of a responsible family member. The application requests information regarding family size and composition, family income and assets, citizenship status, current housing status, and special circumstances.

The application process for public housing includes screening out residents who have a history of violent criminal behaviors, permanent sex offender status, disruptive alcohol use, or abuse, manufacture, or distribution of illegal drugs. A criminal background check is required for public housing, but not for Section 8. Resident selection cannot be based on demographic characteristics such as race, religion, gender, age, or disability. The specific criteria and process for resident selection must be displayed in the HUD facility.

Eligibility is based on the following factors: income, category (senior, disabled, family), citizen or legal immigrant status, and the outcome of the resident screening process. The applicant's family income must meet one of three income classifications: lower income (does not exceed 80 percent of the area's median income); very low income (does not exceed 50 percent of the median income); and extremely low income (does not exceed 30 percent of the median income). As of April 28, 2000, at least 40 percent of public housing's units must be occupied by those in the extremely low income category. For Section 8, 75 percent of vouchers must be granted to those in the extremely low income category. (The percentage is higher in the Section 8 program than in public housing because it is household, not development based, and by its very nature promotes a scattered distribution of very low income households.) Level of household income is determined by each family member's anticipated total earned income and income from assets such as bonds, stocks, and savings. Income is adjusted for certain deductions such as the cost of child care and medical expenses.

If applicants are assessed to be eligible, they are notified in writing. The waiting period before an apartment or voucher becomes available varies by locale. In some communities applicants can wait for up to a decade. Lists are kept based on the date of application and any preferences determined by the local housing authority and approved by HUD. In Section 8, waiting lists may even be frozen if there is a great gap between the length of the existing list and the supply of vouchers.

Ongoing eligibility for rental assistance depends on several factors. Households must demonstrate continued income eligibility and report any changes in family earnings and assets. The family must demonstrate it has not had a detrimental effect on the community and that it has paid its monthly rent in a timely manner. Public housing residents required to perform 8 hours per month of community service must have fulfilled this obligation. (There is no community service requirement for Section 8 tenants.) Among those exempt from the community service requirement (which was introduced in the 1998 Quality Housing and Work Responsibility Act) are persons who are 62 years or older, those who are blind or disabled or their caretakers, those who are employed or are in a welfare-to-work program.

## Benefits

Affordable, safe housing is the major benefit received by participants in federal rent-assisted housing programs. For many lower-income families—including those in which more than one adult is employed—skyrocketing housing costs eat up more than 50 or more percent of their budgets. And the condition of low-end private market housing is often unsafe and unsanitary.

Benefits for those who acquire an apartment in a public housing complex include a rent level controlled by federal guidelines. Generally, tenants choose among two approaches for determining their monthly rent. In the first, a flat rent based on regional rents is established by the local housing authority. In the second approach, a percentage of the family's income is used as the basis for rent. Each housing authority also establishes a minimum rent schedule.

Public housing residents also may receive benefits in the form of HUD-funded service programs including the Resident Opportunity and Supportive Services and the Drug Elimination programs. The former provides funds for academic skills, social services, and other supports, and the latter finances activities to improve community safety.

Families with Section 8 vouchers receive rental assistance for housing they themselves find in the private rental market. The voucher belongs to households until they no longer use it. The primary benefit is a rent supplement paid by HUD to the landlord. This rent subsidy or Housing Assistance Payment is equal to the difference between the tenant's contribution (30 percent of family income, adjusted for HUD-determined deductions) and the regional fair market value of the rental unit. If the apartment rents for more than this fair market value, the family pays this difference (in addition to 30 percent of its income). However, the family cannot pay more than 40 percent of its adjusted monthly income for rent. If the apartment rents for less than HUD's fair market value, the family can keep the excess.

In addition to affordable rents, those living in public housing and those receiving Section 8 vouchers share several other benefits. Both receive leases that clearly define tenants' and landlords' rights and responsibilities. Leases in public housing generally provide for month-to-month tenancy; under Section 8, the initial lease is for a 1-year period. Under Section 8, an additional agreement regarding housing assistance payments is signed by the landlord and the local public housing authority. Violations of public housing and Section 8 leases can lead to loss of benefit, that is, termination of the lease and eviction. Tenants cannot be evicted without legal proceedings and a court hearing.

Residence in one public housing apartment does not entitle the tenant to residence in another HUD facility, each of which has its own waiting list. Section 8 vouchers are portable after 1 year of use and can if accepted be used by tenants in the jurisdictions of another housing authority.

Recipients' benefits also include governmental regulations regarding the safety of their housing. Under Section 8, the responsible public housing authority does an inspection of a prospective privately owned dwelling and reinspects the dwelling annually. Under the public housing regulations, housing authorities are responsible for ensuring ongoing sanitary and safe conditions (McDowall, 2001). This includes repairs, compliance with building, housing, and health codes, the safety of all areas of the facility, and the maintenance of utilities. Initial and yearly inspections in both programs check for such conditions as electrical safety, lead-based paint, window conditions, and security.

There also are some guidelines designed to prevent unhealthy over-crowded conditions. HUD rules do not explicitly direct the local housing authorities with regard to such issues as the age children cannot be permitted to share sleeping quarters with parents or at the age different-sex children be given separate bedrooms. HUD does provide standards related to minimum and maximum number of occupants and apartment size. For example, a studio can be occupied by only one person, a one-bedroom by up to two persons, a two-bedroom by two to four persons. HUD rules also permit pets but only in public housing for the elderly or for persons with disabilities. Section 8 families comply with private landlords' preferences with regard to pets.

Benefits can be lost because of noncompliance with the responsibilities detailed in the public housing or the Section 8 lease. Nonpayment of rent, improper care of the apartment, behavior threatening the well-being of the community, substance abuse and other criminal activity, and (in public housing) a failure to comply with community service and self-sufficiency rules are the primary reasons for threatened or actual benefit loss.

The community service requirement was introduced in 1998 by the Quality Housing and Work Responsibility Act; residents of public housing must spend 8 hours a month in community service, an economic self-sufficiency program, or a combination of both. Some tenants are exempt—those 62 or older, those with disabilities and their caregivers, those who are employed or in a welfare-to-work program. This effort to promote responsibility is reflective of the individualistic ethos informing Temporary Assistance to Needy Families (TANF). HUD does not apply this community service rule to Section 8 families.

The so-called one-strike policy was introduced by the Anti-Drug Abuse Act of 1988 and upheld in a 2002 Supreme Court decision (*Department of Housing and Urban Development v. Rucker,* 2002; see Box 4.6). Under this policy, leases can be terminated if a tenant, a member of the tenant's household, or a guest is involved in drug-related criminal activity. The policy covers even those situations in which the tenant was unaware of the activity and also to criminal activity that occurred off the premises.

Benefits, as noted previously, are not guaranteed to all who qualify. Public housing programs are not entitlements; financial and other eligibility criteria are a necessary prerequisite but are not sufficient to ensure the housing benefit. The supply of publicly supported affordable rental assistance units— either through public housing or Section 8—is the key variable in receipt of the benefit. As we have noted, available public housing units are in many regions scarce and waiting lists very long. Section 8 vouchers are not only limited in number but can expire without being used (they are usually valid for 2 months, with two 1-month extensions possible). This is often because families are unable to find landlords willing to meet the governmental regulations involved in renting to voucher holders.

## Due Process

Residents of public housing or those whose rent is subsidized under the Section 8 program are entitled to due process regarding terminations, denial, reduction, or suspension of assistance. These grievance procedures were adopted in 1975. Each housing authority is required to include its hearing policy in the tenant lease.

HUD's due process requirements relate only to housing authority actions regarding individual tenants. They do not cover disputes between tenants or tenants' collective complaints about policies of the housing authority. The procedures may also exempt grievances regarding lease termination because of drug or other activity threatening the community's safety. This exemption is granted by HUD only if it approves the use of local court procedures in these situations.

While the specific hearing procedures are established by the local housing authority, HUD requires that certain elements of due process be followed, including adequate notice regarding the action (for example, termination of lease, eviction); the tenant's right to legal representation; the tenant's right to inspect all records before the hearing and to present arguments, and to confront and cross-examine witnesses.

HUD provides for informal settlement of a grievance prior to a formal hearing. If this attempt to resolve the dispute through an in-person or in-writing presentation to the housing authority office fails to dispose of the issue to the satisfaction of the tenant, she or he may submit a written request for a hearing to the housing authority. This request must be filed within a "reasonable time."

The hearing is conducted before an impartial officer or panel. The hearing officer(s), appointed by the housing authority, cannot be related to the action taken. Tenants must approve the process for selecting the hearing officer or panel. The tenant should be notified in writing of the time and place of the hearing, both of which should be convenient to both the tenant and the housing authority. Hearings can be expedited in situations related to termination of tenancy because of drug-related or other criminal activity. Informal procedures to settle the grievance do not pertain to expedited hearings.

HUD regulations cover special situations. If the tenant has a disability that affects his or her ability to engage in the hearing, the public housing authority must provide "reasonable accommodation" such as an accessible location, a qualified sign language interpreter, and notices accessible to the visually impaired.

Scheduled hearings may be postponed for up to 5 business days if the tenant does not appear. However, hearing officer(s) can determine that failure to appear constitutes a waiver of the right to a hearing.

Decisions are made by the hearing officer or panel and must be rendered in writing, with explanations, and within a reasonable time following the hearing. Both the tenant and the housing authority receive a copy of the decision. According to HUD, the decision is binding on the housing authority unless the decision is determined by the housing authority's board of commissioners to be contrary to federal, state, or local law or to HUD regulations. If the decision is not in favor of the tenant, he or she has the right to take further legal action.

## THE CLIENTS' STORIES

### Paula

I'm a single mom. I'm 36 years old. I have a 15-year-old daughter. Presently, I own my own home. I am very active in the church. I lost my job recently. I'm doing okay. I saw the writing on the wall. When it came it was no surprise to me. There were a lot of people who were totally devastated. My office was down in New York City in the Chelsea area. I would say that about 2 weeks prior I had basically cleared out my whole entire desk and all, in preparation for it. There were no hard feelings.

I was given a very generous severance package, but that comes into play 30 days after you leave. So, I am waiting for the severance package. I am actively looking for a new job, but I have been told by hiring agencies that the market is very tight at this point in time, which I have no problem with. I'll wait. I have gone to outplacement services. I was given a great deal of pointers on my résumé and how to respond in an interview, following up and asking people if they would be references for me. That was a very big plus, because the job market has changed. I have not been out on the job market in over 6 years. I have not applied for unemployment insurance yet. I'll probably go some time this week.

I'm still drawing on faith to help me cope with it. I have had strangers, ministers, and prophets, who do not even know me, have walked up to me and spoken to me about my situation. They have said to me, I will be blessed beyond measure when I get my new job. So, that is forthcoming, and I believe in that, and I'm standing on that. I'm not worried about it at all. I can truly tell you that my previous job was not for my character. I'm a people person, and I wound up in marketing research, which is just really basically crunching numbers all day long. I just prayed and prayed. Then, that's when the opportunity came up with my boss. He said he was leaving and asked me to go with him. That's what helped me to buy my house. He pretty much sat down with me and said to me, "Write your own paycheck. What do you want?" I expressed to him what I wanted. He said, "Fine." Working with him was just a great, great blessing. When I was ready to purchase my house, he said to me that if I could not get a loan on my own credit he would cosign for me, if necessary. We were a blessing in each other's life.

As of right now, I am doing great. I am behind in my mortgage, but once I get my severance pay, that will cover everything. I'm not worried about it at this time. I'm the type of person that I just go out and just keep on going. I'm not one to sit around. I like to stay active. So, when I did lose my job, I said, "Okay, fine, let me go back out in the job market." I just started calling agencies and applying for jobs.

I have my parents, living two towns over, in the same house where I grew up. I have four brothers and sisters. Three of them live out of state. I have five nieces and nephews. I have a few friends. I'm a very outgoing person. But I've just had a lot of situations happen in my life, very few people do I allow to be close to me. I have some from the church, but really no real friends that I pick up the phone and call.

I'm an adopted child. I've been with my family since I was a baby, about a year and a half. I was formally adopted at age 10. The two eldest are their biological children, and the rest of us are adopted. The two youngest ones are half-brother and -sister. They have the same mother, but different fathers. So, I'm the odd man out. I felt like that growing up. I have always felt like the odd person out. It may have something to do with my childhood in those 18 months.

I was with my biological mother. What happened in that situation, what I understand from a friend, and from what I gathered from newspaper articles—my father killed my mother. My mother was a very young woman, about age 30, and my father was in his sixties. Jealousy reared its ugly head, and he took the butt of a rifle and crushed her skull. He didn't hurt me. As a result I was put in foster care. I do have other siblings. I don't know who they are.

I have yearned to find them. When I go to the doctor, they ask if I have any family history of A, B, C, and D. I cannot tell them. It is upsetting when people talk about their mother and great-grandmother and how these characteristics come forth, and how this person looks like that person, so on and so forth. It is disturbing, but in another sense it is a blessing, because I don't know how my life would have been with my mother. I adore my parents. I love my brothers and sisters.

I went to the public high school. School was fine. I was a bookworm. Starting in junior high, through high school, I read romances. They were my best friends. I had tons and tons of them that I read. I enjoyed reading, writing. I did very well in English classes. I took all my business courses in high school. I did quite well in business. I graduated with a diploma in business. From there, I went to college and graduated with an associate's degree in office technology. After that I became an executive assistant.

While I was going to college I lived at home. Once I graduated I moved out. I rented a room in someone's home, lived by myself, always had a full-time job. It was what I could afford on the salary I was making. I moved out of my parents' home, because we had a falling out and it was necessary for me to leave home. I had all the skills to live on my own, so it was no problem. I was about 19. I ended up pregnant at 20.

I did my normal 6 weeks maternity leave. I went right back to work, and she went to a baby-sitter. She was with baby-sitters all the way until she went to school. Around that time I was back in touch with my family. I moved back home briefly, for about 2 years. The last place I had to leave from, it was sudden, and I did not have the money or anything to move into another place since it was sudden. My parents came and said that I could move back home.

During that period, it was hard. You know, renting a room in someone's house, there are just all these rules. You can't do this; you can't do that. You have to be in by a certain time. You can come down and cook at certain times. Some places you couldn't cook at all. It was just eating out a lot. It was difficult. My daughter was not a crying baby at all, which was very disturbing. She would sleep for 12 and 14 hours at a stretch, without waking up to eat, and I would have to literally shake her awake, to feed her. There were some problems when she was a baby that needed to be addressed also.

She couldn't roll over at the age people were supposed to roll over; she couldn't lift her head. They didn't say what it was attributed to when I took her to the doctor. They just called it a developmental delay. They did a little bit of therapy. My mom helped out a great deal in taking her back and forth to the doctor, because I could not take the time off that often. I would have lost my job. She has no residue of the developmental problems. That was just that one time. She is an A student, very bright and all. Right now she is at that stage where she wants to be the center of attention.

I always worked. At times I had a second job to make ends meet. Again, my mom played an integral part in that. She would watch her for me. My daughter is doing fabulous now. She has done her typical teen thing. We went through a rough patch 2 years ago. I learned it had nothing to do with me. It's something she had to go through. Again that's where prayer came in.

She went to seek out her father. I knew that day would come. I had no problem with that. It just disturbed me the way she had gone about finding him. She was cutting classes and school, to go see him, sneaking around. They played father/daughter for about three months. Then he stopped.

I found out about Section 8 sixteen years ago when I went down to Social Services. I had gone down there to apply for child care. That's when they interviewed me for Section 8. I did a little research and found out who services what. I applied for Section 8 and public housing.

I filled out an application describing my background, whether or not I had a boy or a girl, what my income was. They needed tax returns. They did a background check also. My Section 8 came through. Section 8 was going to help me get an apartment. Again, the real estate market was just too high for me to afford an apartment on my own, with the salary that I was making at the time. I was told it was based on the salary. I did the math and all. They would pay the difference.

With Section 8 and public housing, they mailed me the application. They were not nice. I guess some found in the years of working there, the type of people that they dealt with and all, that they just were not nice. When I went down to apply, I was still pregnant at the time. So, I was told I would have to wait until I had the baby and to come back once I had the baby, so they would know what type of housing to put me in, based on the sex of the child. I did come back after I had her. I had to show them the birth certificate. That's when I was told that there is a waiting period of—at that time—5 to 7 years. I said I would apply anyway. She was born in 1987; and they called me in 1990 for an apartment, which was a very quick turnaround. I just had to come up with a security deposit. When my Section 8 came through, that's when my parents said I could move back home. So, I never responded to Section 8. But later I did go from my parents' home to an apartment in public housing. It was necessary, even though they were willing to have me stay at home. The situation still was not comfortable. I knew I had to leave as soon as possible. They gave me a one-bedroom apartment. Their regulations were that same sex would go in a one-bedroom apartment. I gave the bedroom to my daughter, and I slept on a captain's bed in the living room.

The apartment was nice. It wasn't overly roomy, but it suited our needs at that time. It was a three-story walk-up building. There were six flights of steps. I lived on the third floor. There was a laundry room down in the basement. A recreation center was also down in the basement. The whole complex was family. There just weren't very many activities for the children to do. There were people who had lived there generation after generation. The mindset was just very discouraging—very laid back, very I don't care type of attitude. They allowed their children to do whatever they wanted to do—run up and down the steps, running, screaming. The company was also very loud. There were issues of domestic violence. There were issues of unruly tenants. There were issues of smoking, doing drugs around the area. When you came out in the morning, you saw all the paraphernalia on the ground. Drinking and smoking at night. Across the street, there were drug houses. Housing was very slow to address these things.

A lot of people did work in the complex. People have the notion that everyone who is on public assistance is in public housing. That was not the case at all. Most people worked who lived in the complex.

My rent varied, based upon raises. My rent was always pretty high. It was still affordable for me. It went from $400 up to $900, when I left. I was there for 10 years. It afforded me to be able to still have a place to stay if I ever did lose my job. If I ever had a reduction in pay, I was still able to afford my apartment. It did help me out a great deal until I could take that next step and get a higher paying job. In my mind's eye it was always temporary. I would get another place. That's because of all the activity going around. For me, this was not my type of environment, because I grew up in a house, I grew up with brothers and sisters, typical middle-class family. For me, it was only temporary. I know it was very different with other people. They grew up in public housing as a child, they raised their children in public housing, and now they were raising their grandchildren in public housing. So, their mindset was just totally different. A lot of people there were looking for handouts and not wanting to work towards anything. The older tenants described the times when people would help out each other. They would pick up the slack and clean things themselves. They used to have activities for the children. They planted flowers around. The older residents had pride in the community. The next generation—my age group—didn't care.

I know a lot of things they did had to do with funding from the federal government. The money was there for them to do it. Years ago the money was there for them to do the various activities and get materials. But once that funding was cut back, it just seemed that people were not willing to volunteer their time, their talent. It was a matter of well, if they are not paying for it, then we can't do it.

I went from public housing to this beautiful home. I borrowed because I did get the fabulous job that I did that afforded me to get the house. I knew about FHA [Federal Housing Assistance] loans, so I only had to put 3 percent down. It was just a matter of getting approval on a house that I could afford. Again, this is where my faith comes in. I knew it was time to start looking for a house. I had been in public housing for 10 years. My goal originally had been to be there for only 5 years, but I was there twice as long as I had anticipated. To me, things were just deteriorating more and more at public housing. I knew I didn't want to raise my daughter in public housing because of the environment. We had a board of commissioners. They were not doing anything. It was all just political. They really weren't doing anything for the residents. My take on that it was because they did not live there. They went home to their beautiful houses and kind of shut the door on that situation. They were just sitting on a board. That was all.

I was afforded the opportunity to work in public housing, to actually work in the office. So, I saw the other side of it. I was just really appalled the way things were going. There was a board of commissioners. They met every single month. Things just didn't get resolved. We had an executive director who could not do anything, who had to fight for everything in order to implement any type of change. They were not willing to do that change. It wasn't just the mindset of the residents, it was the mindset of the board also. You bring someone in and you're saying you want change, you want better public housing, but when that executive director is giving you the things necessary to implement the change, everyone says no, we can't do that. It is just very difficult. I think public housing could be improved, but it is the people that are on the board who just don't want the change. They want everything status quo, and that's all. It was very frustrating for that executive director.

As far as the drug problem, as far as overcrowding of families, as far as moving people into appropriate units, those type of things, if a person was unruly or anything like that, the eviction process and all of this was such a hindrance into making things go on, as far as improving conditions. They just didn't want to do it.

The rules and regulations were in place, but again a blind eye was being turned. You would have someone move in, 2 weeks later they would move in their boyfriend. The friends are coming. I saw people who had been living there, I would see they had a new apartment. I saw young ladies have baby after baby after baby. They would run down a house and say we have an overcrowded situation. She needs her own apartment. That's how family after family after family would get apartments. The grandmother is in senior housing; the mother is in public housing; the daughter has her own apartment in public housing. It was generation after generation; same people, same families.

My feeling is there has to be more as far as activities. I think that was the biggest problem. There were just not enough activities to get people involved, to have an investment. You are always going to have people say I don't care. I am going to do what I want to do. You will always have people like that. Look at the teenagers. What do you have for them to do, besides hang out all night, besides running around and sleeping with every Tom, Dick, and Harry, besides just drugging and drinking and fighting?

You're raising your children, but there is no proper outlet for them. They cannot get a job until they are 16 most of the time. I feel that between ages 13 and 16 are the most critical years for a teenager. If they have no type of outlet, no type of goals implanted in them, then they are just going to run the streets. That's what most of these girls did—run the streets and party because they had no other outlet. Sometimes they ended up pregnant. I had one woman whose daughter lived with her. The mother was in the bedroom sleeping. The daughter was on the couch. She had three babies living with her mother. Her mother was just shaking her head.

Where are the programs in place that I can get more skills, get more education, so I can find that better job, so I can go out and to get these things so I can better myself and raise my family and get a better apartment, and ultimately get a house? There is just nothing in place. Public housing, on just the merit of getting affordable housing, that is fine. But once you get the people in there, then they are pretty much left to their own devices. I think because they are left to their own devices, that's where all these other things come into play.

High-rises. I think that is a deterrent to people; I think that scares people. I know in some states there are town houses, or garden apartments. It can blend into the neighborhood. It's not a matter of don't go down that street because that's where all the public housing is. Unfortunately, there is that stigmatism to public housing and how people on public assistance are lazy, and they are drug heads, and so on and so forth. If I did develop public housing, the structure would be to blend in with the other houses that were in the neighborhood. Secondly, I would have a great deal of programs in place, from when Billybob is a toddler up until they are ready to go to college or trade school, or something.

If there were services in the complex, it would be a lot easier. I think it would make a big difference. I have seen documentaries on public housing, where they had the services right there in the building. It's convenient. Matter of fact, I was the first resident they did that for, where the residents are the ones who run the program, who work with the people, instead of having someone from the outside do it. That makes the biggest difference in the world. You can say, "Hey, Maryellen, I know about your situation with your daughter, or your husband. Come on down. We have something here that may help you." I know things like that the executive director was trying to do, get some of the programs going. Again, it was stalled.

It was the summer of '99. I said enough is enough. I needed to move out. This is just not working for me. This environment was just not for me. I needed to move forward. It had been 10 years. I contacted a recommended broker and went to brokers myself. At first, I was looking for a co-op. I thought, get the co-op, pay for it, no problem. Again, I had difficulties because they told me I was a black woman; I couldn't afford it; I was wasting my time. They were white brokers. Well, if I'm coming to you saying this is what I want, then that should be end of it. I went to several brokers. There were a couple of black ones, too, and again they said I was a single woman, there was no way I could afford this. Basically, they just played with me. That was a disaster.

I started looking in the paper on my own. I had seen commercials about $3,000 down, no closing costs. I saw one in the paper and called them. They said, "Sure, let's meet." Again, this is where my faith comes in. I knew what type house I wanted. I had never told anyone I went on a Saturday to look at the house. The first thing I saw was the porch with the wrought iron that I wanted. I walked in and stood here. I had seen this heating grate in my dream. When I walked in I wondered why it looked so familiar. The man asked me what I think, and I said, "I really love the house." He said, "Okay we can meet with the attorneys on Monday to sign the papers." I went that Monday to sign the papers, and the house cost me $144,000, whereas I could only get approved for $100,000, no more than $125,000. The owners paid the closing costs, which was $10,000. They were a construction company. They represented banks and lending agencies. The house had been in foreclosure, vacant for over 3 years. They supplied me with an attorney. It was only $3,000 down on the house; I paid $5,000. I didn't have to pay any mortgage fees. The ironic thing about it, that's why I say faith plays a very large part in my life, this house was the one I dreamt about. The Lord put it in my spirit. There are three bedrooms, one bath, basement, not finished, so I have my washer and dryer, beautiful backyard, two-car garage, and kitchen. The kitchen is not new, it just looks that way.

It took 6 months for me to close on this house. This house was a blessing for me. I didn't need my boss to cosign for me. I was able to get it on my own credit report. I didn't have an inspection on it. They had put a new roof on the house. There were a couple of minor things that needed to be done, which they were willing to do. They put the money aside in escrow to do it. There was another house I had taken a look at. That house was way out of my price range. I had that house inspected, so I knew what to look for in this house. I was satisfied with the house, that it was sound. I did it all by myself.

My daughter was not with me. I went all by myself. Unfortunately, my parents, and maybe it's the wrong perception, my parents felt that I was a single mom. I don't think they had very high hopes for me, to attain those things without calling for a husband. They thought there was just no way that you could afford this. When I came to get this house, I never told them. Once I had put the down payment on this house, that's when I told them. Of course, during the 6 months they kept asking when are you going to get the house, you keep talking about it. I don't think they really saw me as getting the house. When I finally closed on my house, I ran back to them and said, "I'm a homeowner." They were happy for me, that I did get the house. They were proud in their way.

So, again, because I'm a single mom, and I'm a woman, there were some challenges when I moved in. I'm the only single woman homeowner on the block. Because they don't see that male figure in my house, there have been challenges.

My neighbor parked his van in front of my house. A gentleman lived in the van. The gentleman would eat, throw the paper in front of my house. He smoked; I had cigarette butts all in front of my house. At one point, a chore of my daughter's was to put the garbage out. She said that when she put the garbage out she smelled urine all on the sidewalk. Even if he parked in front of someone else's house, it would just be for that night, and he would move the next day. My house was the only house that he would continuously park his van in front of. Finally, one day, I got fed up with it and called the police. They actually came to the house, and I told them what was going on. They said to call them if he comes back. They left. People are very observant. When he came back, whomever was home told him that I had called the police. From that point on, the van was not there.

I'm going back to school to get my bachelor's, so again I can better myself. As an executive assistant, I made fabulous money. I have no problem with being an executive assistant, but I want a future. I want a career change. I want to be an event planner. Since I'm the event planner for my church, I do that a great deal and I really enjoy doing that.

As for housing, again, this is where my religious beliefs come in. When I moved in, I knew it was going to be a rental property. I was going to move out, go into the next house. I know in my spirit that real estate is going to play a very big role in my life. That next house I probably will be getting with my husband, when he comes along. That to me is another thing, as far as single women are concerned. Be content with yourself for a little while, instead of being in such a rush. You could have male role models in your child's life, without him necessarily being your boyfriend or just a sugar daddy, or even the child's father. If the child's father is willing, that's fine; if he's not, then find another role model for your child. My brother, my dad, the ministers in my church are role models for my daughter. Take care of yourself; take care of your children. And by taking care of yourself, be content with yourself, further your education, further your skills. Lean on yourself. Don't lean on a man per se, to sit there and build you up into someone you think you should be. You should do that on your own.

I think everyone wants a place to say this is mine. I truly believe public housing is a temporary stepping stone. It's for people who are just starting out in their life. That's not a stopping place. It was never home in that sense. It was just a stopping place for a little while until I could get that apartment, that co-op or a house. I knew that was not where I was going to stay until I go to senior housing. I think that's the thing we need to emphasize to people when they move into public housing, that it is just a steppingstone, and they need to go further. Again, I think education and skills plays a vital role in doing that.

Public housing wasn't my last stop. It may be a little more difficult for people who grew up in public housing. That's all they are surrounded by. I think that perception is important. I think when people's perceptions are broadened, I think that's when they say, "Hey, I need change. I need to better my life." I think that's the biggest thing.

## Theresa

My name is Theresa K. I just moved 4 months ago. We live in a house. And it's a fortunate thing because I've had a housing situation for many, many years and this year, just by a sheer blessing, I was able to move into another house because, until the end, I didn't know where we were going to live.

I work in a community college as a secretary to the African American Studies Department chairperson. I like to call myself an administrative assistant, but they don't allow that title. I really manage the office. I have a lot of responsibility. I interact with the students on a daily basis, advising them, directing them. I'm in a learning environment—that's something that I always loved to do and I am just very fortunate to be where I am.

I have three children. Rashon—he's 16 and he's the oldest. He's a really good kid, but he's been having a lot of trouble in school, and I believe that part of the reason is because I haven't really had any stability with my housing situation. That's been a problem for me for many, many years and I've moved four times over the past 5 years—not by any fault of my own, just because of certain circumstances. And he hasn't really been able to put down any roots. We've been in counseling for many, many years. . . . I had gotten him a mentor at some point and there are a lot of people who have offered a lot of assistance in helping me deal with this. But it hasn't been easy and we are still struggling. I have a 10-year-old daughter, and she'll be going into the fifth grade this year. She's doing very well in school and I believe that I was probably more stable at the point when she and my other child, who is 9, were small, and that the foundation that they had built in the beginning is really helping them excel right now, and I believe that may have something to do with why he's not consistent. My 9-year-old—he's going into the fourth grade and he's doing well. He's just outgoing and I just have to pay a little more attention to him to keep him, you know, focused on what he's doing. But overall, I'm happy with then—they're very healthy. I know I've been blessed. Sometimes it gets really, really frustrating, being a single mom and just trying to be everything but, you know, with the support system that I have in my life, I'm able to manage.

Part of my support system is Family Services. And family members—I have family members still in my life today who stood by me through all my ups and downs, and I have one aunt that I'm very, very close to and we talk on a daily basis. Other single moms and some single dads and just generally a lot of good people that I've met through the years in my newfound sobriety and my newfound life. I'm very fortunate. I had to learn how to trust and to open up and trust, and that's how I built my support—my support systems. Then people get to know me and reaching out when I need help. I didn't know how to do that at one time but I do now.

I was born in Georgia in 1963. My mother came north to work as a domestic, like a lot of young black women were doing at that time. She obviously wanted to try to make a better way. I remember coming to New York when I was 5. My mother had a baby boy and I remember we lived in a little tiny, tiny house. We then lived in a rooming house. It was just her and me and the man she was with at that time. My brothers were back in the South. And I was 7 and maybe we were there a couple of years because I believe she wanted to bring my brothers to New York but she couldn't because we lived in this rooming house. The next thing I know we lived in a welfare motel. They were popular at that time. This had to be around 1971 or 1972 because I was about 8 or 9 years old and I'll never forget this. There were a lot of families there. I knew a lot when I was a kid—more probably than I should have and there were all these families there—just living there like a little community. That's when my brothers came. She brought them and we all lived in this room and I believe there may have been double beds but I remember her preparing our meals on a hot plate. She would make macaroni and cheese and we would have meat. But, you know, thinking back, that stuff was dangerous. You know, we could have been burned. But she was doing what she needed to do to provide for us. We went to school from that welfare motel. There was a bus that would pick us up and take us to the school where all the other children went. I can't remember a lot—I probably blocked it out—but I remember feeling so stigmatized. I knew my life was not normal, you know, because we were in an area where middle-class, white people lived. I remember a girl named Lisa, and we were friends. And I remember going to visit her house one time and those people lived in big, beautiful houses. You know, we lived in the welfare motel and we would go to school, and I can remember that I never wanted people to know, even at that age (I had to be 8 or 9 years old), that that's how my family lived. I was so ashamed of that type of life.

At some point my mother found an apartment in Eastbay. That's how I came to grow up in Eastbay and eventually graduated from high school there. We moved to Eastbay in 1972. I was 9 years old. My mother had a brand new baby boy, who is my baby brother, and we had a three-bedroom apartment and it was great. It was so beautiful. It was in an apartment building with four different apartments, and I had my own bedroom because I was the only girl. My mother had her bedroom and my brothers—they had their bedroom. This place was so beautiful. It was nicely painted—all the colors. And I had a beautiful new bed and everything because at that point they had provided funds for her to furnish the place and everything. And I just thought it was the greatest thing ever, because it was the first time, at the age of 9, that I thought that we had something of our own. And I was so happy there. The school was right down the block—like 2 minutes. It was just perfect. There were other families there, with other children and at that point in time, back in 1972, it was a good time to grow up because everybody looked out for each other—you know, we all played. I didn't even know what drugs were at 9. It was safe—I could go skipping down the street to the store and along the way people would know who I was because they knew my mother. I did know about alcohol, though. Because my mother was an alcoholic. By the time we got into this apartment, somewhere along the line, my mother's drinking problem must have started to really take off. I remember there was a lot of depression. She was a good mother but she was depressed a lot. And I know these terms now because I'm an adult child of an alcoholic and I learned these things. She had these three children. She was in this relationship with this man that was not very attentive to her. And I know I resented that man because my mother was unhappy a lot. And I saw some forms of domestic abuse because my mother would be very upset because he had been running around with other women and disrespecting her and she would get all upset. I don't know if he was that violent, but it would get to a point where he would strike her. He'd strike her and we would get all involved. You know, "Get off my mother" and "You can't do this," and you know, just total dysfunction. And my mother would decline and she would drink and she would drink and she would drink.

My mother had left her mother and sisters in Georgia in a very violent domestic situation and she wanted to do something about that. She brought the entire family to New York and they moved in with her and, boy I'll tell you, I didn't have a room anymore. My mother lost sight of herself and us. We got lost. We—actually I got lost. I knew I was lost amongst all these people because I'm this little 9, 10-year-old girl who's trying to manage this household and people were taking over and, you know, I'm trying to stand up and say, "No, that's not right, this is wrong." And I wasn't able to do anything and I saw what was happening, you know, all our beautiful furniture was all torn up. And it came to a point—by the time I reached the age of 11, 12, and I was in the junior high school, I wouldn't even bring friends home—I was so ashamed. We had holes in the wall and the furniture was broken down. And that wasn't because of wear and tear—that was because of dysfunction. You know—my mother—she was drinking—and I don't know what was going on in that house, but I know that there was no order—there was no order—there was total chaos as far as I was concerned. And I remember as a kid my escapism was reading. I remember I read *Roots* when I was 9. And when they looked for me I was somewhere in the corner, hiding, reading a book. And that's how I got away from all that.

I know we were on public assistance, but I don't really know how they were being supported, but we all ate together and there was never enough of anything. I can remember days when we were hungry and my mother would have to borrow money from people to get lunch meat—just to make a sandwich or something. Most of the time there was a meal because, you know, coming from the South, they know how to put together something, you know, some rice or some chicken or something. But it just wasn't enough. I remember eating meals and I didn't feel like I was full. But there were so many people.

I remember when I had to go to the store with food stamps and buy things. I hated that. It was the worst because if any child saw you spending food stamps, you better believe the whole town, the whole school would know, "You're on welfare, you're on welfare, you're poor." I hated that. I would wait with those food stamps until people I knew would clear out of something—until the coast was clear. And half the time, I would just have to go ahead with what I had to do and then just deal with the consequences because I had built walls, anyway, in order to protect myself. You know, I didn't want to fight them, but if it came down to it, I guess I would just have to because a lot of times there was really nothing I could do— my mother's cooking dinner. "Go up here to the store, get some bread or some milk, or whatever, and get it back home." I couldn't stay there. I had to spend those food stamps.

By the time I reached junior high school I probably had zero self-esteem because I didn't even think I was pretty. And my mother—she really tried a lot. I remember in junior high school, my mother always tried to let me keep up with the rest of the girls. I remember she would come up with like $30 so I could go to the mall and get a pair of shoes or a pair of pants. With her illness of alcoholism and everything, I think my mother did the best she could. She would always say that I had to graduate high school because I guess that was her way of telling me that that was a way out. By that time, though, I believe her disease had really gotten hold of her and she wasn't pushing like, "Okay, I want you to graduate and go to college." She was saying, "Graduate and go into the armed forces, or something, so you can get a house." Because of my low self-esteem, I was wanting to fit in and you know a lot of things that young people were doing at that time. I believe that by the time we reached junior high school, we had been introduced to drinking, beer, cutting classes and stuff. I just wanted to pass my classes. I didn't push myself. And I look back, and I don't remember the teachers pushing me or anybody noticing—I don't know if I had such a good front or if I just swept through the system—'cause I think, "Why didn't anybody notice me and say, 'What could be going on in this young girl's life that we could change?'" And what my life may have been like if someone had noticed there was something wrong.

Even with the cutting class and stuff—you know, I had boundaries. I would get my homework from another student and get my assignment in. I would get the notes and pass my exams, so I made it through school. I had to go to summer school in eighth grade, though, in order to move on to the ninth grade. I hated that, I hated that. It was the worst punishment because I couldn't work and I wanted to work. I wanted to help my mom, I wanted to buy my own clothes, and help my brothers and stuff. I wanted to be good and I wanted to be with the other factions, too, because I grew up in this type of household. So, I didn't know what to do. I was confused. I didn't have a clue, really. I don't know what I was thinking about, I was just floating around, I guess, just trying to fit in. I wanted to be accepted by the intellectuals and I wanted to be accepted by the people who just wanted to do nothing. So that's what I did. I played both sides of the fence.

That's why they didn't notice me. So I went over to the high school. I left my two buddies behind—that we did all those things together—cutting classes and stuff—they didn't make it. So I went up there alone. Somehow I got through my high school years, but I had little self-esteem. I guess I had been told things as a child. I remember, my aunts used to tease me about my legs. They used to say, "Oh, you have these bird legs." So, by the time I reached high school, I was a young woman, but I didn't want to wear dresses because I was ashamed of my legs. I made it through high school by just doing what I had to do. I didn't push myself. I mean it was so easy for me to get through school. I never even really studied. And when I think about what I could have accomplished if I had really applied myself. The only thing I wanted to do was get out of school and get a job. That's all I wanted to do. I knew I just wanted to make money—make life better for me and my family. That's all I thought about. But there was a recruiter from the Army at the door the next day. And I went out there to one of those places where you go and you swear in and you're supposed to leave and all this. And I was on my way to Fort Dix. But I got out there and I backed out. I had sworn in and everything, but then I said, "I can't go because my mother is ill and she needs me." You know, and I just could not bear to leave. So I got out of there and I came back. Now my mother got evicted from that apartment. I remember that day so well because I was still in high school and back then they would stick your stuff out on the street. She wasn't able to find a place and they sent the sheriff in and they stuck all our stuff on the street; it was garbage, but it was all we had in the world. And my school bus stop just happened to be right across the street from the apartment. I'll never forget because I can see it just as plain as day because they had to stand out and watch the stuff. Otherwise people would just come by and take what they wanted to. So when I got off the school bus—there is all in plain sight. So I think I built these walls around me that—it was like—so what, because there was nothing I could do about that. You know what I mean? There was nothing I could do. That image has stayed in my mind all of my life. And three times I've faced eviction by no fault of my own and that mental picture will always come back to haunt me of what happened to my mother.

How could you let a family—a woman and three children be put on the street with all their belongings? Why wasn't there anywhere to go? No motel, no nothing—we were just on the street. We hadn't anywhere to go. If it wasn't for my grandmother, I don't know where the hell we would be at that point. And I was 17 years old. And my poor brothers—oh, my God, those children were just lost. I had one brother who is a couple of years younger. Half the time, we didn't even know where he was. And to this day my brother—he's been in prison all his life—and one of my other brothers has been in and out of the criminal justice system, too. However, now he's married, he has a family, he's trying so hard.

My mother found a place, but it was horrendous. I was working, but I refused to leave my mother. I was her protector. I had gotten a job with the county Head Start, and I went to a business school through the Office of Women's Services. I felt so good—we had a graduation and everything. And I got a certificate. Then I got a job in the town government; it was a great job, a great opportunity. But what happened was I got involved with drugs and I was introduced to a substance and it destroyed my life. I couldn't work anymore. I had a baby at the age of 20.

At the time my son was born, the baby's father's mother had helped us get a room in a rooming house. Oh, it was horrible, deplorable. There were rats down there. And my mother eventually got a house right across the street from this little basement apartment. She got this house and everything and it was okay. It wasn't the greatest house. And she was with this man at this time who was, I know, a gambler—he played the horses. And what a combination of a gambler and an alcoholic. And they had this house, but there was total dysfunction. We all lived there—well, no, they lived there and I had this baby over in this rooming house and the father and I—we were trying to live together as a couple and everything. But he was a young man who had issues. You know, he was like, at that time, what you would consider a street person. He didn't really have a job or anything. I was just looking for love and I was with him. He was very charming. I met him while I was still working. And by the time the baby was born and everything, I had begun using drugs and at some point I lost my job—I didn't have a job anymore.

And somehow we ended up back at the house with my mother. I lost the room because I lost my job and I didn't have the money to pay for the room. And I believe at some point—I think I went on public assistance, but I wouldn't comply—like if you have to go back and recertify. I wouldn't go because I was not being responsible at that time. I was about 22 years old, I was using drugs and I was not responsible. And I stayed over in the house with my mom— and I was over there and I had a baby and my brothers were there. And there was the same chaos and dysfunction that I had always remembered from childhood—the same thing. The house was open, people would come to buy or drink, or somebody needed a place to stay, you know, they could always find a place to stay there. And my mother—her disease was getting worse and worse. I remember one time my mother had like a seizure. And at that time we didn't really know that it was really like a stroke. Her alcoholism was ruining her health. And then she started acting really, really strange. My mother was going through a breakdown, and years later we found out that my mother was a paranoid schizophrenic. But I was into my own addiction at this time so I really wasn't paying any attention.

My disease was full-fledged at that time; I didn't have a job anymore. Because when I had the job I was at least able to basically support my habit and I wasn't able to do that anymore. I started shoplifting—and this is the part I was going to leave out—honestly—I wasn't going to talk about this. But I don't know if it's fair if I do leave it out. Anyway, I started shoplifting to support my habit and I got in trouble. When my son was 2 years old, on his birthday, I went shoplifting to shoplift things for his birthday. I got arrested. It was the first time. And his two grandmothers—the father's mother—she came and they let me go because it was my first time. But it was just, you know, the beginning for me. And this happened from the time my son was 2 until the time my son was 8 years old. I was in and out of his life for petty larceny. I was at the local jail—in and out—because of my addiction. I ended up facing state time because I got mixed up with some people, just trying to support my habit—that's all I wanted to do, and I ended up in a sweep—in a drug sweep.

Each time I went, it's in the record—I told those people, "The reason I'm here is because I'm a drug addict. I don't belong here, I don't belong here." They never offered me any treatment. When my daughter was born, she had drugs in her system and I had to leave her in the hospital and that's when they came to me. They acted like I had done something wrong and I know that what happened was wrong, but I didn't feel responsible. I was out of control. I just wanted somebody to help me. And they sent these mean people to tell me that my daughter won't be leaving with me and that I'm the wretched of the earth and that I better do this and I better do that and I better—not how to do this—not "We're going to help you do this. We understand. You have a problem and we're going to do what's necessary to help you get through." Just mean. And I was so scared. I just wanted to die. I didn't know what to do. I really did not have a clue. I was addicted. I was physically addicted. My body was telling me that I needed what I needed. Why didn't they take me from the hospital and put me in rehabilitation? I didn't know what the hell was going on. They took my child and I walked out of the hospital, practically nowhere to go. By that time my mother had gotten evicted from that house. She had a good landlord, but with her disease and his gambling, they weren't paying rent. So she got evicted and she moved in with her sister, which was a total mistake. But that's where I had to go because I didn't have anywhere to go—

I was homeless. I didn't know what to do. And I remember they told me that I had to come to court—that's what they did tell me—"Be at court at 9 o'clock on this day." Was I in court? No. I didn't have money to get there. I was physically ill. I needed to get my next fix. I didn't know what to do. Then my son became a child of neglect but they let me keep him. I still had him for at least another year. And then I had another baby in 15 months.

He was born when I was in jail. He would have been born addicted probably, but I got arrested and that saved him because I spent the entire pregnancy incarcerated. I had these two sons, but my daughter was still in the foster care system, so I came home and I didn't have anywhere to go because I didn't want to go back to my mother's house. Because my mother, at this time, lived in a room. So I went into a shelter with my two sons. I really wanted to do everything I was supposed to do. I had my slate clean and I remember I found a place. And I remember those nuns who ran the shelter, they were saying, "You don't have to take that place. You know, are you sure? You know, you don't have to leave right now. Take your time." And I was like, no, because the kids' father—he had helped me get the place and it was my own place. I thought I was going to be okay, but it was terrible. It was like a little studio. We had to share the bathroom. All these people lived in this place and they had a lot of drugs in that house. And I succumbed to that after a few months. It was over for me. I was not in any treatment program or anything like that. And I lost those two boys. They had to remove them because I wasn't complying. They kept saying, "Get into it." One time, this woman had called me and she said, "I want to come and pick you up and take you to a treatment." I had got my little stuff together and this woman came to our house. The woman who was supposed to come didn't come. Instead, a woman came to take my kids that day and I ran with my children. She came with the police—stormed in with the police. I'm thinking I'm on my way to get some help and she came with the police to take my children and I ran with them. It was really crazy. I don't know where I thought I was going. And I took my children to a woman's house and this woman was a nice woman, too. And she said, "Okay, I'll go to court and take your children for you until you get yourself together." I didn't want these people from Child Protection Services to just take them like that because they were being so cruel to me, why would I want them to have them. But the woman called them. She probably got scared. You know, she knew I had ran with them and she had called when I went to the store to get my baby some milk, and when I came back those people had come and got those kids. They were coming down the stairs with my baby and my son. And that was like the worst day of my life because my son, he just wailed—the 8-year-old. They didn't say nothing to me. They just took the kids. After that, I contacted them to find out about my children. It's like no one even cared about me. And I was charged with neglect, not abuse. I never beat them—you know, I really tried to take care of those kids. But they didn't belong with me. It's just that the way it happened was wrong.

So I was still out there and, you know, I really had lost everything. I didn't care what happened to me—I was just so down. And it was just a very bad area. I was just hoping something would happen to me. But what did happen was I got caught up in a drug sweep and that was the turning point. That was in 1992, and I had to go to prison. And, by the time I made it upstate, they offered me an alternative because it was a first time and they said I could go into this boot camp and it was called shock incarceration. And I did that and I know when I was in prison my whole life passed before me because I knew I didn't belong in a place like that. I could not even believe where I was at. But once I got my strength and I had gone through withdrawal, which was terrible, I knew that that was it for me. One way or the other, I would not return to that life. You know, it really didn't have everything to do with my children, it had everything to do with me, because I didn't want to live anymore. So at that boot camp, and everything, that's where I learned that I had a disease. You would learn why you're the way you are. And I found out that I had a disease called drug addiction and that I was accountable, but I wasn't responsible. I had made a decision when I left there that I would get help. So that's what I did. I came out and my godmother, the surrogate mother whom I had known since I was 7 when my mother lived in that rooming house in Eastbay—she let me stay with her. And I stayed there and I got involved with the fellowship and my kids were away. I went into the treatment program. And I had supervised visits with the kids.

When I came home from the boot camp I was eligible for Social Services because my kids were in the foster care system. They paid my rent, they gave me food stamps. You know, just for me, as one person. I didn't have to deal with Social Services on my own because when there were problems and I found myself running up against a brick wall I would just go to my counselor. The people would advocate for me. And I always think of how there are so many people who don't have anybody to advocate for them. If you don't have anybody to advocate for you, you're in trouble. I don't care how articulate you are.

A lot of times you have everything you need, but they'll say, "This is not good enough. Go back and get the . . . " It was always a problem—like a runaround. My counselors taught me how to send things certified. And I had to learn how to deal with the system and the paperwork. And how to, basically I guess, just have some patience.

I had two very good social workers at Social Services with the Child Protective Services. Those women really believed in me, and they really treated me like a human being. They knew there was a problem that needed to be addressed. They never judged—they weren't mean or anything. I trusted them and they helped me a lot. Those two women did a great job. I went into the treatment program in order to satisfy Family Court because they said I needed to complete that. And it was good I did—I needed that. I finished in 10 months. And I thought they were rushing me. But I was doing what I had to do and I got out in 10 months and then I went back to court.

I was at this woman's house. And the judge told me that the last thing that I needed to do was provide housing for my children, and I was, "Well, how in the world am I going to do that?" And I went back to Family Services and explained to them and they told me to find an apartment and everything and they would help me. And I did—I found an apartment. I got the apartment and the kids were reunited, and that was the start for me. That was 1994. I started school in September of 1994. My kids came home in June of 1994 and I started school full time in September.

It was wonderful and it was scary. I had not a clue of how to parent. I was in the after-care program at this point, over at Family Services. So I was in individual therapy and counseling once a week. And I also was in parenting and the kids were in counseling. We needed a lot of support because to bring us together required a lot of hands. And our family therapist—she helped me a lot with parenting. I was in parenting for 2 or 3 years and I would be in parenting right now if I had the time in my schedule. Because it's just been a learning process. You know, it's only been 6 years.

When the kids came home, I knew that public assistance was not what I wanted with my life. I've always worked, from when I was 14. And I wanted to go back to work, but I knew that I was not going to earn enough money to provide funds and I said, "Well, I'm going to college." So I went and there were bumps all along the way—there were always obstacles. The Department of Social Services paid for child care and transportation. They didn't pay for my college tuition. But they allowed me not to work. They would allow, I think, 2 years of training while they still had that. I just made it because when I graduated in 1996, they stopped that.

But I got my associate's degree in business, word processing. I graduated in May and by August, I had a full-time job. I've been there ever since.

If Social Services had not been able to pay for child care and transportation, I don't know what I would have done. I needed to go to college; I knew I needed those computer skills, which I did not have. I didn't want to go into training—I had been in training, I had all that already. I needed to get a degree. And I tried to go back to school. I enrolled and got a scholarship. Then all these things happened. I found not that my housing situation was unstable. My mother lost her leg that year, and I could not concentrate. I was blocked. I could not go forward. And I got through all that and now, what is this, the year 2000. Time has gone so quickly. That's why I want to be in school. I want to finish school. That's what I know I want to do.

I was in that apartment for about 9 or 10 months. One day there was a knock on the door and a lawyer came and said that it was an illegal residence and that it was going into foreclosure and that I would have to move, even though I had a lease and even though I had all these papers that said everything was legal, and even though the people at Family Services had helped me get into this apartment. These things still happened because there were a lot of people out there taking advantage of people in situations such as mine. And I had to move. That was in '95, and I went to court and they just gave me a little more time, but the property did not belong to the people and I did have to move. I found another place. However, I was desperate and I dealt with the same individual who put me in the first apartment because I couldn't find anything else, and I moved into another situation where, even though the apartment was in the landlord's home, it wasn't considered legal as far as the zoning board and the neighbors and everything—they didn't like that. And I had to move again within 6 months or so; that was very upsetting to me. I was in school full time during all of this. I was in school full time and it was just very, very hectic, trying to find a place, trying to go to school, taking care of the children—and it was just almost too much for me to bear. And then my counselor told me about a program which would offer housing but there were a lot of stipulations attached to it. It was for families who need support. They would offer case management and tutoring and, you know, all of these support systems to help this family settle in. And it was good—in the beginning it was a very good program. We moved into a very nice house, and this was the first time I had lived in a house—ever. I had never lived in a house, and we had our own privacy. There was a yard and it was a very nice neighborhood. The school system was excellent. And everybody was very happy—we were so happy. The interviewing process to move into this house was very, very intensive. It took about 3 months and they were very selective.

They wanted to know everything about me—my family, my friends, and everybody—which wasn't a problem because, you know, there was nothing for me to hide so I was very open and honest with them. I didn't understand at that time that that program was geared for people who were very needy. I had to leave because they just felt that I was not needy enough, you know, to remain there. But it was a very confusing time for me and difficult because I had thought that programs were designed for people to progress and I never imagined that my progress would actually hinder me.

I never thought that I would get evicted because I was graduating from college and I was doing well at my job. I always would say to them, "If I needed any assistance, by all means I would let you know. But if I'm able to go into the classroom and talk to my child's teacher about my child, I don't see any reason why you should be there—unless I wasn't able to do that." And that was a problem for them—they wanted "hands on" in every aspect of my life, and it was stagnating and demeaning to me. I was very disillusioned at that time about what the programs were really meant to do. How do you ever get from point A to point Z if people just won't let you? I had bought a car—I was fortunate enough to finance a car through my credit union and when I told the case manager, she said, "Well, why do you need a car?" And I said, "Excuse me, why do I need a car? Because I'm a single mother, I have three children, I have a job, okay, and it's a necessity. It's a Ford Escort, and it's a used vehicle."

I left there, and found a house in Eastbay. It took a whole year— I was listed with every real estate broker in this county and I started to look elsewhere as well. The housing situation over the past 6 months to a year has been really tight. And everybody knows it. And a lot of the places that I have been shown—they were bad—they were really, really bad—I wouldn't mind taking a step back in my life, but not 25 steps back—you know—it would not have been good for me or my children. Okay? So a lot of places I could not even accept—it was unacceptable—it was slum, unlivable, deplorable. And there were so many people out there taking advantage—just taking advantage. And once again, Family Services—they worked really, really closely with me, but I can tell you right now, they were not able, with all their resources, to help me find anything. And something that I could afford. What happened was, I had been talking to a lot of people, doing a lot of networking. Everywhere I would go, you know, people I would meet—I would let them know about the situation. And someone from over at the college just happened to hear that her colleague's husband's mother had passed and there was a house and she said, "You really should go and talk to them." And, you know, at that point, I don't know, I was really so very, very down and felt, you know, "I'm not going to get it." I was really starting to lose my faith and my drive, and I was really tired, I was almost ready to give up. And she said, "Just go." And I went home, and I prayed and I just got my strength and I went. And I was honest with the lady and I told her that, you know, everything that I was dealing with—that I was on Section 8—and that was another problem— another program that has come under a lot of scrutiny. For some reason a lot of people don't want to deal with them. There's too much involved, too much to do. They don't want to deal with Section 8. I was very up front with her. I said, "I have Section 8 and this is the situation. I can only afford this." And that is very intrusive, you know, for a lot of landlords—that's why they don't want to deal with Section 8. The application is very intensive, extensive. So she said, "Okay, well, I'll talk to my husband." And then—at that point, it was just, you know, I said, "Okay, well, whatever's going to be is going to be. I'm not going to worry myself anymore." Because I was really getting very sick. I was going into a depression over this because I didn't know where I was going to live, I didn't know what was going to happen. I didn't know where we would end up and that's not a good feeling, not knowing where you're going to be tomorrow. And I met with them and I met with her husband and he agreed based on, largely in part, a very good reference from the other colleague, about who I am as a person, and they were very happy to have me as a tenant.

I pay $1,300 a month in rent; I pay almost half my salary in rent. That's why I'm eligible for Section 8.

Back in 1994, while I was in the women's program, there were these Section 8 applications going around. At the last minute, I filled in one because I always wanted to avail myself of opportunities, and when I got the application I was like, "Oh, this would be great because I know my family's coming together and I'm going to have to provide housing and this is something that I could be eligible for." So I filled in the application. That was October 1994, and I rushed to get it in because I think it was the deadline by the time I even knew about this application. So I got that in and I went on with my life and everything. And I was on Social Services after I completed that program. That's how my rent was paid. You know, I got the food stamps and they paid the rent, and I was a full-time student taking advantage of the training program which I don't believe they even have anymore. So I really availed myself of these opportunities at the right time and I'm very, very grateful. That was in 1994.

To keep on getting Section 8, you have to get letters from schools. You have to bring in pay stubs. And the thing about that program also is that if you get a raise, they go up on the rent. So that's why I'm going back to school because I really can't see any way out of my situation until I'm able to advance myself where I can make enough money to buy a house because, even with Section 8, if I get a raise then my rent goes up, so I'm never able to save money—I'm just always in the same spot.

When I moved into this home in Eastbay, I explained all about Section 8 to the landlord. I said, "You know Section 8 did get a bad name by some people, but it's really a good program." And it really is. It protects the landlord and it protects the tenant because they have a separate lease and another contract that says—you know, the landlord has to keep this property in livable condition. If there's a problem, they have to fix it. If the tenant is abusing the property, then the landlord is protected. So the program is really good. I explained that. But a lot of landlords were saying, "No, no, no," that they didn't want to deal with Section 8 and I believe that maybe that's why—they didn't want people telling them—"You fix this property, or else." And not only that, I think there may be some people who don't want to pay taxes.

When you work in Section 8, the government pays a third of my rent or something like that. If you're on Social Services, they pay the entire rent, but if you work, they pay like a third of the rent, or something, directly to the landlord. Section 8 will only allow so much—say like, for a two-bedroom, they'll only allow like $1,080 or something like that and utilities have to be included so that's another thing that landlords don't like because they want to charge more—they want to charge $1,150 and they want you to pay your own utilities—so they don't want Section 8 telling them how much they can charge for their property. That's what happened—people want to charge all this money for these properties because they know that people are desperate. Section 8—they're there to protect tenants and they do, but what's happening is there are a lot of landlords now who just say, "No, I won't deal with them. I just want cash." And they can get it, they can get it.

And now, after I get my next degree, I want a better job. I want to teach. I thought I wanted to teach business education because that's what I've done all my life—so I might as well keep doing that. Or teach in the adult education program—something of that nature. Because I'm really good with people. I want to—I just want to be able to provide for myself and my family without any assistance. You know, things of that nature. That's what I want to do. I just want to live, you know, I just want to live. I know life is full of challenges and changes and I'm not afraid of that anymore. I've been doing that all of my life—probably since I was born. I can adapt to any situation. You know, and I've turned all the negatives into positives. When I started to give up with this bad housing situation, I regrouped and I was, "How in the world can you come so far and give up now? You've been through things unimaginable and now, how can you give up because you can't find a way to live? Regroup and troop on." And that's what I'm doing.

## WHAT OUR CLIENTS TEACH US

Both Paula and Theresa have successfully struggled to overcome problems in living. For both, the search for a safe, private environment—a home—has been a compelling life theme. Each helps us understand the meaning within a life's journey of feeling secure, hopeful, proud in a physical space called "home." Related to this are four common themes expressed in these narratives.

1. *For Paula and Theresa, the search for home has been part of the quest for realized dreams and a dominant contributor to self-image and self-esteem* For Theresa, the search is linked to early experiences. From the rooming house room so small her brothers could not live with her mother to the stigma

of living in a "welfare" motel to the joy of having a real apartment to the trauma of being evicted from it, Theresa's childhood is constructed around memories of the struggle to have "something of our own." Memories of her young adulthood similarly center on her housing conditions. While other aspects of her life are deeply troubling—her mother's and her own addictions, her criminal activity, incarcerations, removal of her children—the dominant ongoing theme is that of securing and losing housing and its impact on her and her family.

For Paula, reconstructing the physical context of her childhood—a house and a yard—becomes a redemptive life goal. She not only desires the purchase of her own house as a way to achieve a secure environment for her daughter, but as a way to gain respect from and be more like her adoptive parents and family with whom she "always felt like the odd man out." She comments that her parents did not believe she could buy a house. Proudly she shares how she negotiates the purchase "all by myself." When she finally closes on it, she "ran back to them" (her parents), and says, "I'm a homeowner." She then reports, "They were happy for me, that I did get the house. They were proud in their own way."

2. *Both of these mothers understand the connection between housing conditions and the development of their children.* Paula moves back to her parents' home because she cannot find housing appropriate to raising her baby; Theresa attributes her son's problematic behavior to her unstable housing situation. Both long for a safe, spacious home to foster their children's healthy growth. They intuitively know what research has found—that substandard housing and homelessness are linked with physical and emotional disorders (Sharfstein, Sandel, & Kahn, 2001; Fitzgerald, 2001; Hwang, 2001). Children who are homeless face serious challenges—educational, social, physical, psychological (Nunez, 2004), and have been shown to be much more likely to suffer from asthma, middle ear infections, gastrointestinal disorders, speech problems, anxiety, depression, and developmental delays (Better Homes Fund, 1999; Redlener & Johnson, 1999).

Particularly challenging is ensuring a quality educational experience for children who are homeless. The McKinney-Vento Act (P.L. 100-77; 42 U.S.C. § 11435 (2)) as amended in 2001 protects their educational rights. Among other provisions, the act requires that local educational agencies make it possible for children who are relocated to a shelter or motel to remain in their school of origin unless the child's parent or guardian objects. Schools must name a staff person to serve as a liaison to assist these children. Barriers to staying in school or enrolling in a new one (for example, the absence of proof of residence or an immunization history) must be removed.

Theresa's and Paula's children, when they were threatened by homelessness, were in a situation shared by far too many children in America. A landmark Urban Institute study (Burt, Aron, Douglas, Valente, Lee, & Iwen, 1999) found that about 1.35 million children are homeless each year, and 60 percent of them were very young—between birth and age 8.

The relationship between lack of housing and involvement with the child welfare system has been established (Courtney, McMurty, & Zinn, 2004; Culhane, Webb, Grim, Metraux, & Culhane, 2003). Recognizing this powerful and costly connection, Congress in 1990 authorized the Family Unification Program (FUP), as part of the Omnibus National Affordable Housing Act (P.L. 101-624). The FUP program provides Section 8 Housing Choice Vouchers for families who are in danger of having their children placed in foster care because of the threat of homelessness and for families whose children cannot be returned from foster care because the parent is unable to locate suitable housing. FUP facilitates collaboration between housing and child welfare agencies and reflects the "housing plus services" model being strongly recommended as the most effective approach to supporting vulnerable families (Cohen, Mulray, Tull, White, & Crowley, 2004).

3. *Paula and Theresa help us learn what it means to receive benefits under housing programs.* Theresa receives case management services from a supported housing program. While she welcomes the housing she receives, she eventually leaves the program—and the house—because she no longer feels she needs close supervision of her and her children's lives. "They," she reported, "wanted 'hands on' in every aspect of my life, and it was stagnating and demeaning to me." With the assistance of a Section 8 voucher, she obtains a house to rent on her own. We learn from her about the need for ongoing income documentation and the frustrating relationship between income and rent: "Even with Section 8, if I get a raise then my rent goes up, so I'm never able to save money—I'm just always in the same spot." She also gives us some insight as to why landlords are often reluctant to accept Section 8 tenants— for example, they can't hide rental income, and their property must meet federal standards. Yet, Theresa secured her house by helping her landlord see advantages in renting to a Section 8 tenant, including the fact that her rental payments are supported by the housing authority.

Paula brings us into the world of public housing where tenancy is guaranteed as long as there is compliance with the lease. She gives her perspectives on the negatives in this system, for example, the potential for intergenerational dependency, substance abuse, overcrowding. Paula notes that many residents were employed and that having residents as housing authority staff can improve landlord-tenant communication. She herself was for a time a housing authority employee. "I was the first resident they did that for, where the residents are the ones who run the program, who work with the people, instead of having someone from the outside do it." (Tenant-housing authority communication also is facilitated by the required election of tenants to the authority's board of commissioners and the HUD-mandated organization of a residents' advisory council.) Paula recommends on-site activities and services as a means to enhance community identity and provide an outlet for youth. Her perspective is supported by the recently reported success of such on-site services (Famuliner, 1999; Metsch et al., 2001). Paula eventually buys her own house, using the federal government's direct home ownership assistance. (The government, through the Rural Housing Service and through HUD, provides direct mortgage loans at low interest rates or guarantees private loans with low interest rates. Through these home ownership programs, mortgage payments, property taxes, and insurance costs are set at a fixed percentage (20–28 percent) of household income.)

4. *Both Paula and Theresa show us how external supports and internal resources help the economically dislocated to cope with life challenges. Both are single parents with a history of problematic relationships with their families of origin.* Both have self-images in part formed by negative feedback from the external and familial environments. Both have life histories marked by economic uncertainty—Paula is currently facing unemployment and has not yet applied for unemployment insurance. Denial may be playing some part in the delay, as might her optimism fueled largely by faith.

And yet, while vulnerable, both exhibit great strength. They have made use of supports appropriate to their needs and personalities. For Paula, reluctant to be open with many others, support has come from her church, her deep faith, and her trusting relationship with her boss. Theresa is far more involved in helping systems because of the nature of her past problems; she has made good use of resources for vulnerable families. A family services agency has, in fact, been her ongoing mainstay. Education as a means to a better life is a perception shared by Paula and Theresa. Both had the merits of academic achievement emphasized and reinforced in childhood. Theresa's mother encouraged her to read; Paula was a "bookworm." Both, despite many obstacles, achieved their associate's degrees and aspire to further education. Their resiliency is reinforced by their sense of themselves as the instrument of their own futures. They are in the process of triumphing, and their homes are a testament to their for coping and growth.

Both narratives suggest the effect on individuals of the absence of a comprehensive national housing policy. In many regions, escalating housing costs and a scarcity of housing stock have squeezed low- and even moderate- and middle-income families out of the housing market. In fact, shelters for the homeless count among their residents people who are employed but can't afford local housing costs. The current federal focus on household-based rent subsidy programs over public housing starts may not be the most effective policy choice of the existing paucity of affordable housing. In the absence of a major national commitment to combating homelessness, we can anticipate increased use of illegal housing, more overcrowding of extended family members in one dwelling, enhanced demands on emergency housing resources, and an increase in people who are homeless in the streets of our cities and suburbs. The potential economic consequences include the escalating emergency housing costs, for example, a motel room for a mother and two children costs about $3,000 for 1 month in one New York suburban county; a shelter for that same family can cost as much as $4,000 per month. There are also the costs attendant to the social, psychological, and physical consequences of inadequate housing and fears of homelessness so vividly described by our clients.

# UNEMPLOYMENT INSURANCE

## THE LEGAL CONTEXT

### Authorizing Legislation

Unemployment insurance is a critical fail-safe mechanism for individuals who become unemployed. The objective of this federal-state compensation program is to grant applicants cash benefits. Unemployment insurance payments (benefits) was developed to provide temporary financial assistance to unemployed workers who meet the requirements of State law. (Department of Labor, 2005)

The federal-state relationship operates to allow federal guidelines to dictate the way that states administer their individual programs. Assuming that states act in accordance with federal mandates, then, one need simply refer to the prevailing state legislation and its associated regulations. For example, Pennsylvania state's unemployment compensation law spells out relevant definitions (some of which are featured in Box 5.1, as excerpted from 43 P.S. § 753) and the requirement of cooperation with the Department of Labor and other agencies (43 P.S. § 767).

| 5.1 | EXCERPTS OF PENNSYLVANIA STATE UNEMPLOYMENT COMPENSATION LAW |
|---|---|

### § 753. Definitions

(g) "CONTRIBUTIONS" means the money payments required to be paid into the Unemployment Compensation Fund by employers, with respect to employment, which payments shall be used for the creation of financial reserves for the payment of compensation as provided in this act. This meaning includes, where appropriate in the enforcement provisions of this act, payments in lieu of contributions required to be paid by employers operating on a reimbursement basis as provided in Articles X, XI and XII of this act. "Contributions" also means, where appropriate in this act, money payments required to be paid into the Unemployment Compensation Fund by employers as provided in this act.

### § 767. Cooperation with Department of Labor and other agencies

(a) (1)  In the administration of this act, the secretary shall cooperate with the Department of Labor to the fullest extent consistent with the provisions of this act, and shall take such action through the adoption of appropriate rules, regulations, administrative methods and standards, as may be necessary to secure to this Commonwealth and its citizens all advantages available under the provisions of the Social Security Act that relate to unemployment compensation, the Federal Unemployment Tax Act, the Wagner-Peyser Act and the Federal-State Extended Unemployment Compensation Act of 1970.

(2)  In the administration of the provisions of Article IV-A of this act which are enacted to conform with the requirements of the Federal-State Extended Unemployment Compensation Act of 1970, the secretary shall take such action as may be necessary (i) to ensure that the provisions are so interpreted and applied as to meet the requirements of such Federal Act as interpreted by the United States Department of Labor and (ii) to secure to this Commonwealth the full reimbursement of the Federal share of extended and regular benefits paid under this act that are reimbursable under the Federal Act.

(b)  Upon request therefore, the department shall furnish to any agency of the United States charged with the administration of public works or assistance through public employment the name, address, ordinary occupation and employment status of each recipient of compensation, and such recipient's rights as to further compensation under this act.

(c)  The department may make the state's records relating to the administration of this act available to the Railroad Retirement Board, and may furnish the Railroad Retirement Board, at the expense of such board, such copies thereof as the Railroad Retirement Board deems necessary for its purposes.

(d)  The department may afford reasonable cooperation with every agency of the United States charged with the administration of any unemployment insurance law.

## Regulatory Authority

As a state-administered program, unemployment insurance regulations are issued by state administrative agencies. Like their federal counterparts, state agencies are authorized, through their enabling legislation, to promulgate regulations that put legislative intentions into effect. They are published in counterpart state publications, as well. For example, the regulations for Pennsylvania unemployment compensation are initially published in the *Pennsylvania Bulletin*—the state equivalent of the *Federal Register*. The *Bulletin* is a weekly publication of the Commonwealth of Pennsylvania that contains proposed and final actions by the governor and state agencies with regulatory authority. All final actions are later "codified" into the *Pennsylvania Code,* a subject arrangement of all state rules and regulations.

An illustrative Pennsylvania state regulation regarding unemployment insurance appears in Box 5.2.

## Case Law

Regarding eligibility for unemployment insurance, the Pennsylvania decision of *Black Lick Trucking, Inc. v. Unemployment Compensation Board of Review,* presented in Box 5.3, discusses an appeal of an unsuccessful claim of several truck drivers who, in the course of their coal-hauling work, refused to cross a picket line for fear for their safety.

## THE PROGRAM CONTEXT

### Overview

A response to the widespread unemployment during the Great Depression, the Federal-State Unemployment Compensation Program was established as part of the Social Security Act of 1935 (P.L. 74-271, Titles 3, 9, 12).[1] Its purpose was and remains to provide the unemployed with a portion of their previous wages, allowing them time to seek a new position. The benefits were also designed to ensure a flow of consumer dollars into the economy during periods of high unemployment (Blaustein, O'Leary, & Wandner, 2000). Currently, 97 percent of all U.S. wage and salary workers are covered by the federal-state unemployment compensation program established 67 years ago or related federal-state programs for groups not included in the original legislation. In the year 2001, 128 million persons were covered by these programs (U.S. House of Representatives Committee on Ways and Means, 2004). As of 2002, the following categories were not generally covered: agricultural workers on "small"

---

1. The first known unemployment compensation program was introduced in Great Britain in 1911.

| 5.2 | PENNSYLVANIA STATE REGULATION ON UNEMPLOYMENT INSURANCE |

**§ 101.105. Notice of hearing.**

(a) If the Board determines that a further hearing is necessary, the tribunal shall give at least 7 days' notice of the scheduled hearing to the parties and their counsel or authorized agent of record, with specific instructions regarding the date, hour and place of hearing, and specific issues to be covered at the hearing.

(b) If hearings on more than one appeal are to be scheduled and conducted jointly, each party shall be notified in his notice of hearing that a joint hearing will be held, that a single record of the proceedings will be made and that evidence introduced with respect to an appeal will be considered as introduced with respect to all.

**Authority**

The provisions of this § 101.105 amended under sections 203(d) and 505 of the Unemployment Compensation Act (43 P. S. § § 763(d) and 825).

The provisions of this § 101.105 adopted August 26, 1970, effective August 27, 1970, 1 Pa.B. 435; amended April 7, 1989, effective April 8, 1989, 19 Pa.B. 1550. Immediately preceding text appears at serial page (126521).

---

farms; the self-employed; household workers who receive less than $1,000 in wages per quarter from an employer; employees of religious organizations; certain student interns; some alien farm workers; some seasonal workers; services rendered to relatives; and railroad workers.

Unemployment compensation is a compulsory social insurance program. Employers and their employees must participate. Unlike public assistance programs, eligibility is not determined by financial need and other personal or family characteristics; instead, benefits are a right attendant to having worked for a defined period of time for an employer who contributed tax dollars to the program. There are certain standards for initial and ongoing eligibility related to reason for job loss, time employed, wages earned, and evidence of job search activities. These are reflective of this country's emphasis on individual responsibility and its concern that "handouts" will deter people from being productive.

The federal and state governments share responsibility for the program. The U.S. Department of Labor, through its Employment Security Administration, has oversight of the separate programs operated by the 50 states, the District of Columbia, Puerto Rico, and the Virgin Islands. Both federal and state statutes cover these programs. The Federal Unemployment Tax Act (FUTA), first passed in 1939, establishes national standards regarding federal financing, covered employment, and administration. Within these minimum guidelines, states are free to design their own eligibility standards, benefit levels, duration of benefits, and basis for financing the state's contribution to the program. While a states' rights ethos has largely prevailed, expansion of the federal com-

| 5·3 | PENNSYLVANIA COURT DECISION ON ELIGIBILITY FOR UNEMPLOYMENT COMPENSATION |

## BLACK LICK TRUCKING, INC.
## v. UNEMPLOYMENT COMPENSATION BOARD
### 667 A. 2d 454 (1995)

*Summary:* *Claimants were employed by Black Lick as truck drivers to haul coal from Lucerne 6, a Helvetia Coal Company Mine in Kent, Pennsylvania, and Lucerne 8, another Helvetia Coal Company Mine in Clarksburg, Pennsylvania, to the Homer City Generating Station. On May 25, 1993, selected locals of the United Mine Workers of America (UMWA) initiated a work stoppage and established picket lines at the Lucerne 6 and Lucerne 8 mines. Claimants were members of UMWA Local 2364, a local which was not directly involved with the strike. On May 25, 1993, Claimants reported to work but refused to cross the picket lines established by the coal miners at the striking mines, alleging that they feared for their safety. No coal was hauled from the mines at Lucerne 6 and 8 during the work stoppage; however, Black Lick obtained jobs for Claimants hauling stones and other material from June 2, 1993 until October 15, 1993, when they were temporarily laid off due to lack of work. The work stoppage ended on or about December 16, 1993. Claimants filed applications for unemployment benefits but were denied.*

This is an appeal by Black Lick Trucking, Inc. (Black Lick) from an order of the Unemployment Compensation Board of Review (Board), which granted benefits to Robert C. Rhoades, Douglas H. Leightley, Floy L. Fennell, Chris L. Sherba, Donald K. Robertson, Steven L. Krall, Gary A. Everhart, Gary G. Painter, Francis J. Boston, Harold M. Toy and Timothy F. Pavelchick (collectively, Claimants), reversing the referee's order which had denied Claimants benefits under Section 402(d) of the Pennsylvania Unemployment Compensation Law, Act of December 5, 1936, Second Exec. Sess., P.L. (1937) 2897, as amended, 43 P.S. § 802(d).

Section 402(d) provides as follows:

An employee shall be ineligible for compensation for any week—(d) In which his unemployment is due to a stoppage of work, which exists because of a labor dispute (other than a lock-out) at the factory, establishment or other premises at which he is or was last employed: Provided, that this subsection shall not apply if it is shown that (1) he is not participating in, or directly interested in, the labor dispute which caused the stoppage of work, and (2) he is not a member of an organization which is participating, in or directly interested in, the labor dispute which caused the stoppage of work, and (3) he does not belong to a grade or class of workers of which, immediately before the commencement of the stoppage, there were members employed at the premises at which the stoppage occurs, any of who are participating in, or directly interested in, the dispute.

The facts are summarized as follows. Claimants were employed by Black Lick as truck drivers to haul coal from Lucerne 6, a Helvetia Coal Company Mine in Kent, Pennsylvania, and Lucerne 8, another Helvetia Coal Company Mine in Clarksburg, Pennsylvania, to the Homer City Generating Station. On May 25, 1993, selected

*continued*

locals of the United Mine Workers of America (UMWA) initiated a work stoppage and established picket lines at the Lucerne 6 and Lucerne 8 mines. Claimants were members of UMWA Local 2364, a local which was not directly involved with the strike.

On May 25, 1993, Claimants reported to work but refused to cross the picket lines established by the coal miners at the striking mines, alleging that they feared for their safety. No coal was hauled from the mines at Lucerne 6 and 8 during the work stoppage; however, Black Lick obtained jobs for Claimants hauling stones and other material from June 2, 1993 until October 15, 1993, when they were temporarily laid off due to lack of work. The work stoppage ended on or about December 16, 1993.

Claimants filed applications for benefits with the Indiana Job Center, which denied benefits pursuant to Section 402(d). Each of the Claimants appealed and a consolidated hearing was held. During the hearing, Black Lick requested the referee to dismiss the appeal, asserting that all of the Claimants had failed to state a reason for their appeal. However, the referee, although he found that the appeals were proper, issued one decision based upon the representative Claimant (but issued separate orders, one for each Claimant) affirming the Job Center's determination.

Each of the Claimants then appealed to the Board, stating that the reason for filing their appeal was "because of errors of law and fact." The Board reversed the referee and granted benefits, holding that Claimants refused to cross the picket line because of fear for their safety. The Board also concluded that the issues addressed by the referee in his decision were not waived by the Claimants because they had filed proper appeals. Black Lick's appeal to this Court followed.

Black Lick raises four issues: (1) whether the appeal of Claimants from the Job Center to the referee should have been dismissed because Claimants failed to identify any reasons for their appeal; (2) whether the appeal from the referee to the Board should have been dismissed because Claimants did not specify the reason for appeal; (3) whether Claimants refused to cross the picket line because of a reasonable and genuine fear of physical harm; and (4) whether Black Lick was required to demonstrate that continuing work was available when Claimants refused to cross a peaceful picket line.

Regarding the first two issues raised, parties are required to state "the reasons for appeal" when filing an appeal from a decision of the job center to the referee. 34 Pa. Code § 101.81 (governing appeals from the Department). Additionally, appeals from the referee to the Board also require that a reason be stated. See 34 Pa. Code § 101.102 ("Information to be included in appeals from decisions of referees . . . shall conform to the provisions of § 101.82 . . ."). "What is sought by the referee or Board is some indication, however inartfully stated, of precisely what error(s) occurred and where the tribunal should focus its attention." * * *

Black Lick relies [contends] that Claimants' failure to specify the reasons for their appeals waives all of the issues. Employer, however, misconstrues our holding [in the *Merida* decision]. In *Merida,* the job center found that the claimant was ineligible for benefits due to willful misconduct pursuant to Section 402(e), 43 P.S. § 802(e).

A hearing was held before a referee at which the employer's witnesses did not participate, but were present outside of the hearing room. Over an objection by claimant's attorney, a second hearing occurred during which the employer's witnesses were permitted to testify. The referee in affirming the job center, did not address the objection to the second hearing. On appeal to the Board, the claimant merely stated that his reason for appeal was that "he didn't agree with the decision" and did not raise the appropriateness of the second hearing. The Board upheld the referee's decision. . . .

In the appeal now before us, although the Claimants' petitions for appeal from the Job Center did not raise any issue specifically, unlike the facts in *Merida*, the issues which were decided by the Job Center were the same issues addressed by the referee, and were subsequently discussed by the Board. Thus, pursuant to Sections 101.87 and 101.107, the referee and Board correctly considered the Claimants' appeals.

Black Lick also argues that Claimants were participating in the labor dispute which caused the work stoppage because they voluntarily choose not to cross the picket line and therefore, were participants in the strike. Specifically, Black Lick asserts that no substantial evidence exists to support the Board's finding that the Claimants' failure to cross the picket lines was due to a reasonable fear of violence. We are constrained to agree.

Claimants are ineligible for benefits under Section 402(d) unless, inter alia, they demonstrate that they did not participate in or become directly interested in the labor dispute; that they are not members of the organization that participated or was directly interested in the dispute. Furthermore, claimants who voluntarily refuse to cross peaceful picket lines are considered to be participating in the strike and are ineligible for unemployment benefits.

In *Unemployment Compensation Board of Review v. G. C. Murphy Co.*, this Court set forth the criteria on which to decide what actions by strikers constitute sufficient evidence to cause a non-striker's refusal to cross a picket line to be voluntary. . . .

Applying the law to the facts of the instant case, we conclude that Claimants have failed to prove by substantial evidence that the picket lines were other than peaceful. The record shows that Rhoades testified that he had not even gone to the mines, the site of the pickets, and that he had merely been verbally threatened. Boston testified that he did not cross the picket line because he had heard rumors of violence at the picket lines, although no witness testified that any violence occurred. Pavelchick and Krall did not testify to any threats or acts of violence at the picket lines. (Only four Black Lick Claimants testified). Lastly, John Smith, a Bud Davis employee, testified that he went to the job site where the picket line was established and that the strikers verbally threatened him.

Based upon this testimony, the Board found that "Claimants . . . did not cross the picket lines because they were fearful for their safety and their families [sic] safety." (Finding of Fact No. 8) Although Claimants' fears may have been genuine, the record lacks any evidence that would support a finding that the threats and rumors of violence were coupled with a show of force on the picket line, which is a requirement in establishing that a refusal to cross the picket lines was involuntary. Thus, Claimants have failed to prove that they involuntarily refused to cross the picket lines. . . . Accordingly, Claimants are ineligible for benefits and the decisions of the Board are reversed.

ponent has been embraced during periods of national economic stress. Both the federal-state extended benefits program and federally administered state loans fund resulted from the recessions of the 1970s and 1980s. Federal law and regulations also expanded coverage or changed procedures for certain vulnerable or overlooked categories of workers. For example, in 2000, legislation passed regarding Indian tribes, domestic violence survivors, and new parents (Kenyon & Lancaster, 2001).

Under FUTA, the federal government collects a tax from covered employers. This amount is equal to 6.2 percent of their federal taxable payroll. However, states that have complied with federal guidelines regarding the unemployment insurance system receive a federal tax credit of 5.4 percent. All states meet these guidelines, and therefore the actual tax rate is 0.8 percent of the federal taxable payroll, with the wage-base cutoff at $7,000 per worker. The federal tax dollars cover administrative expenses and also pay for the federal share of the extended benefits program. Excess revenues are kept in a trust fund. This fund covers loans granted to states whose own trust funds are no longer solvent. State tax systems vary; their taxable wage base can be, and in many states is, above the federal $7,000 level.

The actual tax paid by each employer is related to each employer's "experience rating," that is, the amount of benefits that have been paid to an employer's former employees. Just as with auto insurance, rates rise as the insurance is used. Those who dismiss fewer employees—just as those who are in fewer accidents—are "rewarded" by paying lower unemployment insurance taxes.

The federal treasury's Unemployment Trust Fund contains all unemployment insurance monies. It holds the states' accounts, the Railroad Administration account, the Federal Employment Security Administration Account (covers administrative costs); the Extended Employment Compensation Account (for the federal share of the extended benefits program); the federal unemployment account (monies loaned to state programs); and the Federal Employees' Compensation Account (covers federal civilian and military employees' unemployment insurance programs). States use the interest from the Unemployment Trust Fund to pay benefits to their residents.

While the unemployment insurance system has expanded since 1935 to cover nearly all wage and salary workers, the rate of usage of the benefit by the unemployed has decreased. Whatever measure of recipiency is used (for example, the ratio of U.S claimants to the total number of unemployed, known as the IU/TU), long-term declines are found (Bassi & McMurrer, 1997; Wandner & Stettner, 2000). The IU/TU was only 44 percent in 2002 (U.S. House of Representatives Committee on Ways and Means, 2004), down from a peak of 81 percent in 1975. While some unemployed persons do not meet eligibility standards, many more than this figure do. The question of why the decline—despite the program's nonstigmatizing social insurance status—has been puzzling. Some studies have shown that some persons do not apply because they believe they are ineligible (Wandner & Stettner, 2000). Others studies have found that higher wage earners, those employed in manufacturing, union members, those who live in the Northeast, and those who are job losers (not leavers) are more likely to receive benefits (Barsi & McMurrer, 1997). Shifts in some of these characteristics—fewer persons employed in manufacturing, geographic dispersion—have been cited as contributing to the downward trend in participation rates (U.S. House of Representatives Committee on Ways and Means, 2000). Other proposed factors discouraging application include recent changes in states' eligibility criteria and in federal rules (for example, taxation of benefits).

The implications of low utilization go beyond the individuals who are not receiving the benefits to which they are entitled. The economy is affected because fewer dollars are available to and spent by the unemployed. The extended benefits program is also affected, since the trigger for its implementation is the state's insured employment rate. It is important that the country's workforce be informed about their rights and responsibilities with regard to unemployment compensation.

## Application and Eligibility

Newly unemployed persons apply for unemployment compensation at the office of the state agency responsible for this program. Application should be made as close as possible to the time of separation from work. Under the federal-state partnership, each state establishes its own application procedures. Both telephone and in-person interviews are conducted; in many jurisdictions, a face-to-face first interview is followed by telephone contacts. Establishing eligibility is the responsibility of the claimant. Documentation must be provided to confirm identity, employment history, earnings, and citizenship status. The applicant is asked to bring such items as a driver's license, a Social Security card, photocopies of paycheck stubs, W-2 forms, and/or a voter registration card. Once a claim is filed and approved, the first benefit check is usually received within a few weeks.

If the state agency decides that the applicant is not entitled to benefits, the applicant receives a written notice of determination, which includes the reason for the denial, any actions the applicant could take to become eligible (for example, provide additional documentation), and due process appeal procedures.

Under the federal-state arrangement, the states are responsible for setting specific eligibility rules. However, there are basic guidelines each state must adhere to. These include the following:

1. The applicant must demonstrate that she or he has earned the right to the benefit by having earned a specific amount and/or worked a specified period of time during a one-year "base period" (usually defined as the first 4 out of the past 5 calendar quarters). States vary in the particular requirements; for example, some calculate the income base using a flat figure, others a multiple of the quarter in which the highest wages were earned, still others use a multiple of the weekly benefit amount.

2. This is a social insurance program. Therefore, establishing eligibility does not involve financial means testing. Income from rental properties, bank

savings, stock dividends, the value of property, and earnings of other family members are not considered in assessing eligibility.

3. Work performed during the qualifying base period must be done for a covered employer. Almost all wage and salary workers in the United States are covered by the program established in the 1930s and several other special programs introduced since that time to insure specific categories of employees. Among those usually not covered by any form of unemployment compensation are the following: the self-employed, student interns, seasonal camp workers, faculty during summer months between semesters, professional athletes off between sport seasons, illegal aliens, members of the judiciary, elected officials and legislators, employees of nonprofit agencies that employ fewer than four persons, some agricultural and domestic service workers, and those who provide care for relatives.

4. The applicant's unemployment must not be related to the quality of the worker's performance, the worker's desire to leave for another position or for marital or family responsibilities, or the worker's physical or mental disability. (The latter two are covered by Family Leave and Disability programs.) If a worker is discharged because of misconduct, quits without a just cause, or is out of work because of a strike or lockout, he or she will probably be ineligible for unemployment compensation. Those who lose a position because of such no-fault conditions as cutbacks, closings, reorganizations, or sexual harassment will most likely receive compensation.

5. The applicant must be available for and actively looking for work throughout the entire compensation period. "Availability" includes continuing to be in physical or mental health. "Actively seeking" involves providing evidence that the recipient is actually searching for work. In some states, it also may require registering for work at the State Employment Service. In addition, recipients cannot refuse a job that relates to their previous employment experience and pays a wage equal to the prevailing compensation for such work. Some states disqualify recipients who after 13 weeks refuse a job offer if they can do the work and if the pay rate is at least 80 percent of the individual's high quarter wages during the base period.

Several contemporary programs provide unemployment compensation for categories of employees not covered by the 1935 legislation and others who might not be eligible. The state unemployment agency processes these applications. The programs include:

- *Unemployment compensation for ex-service members* (UCX) Applicants must have an honorable discharge from duty and have served a full term or been released early for a qualifying reason.
- *Unemployment compensation for federal employees* (UCFE) Those who apply must bring proof of federal wages, the notification of personnel action, and the "notice to federal employees about unemployment compensation."

- *Unemployment compensation for those affected by trade readjustment* The Federal Trade Act established Trade Adjustment Assistance (TAA) to provide benefits to those who lost jobs because of trade agreements. The North American Free Trade Agreement (NAFTA) Transitional Adjustment Assistance program was specifically developed for those who lost positions because of the impact on their employers of increased imports from Mexico or Canada or because their employer moved production to one of these countries. A TAA benefit is granted after regular unemployment assistance benefits are exhausted, and a Petition for Trade Adjustment Assistance or a Petition for NAFTA Transitional Adjustment Assistance is filed and approved.
- *Self-employment assistance* for those eligible for regular unemployment benefits and likely not to readily be reemployed is an optional program found in several states. Instead of looking for work, the beneficiary spends time starting a business. Technical assistance and other educational supports are provided.
- *Disaster Unemployment Assistance* is for those whose unemployment or ability to earn a living through self-employment activities is a direct outcome of a major disaster. Applicants can receive this assistance only if they are not eligible for regular unemployment insurance.
- *Coverage for those unemployed because of domestic violence* Some states are now specifically including the need to leave work because of health and safety concerns because of domestic violence as "good cause" for unemployment status. These states are California, Colorado, Wyoming, Oregon, Maine, New Hampshire, Connecticut, New York, North Carolina, and New Jersey (National Organization for Women, 2000).
- *Extended Benefits Program* is designed for those who have exhausted regular benefits during a period of high unemployment. Recipients are not automatically eligible. States inform current recipients of the program following the passage of legislation authorizing the potential additional benefits period. The eligibility criteria differ from the regular program; base period earnings and time qualifications differ, and there are more stringent work search rules.

## Benefits

Unemployment compensation is provided in the form of a weekly cash benefit. The minimum and maximum amounts received vary by state. The benefit an individual is granted is determined by the amount of income the individual earned during the qualifying base period. That the benefit is linked to wage underscores unemployment compensation as an earned right.

The benefit has been developed to replace some, but not all, lost wages. From the inception of the program in the United States, the acceptable wage replacement rate has been seen as equivalent to one-half of the unemployed person's prior weekly full-time wage (up to a state-determined maximum)

(O'Leary & Rubin, 1997). Most often used in computing the benefit are the wages from the base period quarter in which earnings were highest.

Recipients, after they establish eligibility, don't automatically get the benefit. They have to call or send in claims on an ongoing regular basis, usually weekly or biweekly. No claim is filed during weeks when a recipient works more than 3 days or earns more than the maximum benefit. When the beneficiary is reemployed, he or she stops filing a claim. Benefits were made taxable by the Tax Reform Act of 1986 (P.L. 99-514). In some situations, 15 percent of the benefit check is withheld for tax purposes.

**Benefit Duration**    Under federal law, benefits can be given for up to 39 weeks—26 weeks of regular benefits followed by 13 weeks of extended benefits. This federal-state extended benefit program is available to states when unemployment rates reach proscribed conditions. Two states—Massachusetts and Washington—provide 30 weeks of regular benefits, and some states have taken advantage of a law enacted in 1992, the Unemployment Compensation Amendments of 1992 (P.L. 102-318). This legislation provides an alternative formula for triggering extended benefits and also permits an optional 7 weeks added to the 13 weeks of extended benefits. It is important to note we are speaking of maximum duration; most states connect the length of time benefits are received by an individual to past earnings or length of time employed— minimum duration ranges from 4 weeks to the full 26. Here again we have a clear demonstration of the benefit as an earned right.

Inherent in duration limits is the issue of how long wages should be replaced. The program has, after all, from its inception been conceptualized as short term, one existing to give the beneficiary an opportunity to find work. A covert issue is not encouraging dependency. While extension of the state-funded regular benefit period has been proposed, currently there appears to be consensus that a half-year of coverage (26 weeks) is adequate unless unemployment rates are high (in which case the Extended Benefits Program can be used). Support for the current duration plan is found in data on the average benefit duration; in 2002, for example, it was 17 weeks (U.S. House of Representatives Committee on Ways and Means, 2004). There is always going to be the question of what to do to assist those who lose jobs and cannot find replacement work within the allotted time. Some people—those who do not qualify for other income support programs—could find themselves with no source of support.

Once recipients complete the maximum time to which they are entitled to compensation, they can become eligible again for this benefit only by obtaining a job in covered employment and accruing the requisite time and earnings. The percentage of recipients who use up benefits is termed the "exhaustion rate." Generally, the higher the unemployment rate, the higher the exhaustion rate, because jobs are less available. The briefer the potential benefit duration, the higher the exhaustion rate, because the recipient has less time to find a new job (Woodbury& Rubin, 1997). This suggests that the longer a person has to find employment, the less likely all benefits will be exhausted (because presumably the beneficiary is looking for and finds work before benefits run out). Whether the availability of the benefit discourages the job search and return to employment status has been a major theme in the discourse on unemployment insurance. Research has suggested that the average unemployment insurance recipient does not abuse the system (Spiezia, 2000). One analysis has found that extending duration by one week increases usage only by one more day or less (Woodbury & Rubin, 1997, p. 246).

**Benefit Amount** The recipient's benefit is not a dollar-for-dollar replacement of lost wages. Instead, the general coverage replacement is 50 percent of the pretax weekly wage up to a state-determined maximum. Because of this maximum, higher earners receive a lower replacement wage, and the national average weekly benefit amount is lower than 50 percent of the average weekly covered wage.

Actual minimum and maximum benefit amounts are determined by the states, and there is a broad range among them. For example, in the year 2002, the minimum weekly benefit ranged from $1 in New Jersey to $107 in Rhode Island; the maximum went from $133 in Puerto Rico to $760 in Massachusetts (U.S. House of Representatives Committee on Ways and Means, 2004). In setting the maximum benefit, one frequently used guideline is two-thirds of the average weekly wage in the state's unemployment insurance covered employment. In setting the minimum benefit, several states set it at a level that exceeds the 50 percent wage replacement guideline for low-income workers. This recognizes the tremendous financial impact of unemployment on low-wage earners, many of whom have no other source of income.

While the benefit amount is most often determined solely by prior earnings level, about one-fourth of the states factor in the individual's number of dependents. Qualifying dependents for a dependent allowance include children under 18, older children with disabilities, and nonemployed spouses. If both spouses are unemployed, only one can claim dependents. The additional benefit is generally a fixed amount per dependent.

The issue of the benefit level involves complex questions of equity, adequacy, and incentive (Jones, 1997, p. 2416). Using a state wage average does not account for an individual's or a family's needs. Can a partial time-limited wage replacement really fulfill the program's mission of preventing poverty? There is some evidence that more attention needs to be paid to compensation through long spells of unemployment (Woodbury & Rubin, 1997). Balancing adequacy and incentive also has been an unresolved, ongoing issue of attention—is there a level at which benefit receipt actually discourages a return to employment?

## Due Process

If the initial claim is denied, ongoing benefits discontinued, or overpayments or fraud alleged, claimants are notified of their right to contest these actions or allegations through an administrative hearing. The written notice of the action being taken includes instructions on when and where to request a hearing. An employer objecting to the claim of a former employee may also ask for a hearing.

An administrative law judge from the state's Unemployment Insurance Review Board presides over the hearing. At this informal, trial-like proceeding, the parties involved can be represented by a lawyer or advocate. Evidence can be presented and witnesses can testify. The claimant and his or her representative can review the agency's file, cross-examine any opposition witnesses, subpoena witnesses, and make opening and closing statements. Materials supporting the claimant's case can be compiled and presented as evidence (for example, a letter of commendation, a contract, doctors' notes, employee manual, photos).

A decision is usually received within several weeks of the hearing. The decision can be appealed to the appropriate appellate body in the state.

The claimant, pending the hearing decision, should continue to file for benefits. This is because if the judge's decision favors the claimant, he or she is entitled to claim benefits accrued during the period between the receipt of the notice of action and the hearing decision.

## THE CLIENTS' STORIES

### Roy

I live in the suburbs, and I am involved in the garment center. I work for a manufacturer as a sales executive, representing all his dress lines. I have been doing this for the last 28 years.

The work involves speaking to, on a daily basis, and taking care of accounts during market weeks and selling all major accounts— department stores, specialty stores, and chains. They come to me. If I have to go to them once in a while if they can't make it to New York, then I do. Usually they come to New York every market, which is like once a month.

The garment center has been suffering for the last 6 years because retail has been bad. There are a lot of imports, which hurt domestic companies. Domestic companies going into imports for the first time is a very difficult thing. If you don't have a proper agent overseas, then you are always late on deliveries. Then when the goods come in, and if you have cancellations because you're late, then you have to have outlets to get rid of the merchandise, and at a loss, so you're always behind the eight-ball, unless you know what you're doing with imports.

I know buyers. I have contacts with these stores, and that's how I do business. They come in because they know me, they like the merchandise, they purchase it. Hopefully it sells at retail and they'll reorder more. Or if they don't do well, then I help them out with markdowns to make them profitable.

I would say that 80 percent is the rapport that you have with the person you're working with. It's all contacts over the years. You learn that when you're working with a buyer, she has an assistant. You become friendly with the assistant because most of your interaction is with the assistant on the phone. Then usually assistants become buyers. So when you have good relationships with the assistants and they become buyers, they always like the people who treated them nice when they were at the lower end of the totem pole.

Everything changes from season to season. You can do well one season if the line is good. If the line doesn't retail, then you don't do well. Everything is affected that way. Your performance may be great one season, and the next season it's not good. One year maybe I can do $18,000,000 at cost, and the next year maybe I can do 2, or maybe nothing. It varies. So there are no loyalties as far as a boss to an employee, or an employee to a boss. The name of the game in the garment center is what did you do for me lately. You're as good as your last dress. That's what it comes down to. It's just a number game. It's all figures.

If the economy goes down, I don't think people are going to buy dresses. They'll go to buy sportswear, a coordinate. They can buy a blouse, a pant, a skirt. They can alternate the outfits. A dress is a dress, wear it once and that's it.

I was with a company for 19 years, and my performance was excellent. So was the company's. The company started to steadily go downhill because of the economy. They had to let me go. They let a lot of people go. Now they are almost ready to go under completely. This was a company that at its peak did $210,000,000. Now if they do 15 with the same overhead, the same rent, they can't stay in business. It's very hard. So, what happened is that they had to let me go, and it was like a rude awakening, because you think that you find yourself finding a home where you're comfortable doing business—you feel like it's your own. You treat it like it's your own. It hurts when you're with a company for that many years. There is no security in this business.

My family is the best thing I have. I have two sons, and I have a wonderful wife. They are always behind me, which helps. My wife is always there for me 150 percent all the time. So, that's good. My wife works as an administrative assistant, and both my children have good jobs. We have our own home. When we were first married we had an apartment. Eventually we bought a house. I commute roundtrip on the railroad. Sometimes it's fine, and other times it's not, but you get used to it, like everything else.

I was born and brought up in the Bronx. My mother came from Warsaw, Poland, with her sisters and brothers when she was 3 years old. My father was born here. His family came from Russia. I'm an only child. I went to a chiropractic college. I always liked taking care of people, trying to help people. I don't think I had the grades to be a medical doctor, but I was fine as a chiropractor. It was a 6-year program, and I made it in 6. I took Liberal Arts and medical courses—anatomy, physiology, pathology, all the normal medical courses. Then you have to take state boards. You don't treat patients with any type of medication. Everything is done from the spine and the nervous system. I just wanted to take care of people. At that time, I think it was 1965 (I graduated in 1964) I was charging $5 a visit. It was $35 for a full series of x-rays. Today it's different. In those days you came in for a visit. Ninety percent of the time, if you adjusted somebody and they felt better you never saw them again. There was no insurance. So, it was a tough field. A lot of people thought that we were like a pseudo-type doctor. We were like a last resort. If nothing else worked, then maybe they would come to you. I tried for about a year and a half, and just couldn't afford to stay in practice any longer. I sold all my equipment. I tried to buy somebody's practice, but it was a little too expensive, and I couldn't afford it.

Then I went into the restaurant business in Manhattan. We had all business clientele. It was a 5-day a week place, Monday to Friday, no weekends. I bought the restaurant and did very well. I met my wife through a customer who frequented the restaurant. I went to a party that this customer had and that's how I met her. We dated for about a year and a half. We had the wedding in my restaurant. We had the whole block closed off for 250 people. It was planned in only 2 weeks.

I was there for almost 5 years. I sold it and bought a very large place on Long Island. I had it for about $2\frac{1}{2}$ years. It was 7 days a week, which was worse than the first one. I never saw my children.

Then I was going to run a restaurant for somebody. A friend called and he wanted me to come down to the garment center to meet this fellow who was running a company. I wasn't really interested. I didn't know anything about it. He said, "You'll go down and meet him, and I'm sure he'll like you." He made me an offer, and because I didn't have experience in the industry, he told me that he couldn't pay me as much as I was getting, but he would shortly work me up quickly if everything worked out. It was a cleaner type living as far as I was concerned. I was wearing a suit rather than an apron; 5 days a week; normal hours, I would see my family. The rest is history. I've been in the garment center ever since.

I always wanted to get back into chiropractic. I tried to get back into it a number of years ago, but it was very hard to get back in. Once you're established and used to a certain lifestyle, to start all over is very tough to do. I was never able to get back into it. You try not to dwell on certain things and just try to go ahead and do the best you can. I was a really good chiropractor. I just couldn't make a living at the time. I don't fault myself. I just wish I could have stayed in it. I don't have any regrets now. It's past. It was an experience.

I did well at everything. I would say that it's just since 1999 that it hasn't been going very great. I'm making a very nice living now, so I can't complain. It's just that my head is not as successful as my pocket.

The first area in the garment center that is affected when anything is downsized is the sales area, because that's the highest income. So, that's where they have to let most of the people go, since they are paid the most. I was one of the top earners in the company, and unfortunately I had to be let go. In 1999, they called me in and just said we're sorry, but things are not going well for the company. He gave me a very nice severance package, taking care of my medical until I was able to pick up insurance. We left on very good terms. It was not personal, just dollars and cents, black and white. The reality hits you; you get depressed, go back and forth, but the thing is to find another job. There weren't that many jobs in the garment center because people were letting go of people, they weren't hiring,

I was let go the same day, without notice. I didn't see it coming. We were doing whatever we could to help the company. Obviously it wasn't enough. The overhead was too big.

The only thing that was really helpful to me at the time was my wife. You realize that nothing is forever. You realize that sooner or later all good things come to an end, no matter what. You're not really secure financially. Mentally you can be, but when you get shook financially like that it affects your mental state, too. Not that you go off your mind. It's just a tough thing to take. You start looking to see if there is something you did. You can go through a million things, but it's not really you. So you lick your wounds and go on.

I was ready to move on the following week. I just rationalized in my head the reasons why I understood it wasn't me. Whatever business was still being done, I was doing it. It was that it just wasn't enough to substantiate the income I was getting. All the 19 years I was there I would say I had the best relationship with him, and he was one of the toughest guys in the industry. We always respected each other. It wasn't my business or my performance for the company, it was just dollars and cents. He knew that even a cut in pay wouldn't have made a difference, because to give me any kind of cut I would have to be working for nothing, because he couldn't afford it.

There was just a situation there. The company was coming down. Who gets laid off but the people who earn the most money. That's where you have to cut. They're not going to cut out a shipping clerk who makes $200 a week. I didn't understand when it first happened, but then I realized what it was. You don't really want to accept things, but that's what happens. I thought about it for a while. The following week I went and filed for unemployment, the first time ever in my life I went to get unemployment.

I really didn't know what to do. I had spoken to my wife. She knew somebody and called a friend who had a husband who had just been laid off. She told my wife what the procedure was. It was very hard to get hold of them—at Unemployment—on the phone; it just keeps ringing, ringing, ringing. So I went down to the office. You get very nervous. You want to make sure you have that money coming in. I was embarrassed to go down and collect unemployment. I thought I'm entitled. I paid for it. I found out the procedure. I went down on a Monday morning. The line was like around the corner. I got there like 7:30 AM and waited my turn. For me, waiting on line was very depressing. I was there with a suit and tie. Everybody there was wearing jeans. I didn't really talk to anyone until we got inside, a lot of them seemed to be very familiar with the procedure. They had been there before. I was never there. I just asked if I were on the right line. They said, "Yes, just get the forms from the [20 or so] baskets at the wall." You don't know if you're getting the right forms or not, if you've never been there before. Then there was a security guy walking around. He said just take one from each basket. There was nobody there to guide you, just a guy in a security uniform, but he didn't seem to know much. He had an attitude like he couldn't care less either. I go all the papers and sat down at what seemed like picnic tables. You sit down and start making out the forms, which I did. That took about 35–40 minutes, because I wanted to make sure I didn't make a mistake. They ask all kinds of questions.

The forms are not complicated. The only thing that is complicated is that you don't understand what the form is for. Where they tell you, "You're fired, laid off, ever collect unemployment before, have you gotten severance pay, have you gotten vacation pay?" you're not familiar with all these things, because you've never been through it before. So you really have to digest what you're reading, to make sure that you don't make a mistake; because if you get up there, on line, and get to get called on, and the person who is examining your paper sees that you made a mistake you are going to have to go through the whole process all over again. There is nobody to help you when you are making out the forms.

Anyone who isn't highly educated, to fill out the forms, they're in trouble. It's a problem. They should have somebody there, at least to try to explain to people. They do have a film that they try to show you, but if you take time out to watch the film you lose your place on line. You can be there forever. They break at certain hours, and I think they are only there until 3 or 1 or something like that during the day.

I got through the form; then I had to sweat out the time on line. If they don't get to see you at a certain time, you're out. And then you may be on the wrong line, because it's very confusing. One line says information, and there are three or four other lines that say nothing. They have these four or five people. Nobody smiles. They act like they're doing you a favor. They're sitting behind these desks that look like tellers at a bank. The lines are all roped in like in a movie theater. People are just waiting. Then you get interviewed by a person.

They ask you questions like, "Is this the first time?" These are things you have already made out on the form. So now you have to verbalize it. Then they go into the computer and check your background. I think I just brought a normal ID, which I carry anyway, a driver's license. I didn't have to bring anything to verify employment. They ask you these idiotic questions, which you have already written down. They tell you that you will be getting your first check within 4 to 5 weeks; it's retroactive. They give you a book and a phone number to call. Every time you call you call the same day of the week, until midnight. But you must call on that day. They designate a day according to the last four digits of your Social Security number. That's the system. You call on that designated day; and you're talking to a machine asking you these questions, and you put in 1 for Yes and I think 0 for No. They ask you questions like, "Are you applying for the week of the 17th?"; you press 1 for Yes or 0 for No; "Did you work during that week; were you eligible to work during that week; were you prepared to work during that week; did you turn down work during that week; did you pick up any part time work; did you work for any kind of relative?" In each one you have to go Yes or No. You hit the wrong number you have to start all over again. If you lose the number you have to try to dial back, you'll get a busy signal for maybe another hour or so. It's getting late and you figure you're going to miss your day, so you won't get your check. It's a terrible system because you can't speak to anyone on the phone where you get a live person. Now I understand that the office is closing, and they're going to do everything on the phone, which is fine if you had a person to talk to. Then sometimes there's something wrong with the machine, so it takes you a few hours before you can get through, because sometimes something happens to the tape. It's only a machine.

They require that you look for work. Two weeks after you file for unemployment you have an appointment that you have to go to. It is in another place. It is a job-seeking fair type office. They used to have computers you were able to use to find jobs, but they cut that out also. They said people were using the computers for other reasons. They have jobs posted on the wall. When I went there the first time, they lecture and you fill out forms, and they tell you that you don't have to accept any jobs under a certain percentage—I think it was 20 percent—of what you were earning. I raised my hand and said what I was earning, and said 20 percent of that you can't even find anything. They just chuckled. I'm willing to take less. That's okay, but they don't have anything. Anything that's posted on the board is from $4 an hour to maybe $8 an hour tops. It's labor-type work; if you are a salesperson, you are up a creek. They never found anything for me. They say they'll try. I even filled out forms for certain seminars. I never heard from them either. Now, if you can't make that meeting 2 weeks after you file for unemployment, and you don't call, they have a letter stating that if you do not call them to notify them that you cannot make the appointment for whatever the reason, your check will be held up. They always use this as a weapon. Any little thing, they're going to hold up your check; which I guess they are entitled to, but they should know when they are dealing with somebody legitimate. I guess it's hard to find out, because they must get hurt, too, I'm sure. Either way, that was my experience.

What happened with me was I got a letter in the mail, and it said I was denied unemployment because they said I was on a corporation. I was on a corporation many years ago in which I didn't earn any money, then I was off it. But they had it down on record; so they wouldn't give me unemployment unless I had a hearing. I called my congressman, a marvelous man. I spoke to his secretary and told her exactly what happened. She took down all the information. Within 2 hours she called me back and told me that I would be getting my check next week. Sure enough, I got my first check. They were terrific, and I sent them a tremendous thank-you letter.

You just have to be astute and just be stern and follow through and don't take any garbage from anybody. You're entitled to it. You pay for it. They're not giving it to you for nothing, even though they act like they are. People are down in their luck for whatever it may be. It doesn't mean they have to be abused all over the world. They're still entitled to get unemployment. I personally didn't like the system. It worked for me as far as the reimbursement helped me, getting paid every week, getting a check until I got another job. It was definitely beneficial. It was the way it was done I didn't appreciate.

In the system of unemployment, after 13 weeks, they review you. When you get your unemployment book, they have a set-up in the back of the book that you have to fill in all the interviews you go on; also newspaper ads that you call for are considered interviews. You have to put down the day of the interview, how you interviewed, in person, sent a fax, résumé, talked to somebody on the phone, what transpired, got the job, didn't get the job. You have to fill this out. You have to be eligible to go for work every single day. You have to be available for work, not turn down anything, as long as it's in the limit of like I said, under 20 percent you didn't really have to accept. If there aren't that many jobs out there you know you have to take something. You have to fill this out, keep records daily, until you get to the point at 13 weeks, then you have to go in, and I'm sure they go over everything. I never got to that. Luckily I found a job. I think you're allowed 26 weeks to your unemployment. But, if for argument sake, you collect a certain amount a week when you find a job, and then you get laid off again, and you're within the same pay period year, it continues. In other words, if you used up 13 weeks, you have another 13 weeks coming to you. But if you're beyond that pay period, and you have enough paid in, you can go beyond the 26 weeks and start another unemployment, as long as there's enough money paid in. If not, then you're out of unemployment. Sure, it's truly an insurance program.

I tried to find employment outside my industry, but still in sales. I didn't limit myself to sales. I would have done anything, as long as it was legitimate work. There's nothing really beneath me. I didn't have any problems with anything as far as age discrimination. I'm 58. When you hear a lot of people want a lot of young kids, that's not really true. I think that if a person is qualified at what they do, they can find a job. There's always a job with the right person. I went into other areas. I went to job fairs, and I went around giving my résumés to a lot of different people in different industries, in computer industries, mostly things to do for sales. If you can sell, you can sell anything, so it didn't matter. Whatever I thought was decent and could get decent income, that's where I went to those booths. I never heard from one of them. They tell you we'll call next week, but you never hear from them, for whatever the reason half of them are probably full of bologna.

Then I started in my area in the garment industry, which was very slim pickings, but I managed to get a lot of interviews. Finally, I got a job and started working again. It was hard work, looking for work. Sometimes it's demeaning, but you do what you've got to do. That's it.

## Judy

I have been working for many years, except that in January my job was eliminated, my longtime job, and so ever since I have been responding to ads, networking, and trying to find another job that would sustain us as a family.

I have two grown sons, both living out West. One is a lawyer, and one is an outdoor person. He's a hiker and mountain climber and he does carpentry, to give him the free time.

My second husband has two children, same ages as mine—33 and 36. His are married, so we are starting the grandparent role, with his children first. Mine are both married, both got married last year, and so their turn will be coming.

I am the oldest of four children. My early school years were spent at a small private school close to where we lived, so that I had very small classes and individual attention, which I think was important and helpful to me. I later went to public school. I studied literature in college. I went intending to be a French major, because I was president of French Club in high school, but I discovered I probably did better in English. So I changed to literature, and I graduated with a BA in American Literature. After college I became obsessed with the idea that perhaps I should be a teacher. So, I started reading; I started observing friends who were teaching. But then I got married. I was 24, and started having my children. While they were small, and between the two, I enrolled in a master's program, which I did over 5 years, in education at a local university.

It worked because my husband would come home, and he would take over basically, and then I would leave. At that time I had one child, and when the second one was born it was a few weeks before my comprehensive exam, which was the final point of the master's. The baby's first day out was going to my mother's so I could go and take that exam, which I'm happy to say I passed, as he and I studied together. Then I had the degree, but by that time I had also been doing volunteer work a few days a week at a number of places where we could take our children and leave them together with a sitter while we met. So, I had gotten involved in a number of different volunteer activities and advocacy around things like affordable housing. It's actually through that volunteer work and serving on some local and community boards that I was invited to do my first job when my kids were about junior high age, which was to work for a small not-for-profit group concerned with housing. From there I went to work at the Housing Authority for 5 years. I don't know, but I always was conscious of how things were for other people.

I think my parents kind of wanted to know more about what was out there. One of the things they got involved in was what was called a Trialog. It was an interfaith dialog with Protestants, Catholics, and Jews getting together for small meetings in the home to talk about their commonalities, as well as their points of difference.

My dad was a professional engineer, worked for many years. My mom devoted herself to us and to community activities and volunteering. She did some part-time work after that in some different retail kinds of things, but she was not the main breadwinner. My dad was, and they managed to put four of us through college, and we all have master's degrees.

I'm the eldest. My next oldest sister unfortunately experienced some psychological problems, and so although she worked in the city in a number of different ways, and in other cities, she is on Social Security Disability and Medicare now. She does some volunteer work. Our next younger sister is the director of a program for youngsters to experience different career possibilities that also helps them to not drop out of school. My brother is a specialist in historic preservation.

My first husband was an engineer also. We were married for 19 years, and then I was on my own for quite a long time. I began to work part time while I was still married.

I was executive director of a small not-for-profit that helped people who were looking for housing to share rooms to rent. I did what I could to help them make connections with available resources in the community. Even some people who were being released from a hospitalized situation, with psychiatric histories. I found some families at my church that were willing to take them in and rent them a room in kind of a safe situation, better than a boarding house or an adult rooming house situation, which often is not therapeutic. I did that and then I moved into the Housing Authority where I learned the government side of how programs can actually help people. I was a Section 8 coordinator. It was a part-time job that I had for 5 years. I had to interview people. I had to help with the record keeping and the applications.

Through these jobs I got to know a number of people well who were in need of the help that those programs could provide. I could see that they were just ordinary people, some of whom had fallen on hard luck. Many of them didn't know where to turn, and I could see that it was really important to explain to them as much as possible what their options were, what they would have to do, a little bit maybe about how to present themselves. Then, where possible I could advocate for them to follow through on the program, such as Section 8 for widows who had become disabled but who were not yet elderly. They did not have enough income to afford even modest housing or rented rooms that were then available.

I knew I wasn't cut out to be a housing manager. I guess I wasn't so interested in devising budgets and so forth. I moved on when I heard from a friend that a job in a legislative office was opening up. I went to the interview with the legislator and was hired. I said I would be willing to do it part time, and the legislator—a woman—was quite amenable to the idea of getting the best out of people at the level that they could give it. She said, "I'll look for someone else and maybe you could job share." She found another person who had recently begun volunteering in her office and asked the two of us if we would like to share the job, which was a fairly new concept in 1981.

So what we did, we worked out methods for job sharing. We kept a journal of calls that we had made that had not yet been responded to, things that might be happening in the next day or two or follow-ups that the other person could do. There was a sense of teamwork. She was my mentor. My first mentor was at the Housing Authority, a very wise woman who encouraged families who had been living in public housing, which was for the lowest income people, when she felt they were ready to apply for a mortgage and buy a house. I saw at least a dozen families leave the authority and move out on their own. She was just very wise about human relationships, as was my legislative employer.

From there, I got an opportunity to go and work in a bar association. They needed a coordinator for state legislation. I learned that I was good at interacting with the public. I learned to be comfortable in front of an audience of hundreds or it could be thousands. I was on radio programs, TV programs, wrote position papers. I did so many different kinds of things that it took me into new arenas and I learned a lot.

I was then recruited from the bar association by a sister organization, a statewide court reform organization—a very small group that is very focused on improving the courts so they are more coordinated and more accessible, and it is less expensive for people to bring their suits or cases to court or to pursue a case when a wrong has been done to them. I worked in a very focused way with committees of attorneys, deans of law schools, some judges to try to bring these issues to the attention of legislators. I also assisted in the organizing of court monitoring projects in a number of different courts, where you had to find, recruit, and train the volunteers to use the particular kind of observation forms. You had to meet with the judges to set it up and agree to the rules of how it would go and then compile the findings at the end and issue a report to the media, to the judges and everyone in the court, as well as to the public. Because I had actually been such a volunteer years earlier in a court monitoring project, I understood what was involved.

I converted to a part-time job because the commute was wearing me down. But, because I was on my own at that point—my husband and I had separated—I had to look for some other jobs to put together. I found a couple of interesting ones.

One was doing some night and weekend fill-in at a group home for girls. That was an interesting experience. Another one I found through a temp agency was working in what I call the paper bag factory that was actually in my town, tucked away behind a tennis court. I think nobody really knew it was there. They made paper bags and shipped them out by rail freight. I was in the personnel office, helping keep the time records and transmitting the daily production and wastage statistics to the main office. That was my first time in any kind of a factory setting. So I got to know the people and how they thought and also what kind of procedures were adhered to. I thought it was a very useful understanding I gained there.

My friends at that point actually wanted me to go to law school, which I toyed with, but my older son was actually applying and starting at law school himself at that time and I kind of didn't want to steal his thunder. So I didn't go. I enrolled in library school at one point for a short time and then didn't stay with it.

I felt it would be good to try to get a full-time job. I started applying for jobs in an arena where I felt really comfortable which was working with volunteers. I was actually reaching out to local agencies that were needing a volunteer coordinator or something of that sort when I ran into the agency that ultimately hired me. I went to apply for the volunteer coordinator job, but we had a friend who I think had just a completed a term as president of the board of that organization. He said, "You know I think there might be another job there that you would be well qualified for." He spoke to the director, and I put together a résumé, and that's the job I actually got.

I was actually designated to represent the agency, on boards or in committees of coalitions that were working and advocating for issues, such as good health care, equitable welfare reform, and affordable housing. This helped not only the clients that the agency was serving through its many programs, but also the staff of the agency. I took board members with me to visit homeless shelters. We interviewed officials of social agencies and government agencies. We attended conferences and meetings. We spoke out and gave testimony at public hearings.

I attempted to interpret to them, as well as to the staff, the various aspects of the issues that were emerging, or the groups that were on this side and on the other side something else so that they could understand. While we needed to understand that everything has political aspects, we didn't have to get wrapped up, and it was very important that we not get wrapped up, in the partisan sides. I was very comfortable with that and would counsel the administration as well as the board. When I made my presentations I tried very hard to stay on that middle track.

Since I left, colleagues tell me, "We miss you because you were the one who put all the pieces together." "You filled in the gaps." "You always had the background, and you could explain things to us." "You knew where to go for resources." "You brought people together in a positive way."

I felt like I was in some ways the soul of the agency. I was representing the agency out in the community in a way I thought represented its good will and its ability to be helpful, without being overbearing, to meet the needs as they were expressed, and the concerns of the people in the communities. So that brings me round to where I am now, which is as sort of a community person.

I couldn't say for sure that I saw the end coming, but there were certainly other priorities that were being put forth. I think that that need is still there, and they have chosen because of budget constraints last year as they looked forward into this year to not have a funded position to do this. It was a total shock when it happened.

It has been 6 months since I stopped getting a regular paycheck, although, thankfully, this agency was big enough and well-enough established to have a policy of severance pay. I was able to apply for unemployment a week after my job ended, because there is an official waiting week in my state's unemployment law, and then I had to apply for a determination of benefits. I had enough work history, so I was able to actually start receiving them. The severance pay I got was a benefit. I wasn't any longer doing work for the agency, so the two did not conflict.

You can actually apply over the telephone now, with a series of questions that they ask, and you do it on a touch-tone telephone if you wish. I guess you don't have to. I found that to be a very convenient way to maintain myself in the system by reporting in the weeks that I didn't have any work. Then, the check comes within a few days.

I had to report in person for some different kinds of profiling and orientations, and I have to confess that the quality of those was quite variable. The first one, which was an orientation, I got letters from the State Department of Labor that came a few days apart giving me two different assignment dates to go for two different kinds of orientations. One was a profiling orientation, and one was an unemployment insurance to work orientation. They were two days in a row. I called up and asked, "Well, what do I do." They said, "Go to the first one, and tell them about the second one."

I went on the first day, which happened to be a very snowy winter, February day. I got to the place, and they said, "Well, people haven't really come in today. We'll give you credit. Just go to the next one." I took my life in my hands to try to comply, and that one turned into nothing. I went to the one the next day, back at the same office. It was the biggest waste of time. We sat in a room where the man took attendance for about half an hour, and then he talked round and round and didn't really say anything. It was supposed to be assistance in getting back to work, and there were a lot of eager people there who desperately wanted to work. The purpose was to acquaint you with services, job listings, résumé workshops, Internet listings, career guides, labor market material, and important requirements. He gave none of those. Thankfully, from that one I got to attend what they called a re-employment workshop. I had a choice of places to go at four different sites. I thought sure I'm not going back to that place again, so I chose a different one. This one was extremely helpful and detailed. It was so different, night and day, from the other one. They gave me a certificate, a dislocated workers certification from the earlier date that said that I was identified as someone likely to exhaust my benefits according to the profiling system, whether that was because of my age or because of the strange nature of the work that I had done, I'm not really clear. I was told to hang on to that.

Then I thought, well they're giving courses in computers, and maybe I could learn more and upgrade skills if they would let me take a course. So, I made an appointment to speak with a counselor at the Department of Labor. She said to me that she thought I could actually handle the learning by going perhaps to my library, or something like that. She wasn't going to recommend me for a course because she said the courses probably went slower than I would want to go. It turned out that she was an extremely professional and competent and helpful person. She started e-mailing me jobs as she would see them help me revise my résumé to make it a little more professional. Certain dates . . . I had things in the wrong order. She rearranged it so that it looked pretty good.

After a month or more I got a notice to go back to the first place I had been to see a counselor in order to be able to continue the unemployment benefit. I went to see a man there who blessedly was professional as well. He said my résumé looked really good. It looked to him like a $60,000 or $70,000 résumé. He said if I wanted to just try to get a job that I would probably have to change it a little to make it look more like I was suited to the jobs that seemed to be available. To myself I said it was kind of a dumbing down that he was asking for. I felt that it was important to keep them there. So, while I rearranged my descriptive parts of things I had done, I didn't ultimately eliminate much except the very earliest jobs.

The counselors were genuinely interested in trying to help. They suggested resources; they commiserated that it's a very difficult economy. The first counselor I had seen several times said that the economy is still in an uncertain condition right now; that you really need to have Plan A, Plan B, and Plan C. That was really helpful to me because it caused me to step back and think what could be some of my fallbacks. As I began to think about it I realized I'm a very good test taker and I was right there by the Department of Civil Service. So, I went and looked on the wall and saw some jobs posted there. I thought I could do this; I could do that. I got those sheets down and I actually applied to take some civil service tests. Then, the other thing was that I have my teacher certification I got when my kids were small and I never used it. I thought what could I do with that?

I read several newspapers every day. There were several big ads that teachers were needed. I went to two teaching job fairs. At one of those I met somebody who said, "We might be interested in talking with you." I learned over time of doing it that I would say to them right off the bat, "If you're interested in somebody with non-traditional preparation, but with permanent certification, I might be your person," and I handed them a résumé. In other words, I wasn't trying to hide the fact that I did not have actual in-classroom teaching experience, other than my substitute teaching and my student teaching, but that I had life experience in working with less fortunate families and people and that I understood the stresses in communities and the issues that would be impinging on people's lives and that maybe that would be a plus.

It's been a very interesting process. Some of the folks I got to know over many years working have been trying to see if they could do something to help me. I've sent out lots of letters and résumés. Very seldom does even an acknowledgment come back. Once or twice I got those; often in postcard form. And only once did I get a letter that said, "Thank you for your application. We wanted to tell you that although you are qualified, we have decided to hire someone else." It just closes the file. I set up a file for each potential employer that I have reached out to and put materials in there that were related to it. You're left in limbo a lot.

The Department of Labor actually gives you a matrix. They tell you to keep track of the things you apply for, because weeks or months from now somebody could call up and say, "We're calling in response to your application for such and such a job," and you might not even remember that you had applied for it. They also require that we keep a log of our job search. I thought that was helpful. It's like what happened as a result of this one. Did it end in a negative, or is it still pending?

I had to keep showing up for appointments with the unemployment office. The job counselor appointments were about every two weeks for about a month, and this one other counselor at the other original place was just really once. It wasn't like this is your 60-day or your 90-day review or anything. Then, every week with the telephone alert system you would have to call. They would ask have you gone back to work? Have you done any work? Whatever. Have you been available for work? They have booklets that they send you. They even personalize the page that you're supposed to send back, and so on.

But, a lot of it is in bold print or capital letters, and it's pretty high level. There were things where I wasn't clear on what they meant. I would say to field test some of these things with a group if they haven't done that in a while. And, also, because it's so confusing when more people are working either temporary jobs or part-time jobs to think about how they go in and out of a system like this, and what do they really survive on, and what will pay the rent or the mortgage or the health insurance. If our elected officials would pay more attention to how all these pieces do or don't fit together for ordinary folks, including myself, they might be more humble and work harder to try to bring about some coordination that was a little more realistic, such as the need for health insurance for everybody.

There was a group of agencies that reached out to me to help with a very short-term job writing a special grant. For 10 days I worked intensely with them. Therefore, those weeks I did not claim unemployment for the time I was doing that, and then they sent me a form to fill out to confirm that that's what I had done. Then, there's a part of it that they send to the employer for confirmation. I certainly did that. I was not looking to play both sides on this one.

People encouraged me to think about becoming a consultant where you have to patch together all kinds of different things. This is probably a last resort because I'm not old enough for Medicare, and my husband's even younger than I am, even though he's retired. For things like health insurance it would leave us in limbo.

Right now, we've been enormously lucky to have found an insurance program that is for people who either work part time or maybe seasonally or those who are recently unemployed that allows you to join an HMO at a reasonable rate. In fact it was actually a little bit less than half of what I was paying to extend the benefits I had with my former employer under what's called COBRA. This program is sort of a middle ground. They base it on your actual income. We chose a carrier that had at least most of the doctors we were already using, so that we didn't have to totally abandon our health care relationships in order to get this benefit. It's only been a couple of months as of now, but it's an amazing thing.

The state has some programs that are not very well known. Some of them I found on websites or people had told me about. I don't know how people in general would find them out. I was lucky from two sides. I have a friend who works for the Department of Labor that I can ask questions about understanding the law or what some piece of paper means or something. Also, knowing about these programs from the work that I previously did, at least enough to know where to look. If I hear a name or something, I can go on a website and get more information.

It's a little frightening being a recipient. It's fearful in that you want to do it right, but sometimes they will send a form or something will come, especially having to do with health insurance where you don't know if you answer the question and the answer is supposed to be no or yes, or because you misunderstood the question, whether it will kick you out of the system altogether. Those are the times when I would call and try to find somebody to ask. In fact, even at the very beginning, at one point to try to get to a live person we actually called all the way to the state capital to a human rights hotline of some kind where we actually got a person to answer the phone. Then she led us back to somebody who could really help with the question that I had at that time. I guess it's knowing a little bit about the law, but not really knowing how it's interpreted that it's a little awesome and frightening; then, never knowing what's coming next that you're going to be asked to do, but then finally getting to the desk with some of these people and finding out that they are reasonable and they are not doing it just to torment me is reassuring.

I have lots to do. I'm still reading and keeping up with the issues that I have been concerned about. I've stayed as a volunteer on some of the committees and groups because of the personal commitment of mine, not just depending on whether I was getting a paycheck.

Also, I am exploring. I always read the want ads, and I send off some responses with my résumé. Luckily I have a fax in my computer so I can do that from home. The counties have set up very nice one-stop centers. I haven't needed to really go there and do it there. I can use, thankfully, through the good graces of my church, the copy machine there as well.

I've actually done the best I could; tried hard to work on my cover letters and keep looking over my résumé; take them everywhere that I go. I still network with people. People will call me to ask how I am doing and tell me they have so-and-so on the lookout for me. One job actually came along, and actually five different people mentioned it to me. I knew it wasn't appropriate for me because I had done some work in that particular area earlier. But, it was very heartwarming that people were really thinking of me. I've met with people; I've brainstormed with them; I've called them to let them know I am available. Then, one person from the corporate world actually challenged me. "Well, what kind of things do you do well? What kind of things would you like to do?"

So, I actually made a list of things that I thought I could do. It was almost a whole page. I kind of expected that some group would say, "Well, you know, you're a good facilitator and organizer and encourager. We have a spot here you could fit." I could help a small agency to grow, or I could help a group sort out things that aren't very well organized. I am good at putting a public face on things. It just hasn't really come along quite the way I had hoped.

I'm kind of still looking to see what might be out there and which of the opportunities will come to fruition if any. Something has to come. I thankfully am not living day to day, week to week. I have a little bit of small retirement and some resources. I own the house in which I live with my second husband. We have more choices than many people, and I certainly recognize that. I don't live at a high level of anxiety. But it's trying to find a match between what might be available and what would allow me to express my values in the work that I would do. To me that is important because I've always been very proud to represent the organizations for which I've worked in the past and speak in their name or tell others about them and work out ways of cooperation among them.

I would say to people dealing with the unemployment system to try to go to those orientations and things and just ask lots of questions. Even when I have had to call some of these offices or tried to ask if I understood something, most of the people that I've spoken to on the phone have tried to be helpful. I think there's just always an element of fear. It's like what if I do something or forget to do something or I don't do it quite right.

I think you learn from every interview that you have: how to present things or something else that you could try to say, but you just don't know if it's going to be the time when they are ready to hire or who they are looking for. When I read the ads in the paper I think high-level administrative job. If I walked in the door I wouldn't be the one that they would be having in their minds. So, I rule myself out of some. I just don't go for those.

The ideal thing would be to have a choice of several jobs that would be within my value system; that would have decent benefits until such time as I will be eligible for Medicare in whatever form that will be by then. I would like people I guess to take a chance on me. I've always felt that I could persist until people got to know me well enough to know who I really am. Although first impressions are important in interviewing, they are not sufficient. You have to dig much deeper than that. I would like to know as much about the culture of a place that thinks they would like to have me as they might like to know about me. I've always been in more of a service-related field. The chances are probably that is where I should stay. I'm exploring different things.

If there is an educational situation where they would let me or invite me to teach I think I would try it. I had always thought that when I retired I would like to work maybe with adults or other people that just didn't quite make it in the educational system. That would be something that I could give my time and my energy to. The fact that my long-time job that I really loved went out from under me may mean that I have the time to accept this challenge from myself sooner, rather than later. Then I'll just have to wait until I retire to learn to play the cello.

## WHAT OUR CLIENTS TEACH US

Roy and Judy represent the profile of the recipient for whom the program was designed. The benefit was earned through many years working for a covered employer; there was a separation from employment not caused by the employee. The benefit as intended helped support Roy and Judy and their families during the relatively short term unemployment phase. While the compensation was not their only source of income (Roy's wife was employed and Judy's husband has retirement income), it permitted them to remain in their homes and to maintain some semblance of their styles of living while they searched for a new job.

Several common themes emerge which give us some insight into the experience of being out of work and participating in the Unemployment Insurance program.

1. *Applying for and receiving unemployment benefits requires time, energy, commitment, and psychological strength.* Roy and Judy teach us and help us experience the process of applying for and receiving unemployment insurance. With Roy, we are standing in a long line early in the morning, feeling isolated and unsure: "I didn't really talk to anyone until we got inside. . . . A lot of them seemed to be very familiar with the procedure. I was asked if I were on the right line. They said, 'Yes, just get the forms from the [20 or so] baskets at the wall.' You don't know if you're getting the right forms or not. . . . There was nobody there to guide you, just a guy in a security uniform, but he didn't seem to know much." We fill out the lengthy application form. "That took about 35–40 minutes, because I wanted to make sure I didn't make a mistake. They ask all kinds of questions. . . . The only thing that is complicated is that you don't understand what the form is for. . . . You really have to digest what you're reading, to make sure that you don't make a mistake . . . because if you get called on and . . . you made a mistake you are going to have to go through the whole process all over again." We then stand on yet another line: "I had to sweat out the time on line. If they don't get to see you at a certain time, you're out." Finally the interview: "They ask you questions. . . . These are things you have already made out on the form. So now you have to verbalize it. . . . They ask you these idiotic questions, which you have already written down." And, Roy informs us of what follows after an applicant becomes a recipient. He tells us about the frustrating automated telephone call-in procedure to "establish ongoing eligibility. . . . You hit the wrong number, you have to start all over again. If you lose the number you have to try to dial back, you'll get a busy signal for maybe another hour or so. It's getting late and you figure you're going to miss your day, so you won't get your check."

Judy, an experienced Social Service client advocate, focuses her frustration on one of the orientation sessions, which she reports to be "the biggest waste of time." Her anxiety regarding the process is reflected in her showing up for an orientation on a very snowy February day when no one came to work: "I," she says, "took my life in my hands to try to comply." She also refers several times to needing to check on procedures to protect herself from being out of compliance and from being denied help. Despite supportive resources in the community and her own professional experience, she finds some aspects of being a recipient intimidating. "It's a little frightening. It's fearful in that you want to do it right, but sometimes they will send a form . . . where you don't know if you answer the question . . . whether it will kick you out of the system altogether." Judy then reports on her frustration in trying to get a "live" person to answer her queries, once resorting to calling to the state capitol for assistance.

And we hear from both Judy and Roy about job search requirements, including a group lecture, an interview journal, and a personal interview after 13 weeks. While there are procedural variations among states, each imposes requirements that are designed to ensure that recipients remain eligible by adhering to work search and other regulations. As Roy notes, "If you do not call them . . . your check will be held up. They always use this as a weapon. Any little thing, they're going to hold up your check; which I guess they are entitled to, but they should know when they are dealing with somebody legitimate."

2. *Larger societal forces have a direct impact on the lives of individuals.* For Roy, global economic forces, the shift in manufacturing venues, the dominance of discounting in retailing, and economic downturns have all negatively affected the industry and the company in which he was employed. These factors—not Roy's performance—resulted in his company's loss of revenue and Roy's loss of his long-term, well-compensated position.

Similarly, for Judy, her position was eliminated because of budget constraints confronting her agency. These financial pressures were related to an economic recession, the aftermath of 9/11 in which social service resources were diverted into crisis intervention service programs, the tightening of public dollars, and the reduction of philanthropic giving linked to the downward spiral of the stock market. For both Judy and Roy, job loss was a result of forces totally out of their control.

3. *Job loss and financial insecurity deeply impact an individuals' well-being and self-esteem.* Embedded in both stories are hints at the impact of unemployment on perception of self and on psychological health. Roy's matter-of-fact, emotionally guarded statements are hints at the anguish he and his family have experienced. The cold circumstances of his discharge from a place he described as "a home" did, as he notes, "hurt when you're with a company for that many years."

Roy's construction of the termination reflects his struggle. He objectively assesses the situation: "It was not personal, just dollars and cents, black and white." But the feelings bubble up: "The reality hits you; you get depressed. . . . I was let go the same day, without notice. . . ." He eases the pain with inventorying the good things he has: "My family is the best thing I have. I have two sons and a wonderful wife. We have our own home." He demonstrates his coping and resiliency with these perceptive philosophical thoughts: "You realize that sooner or later all good things come to an end, no matter what. You're not really secure financially. Mentally you can be, but when you get shook financially like that it affects your mental state, too. It's just a tough thing to take. You start looking to see if there is something you did. You can go through a million things, but it's not really you. So you lick your wounds and go on."

As Roy describes how he in fact does "go on," once again his psychic pain reemerges as he recounts his experiences at the unemployment office. Coping with reconciling a self-image based on achievement with being in need, he struggles with differentiating himself from other applicants. "For me," he notes, "waiting on line was very depressing. I was there with a suit and tie. Everybody there was wearing jeans. I didn't really talk to anyone until we got inside. . . . A lot of them seemed to be very familiar with the procedure. They had been there before. I was never there."

For Judy, similar expressions of the effect of her loss of position and status can be discerned. Her detailed recounting of her employment history and her accomplishments form a poignant prelude to her narration of her current situation. There is almost a frenetic quality to her story of how she is reinventing herself into an exemplary job seeker: "I've actually done the best I could; tried hard to work on my cover letters and keep looking over my résumé; take them everywhere that I go. I still network with people. . . . I've brainstormed with them. I've called them to let them know I am available. Then, one person from the corporate world actually challenged me. 'Well, what kind of things do you do well?' So, I actually made a list of things that I thought I could do. It was almost a whole page." Her frustration and disappointment are subtly seen. She "kind of expected that some group would say. . . . 'You're a good facilitator and organizer and encourager. We have a spot here you could fit.' It just hasn't really come along quite the way as I had hoped."

Judy and Roy have experienced relatively minor mental health consequences of unemployment. They report no impact on physical health. Others are not as fortunate. The relationship between job loss and related health problems has been well documented (see, for example, Murphy & Athanson, 1999; Emanciley, 2000; Sadova, 2000). Several protective factors emerge in both narratives. Both Judy and Roy have spent time looking for work and structured their days—activities linked with increased mental health for those who are unemployed (Wanburg & Griffiths, 1997). Both were able to see unemployment compensation as a benefit for which they had worked and paid. At least one study suggests that the more the payment is seen as an entitlement, the less the negative impact on health (Rodriguez, 2001). "You're entitled to it," Roy says. "You pay for it. They're not giving it to you for nothing, even though they act like they are." Later, he comments, "If you used up 13 weeks, you have another 13 weeks coming to you. But if you're beyond that and get another job, you have enough paid in, you can start another unemployment, as long as there's enough money paid in. If not, then you're out of unemployment (compensation). Sure, it's truly an insurance program."

As older applicants with long-term attachments to the workforce, Judy and Roy both brought to the unemployment situation strengths including the capacity to mobilize an organized, focused job search. Although Roy and Judy both faced the hazards of being in the job market at an age when the likelihood of retaining one's prior level of income or staying on a career track diminished, Roy did not perceive rejections as related to age discrimination. This may have empowered him to continue the search. Judy, while never mentioning her age, alluded to not seeking certain available positions because "if I walked in the door I wouldn't be the one that they would be having in their minds."

Potential employers' behavior contributes to the erosion of self-esteem. "I've sent out lots of letters and résumés. Very seldom does even an acknowledgment come back. And only once did I get a letter that said, 'Thank you for your application. We wanted to tell you that although you are qualified, we have decided to hire someone else.'"

Despite the obstacles of age, a recession, salary demands, and status deprivation inherent in being unemployed, Roy's and Judy's coping mechanisms functioned well. They, as most recipients, did not abuse the system by trying to prolong the period of benefit receipt. Unemployment insurance did not provide them with a vacation; it gave them the opportunity to put their energies into finding work. Roy brought a philosophical maturity to his quest. "I would have done anything, as long as it was legitimate work. . . . I went into other areas. . . . If you can sell, you can sell anything, so it didn't matter."

And finally, he obtained a new position in the same industry as his prior one: "Finally, I got a job and started working again. It was hard work, looking for work. Sometimes it's demeaning, but you do what you've got to do. That's it."

Judy is still searching, but is bringing her innate optimism and a pragmatic perspective to the process. "The ideal thing would be to have a choice of several jobs that would be within my value system, that would have decent benefits until such time as I will be eligible for Medicare. Then I'll just have to wait until I retire to learn to play the cello."

# 6

CHAPTER | **SUPPLEMENTAL SECURITY INCOME**

## THE LEGAL CONTEXT

### Authorizing Legislation

The Social Security Act of 1935 (42 U.S.C. § 401, *et seq.*) is the legal authority for the Supplemental Security Income (SSI) program. The Social Security Act contains 21 titles, including provisions for Supplemental Security Income for the Aged, Blind, and Disabled (Title XVI). SSI is codified at 42 U.S.C. § 1381, and was enacted to provide benefits to persons aged 65 or older, or who are blind, or who have a disability and lack sufficient income or resources. Specifically, it reads as follows:

> For the purpose of establishing a national program to provide supplemental security income to individuals who have attained age 65 or are blind or disabled . . . Every aged, blind, or disabled individual who is determined under part A to be eligible on the basis of income and resources shall, in accordance with and subject to the provisions of this title, be paid benefits. (42 U.S.C. § 1381a)

This general federal legislative language embodies several key principles, which are most succinctly described in the *Social Security Administration Handbook* (2001):

A. Payments are to be made to aged, blind, and disabled people whose income and resources are below specified amounts. This provides objective, measurable standards for determining eligibility and the amount of payment.

B. Title XVI lays out the right to SSI, the benefit levels, and the eligibility requirements. Disagreements about most aspects of SSI program administration can be handled via an administrative review of the decision, and even this outcome can be challenged ultimately in federal court.

C. SSI benefits are paid under conditions that protect the recipients' dignity as much as possible, and there are no restrictions on how the benefits is spent.

D. The eligibility requirements and the Federal income floor are identical everywhere the program operates (see § 2103). This provides assurance of a minimum income that States and the District of Columbia may choose to supplement.

E. Although some earned income is counted against the SSI income limit, benefit amounts are not reduced dollar-for-dollar as the result of income from work. Thus, recipients are encouraged to work, if possible. (See §§ 2173–2179 for a discussion of work incentives.) Blind and disabled recipients, if they are capable, are referred to the appropriate State vocational rehabilitation agencies for services to help them enter the labor market. (See § 2176 for more information on work incentives for the blind and disabled.) (*Social Security Administration Handbook*, 2001, § 2102.2, as rev. November 2004)

Both adults and children are eligible for SSI monthly benefits, and typically also qualify for related programs, such as food stamps and Medicaid. The benefit level varies, with the standard SSI benefit often supplemented by state benefits. The benefit is awarded only to the disabled individual (this effectively excludes their dependents). As a needs-based program, SSI incorporates strict limits on resources and unearned income. Moreover, the income from persons related to the SSI recipient, such as a spouse or parent, may be "deemed" available (that is, treated as though it were the recipient's), and this may result in lower benefits. The nuances of the eligibility requirements, particularly regarding the meaning of "disabled" and "income" are explicated in relevant regulations.

As mentioned earlier, SSI may be supplemented by state benefits— so-called state supplemental assistance. Many recipients take advantage of the sort of entitlement spelled out in the Pennsylvania state law illustrated in Box 6.1.

## Regulatory Authority

The governing federal regulations pertaining to SSI are found in the *Code of Federal Regulations* (C.F.R.), the compilation of all regulations issued by federal administrative agencies. Specifically, the SSI regulations are located in Title 20 of the C.F.R., Part 416, as depicted in Box 6.2.

| 6.1 | PENNSYLVANIA LAW REGARDING STATE SUPPLEMENTAL ASSISTANCE |

**(2) Persons who are eligible for State supplemental assistance.**

(i)   State supplemental assistance shall be granted to persons who receive Federal supplemental security income for the aged, blind and disabled pursuant to Title XVI of the Federal Social Security Act.

(ii)  State supplemental assistance shall also be granted to persons who are aged, blind and disabled, as defined in Title XVI of the Federal Social Security Act, and whose income, pursuant to the standards and income disregards of Title XVI of the Social Security Act, is less than the combined income of the Federal payments under the supplemental security income program and the State supplemental assistance payments established pursuant to the provisions of this act.

(iii) In establishing the amounts of the State supplemental assistance, the department shall consider the funds certified by the Budget Secretary as available for State supplemental assistance, pertinent Federal legislation and regulation, the cost-of-living and the number of persons who may be eligible.

(iv)  Beneficiaries of State supplemental assistance shall be eligible for cash State financial assistance to cover the cost of special needs as defined by statute and regulations promulgated under this act.

(v)   After the amounts of assistance payments have been determined by the department with the approval of the Governor and General Assembly, the amounts of assistance payments shall not be reduced as a consequence of assistance increases, including but not limited to cost-of-living increases, provided through Federal legislation.

Source: 62 Pennsylvania Statutes § 432

## Case Law

The judicial decisions presented in Boxes 6.3 and 6.4 address different dimensions of SSI, including both adult and child beneficiaries.

Eligibility for children has been especially challenging. Regarding the eligibility of minors to receive SSI, there is the opinion handed down in *Bryant v. Apfel* (1998), presented in Box 6.5. The Eighth Circuit has held that plaintiff child's migraine headaches do not satisfy the requirements for a listed impairment and he is therefore not eligible for supplemental security income (SSI). Plaintiff, a 14-year-old boy, alleges that he is disabled due to a learning disability and migraine headaches. His application for SSI was denied initially and on reconsideration, and he sought administrative review. At the hearing, plaintiff testified that he attends special education classes and has trouble concentrating. He also complained that he suffers from migraine headaches two or three times a week, lasting two to three hours at a time, that make him dizzy, sick to his stomach, and bring on photophobia. The administrative law judge found that, although plaintiff's impairments are severe, they are not of

**6.2**  FEDERAL REGULATIONS GOVERNING
SUPPLEMENTAL SECURITY INCOME

### TITLE 20—EMPLOYEES' BENEFITS
### CHAPTER I—SOCIAL SECURITY ADMINISTRATION
### PART 416—SUPPLEMENTAL SECURITY INCOME
### FOR THE AGED, BLIND, AND DISABLED SUBPART A—
### INTRODUCTION, GENERAL PROVISIONS AND DEFINITIONS
### 20CFR416.110

### § 416.110 Purpose of program.

The basic purpose underlying the supplemental security income program is to assure a minimum level of income for people who are age 65 or over, or who are blind or disabled and who do not have sufficient income and resources to maintain a standard of living at the established Federal minimum income level. The supplemental security income program replaces the financial assistance programs for the aged, blind, and disabled in the 50 States and the District of Columbia for which grants were made under the Social Security Act. Payments are financed from the general funds of the United States Treasury. Several basic principles underlie the program:

(a) Objective tests. The law provides that payments are to be made to aged, blind, and disabled people who have income and resources below specified amounts. This provides objective measurable standards for determining each person's benefits.

(b) Legal right to payments. A person's rights to supplemental security income payments—how much he gets and under what conditions—are clearly defined in the law. The area of administrative discretion is thus limited. If an applicant disagrees with the decision on his claim, he can obtain an administrative review of the decision and if still not satisfied, he may initiate court action.

(c) Protection of personal dignity. Under the Federal program, payments are made under conditions that are as protective of people's dignity as possible. No restrictions, implied or otherwise, are placed on how recipients spend the Federal payments.

(d) Nationwide uniformity of standards. The eligibility requirements and the Federal minimum income level are identical throughout the 50 States and the District of Columbia. This provides assurance of a minimum income base on which States may build supplementary payments.

(e) Incentives to work and opportunities for rehabilitation. Payment amounts are not reduced dollar-for-dollar for work income but some of an applicant's income is counted toward the eligibility limit. Thus, recipients are encouraged to work if they can. Blind and disabled recipients with vocational rehabilitation potential are referred to the appropriate State vocational rehabilitation agencies that offer rehabilitation services to enable them to enter the labor market.

(f) State supplementation. (1) Federal supplemental security income payments lessen the variations in levels of assistance and provide a basic level of assistance throughout the nation. . . . In addition, each State may choose to provide more than the Federal supplemental security income and/or mandatory minimum State supplementary payment to whatever extent it finds appropriate in view of the needs and resources of its citizens or it may choose to provide no more than the mandatory minimum payment where applicable. . . .

## 6.3  |  SIMS V. APFEL

### SIMS v. APFEL
### 530 U.S. 103 (2002)

*Summary: Petitioner, alleging a variety of ailments, applied for disability and Sup-plemental Security Income benefits under the Social Security Act. The state agency and an administrative law judge denied her claims. The Appeals Council denied her request for review, and the district court affirmed denial of benefits. The Supreme Court reversed, stating that Social Security claimants who exhausted administrative remedies need not present issues in a request for Appeals Council review in order to preserve judicial review of those issues.*

Justice Thomas announced the judgment of the Court and delivered the opinion of the Court with respect to Parts I and II—A, and an opinion with respect to Part II—B, in which Justice Stevens, Justice Souter, and Justice Ginsburg join.

* * * The Social Security Act provides that "[a]ny individual, after any final decision of the Commissioner of Social Security made after a hearing to which he was a party, . . . may obtain a review of such decision by a civil action" in federal district court. 42 U.S.C. § 405(g). But the Act does not define "final decision," instead leaving it to the SSA [Social Security Administration] to give meaning to that term through regulations. SSA regulations provide that, if the Appeals Council grants review of a claim, then the decision that the Council issues is the Commissioner's final decision. But if, as here, the Council denies the request for review, the ALJ's [administrative law judge's] opinion becomes the final decision. If a claimant fails to request review from the Council, there is no final decision and, as a result, no judicial review in most cases. In administrative-law parlance, such a claimant may not obtain judicial review because he has failed to exhaust administrative remedies.

The Commissioner rightly concedes that petitioner exhausted administrative remedies by requesting review by the Council. Petitioner thus obtained a final decision, and nothing in § 405(g) or the regulations implementing it bars judicial review of her claims.

Nevertheless, the Commissioner contends that we should require issue exhaustion in addition to exhaustion of remedies. That is, he contends that a Social Security claimant, to obtain judicial review of an issue, not only must obtain a final decision on his claim for benefits, but also must specify that issue in his request for review by the Council. (Whether a claimant must exhaust issues before the ALJ is not before us.) The Commissioner argues, in particular, that an issue-exhaustion requirement is "an important corollary" of any requirement of exhaustion of remedies. Brief for Respondent 13. We think that this is not necessarily so and that the corollary is particularly unwarranted in this case. Initially, we note that requirements of administrative issue exhaustion are largely creatures of statute. . . . Our cases addressing issue exhaustion reflect this fact. For example, we held [in an earlier case] that the Court of Appeals lacked jurisdiction to review objections not raised before the National Labor Relations Board. We so held because a statute provided that "'[n]o objection that has not been urged before the Board . . . shall be considered by the court.'" Here, the Commissioner does not contend that any statute requires issue exhaustion in the request for review.

Similarly, it is common for an agency's regulations to require issue exhaustion in administrative appeals. And when regulations do so, courts reviewing agency action regularly ensure against the bypassing of that requirement by refusing to consider unexhausted issues. Yet, SSA regulations do not require issue exhaustion. (Although the question is not before us, we think it likely that the Commissioner could adopt a regulation that did require issue exhaustion.)

It is true that we have imposed an issue-exhaustion requirement even in the absence of a statute or regulation. But the reason we have done so does not apply here. The basis for a judicially imposed issue-exhaustion requirement is an analogy to the rule that appellate courts will not consider arguments not raised before trial courts. As the Court explained in *Hormel v. Helverin*:

> "Ordinarily an appellate court does not give consideration to issues not raised below. For our procedural scheme contemplates that parties shall come to issue in the trial forum vested with authority to determine questions of fact. This is essential in order that parties may have the opportunity to offer all the evidence they believe relevant to the issues which the trial tribunal is alone competent to decide; it is equally essential in order that litigants may not be surprised on appeal by final decision there of issues upon which they have had no opportunity to introduce evidence. And the basic reasons which support this general principle applicable to trial courts make it equally desirable that parties should have an opportunity to offer evidence on the general issues involved in the less formal proceedings before administrative agencies entrusted with the responsibility of fact finding."

As we further explained in *L. A. Tucker Truck Lines*, courts require administrative issue exhaustion "as a general rule" because it is usually "appropriate under [an agency's] practice" for "contestants in an adversary proceeding" before it to develop fully all issues there. . . . More generally, we have observed that "it is well settled that there are wide differences between administrative agencies and courts," *Shepard v. NLRB*, and we have thus warned against reflexively "assimilat[ing] the relation of . . . administrative bodies and the courts to the relationship between lower and upper courts," *FCC v. Pottsville Broadcasting Co.*

The differences between courts and agencies are nowhere more pronounced than in Social Security proceedings. Although "[m]any agency systems of adjudication are based to a significant extent on the judicial model of decisionmaking," the SSA is "[p]erhaps the best example of an agency" that is not. The most important of [the SSA's modifications of the judicial model] is the replacement of normal adversary procedure by . . . the 'investigatory model.'"

Social Security proceedings are inquisitorial rather than adversarial. It is the ALJ's duty to investigate the facts and develop the arguments both for and against granting benefits, see *Richardson v. Perales,* and the Council's review is similarly broad. The Commissioner has no representative before the ALJ to oppose the claim for benefits, and we have found no indication that he opposes claimants before the Council.

The regulations make this nature of SSA proceedings quite clear. They expressly provide that the SSA "conducts the administrative review process in an informal,

*continued*

| 6.3 | SIMS V. APFEL (CONTINUED) |

nonadversary manner." They permit—but do not require—the filing of a brief with the Council (even when the Council grants review), and the Council's review is plenary unless it states otherwise, § 404.976(a). The Commissioner's involvement in the Appeals Council's decision whether to grant review appears to be not as a litigant opposing the claimant, but rather just as an advisor to the Council regarding which cases are good candidates for the Council to review pursuant to its authority to review a case *sua sponte*. The regulations further make clear that the Council will "evaluate the entire record," including "new and material evidence," in determining whether to grant review. Similarly, the notice of decision that ALJ's provide unsuccessful claimants informs them that if they request review, the Council will "consider all of [the ALJ's] decision, even the parts with which you may agree" and that the Council might review the decision "even if you do not ask it to do so." Finally, Form HA—520, which the Commissioner considers adequate for the Council's purposes in determining whether to review a case, provides only three lines for the request for review, and a notice accompanying the form estimates that it will take only 10 minutes to "read the instructions, gather the necessary facts and fill out the form." The form therefore strongly suggests that the Council does not depend much, if at all, on claimants to identify issues for review. Given that a large portion of Social Security claimants either have no representation at all or are represented by non-attorneys, the lack of such dependence is entirely understandable.

Thus, the Council, not the claimant, has primary responsibility for identifying and developing the issues. We therefore agree with the Eighth Circuit that "the general rule [of issue exhaustion] makes little sense in this particular context."

Accordingly, we hold that a judicially created issue-exhaustion requirement is inappropriate. Claimants who exhaust administrative remedies need not also exhaust issues in a request for review by the Appeals Council in order to preserve judicial review of those issues. The judgment of the Fifth Circuit is reversed, and the case is remanded for further proceedings consistent with this opinion.
It is so ordered.

---

comparable severity to those that would disable an adult. The district court affirmed, and plaintiff appealed.

Finally, in another decision regarding children's eligibility for SSI, *In re Cooke* (1998), an administrative law judge (ALJ) ruled that a child with insulin-dependent diabetes mellitus was under a "disability" as defined in the Social Security Act and thus eligible for child's Supplemental Security Income. The child's SSI claim, originally filed in 1990, was reevaluated after the passage, in 1996, of the Personal Responsibility and Work Opportunity Reconciliation Act (PRWORA; P.L. 104-193), which directed that children found disabled under the former standards must have their cases reviewed under newly enacted regulations.

The new regulations consider a child to be "disabled" for SSI eligibility purposes if the child has a medically determinable physical or mental impairment that (1) results in marked and severe functional limitation and (2) results or can be expected to result in death or impairment for a continuous period of at least 12 months.

| 6.4 | BERGMANN V. APFEL |

## BERGMANN v. APFEL
### 207 F.3d 1065 (2002)

*Summary:* The Eighth Circuit Court held that that the administrative law judge's decision denying plaintiff benefits was not supported by substantial evidence on the record as a whole. Plaintiffs application for disability insurance and Supplemental Security Income benefits was denied initially and on reconsideration. At the administrative hearing, the judge found plaintiff ineligible for benefits due to her work activity and concluded that there was no evidence that she was expected to remain off work for one year. Plaintiff sought review by the Appeals Council and submitted new evidence consisting of letters regarding her mental condition from her treating psychiatrist. According to these letters, plaintiff would be disabled for 12 months or longer and likely could not maintain gainful employment for the next two years. The Appeals Council denied the request for review, the district court granted defendant Commissioner of Social Security's motion for summary judgment, and plaintiff appealed. The Eighth Circuit concluded that plaintiff was entitled to disability benefits and remanded the case.*

OPINION: LAY, Circuit Judge.

### I. Background
Bergmann filed for disability insurance benefits and supplemental security income benefits under Titles II and XVI of the Social Security Act ("Act"), 42 U.S.C. §§ 401–33 and 1381–1383c, respectively. Bergmann alleged a disability onset date of July 17, 1995, citing back pain, headaches, emotional trauma, stress, fatigue, dizzy spells, and rheumatoid arthritis.

After being denied benefits initially and on reconsideration, Bergmann sought an administrative hearing. On May 5, 1997, a hearing was held before an Administrative Law Judge ("ALJ"). The ALJ rendered his decision on July 24, 1997, finding Bergmann ineligible for benefits due to her work activity. Specifically, the ALJ noted that "there is no 12 month period since the alleged onset date of July 17, 1995 when the claimant has not been employed at substantial gainful activity levels." The ALJ observed that, although off work at the time of the hearing, Bergmann had a relatively consistent employment history for the relevant time period and she testified to her intent to try to return to work. Based on this, the ALJ concluded, "there is no evidence that the claimant is expected to remain off work for one year." Thus, the ALJ found Bergmann not disabled and denied her benefits.

Bergmann filed a request for review of the ALJ's decision with the Appeals Council. With her request she submitted supplemental evidence unavailable at the time of the administrative hearing. This additional evidence consisted of, in part, letters from her treating psychiatrist, Dr. Donald W. Burnap, discussing her mental condition and opining that she would be disabled for twelve months or longer and likely could not maintain gainful employment for the next two years. Stating that it "considered" this additional evidence, but failing to expound upon it, the Appeals Council concluded that "neither the contentions nor the additional evidence provides [sic]

*continued*

## 6.4 | BERGMANN V. APFEL (CONTINUED)

a basis for changing the Administrative Law Judge's decision." Consequently, the Appeals Council denied the request for review, making the ALJ's decision the final determination of the Commissioner.

Bergmann then filed an action for review with the district court. On February 20, 1999, the district court issued its Memorandum Opinion and Order granting the Commissioner's motion for summary judgment. This appeal followed.

## II. Discussion

### A. Standard of Review

This court will uphold the Commissioner's decision denying benefits if it is supported by substantial evidence on the record as a whole. "Substantial evidence is less than a preponderance, but enough that a reasonable mind might accept it as adequate to support [the Commissioner's] decision." *Cox v. Apfel.* In determining whether existing evidence is substantial, this court looks at both evidence that supports and evidence that detracts from the Commissioner's decision.

In cases involving the submission of supplemental evidence subsequent to the ALJ's decision, the record includes that evidence submitted after the hearing and considered by the Appeals Council. Thus, in situations such as the present, this court's role is to determine whether the ALJ's decision "is supported by substantial evidence on the record as a whole, including the new evidence submitted after the determination was made." In practice, this requires this court to decide how the ALJ would have weighed the new evidence had it existed at the initial hearing. Id. As we have oft noted, "this [is] a peculiar task for a reviewing court." Id. Critically, however, this court may not reverse the decision of the ALJ merely because substantial evidence may allow for a contrary decision.

### B. Claimant's Work Activity

An individual is "disabled" under the Act if she is unable "to engage in any substantial gainful activity by reason of any medically determinable physical or mental impairment which can be expected to result in death or which has lasted or can be expected to last for a continuous period of not less than twelve months." 42 U.S.C. §§ 423(d)(l)(A) and 1382c(a)(3)(A). The burden of establishing a compensable disability under the Act is initially on the claimant.

In this case, Bergmann alleged a disability onset date of July 17, 1995. According to her employment history, she was employed until this alleged onset date, then was unemployed for a brief period before being employed again from April 22, 1996 until April 4, 1997. On April 4, just a month prior to the administrative hearing, Bergmann initiated a 90-day period of unpaid medical leave. At the administrative hearing, Bergmann testified to her intent to return to work:

> Q: And now you're waiting for the doctor to either release you to go back to work or limit you from going back to work?
> A: Well, Dr. Weaver said I have osterior (Phonetic) arthritis and I don't even know if I can deal with going back to work right now. I'm going to try. I'm going to see if Dr. Winslow will fill [the return to work forms] out for after I go for the MRI tomorrow and maybe return back to work Wednesday.
> Q: Okay, so you want to try to return back to work?
> A: That's right.

Considering Bergmann's work history, and more particularly, focusing on her testimonial intent to return to work, the ALJ found that there was "no evidence" that Bergmann was expected to remain off work for the requisite twelve months.

The district court summarized the situation presented to the ALJ: The ALJ was originally presented with a claimant who (although at the time on unpaid medical leave) had engaged in gainful employment in the recent past. In addition, Bergman [sic] testified that she intended to return to work in the future. Thus, at the time of his decision, the ALJ had not been presented with the possibility that Bergman [sic] would remain unemployed for the continuous period of twelve months or more necessary to establish a lack of substantial gainful activity. If these facts were the only basis for determining whether or not the ALJ's decision was based on substantial evidence, this Court would have little choice but to affirm. Having read the transcript of the administrative hearing and reviewed all of the exhibits submitted at the hearing, this court finds the ALJ's initial determination of no disability to be supported by substantial evidence on the record as a whole. However, this is not the end of our inquiry. As the district court correctly pointed out, the submission of the additional evidence to the Appeals Council complicates the analysis; thus, this court now turns to that additional evidence.

*C. Evidence Submitted to the Appeals Council*
Bergmann argues that the Commissioner erred in failing to give the appropriate weight to her treating physician's opinion that she would be disabled for the requisite twelve months. It is well-settled that a treating physician's opinion is entitled to substantial weight "unless it is unsupported by medically acceptable clinical or diagnostic data."

Dr. Burnap was Bergmann's treating physician and the basis of his opinion is not challenged; consequently, his opinion is entitled to great weight. This court, however, is not faced with the simple question of due-weight to be given a treating physician's opinion; rather, this court must consider that question in light of the fact the evidence was submitted subsequent to the ALJ's decision. 20 C.F.R. 404.970(b) provides:

> If new and material evidence is submitted, the Appeals Council shall consider the additional evidence only where it relates to the period on or before the date of the administrative law judge hearing decision. The Appeals Council shall evaluate the entire record including the new and material evidence submitted if it relates to the period on or before the date of the administrative law judge hearing decision.

Thus, the Appeals Council must consider evidence submitted with a request for review if it is "(a) new, (b) material, and (c) relates to the period on or before the date of the ALJ's decision." Whether evidence meets these criteria is a question of law this court reviews de novo.

To be "new," evidence must be more than merely cumulative of other evidence in the record. To be "material," the evidence must be relevant to claimant's condition for the time period for which benefits were denied. Id. Thus, to qualify as "material," the additional evidence must not merely detail after-acquired conditions or post-decision deterioration of a pre-existing condition.

Prior to the administrative hearing, Bergmann saw Dr. Burnap on June 4, 1996, January 20, 1997, and February 25, 1997. The evidence from these visits indicates

*continued*

a diagnosis of Bergmann's "relatively longstanding depression or dysthymic disorder." Further, the reports note an ongoing deterioration in her condition, and, as early as June 4, 1996, predict that she would not be able to maintain gainful employment over an extended period of time. Subsequent to the administrative hearing, Bergmann again saw Dr. Burnap. The medical reports from these post-hearing visits on August 27, 1997, September 25, 1997, and October 2, 1997, constitute the additional evidence submitted to the Appeals Council. These post-hearing reports continue to discuss the medical condition presented to the ALJ, but provide a more specific and conclusive diagnosis regarding Bergmann's disability and work capacity.

Specifically, the August 27, 1997, report notes that Bergmann's major mental illness remains the same, yet it identifies changes in her condition:

> During the past three weeks she has had no appetite, feels she is losing weight and also sleeps very poorly. . . . During the past seven months she has had no social contact with others and no other personal involvement in any activities outside her mobile home. In the past three weeks she has not been able to do any cooking, housework or any other household activities. She sits in a chair.

This same report notes, "at the present time her condition is significantly worse than it was seven months ago and an obvious factor is the death of her ex-husband several weeks ago."

The September 25, 1997, report again indicates no change in the overall diagnosis, but states "her mental disorder is gradually getting worse. She has now been off work since April 4, 1997."

Finally, the October 2, 1997, report states:

> I can say with reasonable medical certainty that [Bergmann] will be disabled for 12 months and probably much longer. My opinion is based on the nature of her back disorder and level of depression. I have now been following her illness since June, 1996, and during this time her condition has steadily worsened. Without assistance she will soon be in serious trouble and even with treatment she will probably not be able to maintain any sort of gainful employment for at least 2 years.

This additional evidence outlines the progress of Bergmann's condition from before the time of the ALJ's decision and culminates in Dr. Burnap's October 2, 1997, conclusion that she is disabled and cannot maintain gainful employment. This evidence is both new and material to the claim for disability before the ALJ. The evidence is

---

## THE PROGRAM CONTEXT

### Overview

The SSI program is a nationwide federal assistance program administered by the Social Security Administration (SSA) that guarantees a minimum level of income for needy aged, blind, or disabled individuals. Historically, the program has helped many beneficiaries avoid destitution, although the ultimate benefit level still represents only about 70 percent of the federal poverty

new because it describes deterioration and provides, for the first time, a conclusive psychiatric determination of disability and inability to work. It is material because, although it involves deterioration, that deterioration occurred over the course of Dr. Burnap's treatment, specifically including the time period before the ALJ.

Accordingly, the picture presented to the ALJ is significantly altered by the additional evidence. Now the evidence shows a claimant who had engaged in gainful employment in the recent past, who is currently on unpaid medical leave, and, despite her expressed hope, has been unable to return to work. Furthermore, a treating physician has clearly indicated disability and inability to return to any work for a prolonged period. Thus, the ALJ's conclusion that there was "no evidence that the claimant is expected to remain off work for one year" is no longer supported by substantial evidence on the record as a whole.

In *Jenkins*, this court's most recent opinion dealing with the question of "new" evidence, the claimant submitted to the Appeals Council medical reports from a treating physician indicating less residual functional capacity than the ALJ had determined. Relying on the weight to be accorded treating physicians, and the fact that the new evidence undermined the ALJ's sole reason for crediting the non-treating doctor's assessment, the court reversed the finding of no disability. Similarly, the ALJ in the present case emphasized a single reason for his finding—Bergmann's testimonial intent to return to work. Bergmann, however, did not return to work and her treating physician strongly indicates her inability to do so in the foreseeable future; thus, the ALJ's reason for denying a disability finding is no longer supported by substantial evidence.

In light of the weight generally owed treating physicians and the fact that Dr. Burnap's psychiatric evaluation is uncontroverted, this court holds that Bergmann is entitled to disability benefits. However, while Dr. Burnap's opinion is clear regarding a finding of disability and inability to engage in gainful employment for the immediate future, the evidence does not reveal a clear onset date. In addition, Dr. Burnap's opinion is now more than two years old, so we do not know whether Bergmann's condition has improved such that she is no longer disabled and thus, entitled to only a closed period of disability benefits. Such factual determinations are within the province of the Commissioner; thus, this court remands to the Commissioner.

### III. Conclusion

Accordingly, the judgment of the district court is reversed, and the case remanded with instructions to remand to the Commissioner for reconsideration in light of the new evidence and to further afford the parties the opportunity to supplement the record with any additional evidence.

threshold for individuals and 83 percent for two-person households (Social Security Administration, 2000). In January 2001, 6.4 million individuals received monthly federal SSI payments averaging $363. Federal expenditures for cash payments under the SSI program during calendar year 2000 totaled $28.8 billion, and the cost of administering the SSI program in fiscal year 2000 was $2.4 billion (*Social Security Administration Handbook*, 2001, § 2100, *et seq., as rev. November 2004).

| 6.5 | BRYANT V. APFEL |

## BRYANT v. APFEL
## 141 F.3D 1249 (1998)

*Summary:* Donald Bryant, Sr. appeals the district court's grant of summary judgment to the Social Security Administration, affirming the Commissioner's decision to deny his application for children's Supplemental Security Insurance (SSI) disability benefits on behalf of his son, Donald Bryant, Jr. (Donald Jr.). Mr. Bryant applied for children's SSI disability benefits on behalf of his son, Donald Jr., alleging that Donald Jr. was disabled due to a learning disability and migraine headaches. The Social Security Administration denied the claim both initially and upon reconsideration. The Court of Appeals affirmed the lower court's decision.

OPINION: Hansen, Circuit Judge.

At the time of the hearing, Donald Jr. was 14 years old and in the sixth grade. He was attending special education classes and said he had trouble concentrating. He testified that he gets along well with his teachers and friends, with the exception of two or three fights. Donald Jr. complained that he suffers migraine headaches two or three times a week, lasting two to three hours at a time. He said he has had these headaches since he was born. The headaches usually start around 2:00 in the afternoon. He said they make him dizzy, sick to his stomach, and bring on photophobia (a painful sensitivity to light). Relief comes only from the combination of prescription medication and sleep; aspirin and Tylenol had no effect. Donald Jr. is also anemic, which makes him tired and less active than other children.

Although he testified that he had these headaches his whole life, Donald Jr. sought medical attention for the first time in September 1994, just months prior to the hearing. At that time, the results of a CT scan performed on his head were normal, and Dr. Joe Elser diagnosed the headaches as migraine headaches. He prescribed Amitriptyline for Donald Jr. and instructed Donald Jr. to keep a diary of his headaches, to continue the medication for two to three months, to report back on its effectiveness, and to consider further therapy if the medication proved to be unsuccessful. There is no indication that Donald Jr. sought further treatment.

In a 1991 intellectual evaluation recommended by the school system due to his poor academic progress, Donald Jr. scored a verbal IQ of 79, a performance IQ of 93, and a full scale IQ of 85 on the Weschler Intelligence Scale for Children-Revised. The results of this evaluation placed Donald Jr. in the slow learner level of intellectual functioning. Subsequently in 1995, Donald Jr. was reevaluated at the request of his attorney. On this occasion, Donald Jr. scored a verbal IQ of 70, a performance IQ of 71, and a full scale IQ of 69 on the Weschler Intelligence Scale for Children-Revised. These scores placed Donald Jr. within the classification of mild retardation.

Donald Jr.'s fifth grade teacher indicated that he was doing well in school. She said Donald Jr. behaves in an age appropriate manner, that he is polite and interacts well with his classmates, and that he always completes his work assignments. She said he is sleepy at times but concentrates well. Records indicate that Donald Jr. misses school only 3 or 4 times a year due to his headaches.

The ALJ found that Donald Jr. has severe impairments, but that they do not meet or equal a listed impairment. The ALJ then performed an individual functional assessment and determined that Donald Jr.'s impairments are not of comparable severity to those which would disable an adult. Accordingly, the ALJ denied benefits, and the appeals council denied further review.

On behalf of his son, Mr. Bryant sought judicial review of the agency decision. The district court concluded that the ALJ's decision was supported by substantial evidence on the record. Thus, the court granted summary judgment in favor of the Commissioner. Mr. Bryant appeals, arguing that the ALJ's decision is not supported by substantial evidence because Donald Jr. has a listed impairment of mental retardation, evidenced by his full scale IQ score of 69 and his history of migraine headaches.

We review the Commissioner's denial of a child's SSI disability benefits by considering whether substantial evidence supports the Commissioner's decision. Substantial evidence exists when a reasonable mind would conclude the evidence is adequate to support the decision, and we consider evidence that detracts from the Commissioner's decision as well as evidence that supports it.

Consistent with the standards applicable at the time of the ALJ's decision, the ALJ followed a four-step sequential evaluation process for determining whether Donald Jr. was entitled to children's SSI benefits. Using this process, the ALJ determined that (1) Donald Jr. is a student and not engaged in work activity, (2) he suffers from severe impairments including a learning disability and migraine headaches, but (3) his impairments do not meet or equal a listed impairment, and additionally, (4) he does not have an impairment or combination of impairments that are comparable to those which would disable an adult.

On August 22, 1996, prior to the district court's review of the ALJ's decision, the President signed into law the Personal Responsibility and Work Opportunity Reconciliation Act of 1996. This new legislation requires a child to prove that he or she has a "medically determinable physical or mental impairment, which results in marked and severe functional limitations." This is a more stringent standard than the old one. This new standard eliminates the fourth step in the old evaluation process, which previously allowed a finding of disability if the child suffered a "medically determinable physical or mental impairment of comparable severity" to one that would disable an adult. The new standard applies to Donald Jr.'s case, because this case was pending at the time the new legislation was enacted. Nevertheless, we will apply the old standard as did the ALJ, because where a claim was properly denied under the old standard, "it must also be denied under the new, more stringent, standard." We conclude that the ALJ properly denied the claim under the old standard.

Mr. Bryant's only argument is that the ALJ's finding that Donald Jr.'s impairments do not meet the listing for mental retardation is not supported by substantial evidence. A child meets the mental retardation listing and is disabled when the child has "[1] [a] verbal, performance, or full scale IQ of 60 through 70 and [2] a physical or other mental impairment imposing additional and significant limitation of function."

Donald Jr.'s 1995 full scale IQ score of 69 meets the first prong of the listing. The ALJ discounted this score by considering that the result is inconsistent with Donald Jr.'s 1991 full scale IQ score of 85. The ALJ found that the earlier, significantly higher score combined with his appearance and demeanor at the hearing indicate that Donald Jr. is closer to the low normal range than the retarded range of intelligence. Mr. Bryant asserts that the ALJ should not have considered the 1991 score, arguing that it is not sufficiently current for an accurate assessment under the list-

*continued*

| 6.5 | BRYANT V. APFEL (CONTINUED) |

ing. Social Security regulations state "'an arguable deficiency in opinion-writing technique is not a sufficient reason for setting aside an administrative finding where . . . the deficiency probably has no practical effect on the outcome of the case.'" Our review of the record convinces us that substantial evidence exists to support the ALJ's conclusion that Donald Jr.'s headaches impose no more than a slight limitation of function at this time, which is not sufficient to satisfy the second prong of the mental retardation listing. He has missed little school on account of his headaches. His headaches are responding to his medication, which he only recently sought and obtained. Additionally, his school work has been improving, and he gets along well with others at school.

We conclude that Donald Jr. does not satisfy the requirements for a listed impairment, and the ALJ's decision to deny benefits is supported by substantial evidence. Accordingly, we affirm the judgment of the district court.

Specifically, the Annual Report indicates that:

- Throughout the 25-year period ending in 2025, the SSI program is estimated to grow largely due to the overall growth in the U.S. population. By 2025, the federal SSI recipient population is estimated to reach 7.9 million.
- Expressed as a percentage of the total U.S. population, the number of federal SSI recipients remained level at 2.21 percent in 2000, and is projected to remain fairly level at 2.2 to 2.3 percent of the population through 2025.
- Federal expenditures for SSI payments in calendar year 2001 are estimated to total $30.5 billion, an increase of $1.7 billion from 2000 levels.
- Growth in SSI program outlays during the next 25 years is projected to remain relatively modest, in constant 2001 dollars, the cost of the program is projected to increase to $39.7 billion in 2025.
- When compared to the gross domestic product (GDP), federal SSI expenditures are projected to decline over time, from the current level of 0.29 percent of GDP in 2000 to 0.25 percent of GDP by 2025. (Social Security Administration, 2001)

## Application and Eligibility

**Adult Eligibility**    While the SSI program provides a national guaranteed standard income for the aged, blind, and disabled, it is a stringent program. "SSI eligibility standards are rigorous," Greenberg and Baumohl (1996) argue,

> and the determination process is lengthy and complex. The factors used to calculate whether an individual is disabled make it significantly more difficult for an individual to qualify when of prime working age, even if, as a practical matter, the individual is unlikely to find employment in the local labor market. Moreover, the

durational requirement—that disability must be expected to last at least a year or end in death—excludes some seriously disabling conditions. (pp. 72–73)

The eligibility qualifications are straightforward: age 65 is the threshold for elderly recipients; blind is relatively self-defining, but there are allowances for grave vision difficulties short of actual blindness; and disability, which may be physical or mental, assumes an inability to engage in substantial gainful activity and that this impairment lasts at least a year or is likely to result in death. Both children and adults may be deemed eligible under the blind or disability requirements. Under some circumstances it may be possible for someone whose blindness is not severe enough to qualify for benefits to receive assistance based on disability, providing the condition limits or prevents gainful employment. SSI recipients are also typically eligible for food stamps and for Medicaid, which covers costs for doctor and hospital care (Social Security Administration, 2001).

As a means-tested program, SSI eligibility is dependent on income—wages, Social Security benefits, pensions, and such noncash items as clothing, food, and shelter (Social Security Administration, 2001). Married persons may have their spouse's income deemed available, and parental income may figure into the eligibility calculus for minors.

Income requirements require some further clarification. For example, SSI recipients may receive their benefits even though they receive some income; the amount one can earn and still receive SSI varies among the states. Moreover, not all income is counted for SSI purposes. Specifically, SSI does not calculate the following in its benefits equation:

- The first $20 of most income received in a month
- The first $65 a month earned from working and half the amount over $65
- Food stamps
- Shelter obtained from private nonprofit organizations
- Most home energy assistance
- Some wages or scholarships for students (Social Security Administration, 2001)

For those who are disabled yet work, wages used to pay for disability-related items (for example, a wheelchair) or services are not counted against SSI benefits. The same is true for blind SSI recipients (for example, they may be able to discount work-related transportation costs and thus not have such costs included as income). As a general rule, persons who are blind or disabled should make special effort to discover if there are special rules that pertain to their status and might affect their SSI eligibility or receipt (Social Security Administration, 2001).

So-called countable resources for an individual may not exceed $2,000 ($3,000 for a couple) to be eligible for SSI. Among the items that are *not* included among the "countable resources":

- A home and the land on which it's located
- Life insurance policies with face value of $1,500 or less
- An automobile
- Burial plots for beneficiary and immediate family
- Up to $ 1,500 in burial funds
- Items intended for work or to earn extra income, in the case of blind or disabled individuals (Social Security Administration, 2001)

Finally, SSI eligibility requires U.S. citizenship or status as a U.S. national, along with residence in the United States or Northern Mariana islands. If an individual is concurrently eligible for Social Security, she or he must make a separate application, as one can, in fact, receive both benefits if all eligibility requirements are met. Those deemed disabled must also accept vocational rehabilitation services, if offered (Social Security Administration, 2001).

**Children's Eligibility**    The Personal Responsibility and Work Opportunity Reconciliation Act of 1996 changed the definition of disability for children under the Supplemental Security Income (SSI) program.

The definition of disability for children:

- Requires a child to have a physical or mental condition which results in marked and severe functional limitations.
- Requires that the medically proven physical or mental condition or conditions must last or be expected to last at least 12 months or be expected to result in death.
- Says that a child may not be considered disabled if he or she is working at a job that is considered to be substantial work. (However, the law did not change the rules that allow certain children already on the rolls to continue to receive SSI even though they are working.)

*Continuing Disability Reviews*    The law requires the Social Security Administration (SSA) to do a continuing disability review (CDR) to determine whether or not the child is still disabled. The CDR must be done:

- At least every 3 years for recipients under age 18 whose conditions are likely to improve, and
- Not later than 12 months after birth for babies whose disability is based on their low birth weight

The SSA also may do CDRs for recipients under age 18 whose conditions are not likely to improve.

*Evidence of Treatment*    At the time the SSA does a CDR, the representative payee must present evidence that the child is and has been receiving treatment considered medically necessary and available for his or her disabling condition. This is true in every case unless the SSA determines that requiring such evidence would be inappropriate or unnecessary.

If the child's representative payee refuses without good cause to provide such evidence when requested, the SSA will suspend payment of benefits to the representative payee and select another representative payee if it is in the best interest of the child. Or, the SSA may pay the child directly if he or she is old enough.

*Disability Redetermination at Age 18*    Any individual who was eligible as a child in the month before he or she attained age 18 must have his or her eligibility redetermined. The redetermination will be done during the 1-year period beginning on the individual's 18th birthday. SSA will use the rules for adults filing new claims to do the redetermination.

*Children in Certain Medical Care Facilities*    In addition to the definition of disability, the law affects children under age 18 who live, throughout a calendar month, in certain institutions where private health insurance pays for their care. The monthly SSI payment for these children will be limited to $30. Previously, the $30 SSI payment limit applied only when Medicaid paid more than half of the cost of their care (Social Security Administration Handbook, 2001).

**Application Process**    The application process for SSI is relatively straightforward. Individuals must make an appointment to apply, making certain to supply the required documentation (for example, Social Security number; proof of age, residence, and U.S. citizenship; income information; and relevant medical data for determining disability) for verifying eligibility. The disability determination evaluation is perhaps the most stringent dimension of the application procedure, and there are separate stages for adult versus child applicants (Social Security Administration, 2001).

The so-called sequential evaluation process for adult disability determination includes five steps, the application of which are designed to ensure national uniformity and expedient decision making. These steps involve the following determinations. A negative outcome at any one of the stages halts movement to the next level, typically resulting in the denial of the claim:

1. Whether the claimant is performing substantial gainful activity (SGA)
2. The severity of the impairment(s)
3. Whether the impairment(s) meet or equal any listing in the "Listing of Impairments" (a uniform set of medical evaluation criteria for all body systems)
4. Whether the impairment(s) preclude the ability to perform past relevant work, despite the impairment(s), and
5. Whether the impairment(s) preclude the ability to perform any other work

The disability determination process for children varies somewhat from the one used for adults. The objective is the same; namely, to move through a set of standard procedures that ensure national uniformity. As in the adult process, a negative outcome at any stage ends the claimant's process. Unlike the adult process, however, the child is assessed on whether his or her impairment or combination of impairments results in marked and severe functional limitations. For children, then, the steps determine the following:

1. Whether the child is performing SGA
2. Whether the child's impairment or combination of impairments are severe (that is, more than a minimal impact on child's functioning), and
3. Whether the child's impairment(s) meet or medically or functionally equal in severity any listing in the aforementioned "Listing of Impairments"

## Benefits

The maximum federal benefit changes yearly. Effective January 1, 2003, the federal benefit rate is $579 for an individual and $867 for a couple (Social Security Administration, 2002). Some states add to the federal SSI benefit, and SSI payment levels are higher in those states. The states that do not provide state supplemental benefits as of January 2005 are Arkansas, Georgia, Kansas, Mississippi, Northern Mariana Islands, Tennessee, and West Virginia. Payment amounts vary based upon income, living arrangements, and other factors. The administration of the state supplement varies, as well; with some administered by the Social Security Administration, some by the state, and others by both state and SSA.

The Personal Responsibility and Work Opportunity Reconciliation Act of 1996 significantly modified SSI benefits to noncitizens. Specifically, SSI benefits are limited, according to the following categories:

- Citizens or nationals of the United States.
- Certain noncitizens who were lawfully residing in the United States on August 22, 1996, and who are blind or disabled, or who were receiving SSI on August 22, 1996.
- Noncitizens who are lawfully admitted for permanent residence under the Immigration and Nationality Act (INA) and have a total of 40 qualifying quarters of work. Quarters of work acquired after December 31, 1996, cannot be counted if the noncitizen, spouse, or parent received certain types of federally funded benefits based on limited income and resources during that period.
- Certain noncitizens who are active duty members, or who are honorably discharged veterans, of the U.S. armed forces, their spouses, and unmarried dependent children. The unremarried spouse and unmarried dependent child of a deceased veteran also may qualify.
- American Indians born outside the United States who are under Section 289 of the INA, or who are members of federally recognized Indian tribes under Section 4(e) of the Indian Self-Determination and Education Assistance Act.
- Certain noncitizens admitted as Amerasian immigrants under Section 584 of the Foreign Operations, Export Financing, and Related Programs Appropriations Act, 1988. SSI eligibility is limited to the first 7 years after being admitted.

- Cuban or Haitian entrants as defined in Section 501(e) of the Refugee Education Assistance Act of 1980 may be eligible for 7 years from the date their status was granted.
- Certain other noncitizens may be eligible for 7 years after:
  — The date of admission as a refugee under Section 207 of the INA
  — The date granted asylum under Section 208 of the INA, or
  — The date deportation is withheld under Section 243 (h) of the INA (as in effect prior to April 1, 1997), or the date removal has been withheld under section 241(b)(3) of the INA (Social Security Administration, 2002)

Proof of U.S. citizenship status must be provided. Noncitizen applicants who served in the armed forces may also need to provide similar evidence of their military service (Social Security Administration, 2002).

## Due Process

The Social Security Administration provides for an appeal of any adverse decision, including those associated with SSI. The typical appellate procedures include (1) reconsideration, (2) a hearing before an administrative law judge, (3) an appeals council review, and (4) review by federal court. The appeal is limited to so-called initial determinations, which include decisions, rendered by SSA in writing, regarding eligibility, benefits amounts, overpayment of benefits, or receipt of notice of proposed termination of benefits. The process begins with the individual notifying the SSA of the intent to appeal. The appellant may decide to have representation throughout the appeals process.

### Stages of the Appeals Process

*Initial Determination*   The process begins with an official notification, in writing, of SSA's action regarding an application for SSI. This notice is the "initial determination" and is the basis for appeal; it—the determination—is, in fact, what is appealed (Social Security Administration, 2002).

*Reconsideration*   In nearly all states, a reconsideration may be requested in writing by submitting the appropriate forms. The beneficiary or his or her representative has 60 days—from the initial determination decision—within which to request, in writing, the reconsideration. Requests made within 10 days will enable the beneficiary to continue to receive benefits until a decision is made regarding the reconsideration. Appeals of disability cessation must be requested in writing in order for benefits to continue. Ultimately, the SSA will notify the recipient of its decision.

*Hearing*   The reconsideration decision may be appealed by requesting a hearing before an administrative law judge. The beneficiary has 60 days within which to submit the request for hearing form, after which the beneficiary (or his or her representative) may review the file for accuracy and to add new evidence, if necessary. As with the reconsideration, the continuation of benefits during an appeal of the cessation of benefits is contingent upon submitting a written request within 10 days of the hearing. The hearing may be waived, in which case the decision will be based on the ALJ's review of the file evidence. However, the beneficiary, or his or her representative, must be present for the ALJ's review. Travel costs to the hearing will be paid by the SSA, provided the appellant resides more than 75 miles from the hearing.

In instances of disability, the ALJ—or the appellant—may request evidence of medical exams or tests. The ALJ may also call witnesses to help with the hearing process, including those that the appellant may have requested. Both the ALJ and the appellant may pose questions to witnesses. The hearing is recorded, and a copy of the record is available to all parties.

*Appeals Council*    An Appeals Council review of the hearing decision may be obtained by submitting the appropriate form ("Request for Review of Hearing Decision/Order") within 60 days. The appellant or his or her representative may enter new evidence into the file. The Appeals Council reviews the evidence and eventually renders a decision, a copy of which is made available to the parties. One outcome may be to grant the requested review, in which case it will either decide the case or send it back to the ALJ for further action, which could include another hearing and a new decision.

*Federal Court*    While the Appeals Council decision is the final outcome within the context of possible remedies in the administrative process, these decisions can be appealed ultimately to the U.S. District Court, and such actions must be filed within 60 days of the Appeals Council determination. The court will review the evidence and earlier decisions, to determine if there have been errors of law or if the agency has acted beyond the scope of its authority. This occasion for judicial review, however, does not involve another hearing; it is solely an appellate review.

## THE CLIENTS' STORIES

### Martin

Okay, I grew up on a dairy farm. So I'm a Jewish cowboy I guess you could say. It was a very strange situation growing up, I was isolated on a farm, it was about close to 800 acres in the middle of the Pine Barrens basically. And it was away from society, it was away from community, didn't have neighbors. The neighbors I had were my brother and his family, my sister and her family, and it was like my parents were in charge of their work, and their society and their culture, and their choice of who's coming in and out of their lives. And if they don't like the world, they can go back to their world, it was that isolated. I went to a private school, a private Quaker school, so that was a whole different setup than the public school system. And a very good system. But again it was another form of isolation. So it wasn't until getting out into the real world that it's not as peaceful and wonderful as you may think it is. It could be. The thing is I came along so late in life, I questioned everything, I grew up in a racist county, I grew up in a very homophobic town, and a very anti-Semitic town.

I studied music for 3 years in college, working on a harpsichord, gave it up for interior design and architecture. . . . I was married in '84, I had a daughter in '87 and I was diagnosed with HIV in July of '88. And all of a sudden my wife is like, bye, and that was a quick wake-up call. My daughter is 14. I write letters all the time, I write e-mails all the time, I call and leave messages. She doesn't get them. It's very spiteful. My ex-wife is the worst. But, you know, that's the way it goes. It hurts. Moved out of the house a year later, met my partner a month after I moved out in October of '89. We had 9 years together, and he died 3 years ago in July. And I was a full-time care-giver to him for 3 years. In the past 3 years I have been regrouping, going through a transition, doing full-time volunteering for HIV and AIDS patients, cofacilitating a support group, acting as a buddy and mentor for the local agency dealing with AIDS patients. And people kept telling me to go to school for social work. And I'm like, fine, I'll go to school and I'll flunk out and then I'll show them. It's been 20 years since my undergraduate degree. I've been back in school since January taking courses and I keep acing multiple tests, and it's blowing my mind. For the past two months I met somebody, he's a great guy, he has two disabled kids, and an ex-wife who works for a local hospital.

It's probably the happiest I've ever been in my whole life. It's just, things are finally working altogether. I mean I'm surprised I'm here, you know I was told in July of '88 to get my affairs in order and I have 6 months to live. So, everything's good. I'm not on any med-ication except for Xanax, Wellbutrin, that kind of stuff.

I was diagnosed with chronic myopathy in '95. My doctor put me on medication because my counts had crashed for the first time due to stress for a lot of losses in my life. And from the side effects of the medication I couldn't use my hands or feet or that kind of stuff, so I had to give up design. Because my partner and I at the time thought we were going to die anyway, we just like ran our credit cards, blew money, we had a ball. But the bad news was I had to go on SSI 'cause I didn't have any money saved. And it's kind of humiliating, honestly, you know, when you're used to mak-ing good money and a life, and then you have to live below the poverty level, it's very humiliating and, you can get in touch with what really matters.

As an interior designer, as a design coordinator, I worked with a lot of architects from casino work to corporate work to having my own business with my wife at the time, and then it was split up at the time of my diagnosis. I was a consultant with some designers and, basically stopped it in '95 and became fully involved with HIV and AIDS issues and found out that what I chose for my life wasn't a passion anymore. That this seemed to be more in line with my life. I never thought that I would allow it to consume my life because I always said it wouldn't but it's become my life, it just, it works, I guess.

Since 1995, I had to go on disability. It sort of like changed my whole mindset. Because I used to evaluate that I-am-my-job, you know, I think a lot of people do that and it's not true at all.

In terms of my shift to a social work career, originally I thought I wanted to be involved with HIV and AIDS only because of the people that encouraged me, with all the help that that community gave me. But I don't see that as my focus, I don't see that as stretching myself at all. I say this too easily. I have become involved in loss and bereavement and that kind of transition. And I seem to do well at it.

Well, I make other people laugh in the darkest of times, I guess, um, probably from a support group that I cofacilitate on Thursday nights. It works. People call me, um, all the time, I'm online all the time with people, talking to them. I don't know why, but there's just, either it's something I do or my personality or something I say or how I see things that seems to empower people and create change. And that's kind of neat.

My economic circumstances have been a little unusual over the years. I guess until the time I was diagnosed, I was probably making between $75 to $100,000 a year which was a nice salary. Well at least when I was on my own. That was probably from more like '83 to '88. And when I was diagnosed and, my wife left the business, and went through that abandonment, I just went through a huge depression for about a year-and-a-half. So, from that I did consulting work with some architects and designers probably making about $45 to $50,000 a year. And then in '95 when I had to go on disability, it became $500 and something a month, which was kind of strange. But my partner was on Social Security Disability [SSD], so we could make it with the two of us. It wasn't until he passed away in July of '98 that all of sudden I realized that I don't have much money. It is tough. I was just about making it.

With SSD, he was making close to about, if I'm not wrong, almost a $1,000 a month, and I was making like five-something, so for two of us to live off of $1,500 a month it was okay. Plus there was housing assistance, there were food deliveries, um, there was food a lot when he still was alive. There were a lot of things available to HIV and AIDS patients. Now that I'm doing so well, they've taken a lot of these things away.

I can use food stamps, it's not always a lot. It's just, to me, that whole situation of going from one extreme to the other and then having an illness and then being reminded of it by being in a humiliating situation, is very strange. I mean it's a catch-22, it's, I don't want to stay in that situation which is why I'm back in school and my health is good enough to allow me to do this. I mean, when I finish school, I don't know. Could I get sick and die in the middle of it, maybe. But I'm willing to take that chance. Well, it's living on a third of an income that I was used to, that I have become accustomed to with my partner. Luckily I moved into a building where, it was owned by friends of mine, in the art museum area, which is actually very nice, so it cost me $120 a month which is great, so that's affordable. That comes with a rent assistance subsidy through the Tenet action group, which is the AIDS social service agency and tenant housing.

All the services I received were through my case worker from the local AIDS advocacy agency. Whether it was even getting into SSI, getting health benefits, housing, food assistance, everything. I first had contact with them when my partner was getting sick, well actually he was probably one of the first people ever diagnosed with AIDS in this country, and it's lucky he did so well and for so long. So he was one of the very early clients of theirs. And they really helped us out with a lot of things. I didn't know of any other organization that was as good in town for support or what not. And whether it was finding support groups or finding resources, or having somebody advocating for us, they really provided me with a lot and I feel I owe them something, but I don't know if I owe them, like, my majoring in college and going back and working for them the rest of my life like they would like me to. I don't think that's really where I want to go.

My case manager went with me when I went to apply for SSI. She went with me, because of her experience with SSI cases. The AIDS Law Project was helpful, too. If I had gone in on my own I don't think I would have gotten it. I was rejected the first time which I don't think a lot of people are.

Getting rejected the first time tends to scare people off. I think if a person hears, you know, you've been rejected for some reason, they'll just stop and won't pursue it. What I have trouble with is when a person gets ill enough or they can't fight on their own and they're too weak and they can't get anything done, then what happens?

At least it felt like that to me, it felt like . . . I've got to say the things correctly, it seems like the less educated a person is the more chances they have of getting on disability or SSI or welfare or things like that. At least that's what my experience was within that system. If you show up with more education, it's more obvious that you understand what's really going on, I think there's an attitude. Well if you can understand this, then you can work, you know? That's, and I can be way off, but that's the feeling I had.

I was rejected the first time around, and it took about 6 months, then it was retroactive. I didn't want to go on SSI, I didn't want to go on Social Security, I wanted to work, but I couldn't, and there was a part of me, now maybe that was, or maybe that whole energy was brought out that I didn't want to go on it, you know. Because I felt like, if I don't work, and if I can't then, you know, I have no purpose, but at the same time everyone was falling into being a caregiver, and my partner got sick at the same time. So, that was a full-time job. And there was no way I could have worked and done that at the time. So it sort of, in the long run it all worked out.

My sense was that the treatment I received in the SSI office did feel kind of racist. I mean a lot of experiences I have, and I never felt that before. I felt homophobia before, I felt anti-Semitism, but I've never felt bigotry or racism. So, it was a new experience, unintended.

A lot of people have lied and have gotten a lot more benefits, you know, and felt that they were in a position where they had to do it to survive. I didn't do that. You know, I can't do that. They would be like forging bills and things like that, adding in expenses and taking the numbers off. I can't do that. People have admitted to doing it and making out fine. And that's just not where I am. Maybe I'm dumb, I don't know. I'd be better off, maybe.

I can continue to live on SSI while I am a student. I did research that that's no problem, as long as whatever money that is being supplied or given to me for education goes for just education purposes. I am recertified once a year. I have done the recertification myself the past couple of years, and that went pretty well. Going in the office, fine, nothing's changed, bring in, just prove that's all you have for income. Basically a doctor's report that everything is the same, or I'm still declared as disabled, but that's fine. The disability declaration is based on my HIV and myopathy and clinical depression.

I don't know about continuing forever on SSI, you know it's like when a person has full-blown AIDS even though medication can make him get well, and increase their viral load and their T-cells and give them energy and a life again, they're still, once you have that diagnosis, you're diagnosed with that the rest of your life. Now I don't know if something happens where I get better, if I'm still, if that's still a declaration or not. I don't know for sure. I'm afraid to call.

Honestly, I'd have to call like the AIDS Law, giving them like a hypothetical situation. They were the ones that provided me with the information about school, what would happen, and that's how I found out the documentation about the school funds were not hurting at all. Because I am on SSI, I also get help with housing, food stamps, health, and medical. I'm getting like say, I say $60, I think it's like $72 a month in food stamps.

Being on SSI can be humiliating. I still want to do things. I still want to do design, I still want to be able to help people, I will get a few design jobs from old clients, and I can't take the money because I'll get caught, basically. I mean there are ways of course, but, you know, it's like I feel like I'm being watched all the time. My checking account and benefits, and things like that. I have to check in monthly with the housing people, and things like that. Report, it's like a little kid reporting to his parents that he has to be home by 9 o'clock at night all the time, you know. I don't have a savings, I just have a checking account.

I have to show that all I'm getting is SSI income. And nothing more. I think there's like a limit where the most you can ever have in your account at one time is $2,000 before they cut you off. They did cut off our housing in April of '98 which was very strange. My partner died a few months later. And I still don't know why. I remember a letter to him saying that, "You broke your lease and you vacated the premises and we're cutting off your housing assistance." Just out of the blue and it was very strange. And of course, you know, there was an appeal, but they sent the letter at the same date as the appeal, so it was just a ridiculous situation. It really wasn't resolved because, May, June, he died $2\frac{1}{2}$ months later, so it was basically an eviction process and by the time he passed away and I moved it was up, it was under the date, the deadline by a day.

They pay like 80 percent of my housing assistance. The apartment where I'm living could probably be rented out for twice as much as what the housing agency believes the worth of the place is. But the people in our development don't need the money. So it's kind of neat. And there's two other people in the same situation that I am living there. So it works out kinda nice actually.

## Carla

My mother received SSI as a result of remaining married to my father who happened to be in a state hospital and was struggling with mental illness. It's hard for me to remember exactly when I first understood that there was some supplemental income that came to our family as a result of my father's illness or disability. My mother didn't discuss it at all. I just know that this mail would come, and I would pick up the mail. I think she was pretty private, maybe almost secretive to others about the fact that we received that support.

I am certain that she couldn't have really raised us without the additional income. I don't even know that scale of the money at that time that she received.

My sister today turns 47—and so my sister was a recipient of SSI, if I'm not mistaken for the better part of 30 years, from when she was 17 and had a significant episode of mental illness and was taken to a state hospital. There were some lags over the years, when she worked briefly, or she was not eligible for one reason or another, but for the most part, for 30 years she has been a recipient.

Once she was out of the state hospital (she was there for 5 months, maybe longer), she didn't have that capacity initially to work and so there were caseworkers and people who helped her. I became involved in connecting my sister to caseworkers and the social programs. I think her journey through these different systems was made a little easier by the fact that she had my mother who had already experienced and understood at least how she could participate, and then I was committed to my sister getting staff support. I wasn't per se looking for funds for her, but was looking for caseworkers and social workers for her to have in place so that when she came out of the hospital she would have a mechanism for support so she wouldn't just be floating on her own.

I think that initially my sister was embarrassed. I think it wasn't easy for her to figure out how to navigate a system where she was going to be receiving support that she didn't feel she had earned. That changed as she became a more experienced consumer, she would set up less obstacles for those exchanges. The staff became more empathetic, more sympathetic, and it was probably easier for them to do the work they needed to do.

It wasn't easy for her. When she was able first to access SSI, there were other resources that were recommended to her and that she was eligible for, so that something that began at one point sort of broadened to be quite a broader spectrum of services.

I have really taken literal guardianship of my sister. She lives in a community residence and they do not have guardianship, but they are I think partners with her in making her life function. So, she is young enough still and functional enough, that guardianship is less an issue. My sister and her caseworker did ask me to assume responsibility for my sister's SSI benefits in part because my mother was formerly in that role, and that was a complicated negotiation. So, I took that role recently, less than 2 months ago. What I do now is, I have opened up an account that is in her name, but my name is associated with it. I think it's a representative account, so when funds come through I monitor my sister's account, and I write checks. There aren't that many. I write checks that compensate her, the community residence, and also write a check literally to her caseworker, which the caseworker then disseminates to my sister and pays her bills with her.

Some of the funds he would have to pay out would be for her laundry, and they would do that together. And some would be for the straight things she consumed—cigarettes and things like that. You know, at this point of time I'm having faith in him. I've known him for a long time. The monies that I give to him are funds that my sister receives. I did ask him to keep receipts since I'm responsible for the account.

There have been many many over the 30 years, but this particular caseworker has been involved with my sister for a good 6 or 7 years. We knew his family before he became a caseworker for her. I think he is one of the more effective ones. He is dependable and he is thoughtful, and he doesn't act patronizing and condescending to my sister and treats her like a person as anyone who works with clients should—but not all do.

It's my understanding that as a result of my sister applying and then becoming eligible for SSI that she was then eligible for food stamps. In addition to food stamps, there were opportunities that she was made aware of. From time to time she has needed help with her rent. She was eligible for a program which was the best and most holistic program that she has ever been part of and had the most responsive and effective caseworkers and social workers. It was for her son. My sister's son was a little boy. He is now 18, and it was probably 10 to 12 years ago.

And her son, additionally, is a recipient of SSI, and he is a recipient for two reasons. One is his mother—my sister—has mental illness. Secondarily, his father, who my sister met in the program, has a substance abuse issue with alcohol, and maybe some minor mental illness issues. So, my sister's son is additionally a recipient of SSI and, to make it all more complicated, lives with my mother. He is in a foster grandparent relationship with my mother. So my nephew's SSI benefits, like my father's SSI benefits, are funneled through my mother who is his caretaker. My sister's daughter additionally has the same sort of trajectory where my sister has mental illness and gets SSI, and the father of my niece was also an SSI recipient because of struggles with mental illness. So both my sister's children are recipients, or have been recipients of SSI over time.

The daughter is now 22 and no longer eligible for SSI benefits. The son just turned 18, and he will go to college, so as far as I know he will be able to continue to be able to access benefits while he is in college. I am not positive about that fact.

Her son, my nephew, well, he was eligible for other kinds of services because as a result of him living with someone that my sister was living with he was in an abusive situation. So, he got additional services, and I suspect they were not literally tied to SSI, but tied to the expense of being abused.

I arranged them by communicating with the state. Then, from that point forward there were many different things that happened. Among them he was evaluated and received different kinds of intervention. My nephew has someone that works with him through community programs, so he has some relationship to—not a PAL type of a place—but someone. That has actually been a pretty regular service. I don't know what it's called. I think he and his sister have often been eligible for food stamps as well. I don't know if they have continued to receive those over the years. I'm not really sure about that.

I think that my nephew accepts the services as a way of life. You know, since he was a baby he has had to in a way create an artificial relationship with a person who is not a family member and give them access to details about his life. He's done that because he was asked to do that early on with the issue of abuse, and then there were opportunities for therapy and for additional kinds of interaction. I think he accepts them and is a discerning consumer of those services, just as I think I may be as well, since there has been such a multitude of different kinds of people in agencies that we have both encountered. His sister is probably a little less patient and a little bit more skeptical of those interactions and services. I don't think she's ever had anyone that's been particularly that effective. That may be why she's a little more skeptical. She struggles with my sister's mental illness differently than I do, or even her brother does. She doesn't fault my sister for the illness, but she thinks my sister could make changes that would change her life and might have changed her children's lives. I was just talking with her the other day and was saying to her that she has a little more anger and disappointment that's pretty deep, and she is now in her twenties. But I think it was a little easier for me. As a kid I did not have to encounter my father's or mother's mental illness on a daily basis. It was a distant thing, and it was not in my house, because he left us when I was 5. They had to encounter it for a brief period of their early lives and were in a sense not directly neglected, but had issues happen as a result of a mental illness. I wasn't in that position. So, I can see where they would have a different way of processing what the illness is and then who the people are that are sort of paid in a sense to provide services to support or intervene with that illness.

I had the opportunity to know my sister before my sister struggled with mental illness, so I have several senses of who she is and what her capacity is. My sister was relatively fine, really until she was 17. So, I have had the luxury of having known my sister before she was sort of an "other." I am empathetic to her situation. I don't hold my sister responsible for her mental illness. I don't think her children do, but they haven't had the experience of knowing her as a "functional" person and a very multifaceted person before they knew her as a mother who was ill. I think that my mother and my father's mother were quite intelligent in making sure that my sister and I developed a relationship with my father, and my mother subsequently did the same thing with my sister's children, so she made sure that her son and daughter continued to encounter her while she was in the hospital. While she was sort of an "other," and I'll use these words in quotes, and "tainted," you know, not normal as some people might think, she was still someone they encountered. They visited her for Mother's Day. We would go for her birthday. We would do things in the hospital so the hospital did not become the place we didn't understand. We figured out how to interact with them. I think that, my mother, and my father's mother were very wise and ahead of their times in sort of ensuring that the kids continued to interact with their family members. I think that that's not always what people have done in those situations.

I know my sister is very happy, as am I, that we have a relationship. I don't want her to be grateful, because I don't think she should be grateful, or even need to be appreciative, because I want to have a relationship with her just like she wants to have one with me. So, I'm doing it for her and for myself as well. I'm having my kids have a relationship with my father who is their grandfather and having a relationship with their aunt, my sister, too, so that they don't think of her as someone who is not worthy of a relationship.

I think my sister's children love her, and I think they want to have interaction with her, but I think it's painful, so I think it's hard, because it's hard to convince someone to sort of experience pain. I remember that it was hard for me to do that with my father, and he wasn't even in my life in any major way. They have lived with their mother when they were little kids for brief periods of time, and then both of them were taken . . . my mother took responsibility for raising them. It is easier for me to interact with my father. The pain and my identity are not so directly tied to him. My sister would come to their schools. She didn't intend to embarrass them, but she would come to their schools and say she was worried about them and want to make sure she saw them.

I think what anybody who interacts with the system has to learn how to do is be first and foremost an advocate and set aside the feelings that they get of either embarrassment or anger, disappointment. There are times when staff people are either insensitive or disrespectful and can also be patronizing. They do it because they are tired and overworked, and they sometimes forget the human element in the work they are doing. I learned a long time ago to try not to take [it] personally, or to name out loud to the people I have been dealing with how I think they are treating me and how that's preventing us getting something done. There was one staff person who characterized my mother as having abandoned my sister. So, I just helped her know historically that she was inaccurate and that she was also not going to get the kind of support and interaction that she was looking for if she would continue to sort of be disrespectful but that she would need to recognize what the family had done for my sister. I think you have to stay pretty clear about the fact that people are in a service capacity, and they are being paid to do a good job. And if they are not doing a good job you have to help them know how to do a better job. So, that's what I have done over the years. I've learned that, but I've learned that because there have been really good people, too. And those good people have helped me see that there is capacity and the staff people can be really very smart and holistic about their work and not just functionarily doing their work.

I currently have been the person in my family named as the next of kin or whatever for my father. He's in a facility that does every-thing—crosses their t's and dots all their i's and gives me every piece of paperwork I could ever not want. I would monitor his bank account. I talked to them about a health care change that's coming down the pike. The other day, just to answer the question, I got this form that said, "Hey, here's a new health plan. If you want your father to have the opportunity to be part of it you can sign these forms and send it back. Have any questions, call us." I thought I really don't want to have this kind of ongoing, interactive role with my father. It's very artificial and I really am happy to be the only per-son in my family to stay with him. I would rather it not be the case. It's enough to do that. It's enough to make sure that there's a major decision about placement. Is he moving from one facility to another to be checked in with about that, etc. I'll be the person that buries my father probably, and takes responsibility for all those things. But, now, all this minutia, this detail that's directly tied to service. I'm not sure I want that responsibility, and it's new as a result of this facility assuming that I have this role with him.

But they are sort of assuming I do. I just get every single request. If my father has a rash—which he did—on his trunk part of his body, they call me to tell me that. And that is not something I wish to hear or encounter.

What is interesting about getting out from under is the details are one thing, and the function of it is another. What it never gives you the opportunity to do is be your own self and be independent without all the family history and the family difficulties sort of part of it. You can always sort of set it aside and compartmentalize it, but each interaction around your family member continues to be a reminder of what your history is and what your experience and your family's whole sort of broader like impact in life is.

I imagine there are other people who are in this situation. Peo-ple are not very forthcoming and don't discuss this sort of thing with one another. I would expect that there are other people in this situ-ation, just because of the way mental illness is sometimes influ-enced by family. And maybe other disabilities. I can't speak for other disabilities. Our family has been primarily through the issue. Mental illness is the sort of inroad for us.

It's not easy when you're navigating a system that sort of deals with people who are kind of broken. Sometimes the agencies don't mean to treat you as a representative in the same way that they treat their consumers, and I know their intention is not to treat their consumers as if they are broken people, or if they are dysfunctional, but it's sometimes hard for them not to. They should do their best to have their family member be treated with respect in every situation. And if their family member is struggling or acting awkwardly in a situation I would say to the family member, "I know this is hard, and this is difficult." Or talk to them and not act as if they are sort of a problem and creating themselves the obstacle. Let me give you an example. My sister was struggling with her caseworker around this question of money and when could she have her money. I just opened this bank account and her SSI income benefits that come through there, but it's taken a little long for that to get up and running, and there are payouts that have to happen for her rent, etc. So my sister waited for 7 months while she was in the hospital to have any kind of control over her finances. She formally had these SSI benefits, or at least had them through my mother and then didn't have them for 7 months.

There was a hiatus and the hiatus was partly due to some complications at my mother's house. She didn't have money, so she didn't have control of funds, so she was really very frustrated not to have any money. She couldn't buy cigarettes. She had to negotiate things in other ways. By the time SSI benefits kicked back in, she was really wanting to call the shots and have control, and that made sense. When she and her caseworker were talking over money, he said to me, "Oh, your sister has been acting up." I told him that I didn't think she was acting up per se. I just think that for 7 months she has not really had money and not had control over money and had to sort of be at the mercy of whoever would offer her something. I would remind the people who were sort of navigating these services and sort of interacting and acting as an intermediary with other people who are brokering services, remind them that the reason the people might be struggling or frustrated or angry or whatever has less to do with their mental illness and more to do with the circumstance around accessing services. I guess it goes without saying. I think it does behoove the profession and the people who are the brokers to really evaluate what they do. They influence so much.

I guess at the time in the '60s and '70s parents did not discuss with children their income. But I did not know that my mom received SSI benefits until I started to see the letters coming in the mail and later learned about it. I think I don't know if people are ashamed of being the beneficiary of their family members who are disabled. I think that they probably feel a little guilt for receiving the benefits. I'm sure that my mother doesn't feel guilty because she had to raise two children without my father. She had all the responsibility. I'm sure the money didn't feel to her to be unearned money. I think SSI thinks of itself as an agency that's literally almost dispensing funds and sort of providing funds for people who are obviously in need, but I don't think they necessarily look more broadly at what the implications of the receipt of funds means to those who are accessing the services. I don't think people know what to do with receiving what I guess is a sort of charity. I think they get used to it and accept it, but I wonder what it does to their psyche over time. I don't know what it would do to a man, a husband to receive funds as a result of his wife having a disability.

I think it would be useful for the government to have, and maybe they do this, sessions where people who have been beneficiaries talk to others about the things they encounter or to help them figure out how to navigate sort of getting over their issues of maybe embarrassment or shame, navigating the system. I imagine if they are not doing those things these would be functional workshops to have. I don't know if people would come because they might be too embarrassed. Maybe there would be other ways. That's part of the reason I think that program for my nephew worked really well, because I think the woman who was the social worker had indeed herself been as a child in an abusive situation and later understood and have heard from a first hand perspective what it's like to be at the effect of the illness. So, she would bring those two things together and be more than effective in her role.

I think of myself as an informed person, but I don't think I know a lot about that whole system. So, if I don't know very much about that system, I bet people who may have less time to learn about things, less resources, maybe even less education than I have probably would know even less. If there were a way that we as people who are helping consumers of the system could know more about it. I don't get a newsletter that tells me about changes in SSI benefits or advocacy or criteria or anything.

## WHAT OUR CLIENTS TEACH US

For both Martin and Carla, SSI has provided an income support lifeline. Martin is coping with a chronic physical illness (HIV/AIDS), and Carla's father and sister are impaired by what appears to be severe and persistent mental illness. As the court cases cited previously suggest, establishing eligibility for SSI is a challenging process with rejections subject to a complex due process system.

Martin was first rejected, but on a second application accepted. Carla offers no indication that her relatives had difficulty establishing eligibility. We can assume, therefore, that they were assessed as being so disabled that they could not support themselves, would not recover in a year, and/or would eventually die of their disorders.

For these recipients, SSI provided enough income so their basic needs for food, clothing, and shelter were met. SSI was established to ensure that there was a national standard and less stigma for those considered the most worthy of assistance—the poor who are aged, blind, or disabled. We learn from Martin and Carla that even these recipients' experiences are not at times treated with respect and compassion. Martin reports that the treatment he received in the SSI office "did feel kind of racist." Carla notes, "It's not easy when you're navigating a system that sort of deals with people who are kind of broken." Several common themes are woven through both narratives that further our understanding of recipients' experiences:

1. *Clients who are eligible for SSI require not only the income supports provided by SSI, but emotional sustenance and other help from family, friends, and/or social agencies.* For people coping with a severe impairment, psychosocial assistance is often a prerequisite to maintaining a degree of independence. For Martin, an agency serving people with HIV/AIDS offers him a rent supplement and advocacy services. As Martin astutely observes regarding his case manager's efforts, "If I had gone on my own, I don't think I would have gotten it." Yet Martin apparently grappling with expectable dependency issues stresses that he did not know "if I owe them like, my majoring in college and going back and working for them the rest of my life like they would like me to." Carla appears to be the mainstay of her family and in turn looks to the "system" for support. Yet experience indicates that she has had negative interactions with some agencies she turned to for help. "Sometimes the agencies don't mean to treat you as a representative in the same way that they treat their consumers, and I know their intention is not to treat their consumers as if they were broken people, or if they are dysfunctional, but it's sometimes hard for them not to."

Martin reports a favorable relationship with his caseworker, and that positive experience makes a major difference. The worker helped him successfully negotiate the universe of services available to someone receiving SSI. He also reports that his caseworker was his strongest advocate, because as he says, "If I had gone on my own I don't think I would have gotten it." Interestingly, Martin's first SSI application was rejected, but then appealed with the help of his case worker.

> Getting rejected the first time tends to scare people off. I think if a person hears, you know, you've been rejected for some reason, they'll just stop and won't pursue it. What I have trouble with is when a person gets ill enough or they can't fight on their own and they're too weak and they can't get anything done, then what happens?
>
> At least it felt like that to me, it felt like . . . it seems the less educated a person is the more chances they have of getting on disability or SSI or welfare of things like that. At least that's what my experience was within that system. If you show up with more education . . . it's more obvious that you understand what's really

going on. . . . Well if you can understand this, you can work, you know? That's, and I can be way off, but that's the feeling I had.

2. *Martin and Carla's stories tell us of the resiliency of human beings.* It is clear from Carla's narrative that her activities over the years have sustained her sister and other family members. She requires replenishment given the toll her emotional and physical investment must take; support for caregivers of the mentally ill is a recognized need and one that is being met by self-help and professional support programs (Goodman, 2005; Stam & Cuijpern, 2001). Martin, having struggled with illness and a series of losses, moves on, noting that now is "probably the happiest I've ever been in my whole life." He is in graduate school, where he "keeps acing multiple tests, and it's blowing my mind." He has a new romantic interest; he cofacilitates a support group; and he is looking to the future. Yet he does not deny the reality that "once you have that diagnosis you're diagnosed with that the rest of your life."

Martin exhibits both an impressive depth of knowledge about SSI and a resiliency in coping with his life circumstances. He has been coping for the past 15 years with his HIV/AIDS diagnosis and the attendant emotional and economic consequences. His work with friends and others with a similar diagnosis certainly gave him some insight into the vagaries of the Social Services system; indeed, as he suggests, these experiences were the impetus for his return to graduate school:

> Moved out of the house a year [after my HIV diagnosis], met my partner a month after I moved out in October of '89. We had 9 years together, and he died 3 years ago [circa 1999] in July. And I was a full-time caregiver for him for 3 years. In the past 3 years I have been regrouping, going through a transition, doing full-time volunteering for HIV and AIDS patients, cofacilitating a support group, acting as a buddy and mentor for the local agency dealing with AIDS patients. And people kept telling me to go to school for social work. . . . It's been 20 years since my undergraduate degree.

Carla seems to have devoted much of her life to caretaking, yet there is no complaining or self-pity permeating her story. She makes astute observations about working with the system; her empathy and maturity are apparent.

> I think what anybody who interacts with the system has to learn how to do is to be first and foremost an advocate and set aside the feelings that they get of either embarrassment or anger, disappointment. There are times when staff people are either insensitive or disrespectful and can also be patronizing. They do it because they are tired and overworked, and they sometimes forget the human element in the work they are doing. I learned a long time ago to try not to take [it] personally. . . . If they are not doing a good job you have to help them know how to do a better job.

Despite all the years of assisting her family and of dealing with the SSI system, Carla's narrative suggests that misperceptions abound and can further frustrate successful interaction with the SSI program. She reports that her mother, niece and nephew have received SSI because their responsible relative does. However, as we have learned, SSI is an entitlement that is granted only to the person who is financially eligible *and* aged, blind, or disabled. Her mother and niece probably received AFDC or TANF benefits, while her nephew, apparently disabled, might himself be an SSI recipient.

Carla is a knowledgeable consumer, yet even she can be frustrated in her efforts to work within the system. The lesson is perhaps obvious: The SSI system is complex and clients can encounter difficulty trying to navigate it. Knowledgeable social work support, therefore, makes a critical difference. Interestingly, and reflective of her intuitive strength, Carla acknowledges her need for being informed. She comments, "If there were a way that we as people who are helping consumers of the system could know more about it . . ."

# 7 CHAPTER | FOOD STAMPS

## THE LEGAL CONTEXT

### Authorizing Legislation

**The Food Stamp Program: Legislative Goals and Historical Antecedents**
Under U.S.C.S. § 2011, Title 7, Agriculture, Chapter 51, the Food Stamp
Program is declared to be built around the following considerations:

> It is hereby declared to be the policy of Congress, in order to promote the
> general welfare, to safeguard the health and well-being of the Nation's
> population by raising levels of nutrition among low-income households.
> Congress hereby finds that the limited food purchasing power of low-
> income households contributes to hunger and malnutrition among mem-
> bers of such households. Congress further finds that increased utilization
> of food in establishing and maintaining adequate national levels of nutri-
> tion will promote the distribution in a beneficial manner of the Nation's
> agricultural abundance and will strengthen the Nation's agricultural
> economy, as well as result in more orderly marketing and distribution of
> foods. To alleviate such hunger and malnutrition, a food stamp program
> is herein authorized which will permit low-income households to obtain
> a more nutritious diet through normal channels of trade by increasing
> food purchasing power for all eligible households who apply for partici-
> pation. (7 U.S.C.S. § 2011)

As the congressional findings suggest, the Food Stamp Program is driven by the twin goals of raising nutritional levels and enhancing the food purchasing power of low-income households. The ancillary impact on the "orderly marketing and distribution of foods" also reveals congressional determination to place a social program such as food stamps within the context of ordered trade within the nation.

The Food Stamp Program traces its origins to the Food Stamp Plan, which was created in the Depression Era of the 1930s to help families in need. At the time, food assistance was not considered part of the welfare plan, but rather a program "designed to eradicate hunger while improving the nutrition and health of low-income families." As such, it was then and is still helping low-income households buy the food they need for a nutritionally adequate diet.

Beginning as a pilot project in 1961, the Food Stamp Program was introduced by the U.S. Department of Agriculture (USDA) in 43 areas of the United States. Congress passed the Food Stamp Act (Public Law 88-525) on August 31, 1964, which provided for the program's gradual and future expansion (Food Stamp History/Goal, 2001). Spurred by rising unemployment, the Food Stamp Program expanded dramatically in the early 1970s when Congress required that all states offer food stamps to low-income households. By 1975, the USDA was spending approximately $5.9 billion (60 percent of its total budget) for benefits to 19.5 million persons living in this country (Food Stamps: SeniorLAW, 2000). By 1997, the Food Stamp Program was providing more than $19.5 billion in benefits to the needy.

President Bush signed into law on May 13, 2002, the Farm Security and Rural Investment Act of 2002 (Public Law 107-171), which included a nutrition title, the Food Stamp Reauthorization Act of 2002. The new legislation added $6.4 billion in new funds for food stamps and other nutrition programs over the next decade and expanded eligibility for some groups while increasing the benefit amount for others (Food Research and Action Center, 2003).

## Regulatory Authority

There are many regulations pertaining to the Food Stamp Program, all of which are initially published by administrative agencies in the *Federal Register*. Eventually, they find their way into the *Code of Federal Regulations* (C.F.R.), which is the official compilation of all regulations enacted by federal agencies. Specifically, at Title 7 of the C.F.R., Part 260 (and its subsections), one finds the regulatory provisions that generally apply to the Food Stamp Program. A sample regulation dealing with the general purposes and scope, along with several definitions, appears as Box 7.1.

## Case Law

There is considerable case law pertaining to food stamps and the many provisions of the program, of which the decisions appearing in Boxes 7.2 and 7.3 are illustrative. The first, in Box 7.2, deals with timely "mass" versus "indi-

**7.1** | SAMPLE FEDERAL REGULATION
REGARDING FOOD STAMP PROGRAM

*** THE FEDERAL REGISTER ***
TITLE 7—AGRICULTURE
SUBTITLE B—REGULATIONS OF THE DEPARTMENT
OF AGRICULTURE CHAPTER II—FOOD
AND NUTRITION SERVICE, DEPARTMENT OF AGRICULTURE
SUBCHAPTER C—FOOD STAMP AND FOOD DISTRIBUTION PROGRAM
PART 271—GENERAL INFORMATION AND DEFINITIONS
7 CFR 271.1

§ 271.1 General purpose and scope.

(a)  Purpose of the food stamp program. The food stamp program is designed to
promote the general welfare and to safeguard the health and well being of the
Nation's population by raising the levels of nutrition among low-income households. Section 2 of the Food Stamp Act of 1977 states, in part:

> Congress hereby finds that the limited food purchasing power of low-
> income households contributes to hunger and malnutrition among members
> of such households. Congress further finds that increased utilization of food
> in establishing and maintaining adequate national levels of nutrition will
> promote the distribution in a beneficial manner of the Nation's agricultural
> abundance and will strengthen the Nation's agricultural economy, as well as
> result in more orderly marketing and distribution of foods. To alleviate such
> hunger and malnutrition, a food stamp program is herein authorized which
> will permit low-income households to obtain a more nutritious diet through

---

vidual" notification regarding potential denial of food stamp benefits; the second, in Box 7.3, with the definition of *household* for the purposes of receiving
food stamps.

## THE PROGRAM CONTEXT

### Overview

Food stamps remain a valuable resource for economically vulnerable households. They are intended to increase the food purchasing power of eligible
households. Each household is expected to devote 30 percent of its monthly
cash income to food, with the food stamps making up the difference between
the expected contribution to food costs and the amount judged sufficient for
an adequate low-income diet. This amount is set by the U.S. Department of
Agriculture, which places the maximum food stamp benefit at the level of the
lowest cost food plan. This plan can vary by household and is adjusted annually for inflation.

normal channels of trade by increasing food purchasing power for all eligible households who apply for participation.

(b) Scope of the regulations. Part 271 contains general information, definitions, and other material applicable to all parts of this subchapter. Part 272 sets forth policies and procedures governing State agencies which participate in the program. Part 273 describes the eligibility criteria to be applied by State agencies and related processing requirements and standards. Part 274 provides requirements for the issuance of coupons to eligible households and establishes related issuance responsibilities. Part 275 sets forth guidelines for monitoring the food stamp program, analyzing the results and formulating corrective action. Part 276 establishes State agency liability and certain Federal sanctions. Part 277 outlines procedures for payment of administrative costs of State agencies. Part 278 delineates the terms and conditions for the participation of retail food stores, wholesale food concerns, meal services, and insured financial institutions. Part 279 establishes the procedures for administrative and judicial reviews requested by food retailers, food wholesalers, and meal services. Part 280 explains procedures for issuing emergency coupon allotments to certain victims of disasters unable to purchase adequate amounts of food. Part 281 sets forth guidelines for designating Indian tribes as State agencies. Part 282 provides guidelines for initiation, selection, and operation of demonstration, research, and evaluation projects. Part 284 provides for a nutrition assistance program for the Commonwealth of the Northern Mariana Islands (CNMI). Part 285 describes the general terms and conditions under which grant funds are provided to the Commonwealth of Puerto Rico.

HISTORY: [Amdt. 132, 43 FR 47882, Oct. 17, 1982, as amended by Amdt 216, 47 FR 23461, May 28, 1982; Amdt. 248, 48 FR 16832, Apr. 19, 1983; Amdt. 356, 59 FR 29713, June 9, 1994]

As of 2004, 54 percent of eligible persons are served by the program (Cunningham, 2004). This figure underscores that the number of those eligible far exceeds those who actually apply. Participation rates vary and are influenced by program rule changes, other public assistance program requirements, and changes in the economy that can cause either expansions or contractions in the food stamp program. Consequently, state and local governments aggressively reach out to ensure that eligible households meet their nutritional needs, particularly during dire economic times. Moreover, the Food Stamp Program generally helps buttress the economy through the contribution to merchants that results when the program expands during weak economic periods. This economic boost not only helps business by enabling recipients to continue to obtain food but is provided at relatively little cost to the local government.

Participation rates have also been affected by the 1996 welfare reform law (Personal Responsibility and Work Opportunity Reconciliation Act (PRWORA; P.L. 104-193), which reduced eligibility by requiring work activity for some nondisabled, nonelderly childless adults (Cunningham, 2004). The law's focus on accelerating the move from welfare to work resulted in

# 7.2 | ATKINS V. PARKER

### ATKINS v. PARKER
### 407 U.S. 115 (1985)

*Summary: In Atkins v. Parker, the United States Supreme Court addressed an important issue regarding timely notice of potential denial of food stamps and the distinction of "mass" versus "individual" notification and the due process implications. A class action suit was filed by Massachusetts residents, who received benefits under the Food Stamp Act. The residents had been mailed a notice informing them of changes that they might experience in regard to their benefits, as a result of an amendment to the Act. They claimed that the notice had been insufficient, in that it did not provide information as to how individual households would be affected. The question before the courts was whether or not the notice informing welfare recipients about changes in the federal law might result in termination, or reduction of benefits violated any federal or state regulations, or the Due Process Clause of the Fourteenth Amendment. The District Court held that the notice violated the plaintiffs' Due Process Rights under the Fourteenth Amendment, and ordered a reinstatement of their benefits. It was determined that the notice did not provide enough information for individual households to figure out the impact that the amendment might have on them. Additionally, the plaintiffs were not given timely notice, nor was the notice multilingual. The Court of Appeals upheld the unconstitutionality of the notice, yet disagreed with the District Court's decision to reinstate the plaintiffs' benefit. The Supreme Court held that the notice sent to the Massachusetts residents was constitutional. Within this section of the Act it is stated that "mass changes," those that could affect all recipients, do not require individual notification as to how particular households will be affected. It does state that "individual" notices are to be sent, and that the notice "inform them of the change." Thus, the notice was deemed constitutional and not to violate the Due Process Clause of the Fourteenth Amendment, since all households received notice of the change that would take place.*

OPINION: JUSTICE STEVENS delivered the opinion of the Court.

In November, and again in December 1981, the Massachusetts Department of Public Welfare mailed a written notice to over 16,000 recipients advising them that a recent change in federal law might result in either a reduction or a termination of their food-stamp benefits. The notice did not purport to explain the precise impact of the change on each individual recipient. The question this case presents is whether that notice violated any federal statute or regulation, or the Due Process Clause of the Fourteenth Amendment. Unlike the District Court and the Court of Appeals, we conclude that there was no violation.

In an attempt to "permit low-income households to obtain a more nutritious diet through normal channels of trade," Congress created a federally subsidized food-stamp program. The Secretary of Agriculture prescribes the standards for eligibility for food stamps, but state agencies are authorized to make individual eligibility determinations and to distribute the food stamps to eligible households, which may use them to purchase food from approved, retail food stores. The eligibility of an individual household, and the amount of its food-stamp allotment, are based on several factors, including the size of the household and its income. Certifications of eligibility expire periodically and are renewed on the basis of applications submitted by the households.

Prior to 1981, federal law provided that 20 percent of the household's earned income should be deducted, or disregarded, in computing eligibility. The purpose of the earned-income disregard was to maintain the recipients' incentive to earn and to report income. In 1981 Congress amended the Food Stamp Act to reduce this deduction from 20 percent to 18 percent. That amendment had no effect on households with no income or with extremely low income, but caused a reduction of benefits in varying amounts, or a complete termination of benefits, for families whose income placed them close to the border between eligibility and ineligibility.

On September 4, 1981, the Department of Agriculture issued regulations providing for the implementation of the change in the earned-income disregard and directing the States to provide notice to food-stamp recipients. That directive indicated that the form of the notice might comply with the regulations dealing with so-called "mass changes," rather than with the regulations dealing with individual "adverse actions."

In November, the Massachusetts Department of Public Welfare (Department) mailed a brief, ambiguously dated notice to all food-stamp recipients with earned income advising them that the earned-income deduction had been lowered from 20 percent to 18 percent and that the change would result in either a reduction or a termination of their benefits. The notice was printed on a card, in English on one side and Spanish on the other. The notice stated that the recipient had a right to request a hearing "if you disagree with this action," and that benefits would be reinstated if a hearing was requested within 10 days of the notice.

On December 10, 1981, petitioners in No. 83-6381 commenced this action on behalf of all Massachusetts households that had received the notice. They alleged that the notice was inadequate as a matter of law and moved for a temporary restraining order. On December 16, 1981, after certifying the action as a class action, and after commenting that the "notice was deficient in that it failed to provide recipients with a date to determine the time in which they could appeal," the District Court enjoined the Department from reducing or terminating any benefits on the basis of that notice.

The Department, in compliance with the District Court's order, mailed supplemental benefits for the month of December to each of the 16,640 class members. It then sent out a second notice, in English and Spanish versions, dated December 26, which stated in part:

> \* \* \* IMPORTANT NOTICE—READ CAREFULLY \* \* \*
> "RECENT CHANGES IN THE FOOD STAMP PROGRAM HAVE BEEN MADE IN ACCORDANCE WITH 1981 FEDERAL LAW. UNDER THIS LAW, THE EARNED INCOME DEDUCTION FOR FOOD STAMP BENEFITS HAS BEEN LOWERED FROM 20 TO 18 PERCENT. THIS REDUCTION MEANS THAT A HIGHER PORTION OF YOUR HOUSEHOLD'S EARNED INCOME WILL BE COUNTED IN DETERMINING YOUR ELIGIBILITY AND BENEFIT AMOUNT FOR FOOD STAMPS. AS A RESULT OF THIS FEDERAL CHANGE, YOUR BENEFITS WILL EITHER BE REDUCED IF YOU REMAIN ELIGIBLE OR YOUR BENEFITS WILL BE TERMINATED. (FOOD STAMP MANUAL CITATION: 106 CMR:364.400).

*continued*

"YOUR RIGHT TO A FAIR HEARING:
"YOU HAVE THE RIGHT TO REQUEST A FAIR HEARING IF YOU DIS-
AGREE WITH THIS ACTION. IF YOU ARE REQUESTING A HEARING,
YOUR FOOD STAMP BENEFITS WILL BE REINSTATED. . . . IF YOU HAVE
QUESTIONS CONCERNING THE CORRECTNESS OF YOUR BENEFITS
COMPUTATION OR THE FAIR HEARING PROCESS, CONTACT YOUR
LOCAL WELFARE OFFICE. YOU MAY FILE AN APPEAL AT ANY TIME IF
YOU FEEL THAT YOU ARE NOT RECEIVING THE CORRECT AMOUNT
OF FOOD STAMPS."

Petitioners filed a supplemental complaint attacking the adequacy of this notice,
and again moved for a preliminary injunction. In October 1982, the District Court
consolidated the hearing on that motion with the trial on the merits and again ruled
in petitioners' favor. The District Court found that there was a significant risk of
error in the administration of the food-stamp program, particularly with the implementation of the change in the earned-income disregard, and that the failure to provide each recipient with an adequate notice increased the risk of error. In essence,
the District Court concluded that the December notice was defective because it did
not advise each household of the precise change in its benefits, or with the information necessary to enable the recipient to calculate the correct change; because it did
not tell recipients whether their benefits were being reduced or terminated; and
because the reading level and format of the notice made it difficult to comprehend.
Based on the premise that the statutorily mandated reduction or termination of benefits was a deprivation of property subject to the full protection of the Fourteenth
Amendment, the court held that the Due Process Clause had been violated.

As a remedy, the District Court ordered the Department "to return forthwith to
each and every household in the plaintiff class all food stamp benefits lost as a result
of the action taken pursuant to the December notice" between January 1, 1981, and
the date the household received adequate notice, had its benefits terminated for a
reason unrelated to the change in the earned-income disregard, or had its file recertified. The District Court also ordered that all future food-stamp notices issued by
the Department contain various data, including the old and new benefit amounts,
and that the Department issue regulations, subject to court approval, governing the
form of future food-stamp notices.

The United States Court of Appeals for the First Circuit agreed with the District
Court's constitutional holding, indicated its belief that Congress could not have
"intended a constitutionally deficient notice to satisfy the statutory notice requirement," and thus affirmed the District Court's holding that "the December notice
failed to satisfy the notice requirements of 7 U.S.C. 2020(e)(10) and 7 CFR
273.12(e)(2) (ii)." The Court of Appeals held, however, that the District Court had
erred in ordering a reinstatement of benefits and in specifying the form of future
notices.

Petitioners in No. 83-6381 sought review of the Court of Appeals' modification
of the District Court's remedy, and the Department, in No. 83-1660, cross-peti-
tioned for a writ of certiorari seeking review of the holding on liability. We granted
both the petition and the cross-petition, and invited the Solicitor General to participate in the argument. We conclude that the notice was lawful, and therefore have
no occasion to discuss the remedy issue that the petition . . . presents. Because there

would be no need to decide the constitutional question if we found a violation of either the statute or the regulations, we first consider the statutory issue.

The only reference in the Food Stamp Act to a notice is contained in 2020(e), which outlines the requirements of a state plan of operation. Subsection (10) of that section provides that a state plan must grant a fair hearing, and a prompt determination, to any household that is aggrieved by the action of a state agency. A proviso to that subsection states that any household "which timely requests such a fair hearing after receiving individual notice of agency action reducing or terminating its benefits" shall continue to receive the same level of benefits until the hearing is completed.

The language of the proviso does not itself command that any notice be given, but it does indicate that Congress assumed that individual notice would be an element of the fair-hearing requirement. Thus, whenever a household is entitled to a fair hearing, it is appropriate to read the statute as imposing a requirement of individual notice that would enable the household to request such a hearing. The hearing requirement, and the incidental reference to "individual notice," however, are by their terms applicable only to "agency action reducing or terminating" a household's benefits. Therefore, it seems unlikely that Congress contemplated individual hearings for every household affected by a general change in the law.

The legislative history of 2020(e)(10) sheds light on its meaning. As originally enacted in 1964, the Food Stamp Act contained no fair-hearing requirement. In 1971, however, in response to this Court's decision in *Goldberg v. Kelly,* 397 U.S. 254 (1970), Congress amended the Act to include a fair-hearing provision, and in the Food Stamp Act of 1977, 2020(e)(10) was enacted in its present form. The legislative history of the Food Stamp Act of 1977 contains a description of the then-existing regulations, which were promulgated after the 1971 amendment, and which drew a distinction between the requirement of notice in advance of an "adverse action" based on the particular facts of an individual case, on the one hand, and the absence of any requirement of individual notice of a "mass change," on the other. That history contains no suggestion that Congress intended to eliminate that distinction; to the contrary, Congress expressly recognized during the period leading to the enactment of the Food Stamp Act of 1977 the distinction between the regulatory requirement regarding notice in the case of an adverse action and the lack of such a requirement in the case of a mass change. Read against this background, the relevant statutory language—which does not itself mandate any notice at all but merely assumes that a request for a hearing will be preceded by "individual notice of agency action"—cannot fairly be construed as a command to give notice of a general change in the law.

Nor can we find any basis for concluding that the December notice failed to comply with the applicable regulations. Title 7 CFR 273.12(e)(2)(ii) (1984) provides:

"(ii) A notice of adverse action is not required when a household's food stamp benefits are reduced or terminated as a result of a mass change in the public assistance grant. However, State agencies shall send individual notices to households to inform them of the change. If a household requests a fair hearing, benefits shall be continued at the former level only if the issue being appealed is that food stamp eligibility or benefits were improperly computed."

This regulation reflects the familiar distinction between an individual adverse action and a mass change. The statement that a notice of adverse action is not

*continued*

7.2    ATKINS V. PARKER (CONTINUED)

required when a change of benefits results from a mass change surely implies that individual computations are not required in such cases. The two requirements that are imposed when a mass change occurs are: (1) that "individual" notice be sent and (2) that it "inform them of the change." In this case, a separate individual notice was sent to each individual household and it did "inform them of the change" in the program that Congress had mandated. Since the word "change" in the regulation [472 U.S. 115, 127] plainly refers to the "mass change," the notice complied with the regulation.

Since the notice of the change in the earned-income disregard was sufficient under the statute and under the regulations, we must consider petitioners' claim that they had a constitutional right to advance notice of the amendment's specific impact on their entitlement to food stamps before the statutory change could be implemented by reducing or terminating their benefits. They argue that an individualized calculation of the new benefit was necessary in order to avoid the risk of an erroneous reduction or termination.

The record in this case indicates that members of petitioners' class had their benefits reduced or terminated for either or both of two reasons: (1) because Congress reduced the earned-income disregard from 20 percent to 18 percent; or (2) because inadvertent errors were made in calculating benefits. These inadvertent errors, however, did not necessarily result form the statutory change, but rather may have been attributable to a variety of factors that can occur in the administration of any large welfare program. For example, each of the named petitioners, presumably representative of the class, appealed a reduction in benefits. None identified an error resulting from the legislative decision to change the earned-income disregard. But even if it is assumed that the mass change increased the risk of erroneous reductions in benefits, that assumption does not support the claim that the actual notice used in this case was inadequate. For that notice plainly informed each household of the opportunity to request a fair hearing and the right to have its benefit level frozen if a hearing was requested. As the testimony of the class representatives indicates, every class member who contacted the Department had his or her benefit level frozen, and received a fair hearing, before any loss of benefit occurred. Thus, the Department's procedures provided adequate protection against any deprivation based on an unintended mistake. To determine whether the Constitution required a more detailed notice of the mass change, we therefore put the miscellaneous errors to one side and confine our attention to the reductions attributable to the statutory change.

Food-stamp benefits, like the welfare benefits at issue in *Goldberg v. Kelly* "are a matter of statutory entitlement for persons qualified to receive them." Such entitlements are appropriately treated as a form of "property" protected by the Due Process Clause; accordingly, the procedures that are employed in determining whether an individual may continue to participate in the statutory program must comply with the commands of the Constitution.

This case, however, does not concern the procedural fairness of individual eligibility determinations. Rather, it involves a legislatively mandated substantive change in the scope of the entire program. Such a change must, of course, comply with the substantive limitations on the power of Congress, but there is no suggestion in this case that the amendment at issue violated any such constraint. Thus, it must be assumed that Congress had plenary power to define the scope and the duration of the entitlement to food-stamp benefits, and to increase, to decrease, or to terminate those benefits based on its appraisal of the relative importance of the recipients' needs and the resources available to fund the program. The procedural component of the Due Process Clause does not "impose a constitutional limitation on the power of Congress to make substantive changes in the law of entitlement to public benefits."

The congressional decision to lower the earned-income deduction from 20 percent to 18 percent gave many food-stamp households a less valuable entitlement in 1982 than they had received in 1981. But the 1981 entitlement did not include any right to have the program continue indefinitely at the same level, or to phrase it another way, did not include any right to the maintenance of the same level of property entitlement. Before the statutory change became effective, the existing property entitlement did not qualify the legislature's power to substitute a different, less valuable entitlement at a later date. As we have frequently noted: "[A] welfare recipient is not deprived of due process when the legislature [472 U.S. 115, 130] adjusts benefit levels. . . . [T]he legislative determination provides all the process that is due."

The participants in the food-stamp program had no greater right to advance notice of the legislative change—in this case, the decision to change the earned-income disregard level—than did any other voters. They do not claim that there was any defect in the legislative process. Because the substantive reduction in the level of petitioners' benefits was the direct consequence of the statutory amendment, they have no basis for challenging the procedure that caused them to receive a different, less valuable property interest after the amendment became effective.

The claim that petitioners had a constitutional right to better notice of the consequences of the statutory amendment is without merit. All citizens are presumptively charged with knowledge of the law. Arguably that presumption may be overcome in cases in which the statute does not allow a sufficient "grace period" to provide the persons affected by a change in the law with an adequate opportunity to become familiar with their obligations under it. In this case, however, not only was there a grace period of over 90 days before the amendment became effective, but in addition, every person affected by the change was given individual notice of the substance of the amendment.

As a matter of constitutional law there can be no doubt concerning the sufficiency of the notice describing the effect of the amendment in general terms. Surely Congress can presume that such a notice relative to a matter as important as a change in a household's food-stamp allotment would prompt an appropriate inquiry if it is not fully understood. The entire structure of our democratic government rests on the premise that the individual citizen is capable of informing himself about the particular policies that affect his destiny. To contend that this notice was constitutionally insufficient is to reject that premise.

The judgment of the Court of Appeals is reversed. It is so ordered.

## 7.3     ROBINSON V. BLOCK

### ROBINSON v. BLOCK
### 859 F.2d 202 (1989)

*Summary:* The plaintiffs in this case were Cheryl Robinson, who received food stamps, and Philadelphia Citizens in Action, which was a group advocating for welfare rights. Robinson and her son lived in a house owned by her brother. Without Cheryl reportedly having any opinion, her sister and niece, who also received food stamps, moved into the house. Cheryl was sent notice that her benefits would be terminated, unless she filed an appeal. This notice was sent by the Department of Public Welfare (DPW) after they had learned that Cheryl's sister resided at the same address. Cheryl did not file a timely appeal and her food stamp benefits were cut off. The sisters were then notified that they would be included in the same household unit for the purposes of receiving benefits, and Cheryl's sister's name was listed as the recipient. After a caseworker discovered that Cheryl's niece was not living with her mother, the household's benefits were reduced, which lessened Cheryl's benefits. When Cheryl attempted to apply for food stamp benefits again under her own name, she was denied because she did not provide verification that her brother was not living in his house with his sisters. At her appeal hearing, Cheryl reported that she knew her brother's address information was false, which was why she did not wish to provide it. Her caseworker then made two separate appointments for Cheryl to reapply, neither of which Cheryl attended.

In District Court, the plaintiffs claimed that the Pennsylvania DPW and the U.S. Department of Agriculture (USDA) violated the 1981 and 1982 amendments to the Food Stamp Act. The amendments stated that, for the purposes of calculating benefits, siblings living together were to be combined into one household. It was also claimed the defendants' failure to send individual notices of program requirements to both parties living at the same address violated the plaintiffs' due process rights. A third claim was made in regard to the third party verification required by DPW. The plaintiffs stated that in the interview the DPW asks for information not specified on the application for benefits. They also state that DPW did not offer applicants the opportunity to provide alternate ways "to prove eligibility, if a third party refuse[d] to cooperate." It was claimed that the failure to allow for alternatives violated the Due Process Clause, as well as other federal statutes and regulations. The District Court granted the defendants' motion to dismiss the third party verification claim. Summary judgments were granted to the defendants in regard to the claims about siblings residing at the same address and notification of eligibility notices or program requirements.

In the Court of Appeals, the plaintiffs had two claims. The first was that the sibling rule violated the Due Process Clause of the Fifth and Fourteenth Amendments (42 U.S.C. Section 1983) and the Food Stamp Act. While the court did not directly address the issue of violation of the Due Process Clauses, it did conclude that the "same address test used by the DPW and USDA to determine applicants' eligibility was not a valid means of enhancing the statutory sibling rule. The District Court's decision was reversed, and the issue was remanded back to that court in order for a more valid determination of whether or not Robinson and her sister lived together, as to constitute a single household under the Food Stamp Act. The second claim was *that the third party verification requirements violated the Due Process Clause of the Fourteenth Amendment, 42 U.S.C. Section 1983, and other federal regulations and statutes, when a third party was unwilling to cooperate. The Court of Appeals ordered that the District Court's dismissal of that claim be reversed. It remanded the issue back to the lower court, so that plaintiffs could be given an opportunity to provide specific situations in which the defendants had violated their due process right in regard to the federal statutes and regulations.*

OPINION: BECKER, Circuit Judge

This is an action brought on behalf of a class of food stamp and welfare recipients by Cheryl Robinson, a food stamp recipient, and Philadelphia Citizens in Action, a welfare rights advocacy group, challenging the manner in which the defendants, federal and Commonwealth of Pennsylvania officials, have administered certain eligibility and benefit level provisions of the Food Stamp Act of 1964 as amended, ["the Act"] through various federal and state regulations and agency procedures. Plaintiffs' primary claim arises from defendants' interpretation of the 1981 and 1982 amendments to the Act which provided that "siblings who live together" must be combined into one food stamp household rather than treated as separate households for benefit calculation purposes.

Plaintiffs complain that the defendants have created an irrebuttable presumption that siblings who live at the same address in fact live together and therefore constitute one household, in violation of the statute. This is a distinction of significance because, due to the economies of scale that may be realized in group purchase and preparation of food, a single household will receive a lower amount of food stamp benefits than will two or more households with the same total number of members as the single household. Plaintiffs also claim that defendants violated their due process rights by failing to send individual notices of eligibility or program requirements to the head of each family that has been combined under the sibling rule into a single food stamp household.

Plaintiffs raise a wholly separate claim arising out of the requirements of that households seeking eligibility for food stamps, Aid to Families with Dependent Children ("AFDC"), and Medical Assistance ("MA"), must cooperate with the state agency, and that certain information provided in the food stamp application must be verified through, *inter alia,* the use of third-party information or documentation, to establish the accuracy of statements on the application. Plaintiffs complain that the Pennsylvania Department of Public Welfare ("DPW"): (1) engages in a pattern and practice of repeatedly demanding from applicants and recipients information not clearly specified in the benefit application; and (2) denies plaintiffs benefits without offering them alternative means of proving their eligibility when a third party refuses to cooperate, in violation of the Due Process Clause, . . . and of other federal statutes and regulations.

The district court granted the defendants' motion to dismiss the third party verification claim, and granted defendants' motions for summary judgment as to the remaining claims. It also denied plaintiffs' motion for class action certification of the sibling rule and third party verification class claims. Finally, the court denied plaintiffs' motion to amend their complaint to add Annie Alvin and Gloria Pope as plaintiffs.

For the reasons that follow, we conclude that the district court erred in its grant of summary judgment as to the sibling rule claims, in granting the motion to dismiss

*continued*

## 7.3 | ROBINSON V. BLOCK (CONTINUED)

the third party verification claims and in denying leave to amend to permit the addition of Annie Alvin and Gloria Pope as parties; hence we will reverse and remand for further proceedings. In all other respects, including disposition of the notification claim and the motion for class certification, the judgment and orders of the district court will be affirmed.

### I. Facts and Procedural History
#### A. *The Parties*
In their second amended complaint, plaintiffs proposed two classes of plaintiffs. Class A would consist of Cheryl Robinson, Annie Alvin and Philadelphia Citizens in Action and would raise the sibling household claims. Class B would consist of all of Class A plus Gloria Pope, and would raise the third party verification claims.

#### 1. *Plaintiff Cheryl Robinson*
Plaintiff Cheryl Robinson, a food stamp recipient, lived with her eleven year-old son in a three-story house owned by her brother. Cheryl's sister Margo Robinson and her daughter, also food stamp recipients, eventually moved into the house, although Cheryl apparently had no say in the matter. Over the years, Cheryl and Margo had several serious disagreements, and living in close quarters only seemed to exacerbate the existing tensions between them. When DPW discovered that Cheryl was living in the same house as her sister, she was given notice that unless she appealed, her food stamp benefits would be terminated. Cheryl did not file a timely appeal and her food stamp case was closed.

Cheryl and her sister were then notified by DPW, through the County Assistance Office, that under the federal and state regulations they would have to be included in the same household unit for food stamp purposes. The sisters agreed that Margo's name would be designated as "payment name" for purposes of receiving food stamps for the household. At one point, relations between the sisters became so strained that Cheryl asked her caseworker if she could be designated as payment name. The caseworker suggested that Cheryl find another place to live, apart from her sister.

Soon after the Robinsons were combined into a single household for purposes of receiving food stamps, the local caseworker discovered that Margo's daughter was not living with her, as she had claimed. As a result, Margo's food stamp benefits were terminated, thereby also depriving Cheryl and her son of benefits. Cheryl appealed.

At about the same time, the DPW caseworker began to suspect that Cheryl's brother, Keith Robinson, was living with Cheryl, inasmuch as his driver's license and voter registration card indicated his address as being the same as hers. The caseworker gave Cheryl an opportunity to show that Keith lived elsewhere—a burden that was hers—and the caseworker also attempted to establish where he lived. Because Cheryl was unable (or unwilling) to provide verification that her brother was living elsewhere, her reapplication for food stamps was denied. Cheryl again appealed. At her hearing, Cheryl testified that she did not want to provide the caseworker with a copy of her brother's voter registration card or driver's license, which listed her mother's address, because she knew that this information was false.

In light of these various problems, the caseworker made two appointments for Cheryl to reapply for benefits in her own name at a different location. Cheryl failed to, or chose not to, make such a reapplication.

On July 13, 1984, DPW's hearing officer denied both of Cheryl's appeals. The hearing officer stated that DPW's "regulations are explicit in providing that *in no event* is separate household status extended to siblings unless one sibling is elderly or disabled." (emphasis added). After filing this suit for declaratory and injunctive relief, and some seven months after her food stamp benefits were discontinued, Cheryl moved to Michigan; her son remained in Philadelphia. Cheryl also seeks restoration of the benefits allegedly unlawfully denied her.

## 2. Proposed Plaintiff Annie Alvin
Annie Alvin lived with her daughter in a building owned by the Philadelphia Housing Authority. Her sister Sharon and Sharon's son lived in the same building. The sisters had separate cooking facilities, bedrooms, living rooms, kitchens and telephones, but had common doors and stairs. Until February 1984, the sisters had received separate food stamp allotments. However, in February the DPW terminated Sharon's food stamp benefits and advised Annie that she would receive food stamps for a household that consisted of her family as well as Sharon's. Because of this change, Sharon became uncooperative in paying her share of the rent and the utility bills. The friction between them increased to the point where Sharon moved out in September, 1984.

In December 1984, DPW informed Annie that she had received an overpayment of $1,134 in food stamps between April 1, 1983, and February 29, 1984. The basis for this calculation was the "sibling rule": for the period in question, the DPW combined the amount of food stamp benefits received by Annie and Sharon Alvin separately, and then subtracted the amount to which they were entitled as a single household. In December 1984, DPW demanded full repayment, in installments of at least $15 per month. As of this date, the DPW has not pursued collection activities nor reduced Annie's current allotment to recover the alleged past overissuances.

## 3. Proposed Plaintiff Gloria Pope
Gloria Pope, the only plaintiff who is solely a member of plaintiffs' proposed Class B, alleges that the DPW's third party verification procedures were unreasonably applied and that errors were made regarding her benefits which caused delay and inconvenience. In 1984, Pope, who had previously received public assistance, reapplied for AFDC, food stamp, and MA benefits. She was given a form PA 253, requesting various kinds of verification. Pope's application was denied, allegedly because of her failure to provide certain verification information. Pope alleges that this information was not requested on the PA 253.

Pope later reapplied for public assistance. Her application was again denied, this time allegedly because of problems Pope encountered in obtaining adequate third party verification of information she provided the DPW. To continue receiving public assistance, Pope alleges that she must submit to eligibility redeterminations for AFDC and MA, and recertifications of her food stamp eligibility at least once every six months. Moreover, she claims that defendants employ substantially the same policies, patterns and practices in requiring supplemental verification from applicants and recipients.

*continued*

*4. Plaintiff Philadelphia Citizens in Action*

Philadelphia Citizens in Action ("Citizens") was added as a party in the first amended complaint. It is an organization of public assistance recipients which contends that some of its members have been denied food stamps and proper notice of action affecting their food stamps because they live in the same building as a sibling or because they are unable to comply with the DPW's third-party verification requirements. Citizens contends that it has been forced to expend time, money and resources advocating on behalf of recipients denied or threatened with denial of benefits because they resided in the same building as a sibling or because they could not produce the third party verification demanded by defendants. Finally, Citizens contends that many of its members have been or will be harmed by defendants' illegal practices.

*5. The Defendants*

Defendants are John R. Block, the United States Secretary of Agriculture, Walter W. Cohen, Secretary of the Pennsylvania Department of Public Welfare, and Don Jose Stovall, Executive Director of the Philadelphia County Assistance Office.

*B. The Claims and Defenses*

Plaintiffs set forth ten claims in their amended complaint, but these can essentially be reduced to two major claims. First, plaintiffs claim that defendants' implementation of the sibling rule violates the Due Process Clauses of the Fifth and Fourteenth Amendments to the United States Constitution, 42 U.S.C. § 1983, and the Food Stamp Act.

Plaintiffs primarily sought to enjoin defendants from: (1) denying or reducing food stamps to plaintiffs based upon their residence in the same building with their siblings, unless they actually live together; (2) denying plaintiffs' application for food stamps based upon the non-cooperation of a sibling or member of a sibling's household; and (3) delaying or denying AFDC, food stamp, and MA benefits due to applicants' or recipients' failure to promptly provide third party verification where the applicant or recipient cannot obtain prompt third party cooperation. Plaintiffs also sought declaratory relief and restored benefits for the named plaintiffs.

*1. The Sibling Rule Claim*

Eligibility and benefit levels for food stamps are determined by the United States Department of Agriculture, acting through state agencies such as DPW, and are based upon need. Benefits are allocated per household, rather than per individual. The statute defines a food stamp household as "(1) an individual who lives alone or who, while living with others, customarily purchases food and prepares meals for home consumption separate and apart from the others, [or] (2) a group of individuals who live together and customarily purchase food and prepare meals together for home consumption." However, through amendments in 1981 and 1982, Congress amended the Food Stamp Act to provide that "parents and children, *or siblings, who live together* shall be treated as a group of individuals who customarily purchase and prepare meals together for home consumption even if they do not do so, unless one of the parents, or siblings, is an elderly or disabled member." The legislative history to the 1982 amendment notes that the Committee expected that caseworkers "could effectively question claims and that the burden of proof for establishing 'separateness' would be placed on the household, not on the administering agency."

Pursuant to authority granted in the statute, the Secretary promulgated the following regulation, which was in effect at the time the claims that are the subject of the present litigation arose:

> *Household definition.* (1) A household may be composed of . . . (iii) A group of individuals who live together and customarily purchase food and prepare meals together for home consumption. . . . (3) *In no event* shall nonhousehold member status . . . or separate household status be granted to . . . (iv) Siblings (natural, adopted, half or step brothers and sisters), unless at least one sibling is elderly or disabled.

The DPW has adopted nearly identical regulations.

The gravamen of plaintiffs' claim is that while the Food Stamp Act confines the sibling rule to siblings "who live together," neither the federal nor state regulations included the "live together" test in their regulations implementing the sibling rule. While the Food Stamp Act creates an evidentiary issue as to whether siblings are "living together," the regulations implementing the sibling rule appear to eliminate this evidentiary issue, and instead create an irrebuttable presumption that siblings live together, thus constituting one household. More precisely, as plaintiffs clarified their position at oral argument, their claim is that the local DPW offices were and still are applying a "same address" test to determine whether siblings lived together. In response to a hypothetical question posed by the Court, plaintiffs provided an example of the same address test: if one sibling lived on the first floor of a building, and the other sibling lived on the 23rd floor of that building, the siblings, because of the same address test, would be considered to be living together. Although we do not suggest that the type of fact situation described in the hypothetical is at work here, the hypothetical does help to frame the issue.

The Secretary, however, stated at oral argument that he does not apply a same address test, i.e., an irrebuttable presumption that siblings who reside at the same address in fact live together and therefore constitute one household. The Secretary maintains on appeal that despite the difference in wording between the statute and the regulation, "nothing in the Secretary's regulation precludes a claimant from asserting that he or she does not live with a sibling." Plaintiffs respond, however, that the DPW has not changed its regulations to reflect the "live together" component of the statute, and that under the current regulations caseworkers would not accept—indeed, would be precluded from accepting-siblings' claims that they do not live together. At the conclusion of oral argument the Court, sensing that the parties were within reach of agreement, requested each party to submit proposed language of the regulation implementing the sibling rule which would be consistent with the statute. Responding to the plaintiffs' submission, the Secretary stated that he was willing to stipulate to the following, which, he maintained, was based on current law and policy:

> (1) In implementing the "live together" test for siblings, the defendants are required to apply the sibling rule to siblings who are found to live together in light of all the circumstances; (2) defendants are required to offer siblings a rea-

*continued*

sonable opportunity to present evidence bearing on whether they in fact "live together"; and (3) defendants are required to make any necessary adjustments in the allotment of food stamps, including providing retroactive benefits under 7 U.S.C. § 2023(b), and to refrain from alleging overissuances of food stamps to siblings who can show that they do not or did not "live together."

Although the plaintiffs sought a more exacting statement, we view the Secretary's proffer as sharply narrowing the scope of the dispute between the parties over the sibling rule issue. In stating that the sibling rule may only be applied to siblings who are found to live together "in light of all the circumstances," the Secretary and the DPW are conceding that a same address test is an impermissible way to implement the sibling rule and that to apply such a test would be to disregard all the circumstances that must be considered in order to determine whether siblings live together. Unfortunately, however, the defendants' proffer has not obviated the need for this opinion, because the plaintiffs are unwilling to accept it without more detailed protocols for its application. Moreover, there may indeed be situations in which siblings living together, as did the Robinsons and Alvins, could be found not to live together after considering "all the circumstances." Indicia of not living together might include, *inter alia,* separate entrances and locks, separate finances, utility bills and telephones, and essentially separate living quarters. Of course, determining what constitutes living together remains with DPW. The proffer does, however, form much of the basis for our result. * * *

*C. The District Court Memorandum Opinion*
The defendants moved for summary judgment on the merits as to claims one through seven of the amended complaint, i.e., the sibling household issues. As noted, they also moved for summary judgment on grounds of mootness and lack of standing. Neither party moved for summary judgment on the merits of the Class B claim. Therefore, in the absence of affidavits, answers to interrogatories, depositions or other evidence, *see* Fed. R. Civ. P. 56(c), the order dismissing the Class B claims appears in substance to be a dismissal pursuant to Fed. R. Civ. P. 12(b)(6).

In granting defendants' motions as to the sibling rule claim, the district court found the sibling household issue to be "directly controlled" by the United States Supreme Court's decision in *Lyng v. Castillo.* In that case, the Supreme Court held constitutional the statutory distinction, embodied in the 1981 and 1982 amendments to the Food Stamp Act, between (1) parents, children and siblings and (2) all other groups of individuals. As we have explained, the issue is more complex, hence the court erred in finding *Castillo* dispositive.

With regard to plaintiffs' third party verification claims, the district court stated that the individual claims presented were capable of being handled through the administrative hearing process. The court therefore held that plaintiffs' third party allegations failed to state a due process claim and dismissed them, apparently pursuant to Fed. R. Civ. P. 12(b)(6). However, the district court did not address plaintiffs' claim that, notwithstanding the legality of the applicable regulations, the DPW is engaged in a pattern and practice of not complying with those regulations.

## II. The Sibling Rule Issue

In addressing the sibling rule issue, the crucial issues are how the USDA and the DPW implemented the rule in the case of Cheryl Robinson and Annie Alvin, and whether this method of implementing the rule is permissible under the Food Stamp Act. For the reasons given below, we agree with plaintiffs' contention that DPW used a same address test in determining that Cheryl Robinson and her sister and Annie Alvin and her sister lived together. By "same address test" we mean that DPW applied a conclusive presumption that siblings who live at the same address live together for purposes of the Act. We hold that such a test was not a permissible way for the USDA and DPW to implement the statutory sibling rule.

### A. Legislative History of the Sibling Rule

Before 1977, a food stamp household was defined as an "economic unit," a term which took into account the "common living expenses" of all members of a group of people. The Food Stamp Act of 1977 replaced the "economic unit" test with a new test that still remains the focus in determining what constitutes a household: "live together and customarily purchase food and prepare meals together for home consumption." Congress thus made the fact that a group of individuals may share nonfood living expenses irrelevant for purposes of determining whether the group constitutes a household.

In 1981, Congress inserted into the statutory section defining household the provision that "parents and children who live together shall be treated as a group of individuals who customarily purchase and prepare meals together for home consumption *even if they do not do so.* "The 1981 amendment thereby created an irrebuttable presumption that "parents and children who live together" purchase and prepare meals together for home consumption.

In 1982, Congress again amended the Act and added the sibling rule to the definition of household. This amendment merely added the words "or siblings" to the 1981 amendment that created the parent-children rule; the statute now provides that "parents and children, or siblings, who live together shall be treated as a group of individuals who customarily purchase and prepare meals together for home consumption even if they do not do so." This amendment was enacted by Congress in order to extend the step taken in 1981 of "limiting [the] potential manipulation of food stamp rules" that occurs when parents and children claim separate food stamp household status, although they live together, merely by refraining from purchasing food and preparing meals together. The 1982 amendment followed this rationale inasmuch as it was "designed to further limit the number of instances in which household members may manipulate current rules and gain status as separate food stamp households (and receive, thereby, larger benefits), although they live together and depend on one another for support."

We conclude that the 1981 and 1982 amendments did not change the substance of the "live together" test but merely closed loopholes that enabled groups of individuals who lived together, i.e., parents/children and siblings, to be treated as separate food stamp households merely because they did not (or claimed they did not) purchase food and prepare meals together. The amendments created irrebuttable presumptions that (1) parents and children and (2) siblings who live together also purchase food and prepare meals together for home consumption.

*continued*

## 7.3 | ROBINSON V. BLOCK (CONTINUED)

### B. Discussion

As noted earlier, the regulations omit the "live together" language of the Act. The language of the regulations would thus appear to preclude consideration of "all the circumstances" in rendering the "live together" determination, as is required. *See supra* at 209. This interpretation would result in the application of a same address test. The threshold question presented is whether DPW has employed such a test or instead has considered "all the circumstances" surrounding siblings' living situations. If we conclude that DPW did employ a same address test, we must then determine whether such an interpretation of the Act is permissible.

In reviewing the termination of Cheryl Robinson's food stamp allotment, there are undisputed facts in the record from which DPW reasonably could have concluded that (1) Cheryl and her sister Margo lived together; and (2) their brother Keith lived with them. As noted above, Cheryl and her sister lived in the same house owned by their brother Keith. Moreover, Keith Robinson's driver's license and voter registration card indicated that he lived with Cheryl and Margo. Despite Cheryl's assertions to the contrary, she was unable or unwilling to provide DPW, as requested, with notarized verification of her brother's true address. From these facts and others, and taking into account that the burden of proof for establishing 'separateness' is placed on the household, we believe that DPW could have reasonably concluded that Cheryl Robinson lived with her siblings.

However, we cannot be certain that DPW relied upon these facts in reaching its conclusions. We are particularly concerned by the hearing officer's statement that "regulations are explicit in providing that *in no event* is separate household status extended to siblings unless one sibling is elderly or disabled" (emphasis added). This statement essentially tracks the state regulation, and the hearing officer was thereby following DPW regulations that hearing officers may not invalidate or modify a departmental regulation. In other words, the hearing officer felt obligated to base her decision on the state regulations, and apparently she was constrained from considering the "live together" language of the Act.

In light of these regulations and the hearing officer's remarks, we are unable to conclude that the facts noted above were dispositive in DPW's decision to terminate Robinson's food stamp allotment. It seems more reasonable to conclude that DPW followed its regulations that separate household status is not to be granted to siblings, and thereby applied a same address test. Despite the burden placed on households to establish "separateness," we do not believe that this burden has any relevance where the incorrect legal standard has been used by the agency. For similar reasons, it is reasonable to conclude that DPW followed the same methodology in reducing Alvin's food stamp allotment.

As noted earlier, there may indeed be situations in which siblings living in small dwellings could be found not to live together, after considering "all the circumstances." Indicia of "separateness" might include, *inter alia*, separate entrances and locks, separate finances, utility bills and telephones, and essentially separate living quarters. Of course, the "living together" determination remains with DPW.

We concede the difficulty in attempting to ascertain the methodology employed by DPW in rendering its "live together" determination. However, for the reasons noted above, and because we believe caution is necessary where, as here, benefits are terminated or reduced, we conclude that DPW applied a same address test in determining whether Cheryl Robinson and her siblings and Annie Alvin and her sibling lived together. The question with which we are then faced is whether such an interpretation of the Act is permissible.

As a reviewing court, we must reject an administrative construction of a statute if it is "inconsistent with the statutory mandate or . . . frustrate[s] the policy that Congress sought to implement." Our reading of the statutory provision defining household, the legislative history of its various amendments, and the policies behind the several revisions to the definition convinces us that the USDA's and DPW's application of a same address test in implementing the statutory sibling rule is not only inconsistent with Congress' policy in enacting the statute, but also is not a rational interpretation of the statute. The defendants have essentially so conceded.

In reviewing the several amendments to the definition of food stamp household, and the policies behind them, our focus has been limited to determining whether Congress intended that siblings who live at the same address should irrebuttably be considered as living together. Congress has delegated to the Secretary the authority to decide what is meant by the term "living together." The Secretary has chosen not to define the term but to determine which individuals are living together through "the application of a reasonable judgment based on the circumstances of a particular living arrangement." Indeed, at oral argument, plaintiffs' counsel stated that he was not asking the court to enunciate any particular standard for defining the term living together. Because of the congressional grant of authority, our inquiry here is therefore limited to whether a same address test can be construed to be an "application of a reasonable judgment" under *any* circumstances.

As we have explained, to apply a same address test in implementing the sibling rule would run afoul of Congress' intent in treating only groups of individuals who "purchase food and prepare meals together for home consumption" as a food stamp household. In the absence of additional evidence, there is no reason to believe that siblings who merely live at the same address customarily purchase food and prepare meals together for home consumption. Application of a same address test does not prevent the artificial manipulation of food stamp rules—the sole concern of the 1981 and 1982 amendments. It seems unlikely that siblings would choose to live at the same address for the sole reason that they might thereby be able to purchase and prepare food together (and hence more cheaply) yet still maintain, under the regulations, separate household status in order to gain a greater food stamp allotment.

With regard to the sibling rule issue, we will reverse and remand to the district court to determine whether Robinson and her sister, and Alvin and her sister, in fact lived together so as to constitute a single household under the Food Stamp Act. Although evidence that these siblings lived at the same address may be considered in making the "live together" determination, such evidence is not conclusive. The district court should ensure that in implementing the sibling rule, defendants shall, as they have conceded they must: (1) apply the sibling rule to siblings who are found to live together in light of all the circumstances; (2) offer siblings a reasonable opportunity to present evidence bearing on whether they in fact live together; and (3) make any necessary adjustments in the allotment of food stamps, including providing retroactive benefits and refraining from alleging overissuances of food stamps, to siblings who can show that they do not or did not live together. Additionally, the district court should order DPW to issue instructions to its casework-

*continued*

### 7·3    ROBINSON V. BLOCK (CONTINUED)

ers, if DPW has not already done so, that the sibling rule is only to be applied to siblings who live together, and that the fact that siblings reside at the same address is not conclusive evidence in deciding whether siblings live together.* * * [Section III omitted.]

### IV. Conclusion

For the foregoing reasons, we will reverse the judgment of the district court and remand for that court to determine whether plaintiffs and their siblings lived together so as to constitute a single household under the Food Stamp Act. We will further reverse the order of the district court denying plaintiffs leave to amend their complaint to add Annie Alvin and Gloria Pope as parties, and direct that leave be granted. With regard to the third party verification claim, we will reverse the order dismissing the complaint and remand to the district court for further proceedings. In all other respects, the judgment and orders of the district court will be affirmed.

lower participation rates because households that do not receive public assistance are less likely to apply for food stamps. "While most individuals who leave TANF [Temporary Assistance to Needy Families] still qualify for food stamps," Cunningham (2004) argues, "that eligibility is no longer automatic. As a result, some individuals are unaware that they are still eligible . . . and others choose not to apply. In 2001, individuals receiving TANF were three times more likely to participate in the FSP than individuals not receiving TANF" (p. 15).

The interplay between program expansion or contraction and recipient participation is further illustrated in a report on food stamps and working families that cites the central role that food stamps play in supporting working families:

> A family of four earning the minimum wage full-time year-round will only reach 75 percent of the poverty level, even after receiving the Earned Income Tax Credit [EITC]. This family can receive the equivalent of over a third of its earnings in food stamps, bringing the family close to the poverty level. And unlike the EITC, which is usually received in a single lump sum in the year after the low income on which it is based, food stamps are delivered monthly at the time of determined need, and so are available for day-to-day expenses when the family is poor.
>
> But many working families do not receive the food stamps they need. Between 1994 and 1999, the total number of people receiving food stamps declined by 35 percent, from 28 million to 17 million. During this time, the number of people living in poverty declined only 15 percent. Less than half of the decline in food stamp enrollment was due to families becoming ineligible because of rising incomes or welfare reform rules excluding certain groups from eligibility. Most of the decline in enrollment was due to fewer eligible families receiving food stamps. The proportion of eligible individuals receiving food stamps fell from 74 percent in 1994 to 57 percent in 1999.

Worse still, the proportion of eligible working families receiving food stamps-which had always been lower than that of non-working families-also declined. In 1994, 64 percent of eligible working families received food stamps; in 1999, the most recent year for which we have data, this number was 48 percent. In other words, *at the very time when welfare reform was encouraging the transition from welfare for work, the food stamp program was becoming less effective at serving working poor families.* Because state food stamp agencies were already in contact with many of these families, one would have expected the opposite: the large influx of new low-income workers from the welfare rolls should have increased food stamp participation rates among the working poor. (Hayes, 2002, pp. 5–7)

Moreover, recent trends continue to underscore the fluctuation in food stamp participation:

Food stamp participation dipped in January 2005 to 25,458,113, an over-the-month decline of 29,290, but an over-the-year increase of nearly two million people. The Food Stamp Program growth in recent months reflects continuing joblessness, state actions to improve access, and the effects of the food stamp reauthorization implementation.

The number of people participating in the Food Stamp Program in January 2005 was 8.58 million more persons than July 2000, when program participation nationally reached its lowest point in the last decade.

Caseloads dropped through 1998 and 1999 as the economy improved and many states failed to get food stamps to low-income families who had left cash welfare for low-paid work. Caseloads then stabilized and began rising in 2000. Increases in participation since 2001 likely have been driven by improved access to the program in states, including most recently for legal immigrants, and by the weakened economy.

Participation has risen in 44 of the last 49 months. Participation in January 2005 fell in the District of Columbia and rose in 48 of the 50 states compared to a year earlier. (Food Research and Action Center, 2005)

The federal government pays 100 percent of Food Stamp Program benefits. Federal and state governments each cover 50 percent of state administrative costs, and they share the costs of employment and training for food stamp recipients within the state. In fiscal year (FY) 2002, total federal food stamp costs were $24 billion (U.S. House of Representatives, Committee on Ways and Means, 2004). The program provides eligible low-income families with monthly coupons that can be used to purchase food. However, electronic benefit transfer (EBT) systems are quickly replacing the use of coupons. The USDA reports that all 50 states, Washington, D.C., and Puerto Rico are now using EBT systems. The length of participation in the Food Stamp Program is less than 2 years for 71 percent of those receiving food stamps. Half of all new recipients stay on the program no more than 6 months, and 57 percent end participation within 1 year. Receiving food stamps increases the nutritional value of a low-income household's home food supplies by 20-40 percent (Food Research and Action Center, 2005).

According to the Food Research and Action Center (2005), the average monthly participation level in fiscal year 2003 was 21.26 million individuals. The center, noting that the program targets the most needy, further indicates that:

Of all food stamp households in FY 2003 (the year for which the most recent detailed USDA data are available), 55 percent contain children; households with children receive 79.3 percent of all food stamp benefits. 18 percent of food stamp households contain an elderly person, and 23 percent contain a disabled person. Approximately 88 percent of food stamp households have gross incomes below the poverty line ($18,100 for a family of four in 2002). Approximately 38.4 percent of food stamp households have gross incomes below half of the poverty line (Available at www.frac.org/html/federal_food_programs/programs/fsp.html).

## Application and Eligibility

Households that meet the requisite rules are eligible to receive benefits. Individual members must satisfy related work effort requirements and meet citizenship and legal permanent residence tests. Aside from a few exceptions, TANF and Supplemental Security Income (SSI) recipients are automatically eligible for food stamps, as are some recipients of state general assistance programs (U. S. House of Representatives, Committee on Ways and Means, 2004).

Other considerations affect eligibility, and therefore is it important to have a firm grasp of the eligibility requirements, such as those following, which are provided by the Center for Food Research and Action Center (2005):

> Eligibility for the Food Stamp Program is based on financial and nonfinancial factors. The application process includes completing and filing an application form, being interviewed, and verifying facts crucial to determining eligibility. With certain exceptions, a household that meets the eligibility requirements is qualified to receive benefits. A *household* is defined as a person or a group of people living together, but not necessarily related, who purchase and prepare food together. Households, except those with elderly or disabled members, must have gross incomes below 130 percent of the poverty line. All households must have net incomes below 100 percent of poverty to be eligible.
>
> Households must meet certain requirements and provide proof of eligibility to receive food stamps. These requirements are as follows:
>
> 1. Recipient must be a United States citizen or a lawfully admitted permanent resident. The Welfare Reform Act of 1996 ended food stamp eligibility for many immigrants, even those who are lawfully in the United States. The welfare reform act also created time limits on benefits for refugees. Citizens and noncitizens may be eligible. Eligible noncitizens include refugees and deportees for a period of 7 years after they have entered the country or their status is granted, certain battered individuals, and individuals admitted for lawful permanent residents who have a military connection or who can be credited with 40 quarters of work (about 10 years). Refugees, deportees, battered aliens, and lawful permanent residents may also be eligible if they were lawfully living in the United States on August 22, 1996, and were over 65 on that date, are now under 18, or are receiving disability or blindness payments. Additionally, certain Hmong and other Highland Laotians and their spouses and children and foreign-born members of American Indian tribes entitled to cross into Canada and Mexico may also be eligible. The status of noncitizens must be verified.
> 2. Recipient must provide a Social Security number or apply for one.

3. Recipient must meet the income and resource requirements, which include the following:

    a. Households may have $2,000 in countable resources, such as a bank account. Households may have $3,000 if at least one person is age 60 or older. Certain resources are not counted, such as a home and lot. If you receive Supplemental Security Income (SSI), your benefits are not counted. The amount of benefits an eligible household receives depends on the number of people in the household and the amount of their income.

    b. Vehicles are not counted if they meet one of the following criteria: are valued under $4,650, are used over 50 percent of the time for income producing purposes, are needed for long distance travel to work, are needed to transport a disabled household member or are needed to carry most of the household's fuel and water.

4. Work requirements—with some exceptions, able-bodied adults between the ages of 16 and 60 must register for work, take part in an employment and training program to which they are referred by the food stamp office, and accept or continue suitable employment. Failure to comply with there requirements can result in disqualification from the program. In addition, able-bodied adults between the ages of 18 and 59 who do not have any dependent children can get food stamps only for 3 months in a 36-month period if they do not work or participate in a work fare or employment and training program other than a job search. Other members of the household may continue to get food stamps even if this person is disqualified. (Food Research and Action Center, 2005)

## Benefits

Food stamp eligibility, and thus the benefit grant, is associated with household size and the net income available to the household. The monthly allotment is not taxable, nor are state sale taxes applied to food stamp purchases. As indicated previously, receipt of food stamps is not affected by grants from other welfare programs, although some may use food stamp allotments to "trigger" eligibility or otherwise consider the availability of food stamps in determining the benefit level. Moreover, the

> monthly food stamp allotments are tied to the cost of purchasing a nutritionally adequate low-cost diet, as measured by the Agriculture Department's Thrifty Food Plan (TFP). Maximum allotments are set at: the monthly cost of the TFP for a four-person family consisting of a couple between ages 20 and 50 and two school-age children, adjusted for family size (using a formula reflecting economies of scale developed by the Human Nutrition Information Service), and rounded down to the nearest whole dollar. Allotments are adjusted for food price inflation annually, each October, to reflect the cost of the TFP in the immediately previous June. (U.S. House of Representatives, Committee on Ways and Means, 2004)

Current program benefits provide an average of about 90 cents a meal per person.

Allotments are usually issued monthly. The benefit must be provided within 30 days of the initial application and continued without interruption if an eligible household reapplies and fulfills recertification requirements. The local welfare agency may deny an application, also within this 30 day period. Households with immediate need due to little or no income may receive expedited service, typically receiving benefits within 7 days of initial application.

While the program supplies food to meet nutritional needs of recipients, there are limits to the items that may be purchased. A profile of eligible versus ineligible items that may be purchased with food stamps, as defined by the state of Pennsylvania, follows.

### ELIGIBLE FOODS

- Any food intended for human consumption including soft drinks, candy, ice cream, coffee and spices.
- Seeds and plants to grow food for personal consumption by eligible households.
- Meals prepared and served by:
  A. an authorized meal delivery service;
  B. a communal dining facility for the elderly and/or SSI household;
  C. a group living arrangement such as:
     1. a rehabilitation center for drug addicts or alcoholics;
     2. a shelter for battered women and children;
     3. an authorized provider of meals for the homeless; and
     4. an authorized restaurant serving meals to the homeless, elderly or disabled.

### INELIGIBLE FOODS

- Alcoholic beverages, pet foods, and hot foods prepared for immediate consumption (such as barbecued chicken).
- Non-food items such as paper products, soap, household supplies, medicines, and cigarettes. (Pennsylvania Department of Welfare, 2005)

Food stamp benefits may not be used to pay off a bill for food purchased on credit or to pay in advance for the receipt of foods except for purchase from a nonprofit cooperative food-purchasing venture.

## Due Process

A denial of an application for food stamps, or a reduction, suspension, or termination of benefits, triggers an opportunity for a "fair hearing" process. Typically, the party bringing the appeal (the claimant) believes the administrative decision is either incorrect or unfair. The claimant may ask the agency for assistance in filing a fair hearing appeal, must do so within a specified time frame, and may expect to receive a decision from the agency within a specified period of time. While the specific elements of this process vary among the states, all procedures share the following key characteristics (similar to fair hearings in TANF or Medicaid):

- The process begins with the claimant's appeal to the local department of social services.

- The claim may involve requesting a prehearing conference, which affords an opportunity to discuss the claim and achieve an agreement before a fair hearing. The claimant and a representative of the agency are able to explain their positions; if the agency determines its action was incorrect, it will change the decision, but it if finds no error the claimant may then request a fair hearing.
- The fair hearing is a formal proceeding, involving the claimant and his or her representative (which may include an attorney) and an agency representative. The claimant may view his or her case record and other materials on which the agency based its decision, may pose questions to agency representatives, and may present documents that substantiate the claim of unfairness. Benefits usually continue during the fair hearing process and are not reduced or terminated until after the fair hearing is completed.
- The claimant may appeal the fair hearing outcome to a state court, usually within a specified time frame.

## THE CLIENTS' STORIES

### Geraldine

My circumstances and why I end up here was, I was incarcerated in August, and I was released in December. I had Section 8, a beautiful home, right down there in town. Section 8 won't release my voucher or terminate me. They are just not allowing me to use it. Therefore, I couldn't provide appropriate housing for my two children I have with me. My only out, and thank God I am a vet, was to come here to this homeless program for veterans.

They put us to work, and I saved a little bit of money. Then this other agency in the county here, as long as I have a job will help me with my security money, and I will be able to get a foundation and stabilize myself so that I can provide appropriate housing and other things for my two children. They're waiting, so they say, on some paperwork to come from the court so they will know whether to terminate me, but my feeling is that after 7 months, if you are sending paperwork to the courthouse, which is walking distance from this building, if you're not getting any response, then what information you are looking for is not there, so just go ahead and give me my Section 8 so I can get on with my life. I had my Section 8 for 6 years.

If I am successful with all of this stuff, I intend on finishing the program at the VA [Veteran's Administration hospital]. It is to my best interest to finish this program, because it helps me with a lot of things. I got my therapy here. It helps me with my addiction problems. It helped me learn how to maintain and save my money. Different things like that. It helped me find a job, even though I am working under what they call compensated work therapy for a company that makes gun-cleaning kits.

Then, once my compensated work therapy is over, we have a vocational education section and a vocational rehab section that helps me out with my résumés. They take us out on job search, and help us do what they can as far as getting us a job.

I'm having a little bit of a problem, because I'm not used to having basically low-paying jobs. I spent 15 years in the military—3 on active duty, 12 inactive. I have 3 years of college; I took one semester off and never went back. That was 27 years ago. I have a lot of education; raised by schoolteachers. I just got caught up in a grip, everyday life in the concrete jungle, and now it's kind of hard for me to get myself back to where I should be.

I need to go back to school for one thing, because when I left I had a 3.85 average at the college I attended in New Jersey. I also got accepted at a school in Louisiana for my master's in Hospital and Health Administration, and I just didn't go. I have never had, until I came to Pennsylvania, I never had regular blue-collar jobs. I always had government jobs, so I was always able to provide for myself, until I came here and got mixed up in the system. And it's all gone haywire.

I came to Pennsylvania May 23, 1999. I guess about 6 months before I came here I was forced to resign from a job at the VA hospital. I wasn't forced. It was an option. I could either resign, go and get the help that I needed, or don't resign and eventually get fired, which would have made it much worse for me. So I resigned and I came down here, into the substance abuse program. That lasted for about a year, a year and a half.

Then I got back up in the grips [of the street] again. I don't know exactly what made me do the things that I did. Addiction is like a sickness or illness, or however they want to classify it. I know right from wrong, you know. I just couldn't get it together. Any time something bothered me I just went back to my old habits and behaviors. That was I guess around September 2000. It all started up. Maybe a little later, around November, I started dipping and dabbing again. Then one thing lead to another. I had lost my job at the department store where I worked back in January of 2000. It was a job I liked. I enjoyed it, because I love working with people. What happened was I went to H&R Block, which was at the mall. I was working at the mall. I didn't really know, but it's only common sense, that if you're on the clock, you're not supposed to leave the premises, but everyone did it. What happened was it took a little longer than I expected on my 15-minute break. Instead of coming out of the building and coming in through security I shot back to my spot of duty in the Jewelry Department and was spotted on camera coming back in the building. So, I was terminated for theft of company time. From that point on everything went down hill.

It was theft of company time, and I thought I was only AWOL. I thought it was real strange, because I had started working there in

August. I started working there while I was part of this program. I started out at $6.50. By the time the store opened I had my first raise. I started out doing customer service. We put that store together. When I first started working at the store, there wasn't even a first floor. There were no rugs or anything. I stocked all of the second floor, the housewares, the small appliance department, where they had us working, the pots and pans, everything relating to housewares on the shelves, rearranging them and making them appropriate. We had to make sure what was visual for the customer, what would attract the customer's attention when they came into the store, what would or wouldn't make money. I learned a lot. They asked me if I wanted to do houseware stock. I said yes and that gave me a raise. After a month, they asked me if I wanted to do small appliances also. They gave me another raise, plus another responsibility. So, I was doing houseware stock, small appliance stock, opening up all the cash registers, customer service, floor work, covering for lunches, breaks, and everything.

And having my treatment here. I was doing all of this. I like people contact jobs, so that was no problem for me. But by the time they had decided to terminate me I had another raise. I went from $6.50 in August to $8.75 by January 1. At Christmas time they did a progress report, which was off the record scale. It was an excellent progress report. Instead of either chastising me, or suspending me, they just downright fired me. I have been trying to get back there ever since. That kind of hurt me. I figured that if I had done so much, and I was so good and so valuable to this company that they gave me these raises and extra responsibility, why the first time I slipped up they just cut me loose? Then I had to go and get on welfare, which was a big cut.

I didn't come back into treatment after I had left, until March 11 of this year. By that time there was so much other stuff it was either come back into treatment and try to figure out what I missed last time, or end up back in prison.

I'll be 47 in September and most of the people my age either have children that are in or out of college, have grandkids, etc. etc. All of things I'm doing now they did in their late teens and early twenties. Well in my late teens and early twenties I was traveling overseas; I had a house; I was in college. My life was so stable. Once I got introduced to what I call the concrete jungle I liked it. I was 31. I'm a stubborn person. Being that I liked it, and I still do but know that I can't do it any more, and I'm grown, the more somebody tells me what not to do, I consider that as a form of dictatorship. So, I'm going to do what I want to do anyway, like I'll show you.

Getting involved in the concrete jungle means getting involved in the street life, the hustle life. All the things that people dig, now I'm doing it, what people did and outgrew. I'm not going to outgrow it because I'm grown. Society is not going for it, this way or that way, and that way is not the way I should play. So, it's their way, and

I just have to get it out of my head that somebody knows what's good for me, because obviously I don't or I wouldn't be here. I wouldn't be involved in the system. That's what caused me to end up in jail, for 111 days. They came to my house twice in 2 weeks. One time I got out on bail; the second time there wasn't any bail. I probably could have gotten out on bail, but I didn't go to court until December. They sent me down to the county lockup.

I had my children in someone else's care while I was gone. I was on welfare. They were stealing my money, selling my food stamps. My Social Services money was always put into my household. I had strict rules. I was raised with certain principles and morals. I'm not sugar-coating anything that I did. I paid my rent because I needed some place to get high. I paid my electric bill because I needed to see how to get high. I kept food in my house so my kids would never be hungry while I'm trying to do what I want to do for me. They shouldn't bug me they are hungry. My house stayed equipped. All my rooms had TVs. Each one of the kids had their own TV, their own VCR. My money went into the household. In order to support my habit I had to do my hustle. All of this led up to me going to jail. I wasn't working. I was on welfare.

At the time when I had applied for welfare, me and the children weren't staying in the same household; so my plan was to use my Section 8 that they never released to me. In the meantime, I'm still fighting with these people, "Well, give me the Section 8. Let me at least put the girls and myself into a place. Then, if it has to be terminated, at least we would not be separated, living from pillar to post, place to place." By that time I would be stable where I could have found a decent job. If you take the Section 8 or terminate and I have to go to a fair hearing, at least we would have a roof over our heads. They wouldn't do it. I was hurt by that. I believed that maybe Children, Youth and Family could have been more aggressive in convincing them to give me and let me use the Section 8. Instead, Welfare ended up cutting me off because the children and I were not in the same household.

I was forced to put the children in foster care, simply because if I couldn't provide a home for them, they could no longer stay where they were at. If push came to shove, they could have come where I was, but there were already enough children there, and I felt as if I was an inconvenience, even though I was welcomed with open arms. The children used to come and see me there. They would stay the weekend sometimes, but that's different than staying all week.

I talk to my kids at least three times a week. I saw my daughter yesterday morning coming from breakfast with her foster mom, who works here on the hospital compound. They are in a decent home. I knew her from when I was here in '99, so I'm not worrying about them being abused. What I do worry about is my children can have a flip mouth sometimes. I can tell them to do something, but they don't want anybody else to tell them to do something, but that's kids. My oldest is 14, and my baby is 10. My son is still in New York. He's 11.

Getting the cash part of welfare was a little strange compared to the only other state where I had applied and received welfare. Here, you get your money twice a month. There, you get it once a month. You get everything the first of the month. I had no problem getting the food stamps. I had to prove certain things before I could get the cash—which, after not having to prove anything to going to have to prove something was strange, but you do what you have to do in order to receive what you need to survive. It took a while. That's nationwide. If I came today and applied for my stuff, my food stamps would be effective as of today. If I got there before noon-time, I would have my food stamps in the morning. Now they give me all these papers that I have to take to different people to fill out. When I got the cash that would be effective the day that I brought the papers, not the day that I originally applied. That cuts the money down.

Then you have to participate in their program, which is good. Their program that I participated in I took a computer class. It was a job-training program. Their programs are pretty good. One is called the Up Front, which I didn't like. I could have stayed home and read the newspaper. Basically, that's what you do from 9 to 4. You come there and just go through the newspaper and make phone calls. I think that's a waste of time. But, if you don't do it you won't get your cash money.

My baby is emotionally disturbed. So in all actuality, if she would decide to start to act up, I would not be able to work, because nobody wants to take care of her while I work. Therefore, I have to survive off the $367 a month in food stamps. If there were a problem, I would get as far as them disapproving my portion of the grant. I would get $220 a month. So that's $440 a month in cash and $367 a month in food stamps. Out of that $440, you're sup-posed to pay rent. Phone is a necessity nowadays. All your things, your nonperishables, everything is coming out of that $440, and you can't do it. If I were to find me a part-time job, whatever monies I make is deducted from the $440. I'm still not getting ahead. I think that their system here in this sense should be more like the other state I was in. With me and the children I was getting $488. If I went to work, I'm not sure if it was 3 months or 6 months I would still get my welfare check. Then I would be cut off. But they do that so that you could get ahead and won't fall short and have to return and come back to them.

My goal was to come here to the Veterans Administration Hos-pital and get stabilized as far as my addiction and everything; pay attention this time, because I didn't last time, and get my life back on the right track and get one of them long-term jobs, which only pays $5.50 an hour, but there is no tax coming out, and I would have had it for 6 months. They force you to save 70 percent of your money, which was good, and those long-term jobs, as the jobs open up you get first crack at it. That was the plan. As long as I'm here on the compound, if something comes up, I'm right here. They hire from when they post their jobs. Unless it specifically says "Employees only may apply," then they pick from these programs first. This was to my advantage to come here. My coming here [the Veterans Administration Hospital] was not a tough decision to make. To put the kids into foster care was my toughest decision. I knew coming here was easy because I wanted to get it right this time. I thank God for the VA. Who knows? I probably would have ended up back in prison, because then the system just wasn't working for me. Or maybe I wasn't using it right. Whatever it was, it was just taking me too long for me to do the things I had to do, plus deal with my addiction and all the other things I had to do. I had to be someplace where I can just forget about everything, and just work on me. This was it.

I really pretty much wasted my life. And then the drugs kept me from getting all of the things that I enjoyed. Kept me from getting them back. As they say, it's baffling and cunning just kept me in. This is going to help me get it right. It was a 15-year period.

The toughest thing has been the moving forward. I have accepted that I am an addict, that it's out there, and that's what I like to do. But I'm having a hard time accepting the fact that I can't do it any more. Age doesn't have anything to do with it. There's nothing wrong with being a big baby. I think there's nothing wrong with that at all. I do believe that had I not told you I was 47 you would never have known. Whatever makes you happy. I don't be happy, walking around here, not one to talk to nobody, because I'm older or I'm bigger than that. That's not me. Put me down with the real people. Whatever knowledge I have, regardless of what I do, or whatever I know I kick it out there. One of the fellows told me, "You know everything, but you use none of it." I know right from wrong, but all I can do is tell you what I feel is right. If you want to be like me, then do what I do. Don't use it. That's all I could tell you.

## Della

I grew up in the city with my father and my aunt. My father passed away in 1999. I was at the shelter at about 17, little bit before my 18th birthday. I couldn't handle it at the time, so I left. I did graduate from high school in 2001. I was pregnant with twins. I came back to the Emergency Center where I stayed. I lost one twin. I went to the shelter and was on welfare at first until I found a job. I joined the job program, to help us find employment. I found employment for a while, but I saved enough money from the welfare checks to move to transitional where I stayed, and then I found a job at a veterinarian. I was at both places for a total of 15 months. This was about a year after high school. I went to school in a rough area. My father was sick. So the school that I applied, for creative writing, they needed him there to come and sign a couple of things. He wasn't able to come, so my audition I wasn't able to pass. I was worried about him and I wasn't able to go there. He started to get real ill. I was with him more. He passed away the day that I graduated from high school. I went a couple of years to community college. I did a couple of courses there. Then I had my son and wanted to spend time with him. I didn't go back. I found a new home, and got a new job, and kind of steered in the right direction now.

I now work at a charter school. They have a good job program. I have been there since October. I just got off from cash assistance. I'm still on medical assistance and food stamps.

I have been on food stamps since I got pregnant, which was back in 2002. I had a hard time at first getting on there. It was like I had to bring them proof of pregnancy and then they didn't know what set amount to give me, and now that I'm working, they cut me down. For proof for food stamps, I had to bring in a proof of pregnancy; proof of need; identification; Social Security card. For proof of pregnancy I had to bring something from the doctors that said I was pregnant.

My thing with welfare and food stamps is like you have to turn everything in by a certain time, and sometimes you are not able to get that stuff. If I was not ready they put me on suspension and you don't have food and if you have a child it's not your fault. Sometimes it cuts you off and you have to start all over the next month. You're without food. I lived in a shelter. You have to go to a supervisor, and sometimes they are nasty. Sometimes they're not. I had a couple of nasty ones, and a couple of nice ones. But, if you don't hand them the documents, you won't get the food stamps until the next month.

The way they work, you have to have them in by a certain time, for example February 19 at 11 o'clock. If you're not there at 11 o'clock, they sort of put you in a category, and then you go to call for your food stamps, and there is nothing there. You have to do what they say when they say it. It was pretty much the same experience for everybody. You have to follow the rules and regulations. They didn't give me much leeway. I had a suspension not long ago because I didn't give them my lease. But I didn't have my lease yet. They understood, but they weren't going to turn the food stamps on until I gave them the lease. When I finally gave her the lease I was cut down. You have to give pay stubs.

They had a semi-monthly reporting thing going on, and I'm not used to that. I never had to do that. Not knowing, I was keeping them for myself and my records and not turning them in. It was sort of a threat. They wanted papers or they wouldn't give me food stamps.

My food stamp money was cut because I don't pay any rent, plus I have a job. The way welfare is, if you pay rent, they give you more. My rent is zero here for now. I will be rent free until my income amount increases. As I earn more it will still be subsidized.

When I got this job I tried to close my account myself. By the time they finished calculating it, it was not worth it. It's like a clock and it still ticks. My clock is not ticking now that I'm off the cash.

I used up 255 days, and I'm not sure of the maximum. They call you "pre" when you don't really utilize days. "Post" is when you have to have a job to get welfare. It means you have used up all your time and did nothing. Pre also allows you to go to college, and they'll still keep you on the system for cash assistance. I got $102.50 every two weeks for me and my son. I turned that into savings.

I joined the job program—I couldn't just sit home, and my clock stopped. The job program provided me with training sessions—how to fill out a résumé, how to present myself. We had computer class, and I got a certificate. They have a program where they provide you with tokens and stuff to go out to look for a job. When I found a job I was eligible for a program for working mothers. It's a program for working moms that gives them transit checks, something to keep them going and help them with utilities. I'm in the process of filling out the application. I graduated from the job program, found a job. I have him in the day care which is downstairs. I'm working and have so far kept the job for almost 5 months. I like it.

I think that the Food Stamp Program is very helpful. My pay rate is $8 an hour. It started out at 3 hours a day. My son drinks soy milk, which is expensive. I appreciate the little help I do get from welfare. So, it really helps. My food stamps will decrease once my income goes up, unless from what I understand from my caseworker, she said that if I was paying rent, then my food stamps would have gone up. Since I'm not paying any rent, they went down.

I hear from a lot of women in the shelter that they just want to be off on their own, period. They get tired of the hassle dealing with food stamps. Even though you're grateful for what you get. They appreciate it, but what they have to go through to get it. Going to the office, for many hours, knowing you have a lot of stuff to do. For me, for instance, if I have an appointment at 11, I end up staying until 2. The reason for the delay is that they sometimes forget about it. They have other people overlapping your time. A lot of people get frustrated.

My son has come a long way. My son weighed 3 pounds when he was born. The shelter expected me to have twins, bring home two babies. They gave us so much stuff. It was a blessing. The shelter is something you're not used to. You have to depend on somebody else now. You're not used to five women in one room. There is curfew and a lot of rules.

When I got to transitional housing it was like a load off me; a step up. We were in our own unit—a little apartment with a bed, little kitchen area, bathroom—just for the two of us. I got here because "Someone" determined that I was doing what I was supposed to do, I'm making an effort to do something with my life. I'm following rules and regulations. I'm trying to find a job. I'm trying to get out of here. You still have curfew which is 12 o'clock. There is a lot of leeway there. They have a pay phone on each floor. You can give the number out. They still have front desk security down there. You can stay here for 7 years' time.

When I got to community college, I didn't start with my classes on a college level. I had to do some pre-classes, which put me back a bit. I did two years. I have two semesters left. I was going to get into a program at a 4-year college, but I wanted time with my son.

Someday, I think I'll be working in a hospital somewhere. I went to a career school for cardiovascular, and I got a diploma there. At the same time as Community College. I was pregnant, and it got too hard. I enjoyed that. When I get to a 4-year college I know my whole major is going to change. The college has amazing things. They offer a lot of stuff. I have a friend who is in one of the Spanish programs. She is going to Mexico on spring break. She is in a class where they speak only Spanish, so she has to learn the language. I look forward to it.

I had this big dream that I was going to become a pediatrician, go to med school. I still have that dream. I love children. I see other opportunities I didn't know were there when I made my decision in high school.

I'm just taking it step by step. I plan to have a job where they'll offer me benefits. I pray to be off food stamps.

I've worked to pay off whatever—house, bills, my son. I budget my money. With or without welfare, I have to find a way. I know one particular young lady. We are best friends. She got out. I know other ladies who get frustrated. Depends on where you want to go and how you think you are going to get there. I know one young lady. I had a conversation one day. I told her that my clock stopped, in case I needed it in the future. Not to say that I love to, but if an emergency occurs the help will be there. I think that's what welfare really should be. If you're in need of help now; until you get back on your feet. I don't think public assistance is a way of life. I know some ladies who are like that. They sit and watch TV. Kids get day care. They're home.

On a lot of applications for welfare and food stamps, they ask, "Why are you applying?" I always say I am in need of help right now for whatever amount I'm applying for. The case manager and you both sign. It asks, "Where do you expect to be in 10 years?" I always put the same thing. I plan to be in med school—graduating. I plan to be off of assistance. Thank you. I never know what's going to happen the next day, and I don't want to take advantage of something like that. For one, I'm grateful that we have this public assistance, giving money to people who need this. Where else can you find that. When I get a job, I quickly call them—cash off. I don't want to feel all the time that they're helping me. I want to do it.

In the shelter I've seen so many women come and go. It's like they can't handle the pressure after 2 days. And then 2 months later they're back. And in those 2 months, they could have gotten a place by then.

Usually when you appeal, they get back to you really quick. They really do. Not that it makes the situation better, but they get back to you quick. I never appealed. It wasn't a big deal. When you appeal, they call you back right away, saying what the problem is and what to bring in, because the supervisors get involved in it. This is what I heard, that it's really quick. I never appealed anything, and if I ever had to I probably wouldn't. I heard that it may have taken maybe 2 weeks or 3. Most of the women win the appeal, from the ones I know. While waiting for the final outcome of the appeal, actually they do get whatever they set them to have. You'll get that until they decide otherwise. At the beginning of next month, it will be whatever. So, you don't go without.

They put a lot of people on suspension for not turning in pay stubs, or not coming to appointments. They don't know why you're not coming to appointments. Once you're cut off you have to go through the whole process again. You have to fill out the book again. That's a long process.

I think my father played a lot of part in my ability to cope with my current circumstances. I never even imagined my dad leaving my side. I'm in the real world now. Nobody's there to shelter me. Me and my father used to give gifts to the shelter, when I was little. I always had to work for what I wanted. I had to do something to get it. It wasn't just given to me. I had to work hard for whatever I got. And I just get more mature every year. You learn from your mistakes. You have to move forward and see where your position is in life.

## WHAT OUR CLIENTS TEACH US

Geraldine's and Della's participation in the Food Stamp Program has provided them with supplemental income for food. Food stamps helped both women sustain their families' well-being, thus fulfilling the program's mission.

Food stamp benefit levels are directly connected to income and resource levels. As Della notes, because she does not pay rent and has a job, her food stamps have been reduced. This illustrates the dilemma recipients and policy-makers face in packaging benefits—how do you balance eligibility thresholds so disincentives to self-sufficiency are not built into the package? If, for example, moving into the labor force means loss of Medicaid, food stamps, and/or child care, what incentives are there to do so? Transitional child care and medical benefits, as well as jobs that provide sufficient income, child care, and health insurance for working families are needed if people on assistance are to achieve self-sufficiency.

Geraldine and Della are struggling to overcome their problems-in-living. The Food Stamp Program takes on additional dimensions when viewed within the context of their life journeys. Geraldine's story evidences her struggle to use social programs to escape the consequences of her drug dependency. As a veteran she participates in an array of programs through the Veterans Administration, all of which are focused on helping her move beyond her dependency and back into the labor force. Della used the Food Stamp Program to stay healthy and provide her child with nutrition, particularly the soy formula that he needed. Both women offer important insights:

1. *Clients have different perspectives on benefit programs related to their experiences with the administrative agency.* Geraldine successfully dealt with the food stamp bureaucracy and experienced no real difficulty in the application process. She reports "no problem getting the food stamps. . . . If I got there before noontime, I would have my food stamps in the morning." Della's experiences, on the other hand, were uneven, related in part to the provider's attitudes: "You have to go to a supervisor, and sometimes they are nasty. I had a couple of nasty ones, and a couple of nice ones."

Another variable that affected Della, and often affects recipients, was the degree of flexibility evidenced by the benefits administration with regard to such issues as supporting documentation and deadlines. As Della states:

> They way they work you have to have them [the documents] in by a certain time, for example February 19 at 11 o'clock. If you're not there at 11 o'clock, . . . and then you go to call for your food stamps, . . . there is nothing there. . . . You have to follow the rules and regulations. They didn't give me much leeway. I had a suspension not long ago because I didn't give them my lease. But I didn't have my lease yet. . . . They weren't going to turn the food stamps on until I gave them the lease. . . .

These procedural rules are reflective of an administrative posture; they are not dictated by federal food stamp policy. The administering agency could have asked for a note from the landlord regarding the pending lease; the 11 o'clock deadline is an arbitrary requirement. While in some other programs, lowering rolls saves counties and states dollars, the exclusionary posture with regard to food stamps is more difficult to comprehend. The federal government pays 100 percent of the costs of the benefit and part of the administrative costs. The benefit dollars return to the local economy through purchase of food in community stores. It can only be conjectured that the agency's requirements were linked to the larger negative societal and institutional attitudes toward those needing economic supports.

Low food stamp participation rates are an issue in many regions. Client reluctance to access this benefit may very well be related to fear of stigma and of just the kind of experiences that Della recounts.

2. *The receipt of food stamps and their significance in clients' lives needs to be viewed contextually.* For Geraldine, they are a factor as she works to reclaim her life. Food stamps and other social programs are supporting her efforts to escape the consequences of drug dependency. Her participation in the Food Stamp Program takes place within the environment of the Veterans Administration.

For Della, combating homelessness and finding employment have been major issues in her young life. Food stamps have helped her acquire the expensive soy formula her son requires. The Food Stamp Program's impact on moving her to self-sufficiency would clearly not have been effective without the housing and employment supports she receives. There is a synergy to benefit programs. They often are only meaningful in clients' lives when they work together. Housing, employment, and food assistance permitted Della to concentrate her energies on securing and retaining not only a job, but a sense of futurity and hope. On the other hand, for Geraldine, her struggle with housing appears to be blocking her progress.

3. *The resilience of the human spirit is once again evidenced by our clients.* Each of their life journeys has had externally and internally induced barriers to self-sufficiency: drug addiction, parental death, teenage pregnancy, incarceration, loss of children.

Geraldine has a more difficult time seeing herself in a different place. She is still struggling with addiction: "That's what I like to do," she says. "I'm having a hard time accepting the fact that I cannot do it anymore." Yet, she speaks of her ability to get a foundation and stabilize myself. . . . If I am successful with all this stuff, I intend on finishing the program at the VA. . . . I need to go back to school, because when I left I had a 3.85 average."

Della appears to be moving to self-sufficiency. She works at a school and is no longer receiving cash assistance. Medicaid, food stamps, and housing assistance are helping her make the transition. And she holds onto a dream of a college education and a career in medicine. She is realistic about what she needs to do. "I'm just taking it step by step. I plan to have a job where they'll offer me benefits. I pray to be off food stamps."

# MEDICAID

## THE LEGAL CONTEXT

### Authorizing Legislation

Medicaid, which is Title XIX of the Social Security Act, provides medical assistance to individuals and families with low income and limited resources. Enacted in 1965, the program is jointly funded by federal and state governments, with the goal of assisting states in the provision of adequate medical and health-related services to the poor. It is the largest source of funding for medical and health-related services for persons with limited income.

The statutory basis for the program is 42 U.S.C. § 1396, *et seq.* The illustrative excerpt following addresses the appropriations for the program, but also spells out the intended beneficiaries:

> For the purpose of enabling each State, as far as practicable under the conditions in such State, to furnish (1) medical assistance on behalf of families with dependent children and of aged, blind, or disabled individuals, whose income and resources are insufficient to meet the costs of necessary medical services, and (2) rehabilitation and other services to help such families and individuals attain or retain capability for independence or self-care, there is hereby authorized to be appropriated for each fiscal year a sum sufficient to carry out the purposes of this title [42 U.S.C.S. §§ 1396 *et seq.* ]. The sums made available under this section

| 8.1 | REGULATION ON ADMINISTRATION OF MEDICAID |

TITLE 42—PUBLIC HEALTH
CHAPTER IV—CENTERS FOR MEDICARE AND MEDICAID SERVICES,
DEPARTMENT OF HEALTH AND HUMAN SERVICES
SUBCHAPTER C—MEDICAL ASSISTANCE PROGRAMS
PART 431—STATE ORGANIZATION AND GENERAL ADMINISTRATION
SUBPART M—RELATIONS WITH OTHER AGENCIES
42 CFR 431.636

§ 431.636 Coordination of Medicaid with the State Children's Health Insurance Program (SCHIP).

(a) Statutory basis. This section implements—
    (1) Section 2102(b)(3)(B) of the Act, which provides that children who apply for coverage under a separate child health plan under title XXI, but are found to be eligible for medical assistance under the State Medicaid plan, must be enrolled in the State Medicaid plan; and
    (2) Section 2102(c)(2) of the Act, which requires coordination between a State child health program and other public health insurance programs.
(b) Obligations of State Medicaid Agency. The State Medicaid agency must adopt procedures to facilitate the Medicaid application process for, and the enroll-

---

shall be used for making payments to States which have submitted, and had approved by the Secretary, State plans for medical assistance.
HISTORY: (Aug. 14, 1935, ch 531, Title XIX, § 1901, as added July 30, 1965, P.L. 89-97, Title I, Part 2, § 121(a), 79 Stat. 343; Dec. 31, 1973, P.L. 93-233, § 13(a)(1), 87 Stat. 960; July 18, 1984, P.L. 98-369, Division B, Title VI, Subtitle D, § 2663(j)(3)(C), 98 Stat. 1171.)

## Regulatory Authority

The regulations pertaining to Medicaid can be found in the *Code of Federal Regulations*, in several parts of Volume 42. Box 8.1 addresses the coordination of Medicaid with the state children's health program.

## Case Law

The representative case law presented in Boxes 8.2 and 8.3 focuses on key dimensions of the Medicaid program, including the purpose and intent of Medicaid, the right to so-called due process protections in relation to denials of benefits, and the validity of regulations regarding the use of Medicaid funds to reimburse states for the cost of abortions.

ment of children for whom the Medicaid application and enrollment process has been initiated in accordance with § 457.350(f) of this chapter. The procedures must ensure that—

(1) The applicant is not required to provide information or documentation that has been provided to the State agency responsible for determining eligibility under a separate child health program under title XXI and forwarded by such agency to the Medicaid agency on behalf of the child in accordance with § 457.350(f) of this chapter;

(2) Eligibility is determined in a timely manner in accordance with § 435.911 of this chapter;

(3) The Medicaid agency promptly notifies the State agency responsible for determining eligibility under a separate child health program when a child who was screened as potentially eligible for Medicaid is determined ineligible or eligible for Medicaid; and

(4) The Medicaid agency adopts a process that facilitates enrollment in a State child health program when a child is determined ineligible for Medicaid at initial application or redetermination.

**HISTORY:** [66 FR 2490, 2666, Jan. 11, 2001; 66 FR 11547, Feb. 26, 2001; 66 FR 31178, June 11, 2001; 66 FR 33810, June 25, 2001]

**AUTHORITY:** Sec. 1102 of the Social Security Act, (42 U.S.C. 1302).

In *Atkins v. Rivera* (1986), the U.S. Supreme Court addressed the question of whether the federal government must share the cost of Medicaid with states that elect to participate in the program, and, in return, whether participating states are to comply with requirements imposed by Medicaid statutes. *Catanzano v. Dowling* (1995), a circuit court decision, deals with the issue of home health care coverage under Medicaid. As noted earlier in *Goldberg v. Kelly* (1970), the U.S. Supreme Court has announced that government-assistance program recipients are entitled to some kind of hearing prior to termination of benefits. In the Medicaid realm, *Catanzano v. Dowling* (1995), the Second Circuit Court of Appeals heard a claim wherein Michael Dowling, in his capacity as Commissioner of the New York State Department of Health, appealed an order entered on July 28, 1994, in the U.S. District Court for the Western District of New York denying a motion to amend a preliminary injunction previously granted in favor of Michelle Catanzano and other applicants for home health care services under the Medicaid program, 42 U.S.C. §§ 1396 *et seq.* In its decision and order, the District Court determined that decisions made by certified home health agencies to deny or reduce the amount of home health care prescribed for Medicaid recipients are "state actions" that trigger the recipients' federal fair hearing rights. The Circuit Court affirmed the order of the District Court.

| U.S. SUPREME COURT DECISION
ON MEDICAID BENEFITS

## ATKINS v. RIVERA
### 477 U.S. 154 (1986)

*Summary:* This case concerns the means by which a State may calculate eligibility for medical-assistance benefits (Medicaid) under Title XIX of the Social Security Act. In Massachusetts, persons who lack sufficient income, measured on a monthly basis, to meet their basic needs automatically qualify for Medicaid. The Commonwealth, however, also provides Medicaid benefits to persons who earn enough to meet their basic needs, but whose medical expenses within a 6-month period consume the amount by which their earnings exceed what is required for basic needs. Construing the Act's (i.e., Title XIX of the Social Security Act) requirement that assistance for the two groups be calculated using the "same methodology," the Massachusetts Supreme Judicial Court held invalid the Commonwealth's use of a 6-month period for measuring medical expenses. The court ruled that inasmuch as a 1-month period is used to measure the income of those with insufficient means, an identical period must be used to measure medical expenses for persons in the state applying for benefits. Because this holding conflicted with rulings of two Federal Courts of Appeals, the United States Supreme Court agreed to hear the case. The Supreme Court held, unanimously, that the Massachusetts choice of 6 months for the spenddown period under 1396a(a)(17) did not violate federal Medicaid laws, where (1) the Medicaid statutes were silent as to how many months' excess income a state may require an individual or family to contribute to medical expenses before Medicaid coverage of further medical expenses begins; (2) the provision in 1396a(a)(10)(C)(i)(III) for the "same methodology" was not intended to control the length of the Medicaid spenddown period [explained below]; (3) the Secretary's interpretation of the spenddown period in 435.831 was consistent with congressional intent and was entitled to legislative effect; and (4) under 435.831, Massachusetts was free to choose a 6-month spenddown period.*

**OPINION BY:** BLACKMUN

Medicaid, enacted in 1965 as Title XIX of the Social Security Act, 79 Stat. 343, as amended, 42 U.S.C. § 1396 *et seq.* (1982 ed. and Supp. II), is designed to provide medical assistance to persons whose income and resources are insufficient to meet the costs of necessary care and services. The Federal Government shares the costs of Medicaid with States that elect to participate in the program. In return, participating States are to comply with requirements imposed by the Act and by the Secretary of Health and Human Services.

States participating in the Medicaid program must provide coverage to the "categorically needy." 42 U.S.C. § 1396a(a)(10)(A) (1982 ed. and Supp. II). These are persons eligible for cash assistance under either of two programs: Supplemental Security Income for the Aged, Blind, and Disabled (SSI), 42 U.S.C. § 1381 et seq. (1982 ed. and Supp. II), or Aid to Families with Dependent Children (AFDC), 42 U.S.C. § 601 et seq. (1982 ed. and Supp. II). Congress considered these persons "especially deserving of public assistance" for medical expenses, because one is eligible for AFDC or SSI only if, in a given month, he or she earns less than what has been determined to be required for the basic necessities of life. AFDC and SSI assistance are intended to cover basic necessities, but not medical expenses. Thus, if a person in this category also incurs medical expenses during that month, payment of those expenses would consume funds required for basic necessities.

A participating State also may elect to provide medical benefits to the "medically needy," that is, persons who meet the nonfinancial eligibility requirements for cash assistance under AFDC or SSI, but whose income or resources exceed the financial eligibility standards of those programs. Under 42 U.S.C. § 1396a(a)(17), the medically needy may qualify for financial assistance for medical expenses if they incur such expenses in an amount that effectively reduces their income to the eligibility level. Only when they "spend down" the amount by which their income exceeds that level, are they in roughly the same position as persons eligible for AFDC or SSI: any further expenditures for medical expenses then would have to come from funds required for basic necessities. * * *

A State electing to assist the medically needy must determine eligibility under standards that are "reasonable" and "comparable for all groups." 42 U.S.C. § 1396a(a)(17). In addition, and significantly for present purposes, state plans for Medicaid must describe

> "the single standard to be employed in determining income and resource eligibility for all such groups, and the methodology to be employed in determining such eligibility which shall be the same methodology which would be employed under [AFDC or SSI]." 42 U.S.C. § 1396a(a)(10)(C)(i)(III).

Respondent Rivera is employed outside her home and is the mother of two children. She receives no medical benefits from her job, and earns an amount slightly in excess of that which would permit her to qualify for AFDC. In 1983, Rivera applied to the Massachusetts Department of Public Welfare for Medicaid. Massachusetts has chosen to participate in the Medicaid program, Mass. Gen. Laws § 118E:1 et seq. (1984), and also to provide coverage to medically needy persons.

To determine Rivera's eligibility for Medicaid, the Department first calculated her gross monthly income. See 106 Code of Mass. Regs. (CMR) §§ 505.200, 505.210, 505.320 (1985). Next, the Department prescribed certain deductions and disregards to arrive at her monthly "countable income" of $535.30. See 106 CMR §§ 505.200 and 506.100-506.200 (1985). See also 42 CFR § 435.831(a) (1985). Rivera's monthly countable income exceeded the Medicaid eligibility limit by $100.30. See 106 CMR § 506.400 (1985). See also 42 U.S.C. §§ 1382(c)(1) and 602(a)(13) (1982 ed. and Supp. II). As a result, she did not qualify for Medicaid at that time. She would be able to qualify at a later date, provided her excess income was subject to being consumed or spent down by medical expenses.

Massachusetts has adopted a 6-month period over which the spenddown is calculated. Mass. Gen. Laws § 118E:10 (1984); 106 CMR §§ 506.400 and 506.510 (1985). This is the maximum permitted under the federal regulations. See 42 C.F.R. § 435.831 (1985). Accordingly, the Department multiplied Rivera's excess $100.30 by six; she thus could receive Medicaid during the 6-month period beginning with the date of her first medical service only after she spent down $601.80 on medical expenses. The Department's decision denying assistance was upheld by the Welfare Appeals Referee.

*continued*

Rivera then sought injunctive relief in State Superior Court against use of the 6-month period. She argued that the 6-month period for calculating the income of medically needy applicants violates the "same methodology" requirement of 42 U.S.C. §§ 396a(a)(10)(C)(i)(III) and 1396a(a)(17) (1982 ed. and Supp. II), because the Act mandates that AFDC and SSI determinations be calculated on the basis of income earned in a 1-month period. The use of the shorter period would have permitted Rivera to receive Medicaid after incurring only $100.30 in medical expenses. * * *

The Supreme Judicial Court, by a unanimous panel vote, held that the Massachusetts requirement for a 6-month spenddown period was invalid. It relied in part on a ruling by the United States District Court for the District of Massachusetts sustaining an identical challenge to the Department's 6-month spenddown regulation. Although noting that eligibility determinations for the categorically needy do not involve spenddowns, the court observed that such determinations do require the use of a 1-month computation period. Therefore, it concluded, in providing that the "same methodology" be employed, the Act requires that a 1-month period be applied in eligibility calculations for the medically needy.

Respondents contend that the Secretary's regulation, and Massachusetts' 6-month spenddown enacted pursuant thereto, are "manifestly contrary to the statute." Respondents point to another section of the Act, 42 U.S.C. § 1396a(a)(10)(C)(i)(III), [*163] requiring that a State's plan describe "the single standard to be employed in determining income . . . eligibility . . . and the methodology to be employed in determining such eligibility, which shall be the same methodology" employed under SSI or AFDC. To respondents, this statutory language is an express congressional mandate that the same methodology, here the 1-month budget period, be applied to eligibility determinations for the medically needy. This requirement, the argument goes, operates as an express limitation on the Secretary's authority to regulate the state administration of spenddowns. Similarly, it is a direct restriction on the States, requiring them to use a 1-month period in which the medically needy must spend down, on medical expenses, their excess income. * * *

When Medicaid was first enacted, Congress did not require that the "same methodology" be used for determining the eligibility of categorically and medically needy individuals. Instead, it required only that a State's Medicaid plan use "com-

# THE PROGRAM CONTEXT

## Overview

Medicaid is the jointly funded federal-state program that pays for medical assistance for certain persons with low incomes and limited resources. The shared funding arrangement assists states in providing medical and health-related services to the country's poorest people. The so-called *Green Book*, a comprehensive description of federal social programs under the jurisdiction of the U.S. House of Representatives Committee on Ways and Means, encapsulates the contours of this important program:

parable" standards for both groups. The Secretary and several Courts of Appeals interpreted the original "comparability" language to require virtually identical treatment. See, e.g., 38 Fed. Reg. 32216 (1973), originally codified as 45 CFR § 248.2. Notably, no one advanced the claim that this "comparability" language prevented States from using a spenddown period of up to six months. * * *

Congress concluded that the administrative and judicial interpretation of the "comparability" provision denied States necessary flexibility to set eligibility standards and to adjust the scope of services to fit the varying requirements of medically needy persons. Thus, as part of the Omnibus Budget Reconciliation Act of 1981 (OBRA), 95 Stat. 357, Congress amended the Medicaid Act by deleting the "comparability" requirement. After the amendment, a State was required only to include in its plan for the medically needy "a description of . . . the criteria for determining eligibility of individuals . . . for medical assistance." OBRA § 2171(a)(3)(C)(i), 95 Stat. 807. * * *

The regulations promulgated by the Secretary accordingly left the States free to use eligibility standards that were unrelated to the standards used in AFDC or SSI, as long as the standards were "reasonable." The Secretary's regulations did not address treatment of excess income for the medically needy or the calculation of spenddowns. Despite the various changes that followed OBRA's passage, many States continued to use a 6-month spenddown, in conformity with the still-existing regulation permitting that choice. * * *

Thus, the "same methodology" proviso was designed to correct a problem wholly unrelated to the 6-month spenddown, which had remained in force from the inception of Medicaid. The proviso operated solely to invalidate the post-OBRA regulations permitting the income and resource standards in state Medicaid plans to deviate from those used in the AFDC and SSI programs in "such matters as deemed income, interest, court-ordered support payments, and infrequent and irregular income." See 46 Fed. Reg. 47980 (1981). Treatment of excess income and the calculation of spenddowns were left untouched by the "same methodology" proviso.

The Medicaid Act itself is silent as to how many months' excess income the State may require an individual or a family to contribute to medical expenses before Medicaid coverage of further medical expenses begins. The Secretary's interpretation of the Act is consistent with congressional intent, and under that interpretation Massachusetts is free to choose a 6-month spenddown. Accordingly, the judgment of the Supreme Judicial Court is reversed.

It is so ordered.

---

Medicaid is a program that is targeted at individuals with low-income, but not all of the poor are eligible, and not all those covered are poor. For populations like children and families, primary and acute care often are delivered through managed care, while the elderly and disabled typically obtain such care on a fee-for-service basis. Nationwide, Medicaid finances the majority of long-term care services. Such services include, for example, nursing home care and community-based services designed to support the elderly and disabled in their homes. Recently, some States have begun to integrate Medicare and Medicaid financing and/or coordinate acute and long-term care services for these populations. (U. S. House of Representatives, Committee on Ways and Means, 2004)

<table>
<tr><td>8.3</td><td>CIRCUIT COURT DECISION ON MEDICAID RECIPIENTS' RIGHTS</td></tr>
</table>

## CATANZANO v. DOWLING
### 60 F.3D 113 (1995)

*Summary:* This appeal arises out of a challenge to the system by which New York State provides home health care benefits under the Medicaid program. The Medicaid program, through which the federal and state governments provide health care and services to needy individuals, is subsidized by the federal government and is administered by the states. A state participating in Medicaid must offer home health care services as part of the program. These services can include assistance in dressing, bathing and preparation of meals, as well as the provision of medication and other services. Home health care is prescribed, as are other forms of medical treatment, by the patient's treating physician, and the prescription can range from brief daily visits to around-the-clock monitoring by an aide or nurse.

**OPINION:** MINER, Circuit Judge:

In New York, home health care services under Medicaid must be provided by certified home health agencies ("CHHA"). See N.Y. Pub. Health Law §§ 3602(3), 3614(1). CHHA are home care providers that are licensed and regulated by the State, and, pursuant to federal regulations, CHHA must comply with state as well as federal law. See 42 C.F.R. § 484.12(a).

Although a patient's treating physician prescribes the form or amount of required home health services, CHHA employ their own professional medical staff of nurses who, pursuant to state law, make their own determinations as to the medical necessity and appropriateness of home health services.

In the summer of 1989, the named plaintiff, Michelle Catanzano, who was disabled at the time and receiving prescribed twenty-four-hour-a-day home health care, was hospitalized. Upon her discharge from the hospital, the CHHA responsible for her care unilaterally decided to reduce her home health care services from twenty-four-hour-a-day to twelve-hour-a-day care. At that time, state law required that if a determination of a CHHA conflicted with that of a patient's treating physician, the local Department of Social Services ("local DSS") referred the matter to an independent physician (or "local professional director"), who made the final determination as to the necessary amount of care. In the case of a referral to a local professional director, the patient was entitled to receive notice that a determination was to be made, a hearing on the matter, and aid-continuing rights as required by federal and state law ("fair hearing rights"). These rights, which have their roots in *Goldberg v. Kelly,* are mandated by federal regulation whenever the state agency responsible for the administration of Medicaid decides to reduce, deny, or suspend benefits.

Although Ms. Catanzano's treating physician disagreed with the CHHA's determination, the determination was implemented without being referred to a local professional director, and Ms. Catanzano was not accorded her fair hearing rights. As a result, she filed this action in 1989 to enjoin the Monroe County DSS, the agency with responsibility for Ms. Catanzano's Medicaid services, from making any reductions in home health care without according her a fair hearing. The district court granted the injunction in part, finding that, under state law, every dispute between a CHHA and a treating physician was to be resolved by a local professional director, and that state law required the provision of fair hearing rights in all such cases. The district court also held that the denial of services without fair hearing rights deprived Ms. Catanzano of her federal constitutional right to due process. The district court's order was affirmed by this court in March of 1990. * * *

Where, as here, a plaintiff seeks to stay governmental action taken in the public interest pursuant to a statutory scheme, a district court may grant a preliminary injunction only where the plaintiff can show irreparable injury and a likelihood of success on the merits. We review the district court's issuance of the preliminary injunction for an abuse of discretion, which "typically consists of either applying incorrect legal standards or relying on clearly erroneous findings of fact." Here, the central issue is whether the district court correctly concluded that the CHHA's actions should be deemed state action.

The parties do not dispute that Medicaid applicants and recipients are entitled to fair hearing rights when a decision is made by a state agency that adversely affects their right to receive benefits. The Medicaid statute, 42 U.S.C. § 1396a(a)(3), requires that the state plan must "provide for granting an opportunity for a fair hearing before the State agency to any individual whose claim for medical assistance under the plan is denied or not acted upon with reasonable promptness." In addition, federal regulations require that, whenever the state agency takes action to terminate, suspend, or reduce Medicaid eligibility or covered services, an applicant or recipient receive a fair hearing that meets the due process standards enunciated in *Goldberg v. Kelly.*

It is fundamental, however, that "the action inhibited by the [due process clause] of the Fourteenth Amendment is only such action as may fairly be said to be that of the States." Therefore, the due process fair hearing rights required by the statute and regulations are triggered only when the adverse actions are implemented through state action. We therefore turn to whether the CHHA's decisions to deny or terminate Medicaid benefits should be deemed "state actions" that trigger plaintiffs' fair hearing rights.

As noted above, in the first two steps of its assessment, the CHHA determines whether the prescribed services "can maintain the recipient's health and safety in the home," and whether the recipient's needs can be met by employing certain alternative services. Determinations by CHHA in these instances are not forwarded to a local DSS for ratification or approval. The district court held that CHHA action in these circumstances was the equivalent of state action, stating:

> The State and County defendants exercise significant control over the CHHA. They pay for covered services, regulate their activities, issue directives which cannot be ignored and created the legal framework which governs their activities. It is only in the framework of N.Y. law and the state regulations that CHHA make determinations concerning home health care for a Medicaid applicant or recipient.

The district court concluded that it is "patently unreasonable to presume that Congress would permit a state to disclaim federal responsibilities by contracting away its obligations to a private entity." In the face of this persuasive reasoning, the

*continued*

| 8.3 | CIRCUIT COURT DECISION ON MEDICAID RECIPIENTS' RIGHTS (CONTINUED) |

State argues that CHHA are private entities that make only independent professional judgments regarding the care that each patient requires, and therefore that no fair hearing rights are triggered by their determinations. We disagree with the State, and conclude that, with respect to determinations made under steps one and two, CHHA action is state action that triggers plaintiffs' due process rights.

In *Blum v. Yaretsky,* the United States Supreme Court was presented with the question whether decisions made by physicians and other agents of nursing homes to transfer or discharge Medicaid recipients amounted to "state actions" that triggered due process protections. There, federal regulations required nursing homes that participated in Medicaid to establish in-house utilization review committees ("URC"), whose functions included periodically assessing whether patients were receiving the appropriate level of care, and whether patients' continued stays at the institution were justified. In some cases, however, decisions as to the length of required stay were made by administrators of the nursing homes or by the patients' attending physicians, and these decisions were distinct from those made by the URC. At issue in *Blum* was whether the latter decisions, those made by the nursing home administrators or patients' attending physicians, were state actions.

In its analysis, the Supreme Court stated that "a State normally can be held responsible for a private decision only when it has exercised coercive power or has provided such significant encouragement, either overt or covert, that the choice must in law be deemed to be that of the State." In holding that the decisions by the administrators and private physicians were not state actions, the Court noted that

---

Medicaid is a state-administered program; each state sets its own guidelines regarding eligibility and services. The Center for Medicare and Medicaid Services, a federal agency within the Department of Health and Human Services co-administers the Medicaid program with the states.[1] An individual may apply for Medicaid in the state public welfare or Department of Social Services or Social Security Office. Some states also permit applications via the Internet, by telephone, or at locations in the community, such as community health centers. It is sometimes possible to qualify for payment of services provided up to 3 months before the month of the initial application for Medicaid.

The application is often made in conjunction with an eligibility determination for other social programs, such as Temporary Assistance to Needy

---

1. This entire section draws liberally on materials from the Centers for Medicare and Medicaid Services, which in turn are derived from original sources, that is, Title XIX of the Social Security Act, also referenced as 42 U.S.C. § 1396 *et seq.* The law is voluminous, and variability across state Medicaid programs is the rule, not the exception. The complexity of Medicaid presents an enormous challenge for anyone attempting to make generalizations about the program. Therefore, extensive reliance on these materials from the center makes for a more manageable review of the program elements from a reliable source.

"the State is [not] responsible for the decision to discharge or transfer particular patients. Those decisions ultimately turn on medical judgments made by private parties according to professional standards that are not established by the State." Moreover, the Court noted, "there is no suggestion that [the decisions at issue] were influenced in any degree by the State's obligation to adjust benefits in conformity with changes in the cost of medically necessary care." The Court explicitly noted, however, that determinations made by URC were "not part of the case." * * *

In light of the foregoing, we must reject the State's argument that the CHHA's determinations should not be deemed state action. First, while we recognize that regulation alone does not make a state actor, CHHAs are not simply regulated by the State; rather, they are deeply integrated into the regulatory scheme set up by the implementing regulations, and the administrative directive. CHHA, for example, are the only entities permitted to provide home health care under Medicaid, and are required to evaluate all potential recipients. Significantly, unlike in Blum, the decisions made by the CHHA are not purely medical judgments made according to professional standards. Instead, section 367-j(2)(a)(i) requires the CHHA to determine whether the health and safety of the recipient can be maintained "as defined by the department of health in regulation." Furthermore, the statute provides the specific alternatives that the CHHA is to consider in making the "efficiency" determinations mandated in step two. * * *

In sum, we conclude that the State "has exercised coercive power [and] has provided such significant encouragement . . . that the [CHHA's' determinations in steps one and two] must in law be deemed those of the State, and that the determinations thus trigger fair hearing rights.

For the foregoing reasons, the district court's order is AFFIRMED.

---

Families (TANF) or Supplemental Security Income (SSI). Persons eligible for any of the following programs are automatically eligible for Medicaid without filing a separate application:

- TANF
- SSI
- General Assistance
- Refugee Cash Assistance
- State Blind Pension
- State Subsidized Adoption
- Title IV-E Foster Care
- TANF received for at least 3 months of previous 6 months prior to losing eligibility because of an increase in income from employment or the receipt of child support; Medicaid under these circumstances is limited to not more than 12 months for employment income and not more than 4 months due for support (Pennsylvania Department of Public Welfare, 2005)

Within broad national guidelines established by federal statutes, regulations, and policies, each state (1) establishes its own eligibility standards; (2) determines the type, amount, duration, and scope of services; (3) sets the rate of payment for services; and (4) administers its own program. Medicaid policies for eligibility, services, and payment are complex and vary considerably, even among states of similar size or geographic proximity. Thus, a person who is eligible for Medicaid in one state may not be eligible in another state, and the services provided by one state may differ considerably in amount, duration, or scope from services provided in a similar or neighboring state. In addition, state legislatures may change Medicaid eligibility and/or services during the year.

## Application and Eligibility

Medicaid does not provide medical assistance for all poor persons. Under the broadest provisions of the federal statute, Medicaid does not provide health care services even for very poor persons unless they are in one of the groups designated following. Low income is only one test for Medicaid eligibility for those within these groups; their resources also are tested against threshold levels (as determined by each state within federal guidelines). Medicaid eligibility is limited to individuals who fall into specified categories. The federal statute identifies more than 25 different eligibility categories for which federal funds are available. Although most persons covered by TANF will receive Medicaid, it is not required by law. That is, Medicaid is not tied to the 5-year limit on TANF. A recipient may continue to be eligible for Medicaid even after the 5-year limit is reached.

States generally have broad discretion in determining which groups their Medicaid programs will cover and the financial criteria for Medicaid eligibility. To be eligible for federal funds, however, states are required to provide Medicaid coverage for certain individuals who receive federally assisted income-maintenance payments, as well as for related groups not receiving cash payments. Federal funds are not provided for state-only programs. The following enumerates the mandatory Medicaid "categorically needy" eligibility groups for which federal matching funds are provided:

- Individuals who meet the requirements for the Aid to Families with Dependent Children (AFDC) program that were in effect in their state on July 16, 1996, or—at state option—more liberal criteria
- Children under age 6 whose family income is at or below 133 percent of the federal poverty level (FPL)
- Pregnant women whose family income is below 133 percent of the FPL (services to these women are limited to those related to pregnancy, complications of pregnancy, delivery, and postpartum care)
- Supplemental Security Income recipients in most states (some states use more restrictive Medicaid eligibility requirements that predate SSI
- Recipients of adoption or foster care assistance under Title IV of the Social Security Act
- Special protected groups (typically individuals who lose their cash assistance due to earnings from work or from increased Social Security benefits, but who may keep Medicaid for a period of time)
- All children under age 19, in families with incomes at or below the FPL
- Certain Medicare beneficiaries

States also have the option of providing Medicaid coverage for other "categorically related" groups. These optional groups share characteristics of the mandatory groups (that is, they fall within defined categories), but the eligibility criteria are somewhat more liberally defined. The broadest optional groups for which states will receive federal matching funds for coverage under the Medicaid program include the following:

- Infants up to age 1 and pregnant women not covered under the mandatory rules whose family income is no more than 185 percent of the FPL (the percentage amount is set by each state)
- Children under age 21 who meet the AFDC income and resources requirements that were in effect in their state on July 16, 1996
- Institutionalized individuals eligible under a "special income level" (the amount is set by each state—up to 300 percent of the SSI federal benefit rate)
- Individuals who would be eligible if institutionalized, but who are receiving care under home and community-based services waivers
- Certain aged, blind, or disabled adults who have incomes above those requiring mandatory coverage, but below the FPL
- Recipients of State Supplementary Income payments
- Certain working-and-disabled persons with family income less than 250 percent of the FPL who would qualify for SSI if they did not work
- Tuberculosis(TB)-infected persons who would be financially eligible for Medicaid at the SSI income level if they were within a Medicaid-covered category (however, coverage is limited to TB-related ambulatory services and TB drugs)
- Certain uninsured or low-income women who are screened for breast or cervical cancer through a program administered by the Centers for Disease Control. The Breast and Cervical Cancer Prevention and Treatment Act of 2000 (Public Law 106-354) provides these women with medical assistance and follow-up diagnostic services through Medicaid.
- "Optional targeted low-income children" included within the State Children's Health Insurance Program (SCHIP) established by the Balanced Budget Act (BBA) of 1997 (Public Law 105-33)
- States are also required to provide coverage to refugees for the first 7 years after entry into the United States; asylees for the first 7 years after asylum is granted; certain individuals whose deportation is being withheld by the Immigration and Naturalization Service for 7 years after the deportation is first withheld; lawful permanent aliens after they have been credited with 40 quarters of coverage under Social Security; and immigrants who are honorably discharged U.S. military veterans, active duty military personnel, and their spouses and unmarried dependent children who otherwise meet the state's financial eligibility criteria. In addition, states are required to provide emergency Medicaid services to all legal and undocumented noncitizens who meet the financial and categorical eligibility requirements for Medicaid.
- "Medically needy" persons

The medically needy (MN) option allows states to extend Medicaid eligibility to additional persons. These persons would be eligible for Medicaid under one of the mandatory or optional groups, except that their income and/or resources are above the eligibility level set by their state. Persons may qualify immediately or may "spend down" by incurring medical expenses that reduce their income to or below their state's MN income level.

Medicaid eligibility and benefit provisions for the medically needy do not have to be as extensive as for the categorically needy, and may be quite restrictive. Federal matching funds are available for MN programs. However, if a state elects to have a MN program, there are federal requirements that certain groups and certain services must be included; that is, children under age 19 and pregnant women who are medically needy must be covered, and prenatal and delivery care for pregnant women, as well as ambulatory care for children, must be provided. A state may elect to provide MN eligibility to certain additional groups and may elect to provide certain additional services within its MN program. Currently, 38 states have elected to have a MN program and are providing at least some MN services to at least some MN recipients. All remaining states utilize the "special income level" option to extend Medicaid to the "near-poor" in medical institutional settings.

The Personal Responsibility and Work Opportunity Reconciliation Act (PRWORA) of 1996 (Public Law 104-193) made restrictive changes regarding eligibility for SSI coverage that impacted the Medicaid program. For example, legal resident aliens and other qualified aliens who entered the United States on or after August 22, 1996, are ineligible for Medicaid for 5 years. Medicaid coverage for most aliens entering before that date and coverage for those eligible after the 5-year ban are state options; emergency services, however, are mandatory for both of these alien coverage groups. For aliens who lose SSI benefits because of the new restrictions regarding SSI coverage, Medicaid can continue only if these persons can be covered for Medicaid under some other eligibility status (again with the exception of emergency services, which are mandatory).

PRWORA also affected a number of disabled children, who lost SSI as a result of the restrictive changes; however, their eligibility for Medicaid was reinstituted by Public Law 105-33, the Balanced Budget Act of 1997 (BBA). Title XXI of the Social Security Act, known as the State Children's Health Insurance Program, is a new program initiated by the BBA. In addition to allowing states to craft or expand an existing state insurance program, SCHIP provides more federal funds for states to expand Medicaid eligibility to include a greater number of children who are currently uninsured. With certain exceptions, these are low-income children who would not qualify for Medicaid based on the plan that was in effect on April 15, 1997. Funds from SCHIP also may be used to provide medical assistance to children during a presumptive eligibility period for Medicaid. This is one of several options from which states may select to provide health care coverage for more children, as prescribed within the BBA's Title XXI program.

Medicaid coverage may begin as early as the third month prior to application—*if* the person would have been eligible for Medicaid had he or she applied during that time. Medicaid coverage generally stops at the end of the month in which a person no longer meets the criteria of any Medicaid eligibility group. The BBA allows states to provide 12 months of continuous Medicaid coverage (without reevaluation) for eligible children under the age of 19.

The Ticket to Work and Work Incentives Improvement Act of 1999 (Public Law 106-170) provides or continues Medicaid coverage to certain disabled beneficiaries who work despite their disability. Those with higher incomes may pay a sliding scale premium based on income.

## Benefits

Title XIX of the Social Security Act allows considerable flexibility within the states' Medicaid plans. However, some federal requirements are mandatory if federal matching funds are to be received. A state's Medicaid program must offer medical assistance for certain *basic* services to most categorically needy populations. These services generally include the following:

- Inpatient hospital services
- Outpatient hospital services
- Prenatal care
- Vaccines for children
- Physician services
- Nursing facility services for persons aged 21 or older
- Family planning services and supplies
- Rural health clinic services
- Home health care for persons eligible for skilled-nursing services
- Laboratory and x-ray services
- Pediatric and family nurse practitioner services
- Nurse-midwife services
- Federally qualified health center (FQHC) services, and ambulatory services of an FQHC that would be available in other settings
- Early and periodic screening, diagnostic, and treatment (EPSDT) services for children under age 21

States may also receive federal matching funds to provide certain *optional* services. Following are the most common of the 34 currently approved optional Medicaid services:

- Diagnostic services
- Clinic services
- Intermediate care facilities for the mentally retarded (ICFs/MR)
- Prescribed drugs and prosthetic devices
- Optometrist services and eyeglasses
- Nursing facility services for children under age 21
- Transportation services
- Rehabilitation and physical therapy services
- Home and community-based care to certain persons with chronic impairments

The BBA included a state option known as Programs of All-inclusive Care for the Elderly (PACE). PACE provides an alternative to institutional care for persons aged 55 or older who require a nursing facility level of care. The PACE team offers and manages all health, medical, and social services and mobilizes other services as needed to provide preventative, rehabilitative, curative, and supportive care. This care, provided in day health centers, homes, hospitals, and nursing homes, helps the person maintain independence, dignity, and quality of life. PACE functions within the Medicare program as well. Regardless of the source of payment, PACE providers receive payment only through the PACE agreement and must make available all items and services covered under both Titles XVIII and XIX, without amount, duration, or scope limitations and without application of any deductibles, copayments, or other cost sharing. The individuals enrolled in PACE receive benefits solely through the PACE program (Center for Medicare and Medicaid Services, 2005).

## Due Process

Medicaid beneficiaries have the right to appeal if their Medicaid services are reduced or terminated and when their Medicaid benefits are denied or delayed. These rights are grounded in the U.S. Constitution, particularly the guarantee of the right to due process. State procedures to protect this right vary but, as with the TANF, SSI, and Food Stamp programs, generally provide for a "fair hearing" that contains the following features:

- Notice in writing when a benefit is denied and generally before the date of a proposed termination or reduction of services.
- A right to a hearing before an impartial decision maker concerning denials, reductions, terminations, or delays in Medicaid benefits, and a right to a written decision of the hearing request. If not satisfied with the hearing decision, Medicaid beneficiaries can appeal to a state court.
- In cases involving a reduction or termination of care, Medicaid beneficiaries can usually get services continued pending the final hearing decision if they make a timely request for continued services.
- Besides seeking redress through a state fair hearing process, Medicaid managed care enrollees may complain to their managed care plans through in-plan grievance procedures. Under federal regulations, the in-plan grievance procedures must be approved in writing by the state, provide for prompt resolution of grievances, and ensure the participation of employees in the managed care plan who have authority to correct problems. In-plan grievance procedures do not take away beneficiaries' right to request Medicaid fair hearings.

## THE CLIENTS' STORIES

### Rita

I currently live with my significant other and with my daughter, whom I have full custody of. Her father lives in another state. I just got my master's degree in social work, and I'm employed by the federal government, and my life is good. I just bought a new car, which I'll be picking up tomorrow night, so that's exciting. But it wasn't like this a few years ago.

My significant other owns a home, and he basically supports the household. We have four bedrooms, and it's a very nice home in a *Leave It to Beaver* kind of neighborhood. All the houses are basically the same, but it has a decent school district, and it was a great place for my daughter to go to school and make her friends and connect to the community. For me it was the best move I made in my life.

I was born in Coney Island. My parents were working people. They both came out of ghettos, neighborhoods that we wouldn't want to walk in today if we could avoid them. They were poor, very impoverished people. My father was on public assistance when he was a young boy. They are both Jewish, and they know each other since they are 13 and 15 I believe. My mother insisted my father go to hairdressing school when he came out of the Army. He was a musician and didn't know what to do. So she said come be a hairdresser with me. So they became hairdressers. They had one business in Brooklyn on Mermaid Avenue. Then they had another business when we moved out here to the Island. They kept moving up houses as the business grew. Life got a little easier, but my father was always a very insecure man. I think when you are on public assistance, at a point in your life it creates a tremendous insecurity that takes a long time to overcome and feel comfortable with.

I have an older sister, 2 years older, who was basically the perfect child, the good one. She did everything that she was supposed to at the time, very bright, all those things. We hated each other as kids. Now we are incredibly close.

My family moved from the city; we kept moving. Eventually, we moved to a town where my parents ran a shop for 20 years. We went to school. I had two kindergartens, or two first grades and two second grades, it seemed like for a couple of years running. That was very unsettling. I always felt like the new kid, and I hated that. It was not a good time, and I think it made some bad formations there. I guess by the time I was 16 I knew that I had to get away from that house. I couldn't do it. So, I ran away and married the first guy who came along, and he was very mentally abusive and very bizarre. That marriage was annulled, thank God.

When I had come home after I ran away my father said, "You can't just sit around the house. If you're not going to school, you've got to go to hairdressing school and get your license and at least work in my shop." So, I went to hairdressing school, with my eyes closed, sailed through it, and passed. I started to work in the shop with my parents. I was extremely proficient, extremely talented, if I do say so myself. I had a clientele in no time. It was a competitive thing. When my father got sick, he took to his bed and I had to run the shop with my mom, which was no problem. It was a natural thing for me.

I met my second husband, a nice Jewish boy. My parents were thrilled. A customer's son, very cozy situation. I married him, didn't want to marry him, but again I married someone I didn't want to marry. The second wedding was in a temple yet. It was unbelievably beautiful. We had our daughter, and life was good for the first few years. But I was still working for my parents and I got to the point where I told my parents, "I can't work for you guys anymore." I didn't enjoy it. My father would still pull rank. He would scream at me. We would have horrible fights, and I couldn't stand it. I'm not saying I'm that easy to get along with. So, I told them I was going to look for a job somewhere else. That was a Saturday night.

The next week I came into work, and they said to me, "We've made a decision. We're going to sell the house and sell the business. We've decided we want to move to Florida." Eventually my decision was to buy the shop from them and to run it myself. I bought it from them and I renovated it. I gutted it. The man I was married to was a custom cabinetmaker. People would stop in just to see it. And most people knew me since I was 9, when I first went into the shop. So there was like a lot of community feeling about the shop. It was a family place, and we did incredibly well. That went on for 7 years. My daughter was in day care from the time she was a month old because I always managed to find husbands who don't make a lot of money. Which is fine. So I did what I had to do.

So what happened was I started in with a therapist who was wonderful, and all this memory came up, but at the point that it came up I would not get into it with her. I left therapy instead. Then I divorced my second husband. My daughter was 5, and that was horrible. That was when it really started to spiral down. I had to work 7 days a week at that point in order to pay the bills.

When I went to sign up for Medicaid, I had a growth, a lump, in my personal area. I knew I had to get this looked at immediately. I didn't have medical care for years. My daughter was covered under her father. Then for some reason he decided that he was moving or whatever he was doing, and he took her off the insurance. I started to educate myself: Child Health Plus, different things. She was settled with the Child Health Plus, which was a wonderful program for people who are struggling. Then I went to public assistance. I have to say that after I got through the initial horrible experience of waiting on the line, the phone calls that I had to make, they took me right away to a doctor.

How did I know where to go? I think I looked it up in the phone book. How did I know there was such a program? I don't know. I just knew I guess from my years in the shop. The thing about it is that it was something that was for other people. That wasn't for me.

According to my dad, losers, lowlifes, those are the kind of people who are on PA [public assistance]. Well, hey, Dad, self-fulfilling prophesy, here I am. So, I'm not sure how I knew, but I called. I guess I called information, got the Department of Social Services. I knew that's what it was called. I may have looked it up online. I told them what my problem was, that I had a growth that needed to be looked at, and that I had no insurance. They said to come down and fill out the papers. So, of course, going through the door was horrible and to stand on line. There were all those years that I went without medical care . Sometimes I went to a doctor and never paid the money and did what I had to do. If I had a toothache I would wait until it was excruciating and have the tooth pulled, which was stupid, of course, but that's what I did. Regular check-ups didn't happen until the last 2 years. My daughter did go. She always had whatever she needed.

So, walking into Welfare that first time: first of all, I was immediately struck by the fact of this huge building. You have to walk down about 30 steps. All I could think was, "This is the bowels of the world here. This is where I am." So, I had a bad attitude about it. Walked in, stood there, the tears, it was a mob scene. The line snaked around. If I tell you, you waited 3 hours until you got to the window. They tell you to come at 9:30, you're lucky if they saw you by 11:30–12 o'clock. It was insane. I finally got to the window. First I went to one window, a quick line. They asked me, "Do you have any assets?" Yeah, I had a Jeep, it was already 6–7 years old. "Well, that's an asset. That put you over the limit. You're not entitled to public assistance." That's what the guy told me. I said, "All right, but what about Medicaid?" He said, "That you might be entitled to. Go to the next line."

I didn't know what I was going to apply for. I was going to go for the full tilt at that time, seeing what I was eligible for, but I ended up with just Medicaid. When I finally got on the line and got to the window, the woman said to me, "Take your daughter off the insurance that she's on. The two of you will get benefit money, and you'll have benefit cards." I looked at her and said, "I don't want that. I just want Medicaid. That's already really bad." They gave me the Medicaid. The application process was pretty quick because they knew it was a medical emergency, so it was less than 30 days that the card came in the mail. Of course if I was bleeding I would have bled to death in those days, but I figured I could live 30 days with a growth. In the meantime I set up all the appointments so I was ready to go.

Then, of course, going back and getting recertified every 6 months, once a year, whatever it was in those years. What you couldn't help but notice at that point was that the decline of people on the lines. I wasn't a social worker then. I was in community college studying English to be a writer or sociology. That always interested me and does link to what I do now. You couldn't help but notice there were less and less people. It was while I was sitting in a sociology class that I started to talk about my experience on the line and how I felt. The teacher was drawing it out and being encouraging. There were other young women in the class who needed assistance in terms of Child Health Plus, and they didn't know what to do with young kids. I suggested you could do this and that.

At DSS the first woman was very nice, and I couldn't help but think that she's treating me nicely because I'm white. That's what I thought, because she was white and she spoke perfect English. She was definitely a native of America. However, then I got stuck with a caseworker from hell. I don't even remember her name. She was a nightmare. She smelled of liquor sometimes. She was dirty. I was mortified that I had to deal with her, and she was as nasty as they came. The thing about that, though, I went through other things. I would go to the doctor's office and wonder. The first time I found out I was a diabetic and had to see the doctor, I was sitting in the office thinking, "Does it say Medicaid on my file?" I wanted to know. He walked in. His mother and father are my parents' best friends. He didn't remember me because he hadn't seen me in 40 years. He didn't connect the name at first. I broke a sweat and said, "Let me ask you something. Do you know who is Medicaid and who is not?" I started asking him all these questions. He was looking at me like, "Who are you?" He answered, "I never know." I asked, "Well, how do you end up with a Medicaid patient?" He answered it goes into a pool. "Whatever companies I work with insurance-wise, I get a certain percentage of people who are Medicaid. That's how it works. Do you feel better now?" I answered I was just curious, and by the way I am, and introduced myself. The color ran out of his face. We have since become very good friends. But there's that paranoia that goes on when you're on Medicaid. Am I going to be treated differently?

Then I had to fix my teeth. That was the worst part of Medicaid. Medicaid will pull your teeth, but they won't pay to replace them. So I had to have a bridge made, seven teeth later, in the back. The dentist there was not nice. He was horrible. That was not my imagination. I mean your teeth are hurting like that, you know the way they did things, it was like meatball surgery.

Even when they removed the growth, when I had to go the clinic at the medical center, I could not believe it. I felt like cattle, like one of the herd. Thank God I got a nice doctor. She was a young woman. The first doctor who looked at me said, "Well, there's nothing we can do for her." It was blocking the passage. This young girl said, "Well, I'm sorry there is something we can do for her, and we're going to figure it out." She just went and got the top gynecologist in the hospital, brought her—another woman, of course—to where I was, showed her what the problem was. She told her what to do and how to do it. It could be done locally in the office. I went back and had it done. I was scared to death that I was going to die of a staph infection. Because if you would see the amount of people, the amount of traffic that a place like that got. So that was an ordeal, and I felt horrible. That was like a real low point. Then it just started to build up again. I hated once a year going. I would still cry every time I had to go into that building.

The waiting room was horrible. First of all, it's a little dirty, scuzzy to say the least. Interviews were held at DSS in the cubicles, very rote. You sit across. There's a grimy stanchion, and you're sitting opposite her. There's like a plastic glass between us, and it's filthy. That's a very good analogy and very good point, and it may set up how you feel. Because you feel on the other side. You're on the other side. You're over there; I'm over here. There's grimy glass between us, and I need something, benefits from you. My hand is out. So, yes, it feeds into that whole feeling of down, depressed, desperate. It's a very routine interview. They ask you questions, very unemotionally. They don't give a s___ about how you're feeling, if you're crying, whatever. They tell you, this, that.

Of course, I was a master at keeping the records straight. I had everything organized in folders. They wanted to see that I was in school and this and that. It got to the point that the third time I went back to recertify, the woman just opened it and said, "It's all here, right?" I said, "Everything in duplicate." She said good-bye, and that was it. For me it became a business almost. The last time I went to see her, I knew that I had to see her to close out my case. Of course, she was late, as usual. I was fit to be tied. I said I have to get back to work, and I told you that on the phone. Very degrading. Full of shame. Five years of feeling that way.

People aren't educated about choice as a Medicaid recipient. They don't know. You could get managed care. When you're standing on line, the girls with the clipboards come around from the different insurance companies. They ask you if, instead of going to the clinic at the hospital, would you like to have a private practitioner, a family doctor. Who wouldn't say yes to that? So you *do* have choices. You can be treated like a regular patient. But most of the people there didn't know that.

Let me tell you about filling out that form. You need a college degree. It's a good thing I was in school, because you need it to fill it out. It's very complicated. The questions are not clear. They could really revamp that form. They need to. The information they want to gather could be much better stated than it is.

I think what happens is that a lot of people don't fill it out properly and are sanctioned for that reason. I think that's what happened. That sent a message that there were just no benefits available, which is part of the reason today I believe why you don't see masses of people there. People just don't think it's available any more. And then to ask a worker—forget that. They're not going to take time to help you, because they have hundreds of people behind you.

What they need to do when people come in and pick up the forms, there should be some type of orientation program at that point. However they want to set it up. I think it should also be more user friendly. Why can't it be set up like Motor Vehicle, with the numbers and the timing? They need an orientation program where it's bilingual. Those who don't speak English, if we're going to have these people come into this country, we have to help them the best we can to get what they need. They would tell them, this is what you are entitled to; this is how you are eligible; this would make you ineligible. Set it up for them. There should be people on the lines that if somebody has a question—the way they walk around asking which health care is wanted—then they should also ask, "Do you need any help? Can I help you with this?" Of course, that's very idealistic. They don't want you to get comfortable there.

What did I learn about Medicaid? You can get eyeglasses, which I never got. I was afraid I would be blind. I didn't go for the eyeglasses after the tooth experience. The tooth experience was the worst. There are certain dental services they won't do, such as tooth replacement, which means that if you are fortunate enough to get off the system, you're going to go for your job interview minus seven or eight teeth. The dental was an area that required pamphlets, whatever. Of course, by the time I read about that my few teeth were already missing, and it was too late. Thank goodness they have dental implants now. Someday I could do that. The thing about the prescription drugs. You are only allowed under Medicaid $x$ amount of pills. I couldn't go in and buy 3 months at a time. They want you to come in once a month and buy your pills monthly. That runs through all insurance companies, so that's not just a Medicaid thing. Another thing was the treatment of the pharmacist when they see you are with Medicaid. They were terrible offenders. It got so bad at one point. And every time I went in there the guy would say, "Oh, you're a Medicaid," and he would scream it out. It's like when you were a kid and had to buy tampons for somebody, and you didn't want anyone to know. There, he's screaming out at the top of his lungs. I resented it tremendously. There was no need to announce that. Give me my medicine. Here's my card. I'm entitled to this, and good-bye. That was an ordeal. It got so bad. I forgot which but I ran out of pills or left them somewhere, and I needed more. I didn't have a new prescription, and the doctor was away, a whole series of events. I called him up like a person and said, "These are the circumstances and I need more pills." "But you're on Medicaid," he says to me. "I don't know if I can help you out. You have to have the prescription."

I didn't go to any specialists on Medicaid, and I don't think I would have felt comfortable at all. For my diabetes, I was with the family friend doctor, so I felt in good hands. For my gynecological problem, I went back because my gynecologist, who delivered my daughter, was on the plan. When I called up and walked in, he asked, "Where have you been for the last few years?" I said, "Don't ask. Meatball surgery at the medical center." He said, "Well, welcome home." I said, "Thank you." They used to ask, how come there's no copay on your card. I used to say, "Just lucky I guess." I didn't want to tell them. I would feel awkward. I feel like this guy is working for free. So I wouldn't say anything. That was nice when I got to go back to him.

I was glad the program was there, now that I'm looking back on it and have learned about the safety net. Yes, that's what those programs are there for. Not to use and abuse, as a habitual thing, that some of these people unfortunately do, for whatever their reasons are, but for people who sometimes just fall through the cracks, for whatever the reasons are. That that program was there to help me, I'm very grateful for that. Yes, it needs improvement.

## Meredith

I've been disabled since May, '95. I was working as a mail clerk. I moved up to a tax examiner. I was there from '89 to '91 when I got pregnant with my first child, and start getting sick. And I just stopped going unfortunately. And between '91 and '95, I started having children. From '95 on, I had caught HIV positive. But then I started getting an opportun[istic] infections and they made me have to apply for disability.

I left school in 1979, then I went to maybe it was like Youth Corps it was called. You went to school for 3 hours, then we went to work, there was a job and I was at the Navy yard. And then I passed the test in '81. If I had stayed in school I would've graduated in '80. But I got my GED in '81.

I receive food stamps and welfare for my children. We get, well since I have five, I get $240, $294 every 2 weeks, and I receive $300 a month in food stamps. I budget it. I'm a good budgeter. I have no other choice 'cause I'm a single parent.

In terms of my living situation, I have some subsidy. You have to have a case manager and you have to be not on drugs and you go once a month and show them that you paid your utility bills on time and all you do is what you're supposed to do, you stay there a lifetime. If you're not satisfied where you live at, you have to stay there for a year and then you can relocate.

Doing what I'm supposed to be doing means keeping up with, yeah, paying bills and keeping up with my case manager, Or, if I don't see him or somebody, I talk to him on the phone, at least once a month letting them know I'm doing okay. You're going to your medical appointments, taking your children to their medical appointments, making sure they going to school on a daily basis. Yes, I love where I'm at now. It could be larger, but I love it.

Well, at first I was in my drug addiction and I wasn't worrying about anything. But when I went to get help in 1998 and apply again, they denied me. And I was very sick and I didn't know that I was eligible because I had opportun[istic] infections and then when I found that out, I started going to my doctor monthly and she signed a paper stating what kind of opportunities of infections I had. Then they appealed it and it went through. From 1998 to June '99, that's when I received it.

I got a letter in the beginning of June saying it went through and I was eligible, but as the results came, the doctor said I need a representative to make sure that I pay my bills like I supposed to because I just came out of recovery. My sister, my case manager, and I had to go to the SSI building and she had to sign papers to be my representative. She just writes out checks to pay all my bills and then she gives me the difference. And I budgets that.

'Long as they's going all right. They say to me, as long as I feel I'm being treated right, if I don't feel like I'm being treated right, then to call the agency and I could get someone else for a representative. And I'm fine. No, I think a part of it is they had in my records that I was, when I signed up I was an inpatient for drugs, and I wasn't paying my bills like I used to, like I was when I was in drugs. I didn't pay my bills so I would think they don't think I was independent.

I been using [drugs] since 13 years before I got help. The hardest part, it sounds like, was just going through the application, the appeal process to get it. Medical records, and whatnot. The legal advocacy agency was faxing information to my doctor and to my case manager and they was doing it, the transaction. And I was just signing what I had to sign.

My life before participating in these programs like SSI and Medicaid was real bad. It was terrible 'cause I was in drugs. It is terrible. That's nothing to brag about or talk about. Yes, I was a workaholic then. I used to love working. And I used to, like, if I had a day off, I wish I was in work, so I be trying to find something to do, like I used to braid hair on the side. I just had to be doing something. That's why I didn't even have my first child until I was 29. I just like, I felt independent to myself.

But I was also using drugs while I was working, and I was like taking days off, I was like, I felt myself going down, then I popped up, then I had to stop. All my life was about was getting the drugs or something. That's all my life was about. I was working until '91. After then I was doing anything to get the money. SSI worked . . . right, but I wouldn't have been worried about it. I ain't had time to see doctors to find out what was wrong with me 'til the end. I woke up and knew that I was dying and then I felt myself neglecting my children and I had to stop. 'Cause my children come first after me. My sister had them while I was in recovery.

When I compare my life before SSI and Medicaid with after, I'll say once these programs came it gave me a wake-up call that there is life. I felt like I may always have what I want, like food, clothing, spending change to get to my support groups. The case manager did wonders for me. I need her. I know I do. 'Cause if I didn't have any case manager I don't think I could be sitting at this table today. I'd be dead. She woke me up and let me know there is life.

The last one with me, she calls me. I was surprised at first when she called me. Of course when she told me she called to say she was going to resign, I broke down on the phone, and she did, too, but she gave me spirit, tell me keep my head up, she know I able to keep on by myself. I don't need her now. She was just a pushy, but she always had, how do you say it, she always had faith in me, that there was something good about me. She calls to make sure that I was going to my medical appointments like I supposed to, asked if I'm comfortable where I live at, but then she let me know different things that I'm available for.

In the future, I always had my mind on being a case manager, so I can help people the way this person help me. But I'm afraid of one thing. I don't have no child care for me to get this where I want, and then I'm afraid that if SSI would stop me, and my benefits, and then I probably don't have no benefits. So I don't know which way to go from here.

I may be sickly so much I don't want to try to go back to work. Then I'm going to have to all go through this SSI situation again. I never talked to her about that. And I be so tired a lot, that's why I don't really put my foot up to go. Other people doing it and they might don't have all the opportuni[stic] infections that I do. I might not be in that you know category. Hopefully I stay healthy enough to be around for my children to have children themselves, so I can see my grandchildren.

I'm on medicine now, which is paid for by my medical assistance [Medicaid]. Since I'm on SSI, I'm eligible for welfare medical assistance. That's my health. That's medical assistance, food stamps, and cash. And I'm eligible for medical assistance. I have no way of stopping my health, I'm learning that too. So I just went on a retreat for mothers who have HIV, and they was talking about how we should tell our children before others, so they don't wind up hearing it from somewhere else. I'm working on that.

Well, they say you should tell your child before they hear it somewhere else, but I told my doctor that I prefer my children's camp, where it's children that's eligible to go there if they infected or affected. They asked what would we like the camp to do for us, and I said to let my children know the positive things about HIV and AIDS and I promise that when they come home, since they know about, you know, what it is, I'll be able to let them know that they mother have it, because I'm scared to tell them about it now, and they hearing this negative stuff out in the street. I don't know what would happen when I tell them. So I said when they come home this summer from camp, then I can let them know since they know the positive things about it.

They went last year, I sent them last year because I thought, because when they came home I asked one of the oldest boys, "Did you learn about AIDS?" He said, "No, why you asking me?" "Well, when I went on this retreat this Friday [I was told that] they did talk about that in groups," but my son [said differently], 'cause I do not come out and talk, I hold things in, and they say my son taking that from me, holding things in. They just waiting to see what I, when I tell them. So both of us are like, "When you going to tell me is when I'm going to tell you."

I always tell them that medicine is there so I can live longer, be with them. And like if I'm bleeding or something, I tell them don't touch my blood because they'll get sick and have to take medicine like me. I be thinking they would ask why, but they just don't say why. 'Cause I won't lie to them. If they don't ask why, and they don't touch my medicine, like a lot of people say, don't leave medicine around children, they just love the stuff on my dresser but they don't bother it.

All that's in my mind is I just want to be here to see my children all get grown so I won't have to worry about, if I started getting to that stage where I'm starting getting sick, I'd be worrying about what's going to happen, who's going to take care of them, or if they get separated. All that's to see them get all grown, to raise themselves. I'm supposed to have, write out a guardianship and let them know, but I can't get to that point 'cause I feel like if I write that up then the AIDS might start going down. I feel normal unless I'm talking to someone about HIV, because I don't feel sick since I take my medicine and don't take drugs. I want to write out, if something was to happen, who I would want my children to go with and to let the doctors do everything there is to do to try to keep me alive.

I talk to my oldest a lot letting him know how to be positive and try to get him joining things like the Boy Scouts I got him in, trying to let him learn how to be with the right people and try to talk to him, like I see something on TV talking about drugs, and I was like, "Don't go that way." I'm trying to show him the good ways of life and let him know how to be strong. Don't keep depending on me because one day I might not be around, you got to look out for your younger sisters and brothers. I try to keep him independent. The other children, all want to be like him. That's a good example for them to have.

## WHAT OUR CLIENTS TEACH US

Both Rita and Meredith demonstrate resiliency. Each reports a willingness to cope with her economic and health challenges. Each thinks about or takes the requisite steps to regain her health and economic self-sufficiency.

Each participant took a different path to her current status as program participants. Rita clearly reveals that even stable employment is no guarantee against requiring government largess. That she was able to leverage her work experience as a beautician into a plan for pursuing postsecondary higher education reveals her innate strength. Rita learned how to stabilize her own and her daughter's existence while she received Medicaid. Meredith was less fortunate in this regard, having to depend on both Medicaid and SSI and related programs to make ends meet for her and her children. For Meredith, the receipt of Medicaid was associated with her disability status, as evidenced by her receipt of SSI, and thus any meaningful labor force participation was effectively precluded.

Both women evidence a clear appreciation of their life circumstances within the context of earlier life ambitions. Rita's ambitions were expressed through her successful partnership with her father in the beauty business and her willingness to take it over when her parents decided to move to Florida. Meredith was a self-described "workaholic" who clearly received gratification from her attachment to the labor force. Both participants see work as a marker for their attachment to related social values, such as personal responsibility, and as evidence of their determination to care for their families.

Both Rita and Meredith reveal a deep understanding of the nuances of negotiating the system, and both have definite opinions about the actors with whom they have made contact during the course of their requests for assistance. Rita clearly knew the services she required and those to which she was entitled and managed to accommodate workers she found offensive. Her account of the settings in which she applied for services and her treatment by assorted workers is revealing: it says much not only about the conditions under which one receives services but also the sense of personal resolve that a recipient must bring to these circumstances. Meredith's story suggests the benefits of having a dedicated case manager, one who is able to ease the journey through the system and who, as in Meredith's case, takes a personal interest in your well-being. Meredith says:

> I'll say once these programs came it gave me a wake-up call that there is life. I felt like I may always have what I want, like food, clothing, [etc.]. The case manager did wonders for me. . . . If I didn't have any case manager I don't think I would be sitting at this table today. I'd be dead. She woke me up and let me know there is life.

Both participants suggest that asking for aid can be somewhat degrading, but neither indicates that this short-term feeling is permanently stigmatizing. They appear to know the difference between their self-perception as individuals versus their self-perception as a service recipient. They both, essentially, seem to do what is necessary without feeling like they must sacrifice their entire self-esteem. They know that one must "play along" to some degree in order to receive benefits, but neither accepts the notion that the mere receipt of services is evidence of personal failure or ambition. Indeed, they both seem to suggest that their very ability to negotiate the system is a marker for personal responsibility and ambition. And while these contacts with the system were not without their frustrations and associated feelings of shame, it is clear both participants felt positive about being able to surmount any system obstacle, as this quote from Rita demonstrates:

> My hand is out. So, yes, it feeds into that whole feeling of down, depressed, desperate. It's a very routine interview. They ask you questions, very unemotionally. They don't give a s___ about how you're feeling, if you're crying, whatever. . . . Of course, I was a master at keeping the records straight. I had everything organized in folders. They wanted to see that I was in school and this and that. It got to the point that the third time I went back to recertify, the [worker] just opened it and said, "It's all here, right?". . . For me it became a business almost.

Both Rita and Meredith have depended on Medicaid to cope with complex medical problems. For Rita, Medicaid provided treatment for a potentially life-threatening gynecological condition; for Meredith, Medicaid and the other benefits she is receiving are sustaining her life as she struggles with AIDS. This program's relevance to its recipients is self-evident: each of us can understand the fear and anxiety related to being ill and without access to health care. It is not difficult to feel Rita's toothache and the pain that intensified until extraction was the only—and cheapest—option. It is not difficult to empathize with Meredith's painful recognition that she "may be sickly so much" that she cannot go back to work and risk losing her medical benefits.

Our clients who have received medical benefits under Medicaid also teach us:

1. *Medicaid, as other benefit programs for the economically dislocated, comes with differentially experienced challenges and restrictions.* Rita reports that because she had an emergency she was certified in less than 30 days. The real challenge for her was her shame in having to depend on Medicaid. "There's that paranoia that goes on when you're on Medicaid. Am I going to be treated differently?" she asks. Rita also questions the quality of care that Medicaid recipients receive: "When I had to go to the clinic, I could not believe it. I felt like cattle, like one of the herd. . . . The first doctor who looked at me said, 'Well, there's nothing we can do for her.'" She also comments on limitations to the kind of care permitted: "Then I had to fix my teeth. That was the worst part of Medicaid. Medicaid will pull your teeth, but they won't pay to replace them."

Meredith, on the other hand, does not comment on bureaucratic or benefit obstacles, although some undoubtedly affected her. This may be related to the fact that, for her, Medicaid and the medicines it provides are keeping her alive. She is fighting to be "around for my children to have children themselves," and "welfare medical assistance . . . that's my health." Her energy is focused on a struggle for life and well-being. The benefit programs she receives are her lifeline and, as she said, they "did wonders for me."

As both narratives suggest, the complex processes and issues described in the legal cases presented and in the description of the Medicaid program are not the concerns of these recipients. Rita and Meredith—and we suspect most other recipients—see Medicaid through the lenses of their life stories, challenges, concerns, and coping capacities.

2.  *The two interrelated themes that run through so many of our life stories—clients' concern for their children and the hope for a better future—are again expressed here.* Children are the reason the clients have worked to improve their lives and are a major reason they give for accepting benefit programs. For Meredith, compliance with AIDS protocols and staying drug-free are motivated by her children: "All that's in my mind is I just want to be here to see my children all get grown so I won't have to worry about, if I started getting to that stage where I'm starting getting sick, I'd be worrying about what's going to happen, who's going to take care of them, or if they get separated." She struggles with when and how to tell her children about her condition, even sending them to a camp for children "infected or affected" by the disease. As she observes, speaking of her oldest son's reluctance to discuss AIDS, "So both of us are like, 'When are you going to tell me is when I'm going to tell you.'" Rita's commitment to her young daughter was succinctly stated with regard to medical care: "My daughter did go [to the dentist]. She always had whatever she needed."

And our clients who receive Medicaid, as our other clients, teach us about the hope and resilience that propel human beings into the future, no matter how bleak the present. Rita, despite her negative experiences, is "grateful" Medicaid "was there to help me." She successfully copes with abuse, divorce, poverty, and "just got my master's degree in social work . . . and my life is good." Meredith, while struggling with AIDS, remains optimistic and future oriented. She dreams of being a case manager who will help others as she has been helped by her case manager. But her more realistic and repeatedly expressed hope is to empower her oldest child so he can be there for his siblings. "I'm trying to show him the good ways of life and let him know how to be strong. . . . [I try to teach him not to] keep depending on me because one day I might not be around."

# 9

# CONCLUSION

*Helping Clients Cope
with Hard Times*

In the preceding chapters we have been introduced to six social welfare programs designed to help the economically dislocated meet the
need for life-sustaining food, clothing, shelter, and medical care. We
have also met a number of consumers of these publicly funded programs, each of whom, in sharing a life narrative, has given us insight
into the meaning and experience of being a person in economic distress in a society that holds mixed feelings about those in need. In this
final chapter we cull the common themes and lessons drawn both
from our explorations of the six programs and from our clients' participation in them. We focus on two questions: (1) What have we
learned about this society's response to those experiencing hard times?
(2) What implications can we extrapolate for social work practice
with the economically dislocated?

## AMERICA'S AMBIVALENCE
## TOWARD THOSE IN NEED

We have clearly seen within the programs we have reviewed and
through our clients' experiences the paradox of America's simultane-
ous concern for and disdain of those in economic need. A prevailing
ideological perspective (fed by the Horatio Alger myth and the

276

Protestant ethic) is that the economic vulnerability evidenced by those whom we met is an outcome of personal behaviors and defects. The poor or near-poor are viewed as exhibiting character flaws and making bad choices that keep them on the economic fringe. The literature is replete with scholars representing this particular viewpoint, often encapsulated in the notion of the "culture of poverty's" destructive impact (Kaus, 1992; Kelso, 1994; Leacock, 1971; Lewis, 1969; O'Connor, 2001; Patterson, 2000; Rainwater, 1970; Schneiderman, 1969). Structural causal forces—economic slowdowns, race and other "isms," de-industrialization, the dearth of capital in the inner city, the hazards of the secondary job market—are largely overshadowed by the notion that hard times come to those who are unworthy. Despite the work of scholars such as Wilson (1987, 1996) and Anderson (1999), which demonstrates what happens, in Wilson's words, "when work disappears," we remain captive of a deeply imbedded "us-versus-them," "the poor are not like us" mentality that informs harsh regulations and puny benefits and reflects real ambivalence toward assisting people in economic need.

Janssen (2005), commenting on the "profound ambivalence toward the victims of social problems" has dubbed the United States the "reluctant welfare state" (p. 2). He attributes what he calls the "paradox of punitiveness and generosity" to multiple factors, including the absence of a tradition of radical social change, the strain of conservatism in American politics, and myths regarding social welfare (p. 400). Included are the notion that assistance programs such as those we have reviewed do more harm than good and that private supports are more effective than public. Additionally, we introduced in Chapter 1 Ellwood's (1988) assertion that we suffer a conflict of values—work versus autonomy versus family versus community—that does not serve us well as we try to come to grips with the reality of "poor support." Finally, our culture remains caught in the vortex of political values that propelled Ronald Reagan into the White House and spawned his progeny, including the former Speaker of the House Newt Gingrich, the driving force behind the ill-advised but (temporarily) popular "Contract with America." Criticism of poor women and their families has been elevated, one might argue, to a sport; we stand now a mere 9 years away from "ending welfare as we [knew] it," and there is still mileage to be gained from castigating those we perceive as unworthy of public largess. The results of the 2004 presidential election suggests that in relation to these matters, President George W. Bush may rightly proclaim himself the real heir of the Reagan legacy.

Yet America's strong religious and philanthropic traditions have contradicted and controlled these anti-social welfare forces throughout the 20th century, and an array of social welfare programs have been established and sustained. U.S. society may not respect or trust the economically dislocated, but within limits "we" will provide "them" with food, clothing, shelter, and medical care. The relatively steady retreat of the federal government from social welfare over the past two decades has coincided with a strong upward private philanthropic trends, a phenomenon that betrays our competing impulse to help those we deem "worthy" and simultaneously reprimand their "unworthy" counterparts (National Committee for Responsive Philanthropy, 2002). Notwithstanding, the 2004 national elections demonstrated our split over the role and centrality of "moral values" in public discourse, and this debate has serious consequences for our attitudes about those who fall on hard times.

Traditionally, we have been more generous with and accepting of those in life circumstances that we can see as beyond the individual's control—the elderly, the visually impaired, the disabled, children. The seemingly dependent status of these groups ensures our sympathy; we even know people like them or, better still, have them as members of our families. Yet even in programs for those seen as more meritorious of aid, we can detect societal ambivalence. Note, for example, Supplemental Security Income's (SSI) complex, stringent eligibility standards, the minimal provision of housing for the disabled, and the Temporary Assistance for Needy Families (TANF) full family sanction regulations that withdraw assistance from children because of behaviors of their parents.

Our clients have directly experienced the "reluctant welfare state." They have told us how they had to prove their worthiness: long lines; long waits; long, complicated application forms; extensive supporting documents; disdainful treatment by public providers.

Societal ambivalence regarding those in need has, in recent years, been most sharply experienced by those receiving TANF benefits, the program most identified with what society negatively terms "welfare." A group once deemed among the most deserving of the poor—women who are impoverished and their children—has become the object of legislation and regulations designed to reform their character and behaviors. In 2005, as the 1996 enacting legislation is being reviewed for legislative action, legislators from both major parties are evaluating even more stringent work requirements.

While TANF has become the focus of the most punitive impulses toward those in need, America has not abandoned its commitment—reluctant as it may be—to those going through hard times. War on Poverty–era programs such as food stamps, Medicaid, and SSI have essentially continued operating without diminution—and indeed with some expansion—since their inception. While housing policy now emphasizes the private market, and funding is threatened, efforts to relinquish the federal government's active involvement and investment in housing have to date largely failed.

The United States' ideological hesitancy regarding people who are poor extends to its reluctance to investigate and acknowledge the consequences of its legislative and programmatic actions and inactions. Policies and programs are adopted—often as quick political fixes and/or responses to crisis—but not carefully evaluated. Are programmatic goals and objectives being met? And with what results, intended and unintended? A most glaring illustration has been the paucity of formative and summative evaluation data regarding TANF. We hear much rhetoric about so-called success stories of those who have left the welfare rolls. However, we do not know where these individuals are and how they are surviving. We do not know whether and where they are working, whether they have adequate shelter and medical care, whether they are living at or below the poverty line (see Soss, Schram, Vartanian, & O'Brien, 2001, and Vartanian, Soss, Schram, & Baumohl, 1999).

What data are emerging in fact suggests that assumptions underlying the program may be erroneous. Recent research, for example, has revealed that, contrary to the view that TANF would strengthen families, an increasing number of parents and children are living apart because of TANF's time limit policies (Bernstein, 2002).

One rich source of potential data are the recipients of program benefits. Clearly, as we now discuss, the voices we have heard have helped us gain significant insights as to what these programs mean in their lives.

## WHAT OUR CLIENTS HAVE TAUGHT US

We have learned from our clients what it means to be a person in economic distress, to apply for and receive a form of public aid, and with these supports to attempt to move on to realize one's dreams. While each person's life journey is unique, several common insights have emerged that speak to universal aspects of functioning during hard times.

Most resoundingly, our clients' voices reveal a capacity to confront hardship with resiliency and coping strengths. The triumph of the human spirit is felt in our clients' open sharing of their histories, their acknowledging of their own failures and deficits, and their optimistic faith in themselves, others, and the future. Substance abuse, domestic violence, homelessness, AIDS, depression, and loss contribute to their economic distress, but vivid dreams of better times remain. Our narratives clearly support the efficacy of a strengths perspective (Saleebey, 1996) which perceives our clients as resourceful, competent, talented beings. The people we meet do not impress us as hapless victims, but as victors in their quest for support and survival (Goldstein, 1992).

Particularly impressive was how often we find that recipients' future hopes are predicated not on others doing for them but on confidence in their own potential. Our clients clearly contradict the view that benefit programs dampen ambition and fuel dependency. In fact, those with whom we spoke reported that the programs and other helping resources were their means for moving on with their lives. No matter how challenging or frustrating the program might be, our recipients persevered to avoid dependency in the future. Similar strength was demonstrated in our clients' use of other formal and informal resources.

Perhaps most profoundly for us as social workers were the many times clients identified social agencies or individual social workers as having made the difference in their recapturing functional lives. What then do we learn from these clients about effective social work practice with the economically dislocated?

# IMPLICATIONS FOR SOCIAL WORK PRACTICE

A basic lesson our clients have taught us is how social welfare legislative and program policies are inextricably linked with people's lives. We have seen how such policies as the 5-year TANF limit, a reduction in the construction of public housing, or the bureaucratic hassle of applying for food stamps directly affect the daily biopsychosocial functioning of people who are grappling with hard times. Our clients' stories tell us of hopes dashed or elevated by success or failure in acquiring a benefit, and of self-esteem shattered or buttressed by interaction with a resource program and other helping services.

Our clients clearly communicate how agencies and professionals with expertise in helping them access resources have been instrumental in their efforts to cope with the complexities and pressures attendant to applying for and receiving benefits. In fact, social workers have historically been characterized as the professional discipline most legitimately charged with linking clients to resources and contemporary practice models continue to support this as a primary practice function (Hepworth, Rooney, & Larsen, 2005; Wilensky & Lebeaux, 1965).

No matter the setting they are in, the modality they practice, the title they carry, social workers need a working knowledge of how to assist those in need of accessing resources or otherwise negotiating the social welfare system. We next present six principles for engaging in this aspect of professional practice.

*Principle 1: Viewed from an empowerment/strengths perspective, clients are proactive partners in the process of acquiring and retaining resources.* Every interventive act should consider the potential for empowering the client—for example, writing letters with the client, encouraging the client to offer his or her view in a conference. Education is a powerful empowerment mechanism and is crucial when so much depends on familiarity and compliance with legal processes and regulations.

*Principle 2: In terms of clinical practice processes, engagement and assessment regarding resource gaps require keen analytical skills.* Not only must the practitioner be knowledgeable about legal regulations and how the client's situation's relates to them, but he or she must assess or understand the client's psychosocial profile in relation to the resource need. How will the client react to the demands of obtaining or retaining a resource? What will the client's response be to needing the resource? How best can this be shaped into an opportunity for empowering this particular client? How will the client's culture, ethnicity, previous experiences with social programs, age, gender, physical condition, level of psychosocial functioning affect the intervention?

*Principle 3: The values and ethics of the social work profession that emphasize respecting the client's dignity and his or her right to self-determination, confidentiality, and informed consent are especially significant in this area of practice.* Taking action on behalf of the client requires that the client understand what the action means and why it should be taken as well as what risks are involved. Only then can the client make a choice as to whether the action should be taken.

*Principle 4: Professional self-awareness is critical to a successful intervention.* Of particular significance is the worker's "tuning in" to how his or her response to the problematic situation is experienced by the client and the resource provider. If the interventive goal is to elicit a cooperative response from the provider, then the worker needs to communicate and model a collegial position. Indignation and anger need to be reserved and used only when the client's interest cannot be served by a different stance.

*Principle 5: The profession's social mission dictates that social work professionals be concerned with whether a client's private trouble is related to a more pervasive public issue (Schwartz, 1969).*    Is the problem being experienced by your client one that is shared by others? If so, what opportunities are there or need to be created for resolving the problematic issue and ensuring other clients are not affected in the future? One approach permits both the resolution of a private trouble and the pursuit of the related public issue. For example, a social worker in a rehabilitation program for the visually disabled acts on behalf of each of her individual clients, individually resolving their problems with SSI and Medicaid. She also, as a member of a county coalition, actively fights for legislative and administrative reforms. Her knowledge of and passion for the issue derives from her case advocacy work, but her clients ordinarily need not depend on the outcome of the broader intervention for the resolution of their individual problems.

*Principle 6: As in any form of practice, the social worker assumes several roles or postures.*    Chief among these are the roles of teacher, broker, mediator, and advocate, as discussed following.

**Teacher**    As teachers, social workers inform and educate clients about their problematic situation and means to ameliorating or solving it, and the ways they can effectively cope. Practice in this context requires social workers to teach clients about social programs' regulations that affect their eligibility and utilization. What documents must be provided to the agency? What forms need to be completed? What are the requirements for eligibility, and when will you be informed about your eligibility? Who is the person to contact? What are the clients' responsibilities once assistance is obtained? The teaching role needs to focus on active information sharing. As noted before, as a form of professional practice, the teaching process must be guided by respect for the client's dignity and self-determination and with client empowerment as a goal.

Clearly written guidelines can facilitate the learning and teaching. The program's official pamphlets and application forms should accompany these written materials, but unless they are extremely comprehensive and comprehensible they should not substitute for your own material or guidebooks prepared specifically for clients. Reading the guidelines with the client is often an effective teaching approach. Clients, as all of us, learn by practicing a behavior. Preparing clients to be program consumers is facilitated by the technique of role rehearsal—for example, role playing the interview. Having them play both client and worker and reviewing the experience can ensure the actual interview's success. For example, clients can learn how their anxiety and/or anger "feels" to the interviewer and they can experience the kinds of responses which their client's affective state elicits.

Clients can also learn by imitation and identification. The social worker is a role model for clients and as such can teach them effective behaviors. Opportunities may exist in the practice situation for demonstrating such behaviors, such as writing letters or making phone calls to external systems. Instead of doing this work after the client leaves the office, the social worker can make it part of the practice encounter. Call the Department of Social Services with the client present; compose the letter to the Unemployment Insurance Office with the client. The operative word is *with*. Doing "with," not "for" the client will transform the intervention to one in which clients are taught and may grow in their sense of self-efficacy, the sense that they can make a difference in their own lives.

**Broker**   The liaison or broker role is one that has historically been seen as the domain of social work (Wilensky and LeBeaux, 1965). Connecting clients with appropriate community resources is a complex function. The worker needs to get to know the provider organization and its procedures. A helpful technique is to visit and sit in its waiting room, experiencing how clients are treated and noting what you would want clients to know about the agency. The worker should also get to know several key agency personnel and assume a collaborative stance with them. Sometimes professional organizations, community committees, alumni gatherings can provide opportunities for developing professionally based linkages with these colleagues. Often, a productive relationship with the resource provider emerges from the work done on behalf of client after client. This working partnership occurs if—and only if—you as the professional assume a respectful, collaborative posture vis-à-vis the provider agency's personnel.

Clients' abilities to access a resource need to be carefully assessed and the following questions considered: Can the client call for an appointment? Understand directions to get to the agency? Pay for transportation to the agency? Is the client physically or emotionally able to proceed with the in-person or telephone contact with the provider agency? Is accompaniment by the social worker or a case aide required, desirable, or feasible?

**Mediator**   When the client and agency lose sight of where their interests converge, the social worker assumes a mediating posture. That is, the focus is on helping to find the common ground so as to avoid the pressures and pitfalls of a partisan posture. Keeping neutrality in the face of a pending refusal of services for your client calls for heightened self-awareness and continued recognition of the client's best interests. This is all being done in the interest of the client. If, for example, the client has been told she is not eligible for welfare because she did not provide a child's birth certificate, you may decide to call a contact in the eligibility division to remind the agency representative that it legally can accept another available document. As mediator, the worker will also need to encourage the client to quickly provide this document.

**Advocate**   Defining *advocacy* has challenged social workers (Litzelfelner & Petr, 1997), who have viewed it both as the execution of a specific role (Middleman & Goldberg, 1989) and as a continuum of actions and postures assumed on behalf of the vulnerable (Herbert & Levin, 1996; Sosin & Caulum, 1983). For us, the essence of the role of advocate is the worker's activist, partisan stance. Moving beyond being an agent of compromise, the social worker yields neutrality to actively become the champion of the client's position. The advocate role, as Goldberg-Wood and Middleman suggest, is "predicated on the assumption of a conflict situation" (1989, p. 141). Where there is formal or informal harassment, bureaucratic obstacle, and/or organizational unresponsiveness, an adversarial engagement may be necessary. Because a conflictual interaction can short-circuit later communications, the role of advocate should be judiciously assumed, often only after brokerage and mediating efforts have been tried and found wanting. Middleman and Goldberg (1989) refer to this as applying the "principle of least contest" (p. 148).

As an advocate, the social worker represents the client while balancing two significant elements. First, the social worker must be sure that enablement and the client's right to self-determination are not lost amid pressing precipitating needs and pressure for results—"doing for" cannot supplant "doing with." Second, unless agency administration sanctions advocacy, it may be a difficult role choice for the practitioner (Richan, 1991). Indeed, this is one of the reasons why agencies devoted to advocacy have developed and why what is a practice role is at times seen as a field of practice (Reisch, 2002). Current funding mechanisms in which nonprofit agencies depend on public dollars also discourage the use of advocacy aimed at a public agency.

## Macro Practice: The Imperative of Policy Advocacy

Our conversations with those who shared their experiences with us for this text underscore a key reality: individual intervention notwithstanding, the policy environment provides related opportunities to work indirectly on behalf of those on the economic fringe. As Jansson (2003) argues, "Policy practice and policy advocacy are as important to social workers as their other three interventive disciplines: direct service, community, and administrative practice" (p. 1). Policy advocacy and practice reveals yet another dimension of the social-worker-as-advocate function, with special emphasis on the requisite knowledge about social policy formulation, law and its shaping influence on social policy, and government processes. The key role here requires social workers to join the social reform traditions that have historically informed their profession and there by promote social change. The array of competencies necessary to carry out these traditions are considerable indeed, but as Jansson (2003) suggests, the task is as important as it is challenging: policy advocacy and policy practice involve "efforts to help powerless groups improve their lot" and "efforts generally [by social workers] to change policies in legislative, agency, and community settings, whether by establishing new policies, improving existing ones, or defeating the policy initiatives of other people." Each of these are indispensable to promote the well-being of the economically dislocated.

## CONCLUSION

As economic and political threats confront U.S. society at the beginning of the 21st century, hard times for many Americans will continue and will even intensify. Members of the working and middle classes, during recessionary periods, may very well join the poor as consumers of the programs described in this text.

In such an environment, it will be imperative that social workers acknowledge and exercise their role as connectors to system resources. Clients need to know what programs will ease their economic dislocation and how to access them. As of mid-2005, we already have glimpses of gloomy prospects for those in need. For example, even in the face of rising unemployment and minimal job creation, there has been a reluctance to extend unemployment insurance benefits and proposals to expand the stringency of TANF work requirements are likely to be passed by Congress. Moreover, the 2004 presidential elections signaled the public's desire to put in place social welfare policy that may be characterized as punitive.

Hard times provide social work with an opportunity to demonstrate its unique mandate to support the vulnerable, to empower and give voice to the economically dislocated, and where possible to reconnect them to the economic mainstream. Social work, as it fulfills these objectives, must be committed to demonstrations to society that those separated from the labor force are people with hopes, aspirations, and emotions comparable to those who do not require governmental assistance. Giving voice and identity to social program consumers as we have attempted to do in this text can bridge the gap between "them" and "us," and promote the humanitarian administration of social welfare programs for those experiencing hard times.

# REFERENCES

Abramovitz, M. (1997). Temporary assistance to needy families. In R. L. Edwards et al. (Eds.), *Encyclopedia of social work* (19th ed., pp. 311–330). Washington, DC: National Association of Social Workers.

Administration for Children and Families. (2000). *Temporary assistance for needy families (TANF) program: Third annual report to Congress.* Washington, DC: Author.

Administration for Children and Families. (2001, August–December). *ACF News.* Washington, DC: Author. Available at: http://www.acf.dhhs.gov/news/stats/aug-dec.htm

Albert, R. (2000). *Law and social work practice: A legal systems approach.* New York: Springer.

Albert, V. (2000). Reducing welfare benefits: Consequences for adequacy of and eligibility for benefits. *Social Work, 45*(4), 300–311.

American Friends Service Committee. (2001). *Everyone is deserving.* Philadelphia: Author.

Anderson, E. J. (1999). *Code of the streets: Decency, violence, and the moral life of the inner city.* New York: Norton.

Bailey, J. R. (2001, July 17). City won't get true homeless count. *The Columbus Dispatch,* p. B2.

Bassi, L. J., & McMurrer, D. P. (1997). Coverage and recipiency. In C. J. O'Leary & S. A. Wandner (Eds.), *Unemployment insurance in the United States.* Kalamazoo, MI: W. E. Upjohn Institute for Employment Research.

Berger, P., & Luckman, T. (1966). *The social construction of reality.* Garden City, NY: Doubleday.

Bernstein, N. (2002, June 23). Once again, trying housing as a cure for homelessness: Mothers with children are getting preferences in city assignments for subsidized housing. *New York Times,* p. B29.

Bernstein, N. (July 29, 2002). Side effects of welfare law: The no-parent family. *New York Times,* p. A1.

Better Homes Fund. (1999). *Homeless children: American's new outcasts.* Newton Centre, MA: Author.

*Black's Law Dictionary.* (1968). St. Paul, MN: West.

Blaustein, S. J., O'Leary, C. J., & Wandner, S. A. (1997). Policy issues: An overview. In C. J. O'Leary & S. A.Wandner (Eds.), *Unemployment insurance in the United States: Analysis of policy issues.* Kalamazoo, MI: W. E. Upjohn Institute for Employment Research.

Block, F., Cloward, R. A., Ehrenreich, B., & Piven, F. F. (1987). *The mean season: The attack on the welfare state.* New York: Pantheon.

Brandwein, R. (1998). *Battered women, children, and welfare reform: The ties that bind.* Thousand Oaks, CA: Sage.

Brown, R., & Ganzglass, E. (1998). Serving welfare recipients in a "work first" environment. *National Governors' Association Issue Briefs.* Available at: http://www.nga.org/common/issueBriefDetailPrint/1,1434,1857,00.html

Burt, M. (2001). *What will it take to end homelessness?* Washington, DC: Urban Institute.

Burt, M. R. et al. (1999). *Homelessness: Programs and the people they serve.* Washington, DC: Urban Institute.

Butler, S., & Nevin, M. K. (1997). Welfare mothers speak: One state's efforts to bring recipient voices to the welfare debate. *Society for the Study of Social Problems Newsletter,* 3(1).

Casey, T. (1998). *Welfare reform and its impact in the nation and in New York.* New York: Federation of Protestant Welfare Agencies.

Center on Budget and Policy Priorities. (1998). *Analysis of census bureau's income and poverty report for 1997.* Washington, DC: Author. Available at: http://www.cbpp.org/9-24-98pov.htm

Center on Budget and Policy Priorities. (2003). *Key provisions in TANF reauthorization bills passed by the Senate Finance Committee and the House.* Washington, DC: Author. Available at: http://www.cbpp.org/9-22-03tanf.htm

Center on Budget and Policy Priorities. (2005). *Low-income housing vouchers could be cut significantly under administration budget proposals.* Washington, DC: Author.

Center on Budget and Policy Priorities, State Policy Documentation Project. (1999). *Findings in Brief: Time Limits.* Washington, DC: Author. Available at: http://www.spdp.org/tanf/time limits

Center for Law and Social Policy. (1998). *A brief summary of key provisions of the temporary assistance for needy families block grant of H.R. 3734.* Washington, DC: Author. Available at: http://www.clasp.org/publications/clbskp.html

Centers for Medicare and Medicaid Services. (2005). Washington, DC: Author. Available at: http://www.cms.hhs.gov/publications/overview-medicare-medicaid/default4.asp

Charon, J. M. (1985). *Symbolic interactionism: An introduction, an interpretation, an integration* (2nd ed.). Englewood Cliffs, NJ: Prentice-Hall.

Clinton, W. J. (1996, August 22). Signing of Welfare Reform Bill.

Cohen, C. S., Mulroy, E., Tull, T., White, C., & Crowley, S. (2004). Housing Plus Services: Supportive vulnerable families in permanent housing. *Child Welfare,* LXXXIII(5), 509–528.

Courtney, M. E., McMurty, S. L., & Zinn, A. (2004). Housing problems experienced by recipients of child welfare services. *Child Welfare,* LXXXIII(5), 393–422.

Culhane, J. F., Webb, D., Grim, S., Metraux, S., & Culhane, D. (2003). Prevalence of child welfare services involvement among homeless and low-income mothers: A five year birth cohort and study. *Journal of Sociology & Social Welfare* 30(3): 79–95

Cunningham, K. (2004). *Trends in food stamp program participation rates: 1999 to 2002.* Washington, DC: Mathematica Policy Research.

DeBord, K., Canu, R. F., & Kerpelman, J. (2000). Understanding a work-family fit for single parents moving from welfare-to-work. *Social Work,* 45(4), 313–324.

Dworkin. R. M. (1979). How to read the civil rights act. *New York Review of Books,* 26, pp. 37–38.

Economic Policy Institute/Center for Budget and Policy Priorities. (2002). *Pulling apart: A state-by-state analysis of income trends.* Washington, DC: Author.

Edelman, P. (1997, August). The worst thing Bill Clinton has done. *Atlantic Monthly,* 43–50.

Ehrenreich, B. (2001). *Nickel and dimed: On (not) getting by in America.* New York: Metropolitan Books.

Ellwood, D. T. (1988). *Poor support: Poverty in the American family.* New York: Basic Books.

Ellwood, D. T., & Bane, M. J. (1985). The impact of AFDC in family structure and living arrangements. *Research in Labor Economics,* 7, 137–207.

Emanciley, P. (2000). It's depressing. *Human Ecology,* 28(1), 20–23.

Famuliner, C. C. (1999). Help for residents during welfare reform. *Journal of Housing and Community Development,* 546(6), 8–9.

First, R. J., Rife, J. C., & Toomey, B. G. (1995). Homeless families. In R. L. Edwards et al. (Eds.), *Encyclopedia of social work* (19th ed., pp. 1331–1337). Washington, DC: National Association of Social Workers.

Fitzgerald, M. M. L. (2001). Sexual abuse, alcohol, and other drug use, and suicidal behaviors in homeless adolescents. *Issues in Comprehensive Pediatric Nursing,* 24(4), 225–241.

Food Research and Action Center. (2003). *Get ready for food stamp reauthorization in your state.* Washington, DC: Author.

Food Research and Action Center. (2005). *Current news and analyses: Food stamp participation in January 2005 nearly two million above January 2004 level.* Washington, DC: Author. Available at: http://www.frac.org/html/news/news_index.html

Food Research and Action Center. (2005). *Federal food programs: Food stamp program.* Washington, DC: Author. Available at: http://www.frac.org/html/federal_food_programs/programs/fsp.html

Food Stamp History/Goal. (2001). *Food stamp history.* Washington, DC: U.S. Department of Agriculture. Available at: http://www.fns.usda.gov/fsp/rules/Legislation/history.htm

Foscarinis, M. (1996). The federal response: The Stewart B. McKinney Homeless Assistance Act. In J. Baumohl (Ed., for the National Coalition for the Homeless), *Homelessness in America.* Phoenix: Oryx.

Fremstad, S. (2003). *Falling TANF caseloads amidst rising poverty should be a course of concern.* Washington, DC: Center for Budget and Policy Priorities.

Gergen, K. J. (1985). The social constructionist movement in modern psychology. *American Psychologist,* 40, 266–275.

Germain, C., & Gitterman, A. (1980). *The life model of social work practice.* New York: Columbia University Press.

Goldberg-Wood, G., & Middleman, R. (1989). *The structural approach to direct practice in social work.* New York: Columbia University Press.

Goldstein, H. (1992). Victors or victims: Contrasting views of clients in social work practice. In D. Saleebey (Ed.), *The strengths perspective in social work practice.* New York: Longman.

Goodman, H. (2005). Elderly parents of adults with severe mental illness. *Journal of Gerontological Social Work,* 44(1–2), 173–188.

Greenberg, M. (1997). HHS policy guidance on maintenance of effort, assistance, and penalties: Summary and discussion. *Georgetown Journal on Fighting Poverty,* 4(2), 315–322.

Greenberg, M. (2001). From caseload reduction to poverty reduction. *Poverty Research News,* 5(6), 6–9.

Greenberg, M. H., & Baumohl, J. (1996). Income maintenance: Less help now, less on the way. In J. Baumohl (Ed., for the National Coalition for the Homeless), *Homelessness in America.* Phoenix: Oryx.

Greenberg, M. et al. (2000). *Welfare reauthorization: An early guide to the issues.* Washington, DC: Center for Law and Social Policy.

Greenhouse, L. (2002, March 27). Justices rule drug-eviction law is fair. *New York Times,* p. A20.

Hanks, E., Herz, M. E., & Nemerson, S. S. (1994). *Elements of law.* Cincinnati, OH: Anderson.

Harden, B. (2001, August 21). Two-parent families rise after change in welfare laws. *New York Times,* pp. A1, 24.

Hasenfeld, Y. (2000). Social services and welfare-to-work: Prospects for the social work profession. *Administration in Social Work,* 23(3/4), 185–199.

Haskins, R., & Blank, R. M. (2001). Welfare reform reauthorization. *Poverty Research News,* 5(6), 3–5.

Hatton, D. C. (2001). Homeless women and children's access to health care: A paradox. *Journal of Community Health Nursing,* 18(1), 25–35.

Haveman, R. (1996). From welfare to work: problems and pitfalls. *Focus,* 18(1), 21–24.

Hayes, L. (2002). *Food stamps for working families: Issues and options.* Washington, DC: Food Research and Action Council.

Hepworth, D. H., Rooney, R., & Larsen, J. (2002). *Direct social work practice* (6th ed.). Pacific Grove, CA: Brooks/Cole-Thompson.

Herbert, M., & Levin, R. (1996). The advocacy role in hospital social work. *Social Work in Health Care,* 22(3), 71–83.

Hernandez, R. (March 21, 2000). U.S. welfare limit may put thousands in Albany's charge. *New York Times,* pp. A1, A24.

Hurst, J. W. (1982). *Dealing with statutes.* New York: Columbia University Press.

Hwang, S. W. (2001). Homelessness and health. *Canadian Medical Association Journal,* 164(2), 229–234.

Jansson, B. S. (2003). *Becoming an effective policy advocate: From policy practice to social justice.* Pacific Grove, CA: Brooks/Cole.

Jansson, B. S. (2005). *The reluctant welfare state: American social welfare policies—past, present, future.* Pacific Grove, CA: Brooks/Cole.

Johnson, A. K. (1995). Homelessness. In R. L. Edwards et al. (Eds.), *Encyclopedia of social work* (19th ed., pp. 1338–1347). Washington, DC: National Association of Social Workers.

Jones, L. R. W. (1997). Unemployment compensation and workers' compensation. In R. L. Edwards et al. (Eds.), *Encyclopedia of social work* (19th ed., pp. 2413–2417). Washington, DC: National Association of Social Workers.

Katz, M. B. (1989). *The undeserving poor: From the war on poverty to the war on the welfare.* New York: Pantheon.

Kaus, M. (1992). *The end of equality.* New York: Basic Books.

Kelso, W. A. (1994). *Poverty and the underclass: Changing perceptions of the poor in America.* New York: New York University Press.

Kenyon, R., & Lancaster, L. (2001). Changes in unemployment insurance legislation in 2000. *Monthly Labor Review,* 124(1), 29–34.

Kramer, F. (1998). The hard-to-place: Understanding the population and strategies to serve them. *WIN Issue Notes* 4. Available at: http://www.welfare:nfo.org/hard to.htm

Leacock, E. B. (1971). *The culture of poverty: A critique.* New York: Simon & Schuster.

Levin, T. (2001, July 31). Surprising result in welfare-to-work studies. *New York Times,* p. A16.

Levy, F. (1987). *Dollars and dreams: The changing American income distribution.* New York: Russell Sage.

Lewis, O. (1969). *Five families: Mexican case studies in the culture of poverty.* New York: Basic Books.

Litzelfelner, P., & Petr, C. G. (1997). Case advocacy in child welfare. *Child Welfare,* 40(4), 392–402.

Loprest, P. (2003). *Fewer welfare leavers employed in weak economy.* Washington, DC: Urban Institute.

Lyon, E. (1998). Poverty, welfare, and battered women: What does the research tell us? *Welfare and Domestic Violence Technical Assistance Initiative.* Washington, DC: National Resource Center on Domestic Violence. Available at: http://www.vaw.umn.edu/vawnet/welfare.htm

Mannix, M. R., Cohan, M., Freedman, H. A., Lamb, C. & Williams, J. (1999). Welfare litigation developments since the Personal Responsibility and Work Opportunity Reconciliation Act of 1996. *Clearinghouse Review,* January–February.

Marshall, N. L. (1997). The Welfare Reform Act of 1996: Political compromise or panacea for welfare dependency? *Georgetown Journal on Fighting Poverty,* 4(2), 333–345.

Martin, R. R. (1995). *Oral history in social work.* Thousand Oaks, CA: Sage.

Martinson, K., & Strawn, J. (2003). *Build to last: Why skills matter for long-run success in welfare reform.* Washington, DC: Center on Law and Social Policy.

McDowall, B. D. (2001). Measuring and improving the quality of HUD-assisted housing. *Journal of Housing & Community Development* 58(2), 18–21.

Metsch, L. R., Wolfe, H. P., Fewell, R. et al. (2001). Treating substance-using women and their children in public housing: Preliminary evaluation findings. *Child Welfare* 80(2), 199–220.

Meyer, C. H. (1983). *Clinical social work in the ecosystems perspective.* New York: Columbia University Press.

Middleman, R. R., & Goldberg, G. (1989). *Social service delivery: A structural approach to social work practice.* New York: Columbia University Press.

Murphy, G. C., & Athanson, J. A. (1999). The effect of unemployment on mental health. *Journal of Occupational and Organizational Psychology,* 72(1), 83–100.

National Association of Social Workers. (2004). TANF reauthorization delayed once again. Washington, DC: Author. Available at: http://www.naswdc.org/advocacy/updates/2004/040204.asp

National Committee for Responsive Philanthropy. (2002). *The state of philanthropy, 2002.* Washington, DC: Author.

National Conference of Catholic Bishops. (1986). *Economic justice for all: Pastoral letter on catholic social teaching and the U.S. economy.* Washington, DC: Author.

National Institute for Literacy. (1998). *Policy update: Learning disabilities and welfare-to-work.* Available at: http://www.nifl.gov/nifl/policy/updates/98-08-11.html

National League of Cities. (2003). *Trends, policies and economic conditions affecting poverty in America's cities and towns: A discussion paper.* Washington, DC: Author.

National Low Income Housing Coalition. (2001). *2001 advocate's guide to housing and community development policy.* Available at: http:/www.nlihc.org/advocates/publichousing.htm

National Low Income Housing Coalition. (2005). An initial estimate of people with housing problems from the 2003 American Housing survey. Research Note #05-01. Washington, DC: Author.

Nelson, S. (2004). *Trends in parent's economic hardship.* Washington, DC: Urban Institute. Available at: http://www.urban.org/url.cfm?ID=310970

Newman, K. S. (1993). *Declining fortunes: The withering of the American dream.* New York: Basic Books.

Nunez, R. (2004). *A shelter is not a home or is it? Lessons from family homelessness in New York City.* New York: White Tiger Press.

O'Connor. A. (2001). *Poverty knowledge: Social science, social policy, and the poor in twentieth-century U.S. history.* Princeton, NJ: Princeton University Press.

O'Hare, W. (1996). *Poverty in America : Trends and new patterns.* Washington, DC: Population Reference Bureau.

O'Leary, C. J., & Rubin, M. A. (1997). Adequacy of the weekly benefit amount. In C. J. O'Leary & S. A. Wandner (Eds.), *Unemployment insurance in the United States.* Kalamazoo, MI: W. E. Upjohn Institute for Employment Research.

O'Leary, C. J., & Wandner, S. A. (2000). *Unemployment compensation and older adults.* Washington, DC: U.S. Department of Labor, Office of Policy and Research Employment and Training Administration.

Olson, K., & Pavetti, L. (1997). *Personal and family challenges to the successful transition from welfare to work.* Washington, DC: Urban Institute. Available at: http://www.urban.org/welfare/report/htm

Oregon Center for Public Policy. (2004). Oregon downturn 47 months and counting while Oregonians dream. Silverton, OR: Author. Available at: http://www.ocpp.org/2004/nr041112.htm

Patterson, J. T. (2000). *America's struggle against poverty in the twentieth century.* Cambridge, MA: Harvard University Press.

Pear, R. (2002, September 25). Number of people living in poverty increases in U.S. *New York Times*, pp. A1, A19.

Pearce, D. (2000). Rights and wrongs of welfare reform: A feminist approach. *Affilia: Journal of Women and Social Work,* 15(2), 133–153.

Pennsylvania Department of Welfare. (2005). *Food stamp benefits.* Harrisburg, PA: Author. Available at: http://www.dpw.state.pa.us/LowInc/FoodStamps/003670291.htm

Powers, E.T. (2003). Children's health and maternal work activity: Static and dynamic estimates under alternative disability definitions. *Journal of Human Resources,* 38, 3.

Rainwater, L. (1970). *Behind ghetto walls: Black families in a federal slum.* Chicago: Aldine.

Redlener, I., & Johnson, D. (1999). *Still in crisis: The health status of New York's homeless children.* New York: Children's Health Fund.

Reisch, M. (2002). Legislative advocacy to empower oppressed and vulnerable groups. In A.R. Roberts & G. Green (Eds.), *Social workers' desk reference* (pp. 545–551). Oxford, UK, and New York: Oxford University Press.

Richan, W. C. (1991). *Lobbying for social change.* New York: Haworth.

Robinson, G. O., & Gellhorn, E. (1972). *The administrative process.* St. Paul, MN: West.

Rodriguez, E. (2001). Keeping the unemployed healthy. *American Journal of Public Health,* 91(9), 1412–1413.

Sadova, S. W., O'Connor, R., & McCreary, P. R. (2000). Employment status and health in young adults: Economic and behavioral mediators. *Journal of Health Psychology,* 5(4), 549–560.

Saleebey, D. (1992). *The strengths perspective in social work practice.* New York: Longman.

Schneiderman, L. (1969). *The culture of poverty: A study of the value-orientation preferences of the chronically impoverished.* Ann Arbor, MI: University Microfilms.

Schumacher, R., & Greenberg, M. (1999). *Child care after leaving welfare.* Washington, DC: Center for Law and Social Policy.

Schwartz, J. E., & Volgy, T. (1992). *The forgotten Americans.* New York: Norton.

Schwartz, W. (1969). Private troubles and public issues: One social work job or two? *Social Welfare Forum.* New York: Columbia University Press.

Scharfstein, J., Sandel, M., Kahn, R. et al. (2001). Child health at risk while families wait for housing vouchers. *American Journal of Public Health,* 91, 1191–1192.

Shulman, L. (1999). *The skills of helping individuals, families, groups, and communities* (3rd ed.). Itasca, IL: F. E. Peacock.

Smith, P. K., & Yeung, W. J. (1998). Childhood welfare receipt and the implication of welfare reform. *Social Service Review,* 72(1), 1–16.

Solomon, B. (1976). *Black empowerment: Social work in oppressed communities.* New York: Columbia University Press.

Social Security Administration. (1997). *Social Security handbook.* Washington, DC: Author. Available at http://www.ssa.gov/OP_Home/handbook/

Social Security Administration. (2001). *Social Security handbook.* Washington, DC: Author. Available at http://www.ssa.gov/OP_Home/handbook/

Social Security Administration. (2002). *Social Security handbook.* Washington, DC: Author. Available at: http://www.ssa.gov/OP_Home/handbook/

Sosin, M., & Caulum, S. (1983). Advocacy: A conceptualization for social work practice. *Social Work,* 28(1), 12–17.

Soss, J., Schram, S., Vartanian, T. P., & O'Brien, E. (2001). Setting the terms of relief: Explaining state policy choices in the devolution revolution. *American Journal of Political Science,* 24, 69–86.

Spiezia, V. (2000). The analysis of technological change and employment. In M. Vivarelli & M. Pianta (Eds.), *The employment impact of innovation : Evidence and policy.* London and New York: Routledge.

Stam, H., & Cuijern, P. (2001). Effects of family intervention on burdens of relatives of psychiatric patients in the Netherlands: A pilot study. *Community Mental Health Journal,* 37(1), 179–187.

Statsky, W. (1975). *Legislative analysis: How to use statutes and regulations.* St. Paul, MN: West.

Statsky, W. (1984). *Legislative analysis and drafting.* St. Paul, MN: West.

Sweeney, E. et al. (2000). *Windows of opportunity: Strategies to support families receiving welfare and other low-income families in the next stage of welfare reform.* Washington, DC: Center on Budget and Policy Priorities.

U.S. Census Bureau. (2001). *Statistical abstracts of the United States.* Washington, DC : U.S. Department of Commerce, Economics and Statistics Administration, Bureau of the Census.

U.S. Census Bureau. (2003). *Dynamics of economic well-being: Poverty 1996–1999.* Washington, DC: U.S. Department of Commerce, Economics and Statistics Administration, Bureau of the Census. Available at: http://www.census.gov/hhes/www/sipp96/sipp96.html

U.S. Census Bureau. (2004). *Income, poverty, and health insurance coverage in the United States: 2003.* Washington, DC : U.S. Department of Commerce, Economics and Statistics Administration, Bureau of the Census. Available at: http://www.census.gov/hhes/www/income.html

U.S. Conference of Mayors. (2004). *Hunger and homelessness survey: A status report on hunger and homelessness in American's cities.* Washington, DC: Author.

U.S. Department of Health and Human Services. (2001). *Fact sheet.* Available at: http://www.hhs.gov/news/press/2001pres/01fswelfarereform.html

U.S. Department of Labor, State Unemployment Insurance. (2005). Available at: http://www.workforcesecurity.doleta.gov/unemploy/uifactsheet.asp

U.S. House of Representatives, Committee on Ways and Means. (2000). *Green Book* (pp. 357–462). Washington, DC: U.S. Government Printing Office.

U.S. House of Representatives Committee on Ways and Means. (2004). *Green Book.* Washington, DC: U.S. Government Printing Office.

Vartanian, T. P., Soss, J., Schram, S., & Baumohl, J. (1999). Already hit bottom: General assistance, welfare retrenchment, and single male migration. In S. Schram & S. H. Beer, *Welfare reform: A race to the bottom?* Washington, DC: Woodrow Wilson Center Press. (Also in *Journal of Sociology and Social Welfare, 26,* 151–174.)

Vissing, Y. (1996). *Out of sight, out of mind: Homeless children and families in small town America.* Lexington: University Press of Kentucky.

Wanberg, C. R., & Griffiths, R. F. (1997). Time structure and unemployment: A longitudinal investigation. *Journal of Occupational & Organizational Psychology, 70*(1), 75–96.

Wandner, S. A., & Stettner, A. (2000). Why are many jobless workers not applying for benefits? *Monthly Labor Review, 123*(6), 21–32.

Weaver, D., & Hasenfeld, Y. (1997). Case management practices, participants' responses, and compliance in welfare-to-work programs. *Social Work Research, 21*(2), 92–102.

Wijnberg, M. H., & Weinger, S. (1998, March–April). When dreams without resources fail: The social support systems of poor single mothers. *Families in Society,* 212–219.

Wilensky, H. L., & Lebeaux, C. N. (1965). *Industrial society and social welfare: The impact of industrialization on the supply and organization of social welfare services in the United States.* New York: Free Press.

Wilson, W. J. (1987). *The truly disadvantaged: The inner city, the underclass, and public policy.* Chicago: University of Chicago Press.

Wilson, W. J. (1996). *When work disappears: The world of the new urban poor.* New York: Knopf.

Woodbury, S. A., & Rubin, M. (1997). The duration of benefits. In C. J. O'Leary & S. A. Wandner (Eds.), *Unemployment insurance in the United States.* Kalamazoo, MI: W. E. Upjohn Institute for Employment Research.

Wolff, E. (2002). *Top heavy : The increasing inequality of wealth in America and what can be done about it.* New York: New Press.

Zedlowski, S. R. (2003). *Work and barriers to work among welfare recipients in 2002.* Washington, DC: Urban Institute.

# TABLE OF CASES

# INDEX